This is an important contribution to public relations scholarship as it strongly positions the field outside the liberal democratic and corporatist norm, with emphasis on dialogue in divided societies supported by national and situational case studies.

Tom Watson, *Emeritus Professor, Faculty of Media & Communication, Bournemouth University, UK*

This book opens up ways of seeing how public relations and communication operates in complex, fraught environments where the idea of setting clear objectives, targeting audiences, delivering slick messages, are continually undermined by the fluid contexts of conflict and division. It will be an important addition to the growing body of work on public relations beyond the organisational context.

Lee Edwards, *Associate Professor, Communication Studies and PR, University of Leeds, UK*

International Public Relations

International Public Relations: Perspectives from deeply divided societies is positioned at the intersection of public relations (PR) practice with socio-political environments in divided, conflict and post-conflict societies. While most studies of PR focus on the activity as it is practised within stable democratic societies, this book explores perspectives from contexts that have tended to be marginalized or uncharted.

Presenting research from a diverse range of societies still deeply divided along racial, ethnic, religious or linguistic lines, this collection engages with a variety of questions, including how PR practice in these societies may contribute to our understanding of PR theory building. Importantly, it highlights the role of communication strategies for actors that still deploy political violence to achieve their goals, as well as those that use it in building peace, resolving conflict, and assisting in the development of civil society.

Featuring a uniquely wide range of original empirical research, including studies from Israel/Palestine, Mozambique, Northern Ireland, former Yugoslavia, former Czechoslovakia, Spain, Malaysia and Turkey, this groundbreaking book will be of interest not only to scholars of public relations, but also political communication, international relations, and peace and conflict studies.

Ian Somerville is a Reader in Media and Communication at the University of Leicester, UK.

Owen Hargie is Professor of Communication at Ulster University, UK.

Maureen Taylor is Director of the School of Advertising and Public Relations in the College of Communication and Information, at the University of Tennessee, USA.

Margalit Toledano, APR, is a Senior Lecturer of Management Communication at the Waikato Management School, New Zealand.

Routledge New Directions in Public Relations and Communication Research

Edited by Kevin Moloney

Routledge New Directions in Public Relations and Communication Research is a new forum for the publication of books of original research in PR and related types of communication. Its remit is to publish critical and challenging responses to continuities and fractures in contemporary PR thinking and practice, and its essential yet contested role in market-orientated, capitalist, liberal democracies around the world. The series reflects the multiple and inter-disciplinary forms PR takes in a post-Grunigian world; the expanding roles which it performs, and the increasing number of countries in which it is practised.

The series will examine current trends and explore new thinking on the key questions which impact upon PR and communications including:

- Is the evolution of persuasive communications in Central and Eastern Europe, China, Latin America, Japan, the Middle East and South East Asia developing new forms or following Western models?
- What has been the impact of postmodern sociologies, cultural studies and methodologies which are often critical of the traditional, conservative role of PR in capitalist political economies, and in patriarchy, gender and ethnic roles?
- What is the impact of digital social media on politics, individual privacy and PR practice? Is new technology changing the nature of content communicated, or simply reaching bigger audiences faster? Is digital PR a cause or a consequence of political and cultural change?

Books in this series will be of interest to academics and researchers involved in these expanding fields of study, as well as students undertaking advanced studies in this area.

A full list of titles in this series is available at: www.routledge.com. Recently published titles:

Social Media and Public Relations
Fake friends and powerful publics
Judy Motion, Robert L. Heath and Shirley Leitch

Public Relations and Participatory Culture
Fandom, social media and community engagement
Amber Hutchins and Natalie T. J. Tindall

International Public Relations

Perspectives from deeply divided societies

Edited by
Ian Somerville, Owen Hargie,
Maureen Taylor and Margalit Toledano

LONDON AND NEW YORK

First published 2017 by Routledge

2 Park Square, Milton Park, Abingdon, Oxon OX14 4RN
605 Third Avenue, New York, NY 10017

Routledge is an imprint of the Taylor & Francis Group, an informa business

First issued in paperback 2021

British Library Cataloguing in Publication Data
A catalogue record for this book is available from the British Library

Library of Congress Cataloging in Publication Data
Names: Somerville, Ian (Reader in Media and Communication), editor.
Title: International public relations : perspectives from deeply divided societies / edited by Ian Somerville, Owen Hargie, Maureen Taylor and Margalit Toledano.
Description: Abingdon, Oxon ; New York, NY : Routledge, 2017. | Series: Routledge new directions in public relations and communication research | Includes bibliographical references and index.
Identifiers: LCCN 2016010186| ISBN 9781138860131 (hardback) | ISBN 9781315716749 (ebook)
Subjects: LCSH: Public relations and politics–Cross-cultural studies. | Public relations–Cross-cultural studies.
Classification: LCC JF1525.P8 I574 2017 | DDC 659.2/9327–dc23
LC record available at https://lccn.loc.gov/2016010186

ISBN: 978-1-138-86013-1 (hbk)
ISBN: 978-0-367-34068-1 (pbk)

Typeset in Times New Roman
by Taylor & Francis Books

Ian Somerville: For Sahla and Emily.
Owen Hargie: For Patricia.
Maureen Taylor: For MLK.
Margalit Toledano: For Palestinians and Israelis who believe in and work for dialogue, reconciliation, and peace.

Contents

List of illustrations

Figures

Tables

List of contributors

Zeti Azreen Ahmad is an Assistant Professor at the Department of Communication, Kulliyyah of Islamic Revealed Knowledge and Human Sciences (KIRKHS), International Islamic University Malaysia (IIUM). She is currently Head of the Communication Department, KIRKHS. She holds a B.HSc. (Communication) and M.HSc. (Communication) (International Islamic University Malaysia). She obtained her doctoral degree from Stirling University, Scotland. Her doctoral thesis was on Public Relations and Corporate Social Responsibility: Malaysian Perspectives. At present, she is engaged in several research projects on media and youth, social mobility study, public relations, new media and corporate social responsibility (CSR).

A. Banu Bıçakçı received her doctoral degree in Public Relations from Anadolu University, Turkey, in 2009. She is currently an Associate Professor at Yeditepe University's Public Relations and Publicity Department where she has been lecturing since 2006. Bıçakçı has been a guest lecturer at the international MBA Communication and Leadership programme, Quadriga University of Berlin, for two years. Her research interests include history of public relations, corporate social responsibility, city branding, and sustainability. She has authored numerous book chapters and periodical articles both in English and Turkish. Some of her publications are 'Milestones in Turkish PR History' published in the *Public Relations Review*; 'Communicating Social Responsibility: A Look at Turkish Corporate Websites', published as a chapter in *Digital Transformations in Turkey* (ed. B. Akdenizli, Lexington, 2015). Dr Bıçakçı recently co-authored a chapter titled 'A Theoretical Approach for Sustainable City Brands: Multilateral Symmetrical Communication Model' in an upcoming international book (IGI Global, 2016). Bıçakçı is currently on the advisory boards of *Public Relations Review* and the *Journal of Public Relation Research*'s special issues on PR History. She is a member of EUPRERA, ECREA and IAMCR.

İlker Cenan Bıçakçı is Professor and the Dean of the Faculty of Communication at Yeditepe University, Istanbul, Turkey. He currently teaches 'Advanced Studies in Public Relations', 'Media, Globalization and

International Media Structures', and 'Public Speaking'. His areas of interest include ethical/critical issues in public relations, consumption culture and globalization, art sponsorship in the process of globalization, political public relations, social psychology, and intercultural communication. Bıçakçı has published journal articles and book chapters as well as monographs on communications and public relations such as *Communications and Public Relations: A Critical Approach*, updated 7th edition (Media Cat Books, 2008) and *Our Communication World* (Media Cat Books, 2001). He recently co-authored a chapter titled 'The Use of Media in Activist Public Relations: Framing the "Defending Our Honour" Movement' in the edited collection, *Communication Ethics in a Connected World: Research in Public Relations and Organisational Communication*, eds A. Catellani, A. Zerfass, R. Tench and PIE (Peter Lang, 2015). Bıçakçı currently serves on the advisory board of the *Global Media Journal*, Turkish edition. He is a member of EUPRERA and ECREA.

Alexander Buhmann is an Assistant Professor in the Department of Communication and Culture at BI Norwegian Business School. His current research focuses on corporate communication, public relations, and public diplomacy. He is particularly interested in how variances in the (cognitive and social) construction of large collectives as agentic entities impact how people process information and attribute responsibility and legitimacy to these collectives. Additionally, Alexander specializes in measurement and evaluation in public relations, public diplomacy, and communication research. Alexander holds an M.A. in media studies from the University of Siegen (Germany) and a Ph.D. in communication from the University of Fribourg (Switzerland).

Gisela Conçalves is Head of the Department of Communication and Arts at the University of Beira Interior (UBI, Covilhã, Portugal). She develops her research activity at LabCom.IFP – a communication, philosophy and humanities research centre. In 2014 she was elected vice-chair of the Organizational and Strategic Communication section of ECREA. Her current research interests are public relations theories, communication ethics and government communication. Her work has been published in a wide range of public relations and communication management journals and in various edited collections.

Xavier Ginesta is a full-time Lecturer in the Business and Communication Faculty of the University of Vic-Central University of Catalonia (UVic-UCC), and Faculty Vice-Dean Promotion and External Relations. He has been a research fellow in the Autonomous University of Barcelona (UAB), where he was part of the staff of the Political Documentation Centre (CEDOC-UAB). During his time there he wrote his doctoral thesis and taught in the Journalism and Communication Department. He is a member of TRACTE research group (UVic-UCC). His major research areas are political communication and sport communication. He has written five books, including *La Catalunya del Plebiscite* (2013), an analysis of the 2012 Catalan electoral campaign. As an academic researcher, he has published in international journals such as *American Behavioral Scientist*; *Soccer and Society*; and the *American Communication Journal*. As a journalist, he currently publishes political analysis in *El Punt Avui* and the online version of *El Periodico de Catalunya*.

Owen Hargie is in the School of Communication at University of Ulster. He is a Chartered Member, Registered Practitioner, and Associate Fellow of the British Psychological Society. He is an Elected Member of the prestigious Royal Norwegian Society of Sciences and Letters, and a Fellow of the UK Academy of Social Sciences. He has been Associate Professor at a number of UK and European universities. He has published 70 book chapters, 126 articles in refereed journals, 11 major research reports, and 22 books, including: *Key Issues in Organizational Communication*; *Communication Skills for Effective Management*; *Skilled Interpersonal Communication: Research, Theory and Practice*; and *Auditing Organizational Communication: A Handbook of Research, Theory and Practice*. He acts as consultant in communication for numerous public and private sector organizations. In 2007 he was awarded a Senior Distinguished Research Fellowship by the University of Ulster in recognition of his research contributions over three decades.

Denisa Hejlová is a leading Czech scholar and communication consultant. She focuses on research, education and practice in public relations, public affairs, trust management or fashion marketing. Since 2011, she's been heading the Department of Marketing Communication and PR at the Charles University in Prague. Denisa pioneered academic research in fields of public relations, history of PR and public affairs in the Czech Republic. She is also active in the international network; in 2014 she spent a semester as Fulbright visiting scholar at Columbia University in New York. She is a member of the European PR network EUPRERA and she loves to visit Japan, where she studied at Tokyo University of Foreign Studies.

Pelin Hürmeriç is an Associate Professor and Head of the Department of Public Relations and Publicity at Yeditepe University, İstanbul, where she has been a faculty member since 2001. She graduated from Marmara University, Department of Public Relations and Publicity. She received her M.A. degree from Yeditepe University, Department of Public Relations and Publicity. In 2009, she completed her doctoral degree in Public Relations and Publicity at Marmara University. She is on the editorial board of *Global Media Journal*, Turkish edition, and *International History of Public Relations Conference*. She is the co-author of the article 'Milestones in Turkish Public Relations History', published in *Public Relations Review*. She is also the co-author of the chapter 'Ethics Statements of Public

Relations Agencies in Turkey: How Do Turkish PR Agencies Present Themselves on the Web?' published in the edited book *Communication Ethics in a Connected World: Research in Public Relations and Organisational Communication*. She has been giving lectures as a guest lecturer in the International MBA Communication and Leadership Programme at Quadriga University of Berlin for two years. Her research interests are in the fields of corporate communication and history of public relations. She is a member of EUPRERA and ECREA.

Syed Arabi Idid is at the Department of Communication, Kulliyyah of Islamic Revealed Knowledge and Human Sciences, International Islamic University Malaysia (IIUM). He became Dean of the Research Centre in July 2001 and was later appointed as Rector of IIUM from 1 June 2006 until 31 May 2011. He holds a B.A. (University of Malaya), M.A. and Ph.D. (University of Wisconsin–Madison). He is a member of the Board of Directors and member of the Asian Media Information and Communication Centre (AMIC). He is also one of the founding members of the Asian Network for Public Opinion Research (ANPOR), and a member of the World Public Opinion Research Association (WAPOR) and International Communication Association (ICA). He was a president of the Commonwealth Association for Education in Journalism and Communication. At the local level, he was once the president of the Malaysian Communication Association, and the president of the Institute of Public Relations Malaysia (IPRM). He was also a judge for several years in selecting the best journalists organized by the Malaysian Press Institute (MPI). He has conducted several public opinion studies and is also involved in marketing research. His research interests include conducting public opinion studies, public relations, and international communication.

Diana Ingenhoff is currently Head of Media and Communication Research and Vice-Dean of the Faculty of Economics and Social Sciences at the University of Fribourg (Switzerland). Since 2014 she has been President of the Swiss Association of Communication and Media Research (SACM), for which she has been a member of the executive board since 2009. She is a scientific member of the steering board of the Swiss foundation for media quality, and responsible for an annual quality rating of Swiss news media. In 2015 she received a Page Legacy Fellowship in Global Public Relations from the prestigious Arthur W. Page Center. Previously she was head of the Center for Corporate Communication at the Institute for Media and Communications Management at the University of St. Gallen from 2002 to 2005, where she earned her Ph.D. with a dissertation on issues of management in international corporations, which was awarded by the SACM. Her research and teaching responsibilities include organizational communication, media economics, and international public relations, especially with regard to public diplomacy, reputation research, responsibility communication, and new technologies. Her research has been published in international journals and edited collections and she has been the recipient of several international awards for research excellence.

Pauline Irving is a Senior Lecturer in Communication at the University of Ulster, whose main research and teaching interests are in crisis management at personal and organizational levels. Recently she was part of a pan-European project aimed at developing effective crisis communication strategies in the aftermath of terrorist attacks. The resultant strategy was disseminated in the form of a crisis communication manual which is now in use by public authorities throughout Europe. Pauline has a wide range of research publications and has been an invited speaker at both national and international conferences.

Michael Kent is at the School of Advertising and Public Relations in the College of Communication and Information at the University of Tennessee. Kent conducts research on new technology, mediated communication, dialogue, international communication, and web communication. An internationally recognized scholar, Kent has published dozens of articles, books, and book chapters, and is among the most influential and cited scholars in public relations. His research has appeared in public relations, management, and communication journals including *Public Relations Review, Management Communication Quarterly, The Journal of Public Relations Research*, *Gazette*, *Communication Studies*, *Critical Studies in Media Communication*, and others. Kent Received his doctorate from Purdue University, and his Master's from the University of Oregon.

David Klimeš is an Assistant Professor at the Department of Marketing Communication and PR at the Charles University in Prague. The main areas of his scientific interest are history of communication and marketing, new media, and journalism. He is an author of books describing the phenomenon of infotainment, development of Czech humanitarian aid, and the political life of former Czech president Václav Klaus. He is also a columnist for Czech newspapers. He is a trainer of many communication and media literacy workshops in the Czech Republic and abroad.

Stélia Neta João Mboene has worked in the Public Relations Department of the Ministry of Economy and Finances of Mozambique since 2006, and in 2015 she was appointed National Director for the Institutional Coordination and Image. She has a degree in Journalism (Coimbra University) and an M.Sc. in Strategic Communication (University of Beira Interior). Currently she is working on her doctoral thesis in Communication Sciences on the theme of Mozambique Government Communication, at the University of Beira Interior.

Charis Rice is a Research Associate at Coventry University's Centre for Trust, Peace and Social Relations (CTPSR). Charis received a competitive scholarship to undertake her Ph.D. at the University of Ulster, where her thesis examined government communication in Northern Ireland, namely the relationships between political and media actors in this process and the implications for a post-conflict society. She has lectured in the areas of government and political communication, and on various public relations topics. Charis' research in these areas has been published in *Public Relations Review*, the *International Journal of Public Administration* and edited books. Her current research interests include exploring trust, power and communication at an interpersonal and institutional level. Charis has particular interests in the role of ministerial special advisers in governments, especially in complex governments or deeply divided societies. She believes that exploring the roles and relationships of elite actors and organizations, such as government and the media, is paramount to understanding the workings – and health – of democratic societies. Charis is a member of the International Communication Association (ICA), European Communication Research and Education Association (ECREA), as well as the European Group for Organizational Studies (EGOS).

Liane Rothenberger is a Senior Researcher and Lecturer at the Institute of Media and Communication Science, Technische Universität Ilmenau, Germany. She earned her doctorate at the Catholic University of Eichstätt–Ingolstadt, Germany, in 2008. Her research interests include journalism studies, normative influences in communication scholarship, intercultural and international communication, and crisis communication with a focus on (online) communication of terrorist groups. Liane Rothenberger is a member of the International Research Group on Crisis Communication (IRGoCC). As a freelance journalist she has worked for several media, including the German weekly news magazine *Der Spiegel*.

Jordi de San Eugenio is at the University of Vic-Central University of Catalonia (Spain). From 2013 to 2014 he was the Vice-Dean of the Faculty of Business and Communication. From 2011 to 2013 he was Head of the Communication Department. He received his Ph.D. (with honours) in Place Branding from Pompeu Fabra University. He holds an M.A. in Environment Management from the University of Girona, a B.A. in Journalism from Pompeu Fabra University, and a B.A. in Geography from University of Girona. His research interests include place branding, public diplomacy, environmental communication and humanistic geography. His articles have been accepted for publication in the *Journal of Rural Studies* and *Place Branding and Public Diplomacy*, among others.

Ian Somerville is a Reader in Media and Communication at the University of Leicester. His research has been published in a range of international journals of public relations, communication, public administration and sociology, including: *Public Relations Review*, *Public Relations Inquiry*, *International Journal of Public Administration*, *International Review for the Sociology of Sport*, *Journal of Communication Management* and in various edited collections. Current research interests include public relations in conflict and post-conflict societies, government public relations, public relations/lobbying in human rights activism and sports communication and social exclusion. He is a member of the editorial boards of *Public Relations Review* and *Public Relations Inquiry.* In 2014 he was elected Vice-Chair of the Organisational and Strategic Communication section of the European Communication Research and Education Association.

Maureen Taylor is Director of the School of Advertising and Public Relations in the College of Communication and Information at the University of Tennessee. Taylor's research focuses on public relations for relationship building in civil society. Taylor has experience in creating and measuring the outcomes of communication campaigns and media development initiatives in post-conflict nations including Bosnia, Croatia, Serbia, Kosovo, Iraq, Liberia, Mozambique and Sudan.

Margalit Toledano is a Senior Lecturer in the Management Communication Department of the Waikato Management School in New Zealand. She was accredited APR by the Public Relations Society of America (PRSA) in 1985 and has been accepted as a member of the PRSA College of Fellows in 2007 and of the Public Relations Institute of New Zealand (PRINZ) College of Fellows in 2012. She has been serving as co-chair CEPR of the PRSA Educational Affairs Committee since 2010. A former president of the Israeli Public Relations Association with over twenty years of experience as a public relations practitioner, including running her own agency, she worked for leading Israeli organizations in the business, non-profit, and government sectors. She was also involved with Israeli non-profits who promoted dialogue with Palestinians and supported actions for reconciliation and peace. She has published a number of articles in leading PR journals, including *Public Relations Review*, on which she serves as a member of the editorial board, and has a number of chapters in the major handbooks of the field. She co-authored, with Professor David McKie, a book on PR in Israel, entitled *Public Relations and Nation Building: Influencing Israel* (Routledge, 2013).

Jordi Xifra is at the Universitat Pompeu Fabra, Barcelona, Spain. His research interests are within the fields of history of public relations, public affairs and public diplomacy. He leads a research group on think tanks' communication management. Xifra is author and editor of more than fifteen books on public relations and public affairs in Spain and South America, including: *Lobbying: Cómo influir eficazmente en las decisiones de los poderes públicos* (1998); *Teoría y estructura de las relaciones públicas* (2003); *Planificación estratégica de las relaciones públicas* (2005); *Los think tanks* (2008); and *Manual de relaciones públicas e institucionales* (2011). He also is co-editor of the *Routledge Handbook of Critical Public Relations* (2015). His articles have been accepted for publication in *Public Relations*

Review, the *Journal of Public Relations Research, American Behavioral Scientist*, and the *Journal of Political Marketing*, among others. In 2004 he founded AIRRPP, the Spanish Public Relations Research Association. He is the co-editor of *Public Relations Inquiry* (Sage).

Foreword

Krishnamurthy Sriramesh

Globalization is not new to the 21st century. Politics (conquering lands), economics (trade), and cultural exchange have been integral to all the eras of globalization – archaic, early modern, and modern. Communication has also been an integral part of, perhaps even central to, human exchanges through all these eras of globalization. Because of the realities of the 21st century, modern globalization is unique in several respects including the infrastructure for communication (ICTs) and the pervasive use of these technologies. It is in this context that one can discern the importance of international (global) public relations by defining *global public relations as: the strategic communication that is practiced by different types of organizations for establishing and maintaining symbiotic relationships with relevant publics, many of whom are culturally diverse*. In this definition, "cultural diversity," rather than "national boundaries," rightly determines the parameters of international (global) public relations. Such an outlook is driven largely by the realities of the 21st century and the cultural melting pots that many nations have become in no small measure because of the mobility of populations owing to a number of factors such as the ease of travel but also other migratory reasons such as economic disparities and conflict. The result is the altered state of cultural diversity among populations in many parts of the world. This has resulted in "nations" existing within national (political) boundaries, a phenomenon that requires much more study by our field. Political boundaries have often been drawn rather arbitrarily anyway, often by colonizing forces. For all these reasons, far from being a "specialty practice," *international public relations* is a dire necessity that has the potential to help us meet the challenges in understanding, and managing, the cultural diversity that defines our times.

This need begs us to question whether the body of public relations has adequately equipped itself to meet this challenge. One of the primary purposes of scholarship is to prepare students to be effective as young professionals who can hit the ground running when they enter the work force. Another key role is to translate scholarship for the benefit of middle and upper level managers who are at the forefront of practicing international public relations. As has been noted repeatedly for over a decade, public relations scholarship, with a history of about half a century, has yet to embrace adequately the importance of *cultural* diversity to effective communication. Ethnocentricity in the public relations body of knowledge can be discerned in such things as the predominant focus on Western experiences driving the bulk of theorizing as well as corporate experiences playing an unjustifiably large role in theory building often entirely ignoring not for profits (NGOs, INGOs, and civil society) and governments and their agencies – two key types of organizations that have practiced international public relations much more often and expansively than corporations. Ethnocentricity also abounds when one examines the tools of knowledge dissemination – textbooks and articles that address key issues related to international public relations.

The editors of this volume, and the authors who have contributed essays, deserve commendation for adding critical pieces to the growing body of knowledge of international public relations. In doing so, this volume helps address some of the above deficiencies in public relations literature. First, this book attempts to reduce ethnocentricity by assessing the use of public relations outside the developed world thus adding wisdom to earlier attempts in this regard. The essays on government public relations also help bring some balance to the body of knowledge that has focused so heavily on corporate public relations. Second, this volume breaks new ground by attempting to address how public relations is used in societies that are, or have been, witnessing conflict. Conflict seems to be pervasive in today's world and effective communication can make a difference in building peace – an area where public relations is yet to make any impact. Cultural diversity further exacerbates exponentially the challenges of building peace in this conflict-ridden world and international public relations can make a difference in that respect as well. Third, this volume's focus on nation-building and nation branding adds a new dimension to the body of knowledge of global public relations building on previous research of over three decades that has discussed using communication to build images of nations. Finally, the essays in this volume contribute to elaborating on the notion of "nations within nations" that has not been discussed as much as it should in international public relations.

The supply for knowledge on international public relations has certainly not kept pace with the increased demand from practice. So, every attempt to add to the body of knowledge should be welcomed with enthusiastic support. This volume goes beyond that basic need by setting new vistas for future studies with the goal of expanding horizons. All those who are passionate about global public relations should applaud every such attempt at building a holistic and comprehensive body of knowledge that will also have relevance to practice. One fondly hopes that this volume will be the harbingers of many more books on this topic.

Acknowledgements

The production of this book has been a collaborative effort with many important contributors. In particular we would like to thank our panel of expert reviewers for their enthusiasm and willingness to read and comment so insightfully on the many contribution submitted for inclusion to this collection. Their input has been invaluable in shaping all of the work presented in this volume and therefore we express our deepest appreciation to the following: Pat Curtin, Scott Davidson, Lee Edwards, Gregor Halff, David McKie, Magda Pieczka, Tom Watson, Dejan Vercic and Rhonda Zaharna.

At Routledge we would like to thank Jacqueline Curthoys, Kevin Moloney, Nicola Cupit, Sinead Waldron, Andy Soutter and Paola Celli for their help in guiding this project from initial conception to completion. The genesis of this book, where many of the contributions were first presented, was a conference sponsored by the Organisational and Strategic Communication section of the European, Communication, Research and Education Association (ECREA) in Belfast, 12 June 2013, and we acknowledge the funding contribution by the University of Ulster's Institute for Research in Social Sciences (IRiSS) and EDConnect which made the conference possible. Finally and most importantly we want to express our gratitude to Professor Sriramesh Krisnamurthy for writing the Foreword to this volume.

1 Introduction

Public relations in deeply divided societies

Ian Somerville, Owen Hargie, Maureen Taylor and Margalit Toledano

Most empirical studies of public relations focus on the activity as it is practised within stable liberal democratic societies such as the USA. Indeed the dominance of theory and models from US scholars has had a hegemonic influence on attempts within the academy to theorize public relations. This raises the important question of the extent to which theory building in this context has an application to the many countries in the world which are divided by deep societal cleavages along racial, ethnic, religious or linguistic lines. A key purpose of this edited collection is to not only reflect on this question but turn it around and explore how public relations practice in divided, conflict and post-conflict societies may contribute to theory building in the field of public relations more generally. Moreover, contributions to the book help to redefine the role of public relations in society by emphasizing its potential contribution to peace building, conflict resolution, and empowering civil society. It will therefore be of interest to scholars in disciplines such as political science, international relations, public diplomacy, nation branding, and peace and conflict studies.

Public relations can be defined as an activity employed by organizations to promote or challenge competing discourses in order to facilitate a favourable position within local, national and global contexts (Daymon and Demetrious, 2013). Such a definition highlights the political role of the practice in purposively influencing the meaning-making process and acknowledges what has been termed the 'socio-cultural turn' (Edwards and Hodges, 2011) in public relations theory. It is the intersection of public relations practice with socio-political environments in divided, conflict and post-conflict societies, which is a key focus of this book.

Although there have been some noteworthy investigations of the environmental factors influencing public relations practice in non-Western contexts and even conflict societies – for example, *The Global Public Relations Handbook* (Sriramesh and Verčič, 2009) includes chapters on Israel and Palestine – as noted above, the liberal democratic context has dominated academic theorizing of PR practice (L'Etang, 2008). Indeed arguably this applies to one liberal democratic society in particular, the USA. In their influential textbook, Cutlip et al. (2000: 448) argue: 'In a very real sense, the purpose of democracy itself closely matches the purpose of public relations. Successful democratic government maintains relationships with constituents, based on mutual understanding and two-way communication.' For Cutlip et al., 'democracy' means the majoritarian constitutionalist democratic model which characterizes the institutional architecture of the USA. Leaving aside the unreflective ideological assumptions, the rhetorical tactic of legitimacy by association produces the danger that PR (or at least certain conceptions of it) and 'democracy' are seen to go hand in hand, with both being viewed as fundamentally American.

A growing number of scholars have argued that US models and US theory have dominated PR scholarship, and not necessarily to the benefit of the field. This domination is typified by the success of the 'Excellence school' or 'Grunigian paradigm' (Pieczka, 2006; Porter, 2010). Gregory and Halff (2013: 419) note that for a considerable period in the history of modern PR education, 'Excellence theory was taught as staple and American models of practice, as conducted by the large consultancies and corporate organizations, held up as exemplars.' Such foundational assumptions of much contemporary PR theory will be questioned and/or challenged by studies in this volume which attempt to counter the still current ethnocentricity in scholarship by encouraging the analysis of PR from the 'margins'. Thus, while it can be positioned within the emerging 'critical school' in the PR scholarship, this collection does not exclude contributions from a technocratic or functionalist perspective, rather it merely regards this as one amongst a range of theoretical viewpoints, all of which potentially offer meaningful analysis. What makes work critical is the demonstration of reflexivity and recognition of the power relations inherent in any public relations activity.

The main aims of this volume will be outlined below, but before doing that it is worth defining some of the key concepts employed in this book. As Wittgenstein (1953) noted, clear definitions are always difficult, and frequently a pointless endeavour, but it is worth explaining what we mean by terms such as 'deeply divided societies', 'conflict' and 'post-conflict' in order to understand the parameters of this volume. According to Guelke (2012) a 'deeply divided society' is one where violence or the threat of violence keeps it divided. Deeply divided societies find making peace and reconciliation difficult, if not impossible, to achieve mainly due to an inability to agree on a common process for decision-making. Although we are largely in agreement with Guelke's definition, it is worth pointing out that Switzerland has a 'deeply divided society' (Hega, 2011) not because there is a danger of slippage into violent conflict but because it is a multi-ethnic, multi-religious and multilinguistic state in much the same way as, for example, Lebanon is. Thus, in this edited collection, a 'deeply divided society' includes, amongst others, conflicted societies, societies which are in a post-conflict phase and societies which may well have had no history of violence for a considerable period of time. It must be acknowledged that all societies in the contemporary late capitalist period are divided societies in the sense that there are (sometimes extreme) economic inequalities. However, because division based on economic criteria is universal it is an area little examined in the literature which focuses on deeply divided societies except where one (ethnic/religious/linguistic) group, for example, promotes discrimination of another group in the economic sphere – through employment law, etc. This specific kind of economic discrimination is not a feature of any of the empirical studies in this collection.

Defining what constitutes a conflict and a post-conflict society is an area of considerable debate. For the purposes of this volume we employ the widely used Uppsala Conflict Data Program definition of conflict as: 'a contested incompatibility that concerns government and/or territory where the use of armed force between two parties, of which at least one is the government of a state, resulting in at least 25 battle-related deaths in a year'. In respect to what constitutes a post-conflict society we draw upon the United States Institute for Peace definition, which refers to a situation in which violent conflict has formally ceased. Such situations are commonly marked by a peace agreement and/or intervention by a third party under a UN or other internationally recognized mandate. However, although conflict has *officially* ceased, some level of violence may well persist. A post-conflict society is likely to have the following characteristics: (1) there has been a cessation of armed conflict; (2) the different parties involved in and affected by the conflict have signed peace agreements; (3) the society has been significantly demilitarized; (4) the society remains polarized. Most deeply divided societies are societies which are experiencing conflict or are recovering from conflict. Public relations plays a role at all levels in such societies, just as it does in the Western liberal democracies where most PR textbooks are written and most PR research is conducted.

This collection has two main aims. First, to present a range of original empirical research from outside the usual Developed World/Global North studies which have dominated current scholarship in the field. Consequently these studies come from conflict societies, post-conflict societies, transitional societies and societies still deeply divided along racial, religious, ethnic and linguistic lines. By focusing on these contexts the chapters give a voice to scholarship from societies which in many cases have been marginalized in current academic literature on PR. The second purpose of this collection is to contribute to theory development and evaluation in the field of PR. Many of the studies in this book raise important questions about the relevance of theory building – and ensuing PR models – developed in liberal democratic societies to the many regions/states in the world which are currently riven by conflict or are attempting to rebuild after conflict. Several of the contributions to this volume reflect on this important question and in doing so problematize aspects of contemporary mainstream public relations theory. In doing so they also address the issue of what public relations practice in deeply divided societies may have to contribute to theory building for the field of PR.

Broadly speaking, the chapters which comprise this collection can be seen to contribute to several intersecting main themes: public relations and nation building; public relations and nation branding; and public relations and peace building. Some chapters focus directly on government communication actors in divided societies; others on the role of PR for civil society actors; and several chapters engage with the issue of communication strategies in societies where those who deployed or still deploy political violence to achieve their goals remain key actors.

Taylor and Kent (Chapter 2: 'Nation building in the Former Yugoslavia: A 20-year retrospective to understand how public relations rebuilds relationships in divided societies') reflect on nation building in two countries that emerged from the Former Yugoslavia. The authors argue that the current structure of a nation state influences the type of public relations enacted, and provide in-depth case studies of two nations in order to explore two different stages of public relations for nation building. In Bosnia, one-way communication channels and infrastructure development were required. In Croatia, nation building meant creating inter-organizational relationships that lead to social capital. Toledano (Chapter 3: 'Dialogue with the enemy: Lessons for public relations on dialogue facilitation drawn from the Israeli–Palestinian conflict') examines the role of public relations practitioners as facilitators of dialogues between opposing parties in deeply divided societies. It draws from Martin Buber's approach to the concept of dialogue and uses evidence from Israeli–Palestinian dialogue groups that were active during the 1990s when the Oslo Peace Process inspired a 'People-to-People' movement. The chapter investigates a specific dialogue case study, which was sponsored by UNESCO, called the Israeli Palestinian Media Forum (IPMF). Toledano provides testimonials from the dialogue facilitator and participants, as well as her own involvement with the case.

In their chapter (Chapter 4: 'Making sense of communication in societies divided by terrorism: Lessons from Northern Ireland') Hargie and Irving employ a sensemaking frame to investigate public relations in the divided society of Northern Ireland. While the sensemaking paradigm has been widely employed within organizational communication, there has been a dearth of application within the PR field, and so this study is timely. Hargie and Irving investigate the concepts of sensemaking, sensegiving and sensenegotiation, and their effects upon public relations. They do so by analysing the context within which terrorism occurs, and by studying the ways in which sense is shaped by the communication strategies of the terrorists, the media and the government, and the effects of all of this upon the public. They show how, in relation to sensemaking, both the interpretations and actions of the different groups can be understood in terms of past frames that are used to understand current events. Their analysis concludes that in divided societies there is a sensemaking schism, and so a major task for all those involved is that of using communication to attempt to bring the warring factions more closely together so that a shared sensemaking frame may begin to emerge. In this regard they develop a 'communication sensemaking jigsaw' model to illustrate how societies can move from division towards unity, based upon sensenegotiations across target groups.

Somerville and Rice (Chapter 5: 'Deliberative democracy and government public relations in a deeply divided society: Exploring the perspectives of Government Information Officers in Northern Ireland.') assess how the comparatively unique consociational political system, designed to produce a functioning democratic government in a deeply divided society, impacts on government public relations in Northern Ireland's public sphere. Drawing on data from elite interviews they analyse Government Information Officer perspectives alongside those of the other key actors with whom these officials regularly interact in Northern Ireland's government–media communicative sphere – ministerial Special Advisers (SpAds) and political journalists. The communicative interactions between these groups are discussed within broader debates about government public relations in democratic societies and in particular in relation to theoretical work on communication and deliberative democracy. They conclude with some reflections on the role in government that PR could play in deploying 'bridging rhetoric' to help Northern Ireland move towards a more authentic deliberative democracy.

The above chapters focus on well-documented conflict regions – Israel–Palestine, the Former Yugoslavia and Northern Ireland – but many contributors to the book explored other important but often overlooked environments. From the context of Switzerland, Ingenhoff and Buhmann (Chapter 6: 'The entity–agent framework as a starting point for international public relations and public diplomacy research') take a conceptual theoretical approach to the concept of 'nation branding' and argue that the scholarly functionalist-concretist approach to this concept is misleading the study of international public relations and public diplomacy. They criticize macro-categorizations such as 'nation' and 'country' as assuming a manifest social entity while ignoring the fact that modern countries are widely pluralistic in a cultural, ethnic, religious and linguistic sense, and can, therefore, be considered as inherently and deeply divided. Instead the authors suggest an entity-agent framework that offers new insights going beyond the common concretism and allowing for the constructedness of the 'country entity' to be factored in. The authors argue that variances in the construction of entitativity and agency are central for international public relations and public diplomacy because they affect the structures and dynamics of how publics perceive certain countries and, as a consequence, influence their expectations and behaviour towards them.

San Eugenio, Ginesta and Xifra's chapter (Chapter 7: 'Catalonia's public diplomacy and media relations strategy: A case study of the Eugeni Xammar Programme of International Communication and Public Relations') also focuses on nation branding and public diplomacy. Their study analyses the international communication and public relations programme known as 'Eugeni Xammar' that has been conducted by the nationalist autonomous government of Catalonia since 2012. The programme's goal was to influence international public opinion to support Catalonia's independence and secession from Spain. This study combines case study methodology and in-depth interviews to assess the key strategic communication aspects and public relations characteristics of the programme. The authors theorize the Eugeni Xammar Programme as a significant case study for public relations scholars to analyse how, for stateless nations, public diplomacy is essential in order to be recognized in postmodern geopolitics.

As noted above, nation building is a theme explored by several contributors to this volume and it has been a crucial endeavour for states emerging from colonial and/or conflicted histories. Mboene and Gonçalves (Chapter 8: 'Government communication in Mozambique: The open presidencies of Armando Guebuza as a public relations strategy to strengthen national identity') explore how a government public relations strategy strengthened national identity in Mozambique. Using a critical discourse analysis of presidential speeches, Mboene identified repertoires of national-unity symbols, narratives and meanings in President Armando Guebuza's meetings with citizens. In Mozambique, the government integrates a relational public relations approach focused on establishing and managing relationships, increasing participation, and encouraging cooperation between the government and people living in rural areas.

In their chapter on Malaysia, (Chapter 9: '1Malaysia "People first, performance now": A critical perspective on the nation building approach in Malaysia's government public relations') Ahmad and Idid present an analysis of an ongoing government programme entitled '1Malaysia' which is designed to promote national unity and harmony between competing ethnic and religious groups. Their study describes the communication challenges typical of such a deeply divided society and questions the effectiveness of a government campaign that involves concealed political rhetoric. The argument is based on a longitudinal study that was carried out over five consecutive years and included 7,848 respondents nationwide. The survey findings demonstrated that '1Malaysia' was interpreted in many different ways by different ethnic groups in Malaysia.

In an analysis of forced and ultimately failed nation building, Hejlová and Klimeš (Chapter 10: 'Propaganda in Czechoslovakia in the 1980s: Life in a ritualised lie') use an historical frame to examine communication strategies that were employed by the state in the former divided society of Czechoslovakia (which in January 1993 was split into the two sovereign states of the Czech Republic and Slovakia). In particular, they investigate the methods and tools of propaganda used by the Communist Party to maintain the pretence that all of the citizens agreed with the extant power arrangement. They elucidate how the authoritarian Communist ruling elite employed both a repressive system and an ideology to create a narrative of a united society. Using critical discourse analysis, Hejlová and Klimeš analyse the production of the press agency of the Czechoslovak government (ČTK) and identify symbolic construction strategies of legitimation, dissimulation, unification and fragmentation, that were utilized by the state to communicate a created message of 'one nation' to the wider public through mass media, cultural events and the education system. While their investigation and findings are rooted in an historical 'moment' they are applicable to a study of the communication strategies employed by authoritarian regimes more generally.

The final two chapters in this collection address issues at the centre of current political and media attention. Bıçakçı, Hürmeriç and Bıçakçı (Chapter 11: 'Bipolar attitudes in Turkish political PR: The Kurdish question') provide an in-depth analysis of how Turkish government and opposition media have covered the Kurdish issue over time. The analysis shows a bipolar shift in government communication and media coverage of the Kurdish resolution process and the recent conflict process. The results of their nine-month content analysis suggest that propaganda, rather than public relations, is the communication practice of the Erdoğan government on the Kurdish question. Rothenberger's chapter (Chapter 12: 'Computer-mediated public relations of ethno-nationalist terrorist groups') focuses on an analysis of the PR goals and strategies of ethno-nationalist terrorist groups in deeply divided societies, as depicted on their websites. She illustrates how, while there is a clear difference between social movements and terrorist groups, particularly in relation to the use of violence, often terrorist groups evolve from social movements and share the moment of 'mobilization'. As a result, she uses a combination of enlarged PR theory and mobilization theory to interpret the use of PR techniques by terrorist groups on the Internet. She presents the findings from a content analysis of the websites of eight different terrorist groups to show how and in what ways they use the Internet to create a virtual room for transmitting their ideas, ideology and perception of the conflict. Rothenberger concludes that terrorists use PR strategies in a sophisticated way to promote and encourage support for their messages, alter extant power balances, and shift blame and responsibility to the perceived 'enemy'. Accordingly, she argues that the PR strategies of governments need to be carefully tailored to the terrorist group and its specific strategies of consensus and action mobilization.

A key feature of this collection is that it contributes original, empirically based studies which offer perspectives from the 'margins' and go some way towards countering the still predominant Anglo-American ethnocentricity which is the focus in much contemporary PR scholarship. This volume will therefore provide a valuable resource for students and scholars in a wide range of disciplines, including communication, political science, international relations, public diplomacy, nation branding, conflict resolution, and peace studies; and especially for students wishing to explore perspectives on public relations from currently marginalized contexts in both the Global North and the Global South.

References

Cutlip, S., Center, A. and Broom, G. (2000) *Effective public relations*. Englewood Cliffs, NJ: Prentice Hall.

Daymon, C. and Demetrious, K. (eds) (2013) *Gender and public relations: Critical perspectives on voice, image, and identity.* London: Routledge.

Edwards, L. and Hodges, C.E.M. (2011) 'Introduction: Implications of a radical socio-cultural "turn" in public relations scholarship', in Edwards, L. and Hodges, C.E.M. (eds) *Public relations, society and culture: Theoretical and empirical explorations.* London: Routledge.

Gregory, A. and Halff, G. (2013) 'Divided we stand: Defying hegemony in global public relations theory and practice?' *Public Relations Review*, 39(5): 417–425.

Guelke, A. (2012) *Politics in deeply divided societies.* Cambridge: Polity Press.

Hega, G.M. (2011) 'The political functions of education in deeply-divided countries: Coming together apart: The case of Switzerland', in T. Hanf (ed.) *The political function of education in deeply divided countries.* Baden-Baden, Germany: Nomos Verlag.

L'Etang, J. (2008) *Public relations: Concepts, practice and critique.* London: Sage.

Pieczka, M. (2006) 'Paradigms, systems theory and public relations', in L'Etang, J. and Pieczka, M. (eds) (2006) *Public relations: Critical debates and contemporary practice.* Mahwah, NJ: Lawrence Erlbaum Associates.

Porter, L. (2010) 'Communicating for the good of the state: A post-symmetric polemic on persuasion in ethical public relations', *Public Relations Review*, 36(4): 127–133.

Sriramesh, K. and Verčič, D. (eds) (2009) *The global public relations handbook: Theory, research and practice.* 2nd edn. Mahwah, NJ: Lawrence Erlbaum Associates.

United States Institute for Peace, www.usip.org/files/resources/sc_chap1.pdf

Uppsala Conflict Data Program, www.pcr.uu.se/research/UCDP/data_and_publications/definitions_all.htm

Wittgenstein, L. (1953) *Philosophical investigations* (trans. G.E.M. Anscombe). Oxford: Blackwell.

2 Nation building in the Former Yugoslavia

A 20-year retrospective to understand how public relations rebuilds relationships in divided societies

Maureen Taylor and Michael Kent

Introduction

Nation building is a process that creates interactions between citizens, between groups, and between the state and other nations. At the most basic level, a nation exists by the consent of a people and a recognition of a common heritage that is communicated by various social practices (Hobsbawm, 1994). Nations in all stages of economic, social and political development implement nation building activities. For instance, well-established, long-standing nations that are hundreds of years old enact activities to celebrate the past and motivate citizen support for the sustainment of the state. Newer, less established nations may employ nation building to create a common national identity for citizens and to galvanize support for future coordinated actions to improve the state. Nation building is never really over as new challenges such as growth, economic trouble, war, or natural disasters force nations to enact communication, relationships and mobilization.

This book focuses on how public relations creates relationships in divided nations. This chapter explores nation building in two nations born out of the wars that broke up the former Federal Republic of Yugoslavia (FRY). Yugoslavia was once considered the model multi-ethnic nation where Bosniaks, Serbs, Croats, Macedonians, Albanians and Slovenians often intermarried and lived in peace. Most historians attribute the ability of the Yugoslavian nation to remain stable to its charismatic but authoritarian leader, Marshall Broz 'Tito', who led the partisan movement that ended the German occupation of the region. When Tito finally gained power, he governed Yugoslavia through a one-party system with all power, including the media, residing with the state (Taylor and Napoli, 2003).

Yugoslavia started to implode following Tito's death, and in the early 1990s a power vacuum emerged. Actors advancing nationalist ideas and embracing real and perceived ethnic and religious differences filled that. Slovenia, Macedonia, Croatia and Bosnia all voted in referendums for independence from Yugoslavia. The wars in Yugoslavia (1991–1995) were a wake-up call to the world, as a nation once considered a model multi-ethnic state in the heart of Europe descended into civil war.

At the end of the wars, Croatia and Bosnia emerged as independent states. Yugoslavia was reduced to Serbia, Montenegro and Kosovo. And by 2006, Montenegro had also voted to leave Yugoslavia, and Kosovo declared independence from Serbia in 2010. Today, seven nations (Bosnia, Croatia, Kosovo, Macedonia, Montenegro, Serbia and Slovenia) now stand where once there was just one, unified, Federal Republic of Yugoslavia.

The Yugoslavian case is theoretically interesting to understanding public relations in divided societies for several reasons. First, the wars occurred at a time of increased interest in international practices of public relations. In the late 1980s and early 1990s, the public relations field was growing. Scholars began to consider how cultural and societal factors might influence the practice of public relations. A 1992 special issue of *Public Relations Review* highlighted new conceptual theories and practices in public relations in Europe (Van Riel, 1992), India (Sriramesh, 1992) and Latin America (Simöes, 1992). Scholars also recognized that the corporate models of public relations as management were not adequate to explain the diverse practices across the world. One of the topics that international public relations scholarship explored was nation building.

Most of the nation building research has come from African or Asian contexts, demonstrating how top-down (one-way) communication from governments to citizens (Pratt, 1985) functions to build a new nation. Karim (1989), for example, viewed nation building in Malaysia as an essential governmental function that helps to build the national character of developing nations. Van Leuven (1996) studied public relations in Singapore and Malaysia. Taylor and Botan (1997), and Taylor (2000a) examined the Neighborliness Campaign in Malaysia and found that nation building campaigns often have unanticipated and detrimental consequences for national identity and unity (Taylor, 2000).

A second reason why the Yugoslav case is valuable to public relations theory development is that scholars were able to observe, study and sometimes even contribute to nation building activities. The international community, including the United States and European Union, provided massive amounts of assistance to Bosnia and Herzegovina, and Croatia. There was a significant effort to 'build' the nations from the outside. Scholars were able to study the nation building process and, in some cases, actually participate in the nation building projects as researchers, trainers and evaluators. Such first-hand experience provided scholars with a deeper understanding of the opportunities and limitations of public relations in nation building.

Finally, a third reason that the Yugoslavian case is interesting is because its successes and failures have provided the foundation for more recent nation building efforts in other post-conflict contexts. The international humanitarian assistance community learned many hard lessons about nation building from the events in Yugoslavia. They were able to apply some of these lessons to Afghanistan (2001–present) and Iraq (2003–present). Although every nation-building project is different, each case provides new layers of insight into how to build or rebuild relationships in a post-conflict country.

This chapter builds on previous research in nation building in Bosnia (Taylor, 2000a; 2000b; 2004) and Croatia (Doerfel and Taylor, 2005; 2009; Taylor and Doerfel, 2003; Taylor and Kent, 2013; Taylor and Napoli, 2008), and reflects on primary data and personal experiences in the study and implementation of public relations in the nation building process in the former Yugoslavia. After 20 years, as scholars and practitioners, communication professionals can now see how public relations has both helped, and in some situations hindered, nation building. The first section of the chapter provides a discussion of the communication and public relations research on nation building. The second section describes two case studies of public relations and nation building in the Former Yugoslavia. The final section considers the implications of the use of public relations in nation building efforts in divided societies.

Nation building and communication

The term 'nation building' is associated with building political institutions in a newly formed (or transformed) state (Huntington, 1968). The goal of these political institutions is to mediate the demands by citizens for services such as roads, schools, fire protection, and personal safety, with the political capabilities of the government. Nation building in this approach most accurately describes 'institution building'. The creation of institutions such as political parties, nonpartisan professional organizations, and nongovernmental organizations (NGOs) supportive of the current government has been an important part of the nation building process.

Karl Deutsch argued that individuals and small groups became nations when various communication media allow people to share common social habits (1963; 1966a; 1966b). For Deutsch, interpersonal and mass communication fosters the social integration of individuals, groups, associations and institutions. Communication channels allow for the transfer of information from one group or network to others and communication builds the relations among people necessary for attaining national goals.

Mediated communication channels such as print, radio, television and today the Internet bring a nation together. Media create a collective consciousness that leads to national integration. However, there is much more to nation building then creating common communication channels because mediated communication alone cannot create a nation. Instead, an approach to nation building that looks at how communication creates *meaning* is a timely endeavor. The political science literature on nation building reflects a political communication bias. Communication is viewed only as a channel or network rather than as a dynamic human process. However, a public relations approach to nation building draws upon a more sophisticated understanding of communication that focuses on how meanings are socially constructed. Media still play a role, but they are not the only form of communication that matters.

Nations as networks of co-created meaning

A public relations approach to nation building picks up where the integrationists left off 50 years ago because it offers a focus on communication and relationships. The political integrationist perspective provides a starting point for a public relations approach to nation building. But a communicative co-creational approach to nation building goes farther because it addresses the meaning of communication rather than the channels of the messages, as that which shapes the collective consciousness of individuals, groups, communities, and the nation.

A new understanding of the relationship building role that communication plays in the nation building process is needed. Public relations offers a valuable lens through which to view the nation building process. Early public relations assumptions held that public relations was a business and management function. However, today there are different perspectives that position public relations as a relationship building and nation building function. For instance, Kruckeberg and Stark (1988) identified public relations as a way to rebuild community. Extending the Chicago School's concept of community Kruckeberg and Stark argued:

> public relations is better defined and practiced as the active attempt to restore and maintain a sense of community. Only with this goal as a primary objective can public relations become a full partner in the information and communication milieu that forms the lifeblood of U.S. society and, to a growing extent, the world.
>
> (1988: xi)

If public relations can be used to rebuild communities in the United States, then it can also be used to create and recreate communities around the world. Moreover, Botan (1992) argued that public relations should be viewed as a tool to build relationships between previously unrelated social systems or as a tool to modify existing relationships between organizations and publics. When communication and public relations are viewed as tools for creating and maintaining relationships nationally, then the nation state emerges as a truly communicatively constructed system. Public relations can support all types of communication, including political communication (Martinez and Kiousis, 2005), business cooperation and relationship building.

We argue that in addition to the interpersonal relationship building function of public relations in nation building, there is also a second role for public relations research and practice to build, sustain and change networks of groups. One theoretical framework in particular, the social network perspective, is useful for taking a 'bird's eye analysis' of relationship research starting from dyadic relationships (individuals and organizations) to inter-organizational networks (populations of organizations), to entire populations of organizations in a nation or global system (the community ecology) (Yang and Taylor, 2015). Network ecology embodies a macro understanding of the many, diverse, relational networks of organizations comprising the nation state. Public relations communication of all kinds (persuasive, political, risk, crisis, CSR, health), and channels (interpersonal, mediated, mass) construct and reconstruct the meaning that creates networks and community social capital.

Social capital creates shared norms or values that create social cooperation in societal relationships. And like economic capital that is already very familiar to most people, the relationships that social capital creates are part of a *relational economy*. Social capital is an outcome of the relationships in civil society (Coleman, 1988; Fukuyama, 2002).

The value of social capital in public relations has recently been explored. Social capital, as Kennan and Hazelton (2006) noted, can be understood at the individual, organizational, or societal levels. Ihlen (2007) argued that the development of social capital is a crucial public relations activity and fits in well with public relations core values such as relationship building. Public relations communication assists organizations in their struggle to access social capital.

Yang and Taylor (2015) positioned social capital as a central concept in understanding public relations' social function across nations. Organizations exist in local and global networks, and Taylor (2009) argued that social capital is created when organizations, groups, publics and individuals work toward shared goals.

We believe that the type of public relations applied in nation building is dependent on the level and type of existing relationship in the nation. For instance, the integrationist approach looked at relationships in newly formed states emerging from colonialism. These new states needed communication channels and one-way messages to coordinate the actions of previously unrelated people. Those messages help create the identity of the nation state and build national unity. As a nation evolves, other public relations strategies may become more dominant in the nation building. For instance, in a nation that already has a strong national identity, public relations may be needed to build stronger inter-organizational relationships across the nation. Collaboration, cooperation, and mobilization may be the end goal of communication in nations with a strong national identity. We argue that the current structure of a nation state will influence the type of public relations enacted, and provide in-depth case studies of two nations (Bosnia and Herzegovina, and Croatia) that emerged from the Former Yugoslavia. The case studies illustrate two of the possible ways that public relations contributes to nation building in divided societies.

Public relations and nation building in Bosnia and Herzegovina, and Croatia

This section provides two in-depth case studies of how public relations has been used in nation building in Bosnia and Herzegovina, and Croatia. Each case study draws upon primary research by the authors as they studied public relations in nation building projects in the post-war period.

Bosnia and Herzegovina's struggle to build a nation

Since the fall of the Berlin Wall and the dissolution of the Soviet Union and Yugoslavia, the political landscape of Europe and much of the world has changed dramatically. Over 20 new sovereign states have emerged throughout Eastern Europe and Central Asia. One new nation, Bosnia and Herzegovina, experienced some of the most painful implications of the changes in Europe, including civil war and genocide (1992–1995), corrupt nationalist governments, and a breakdown of socialist political and economic systems.

As mentioned previously, the nation of Bosnia and Herzegovina was created in 1992 out of the breakup of the Former Yugoslavia, and immediately entered into a three-year civil war (Glenny, 1996). The international community recognized the enormous cost associated with Bosnia's transition out of communism and nationalism. Since 1995, billions of dollars of assistance have been allocated to the physical reconstruction of the war-damaged country. While there has been progress made in rebuilding the infrastructure of Bosnia and Herzegovina, and some success in keeping the three ethnic groups from renewed fighting, the civil society initiatives still show mixed results (Belloni, 2001).

Creating new institutions and communication channels

Public relations has played multiple roles in Bosnia and Herzegovina over the last 20 years. Forms of public relations started off, as in most communist nations, as one-way communication initiatives from governments to citizens. In communist nations, the state controls most aspects of life: state-run media, state-run companies and state-run institutions hinder the creation of community social capital. People do not trust each other, nor do they trust organizations and institutions. Citizens generally only trust close family members and friends.

The 1995 Federation of Bosnia and Herzegovina included two entities: Republika Srpska and the Federation of Bosnia and Herzegovina. International humanitarian organizations started at the beginning as the new nation emerged from the war. The Dayton Agreement created the Office of the High Representative (OHR) to oversee the civilian implementation of the agreement. Local and national leaders who had participated in the war were removed from office or barred from elections. The NATO-led Implementation

Force was responsible for all military aspects of the agreement, including keeping the three groups from renewed fighting. In 1996 the Organization for Security and Co-operation in Europe (OSCE) was charged with organizing the first free elections.

One of the first ways that public relations was used in Bosnia and Herzegovina was to begin to create governmental transparency, and build trust in government and societal institutions, including the mass media. Many international donor organizations funded local groups, helping them to develop mechanisms for watching local governments and institutions (Botan and Taylor, 2005; USAID, 2000). For example, Transparency Bosnia and Herzegovina uses media relations, sponsors events, publishes research and writes reports to promote transparency and accountability in business transactions, informs the general public about the manifestations and problems of corruption – particularly through convening meetings of experts – and monitors compliance with standards of conduct.

A second way that public relations was used in Bosnia and Herzegovina was to create a Bosnian, rather than Croatian, Serbian or Bosniak identity. The rhetorical construction of a national identity is a foundational step in the nation building process. A national identity can be defined as the conscious identification of a group of people with shared national goals. People often have many different identities – religious, ethnic, professional – that define who they are and what values they hold (Kent and Taylor, 2011a). Efforts to build national identity seek to create a loyalty to the nation that supersedes local or ethnic loyalties and helps a nation to maximize its development potential.

Communication campaigns create national identities that allow a nation's people to think together and act together. Communication is a central part of nation building because mediated communication channels act as relationship building tools that bring citizens together and, in times of crisis or threats, can help to unify them. A national identity is a prerequisite to national unity and, therefore, must be part of the initial stages of nation building.

In Bosnia, the Office of the High Representative sought to remove all symbols that identified people's ethnic identity. For instance, there was the creation of a national license plate, a national flag, national rather than ethnic or regional sports teams, a national educational curriculum and a national currency. While these tactics are not necessarily public relations activities, the process of soliciting feedback from citizens to create them, winning public support and implementing them included many public relations activities. Wolfgang Petritsch, who served as the High Representative, has argued that the Dayton framework has allowed the international community to move 'from statebuilding via institutions and capacity-building to identity building', putting Bosnia and Herzegovina on the road to European Union membership (2006).

A third way that public relations was used in Bosnia and Herzegovina was to build inter-ethnic relationships in communities divided by war.

Communication campaigns and inter-ethnic activities seek to address the mistrust and fear of others. Local organizations created opportunities for people of different groups to meet and engage each other.

Finally, public relations was used in Bosnia and Herzegovina by the Bosnian federal government, in cooperation with the business community, to create a unified national image to be communicated to external countries – a national brand (Mamuti and Dzenita, 2014). Nation branding takes place when countries use public relations and mass communication to put forth a vision or image of the nation that they want people to think about first when they hear the nation's name mentioned (Boulding, 1977). Bosnia needed economic investment and major companies are not interested in setting up shop in a country that could descend into civil war again (Kent et al., 2006). In Bosnia there have been several nation branding campaigns aimed at Europe to encourage investment and tell the story of Bosnia as a European nation. Nation branding was also used to help move Bosnia toward European Union membership though the Stabilisation and Association Agreement (SAA).

Public relations played many roles in post-war Bosnia. The one-way communication tactics of media relations, public information, nation branding, and publicity have dominated. One-way information and dissemination tactics have roles to play in post-conflict situations (Somerville and Kirby, 2012). The use of one-way tactics also made sense in the early stages of nation building: Bosnia was at the beginning of the nation building process and it needed foundational communication processes to be created (Taylor, 2000b). Additionally, the post-war period nation-building activities focused on public information such as how to return to your hometown or how to register to vote in a new location. The nation was being glued together by *information* communicated through independent media (Taylor and Kent, 2000).

As the work of building the institutions and communication channels became less pressing, there was a need for higher-level relationship building among the citizens and between Bosnia and its neighbors. At this time, the more co-creational approaches to public relations emerged in the nation building process. The one-way communication practices of public relations have been joined by dialogue and other relational practices to build relationships in the next level of nation building. The case of Croatia provides insight into that next stage of nation building: *social capital and civil society.*

Croatia builds the foundation of civil society and joins the European Union

The Yugoslavian Republic of Croatia was one of the strongest economic, political and cultural republics in the Former Yugoslavia. Croats were the second largest ethnic group in the Former Yugoslavia and had benefited from higher levels of economic development than Bosnians or Serbians. Post-war Croatia was not as deeply divided along ethnic lines as Bosnia and thus started its nation building at a different point.

The conflict creates the birth of a modern nation

For decades, Croatians resented the loss of their cultural autonomy as a member state of the Former Yugoslavia. When Tito died in 1980, Croatia began preparing to leave the federation (Glenny, 1996). Croatia finally declared independence from Yugoslavia in 1991. From 1991 onward, President Franjo Tudjman and the nationalist Croatian National Party (HDZ), dominated the political arena. Tudjman's party's control over the state institutions, media and economy enhanced nationalist ideologies and fomented war. Any opposition to the regime was crushed. In the early 1990s, Croatian forces were active in central Bosnia hoping to build a connection to Croats living in Herzegovina.

In 1995 the leaders of Croatia, Bosnia and Yugoslavia signed the Dayton Peace Accord. A major part of the peace plan was to ensure that democratic elections would be held in each nation. Significant amounts of international humanitarian assistance were devoted to Bosnia and Croatia. As the first case study showed, most of that humanitarian assistance for Bosnia supported the creation of the infrastructure, fundamental institutions and communication channels in the nation. In Croatia, one of the best developed republics of the Former Yugoslavia, there was already existing infrastructure. While some humanitarian assistance was devoted to helping rebuild those areas of Croatia damaged in the war and help people affected by the conflict, the largest part of the assistance was devoted to establishing civil society organizations and independent media in these nations to help facilitate democracy building. This meant a different role for public relations at this stage of nation building. International donors helped to prepare local grassroots organizations for the much anticipated democratic elections. In December 1999, President Tudjman died and new elections were possible. His death created a small opening for reform in the shadow of the continuation of his nationalistic policies.

By 1999, there was a nascent civil society sector of NGOs, an independent media dedicated to political openness, and international donor organizations that devoted human and financial capital to civil society initiatives (USAID, 2000). A network of Croatian NGOs cooperated to create a non-partisan movement to ensure accurate information and fair elections. The 2000 parliamentary election was important to the future of Croatia because it signaled the end of Tudjman's regime and thus was the first time a democratic election was possible. Since that first free election in Croatia's history, NGOs, the media, and INGOs (international NGOs) have continued to engage in civil society activities.

In January 2000, Croatia elected a new parliament and the nationalist HDZ party lost power. With the election of the new Parliament and President Stjepan (Stipe) Mesic, Croatia became a democracy and soon entered into discussions with the European Union for membership of the EU. In the summer of 2000, the new Croatian Parliament was established and Croatia moved into a stabilization period in its nation building.

Social capital and the roles played by public relations in stabilization and nation building

What role has public relations played in this nation building stage? We believe that public relations' contribution to Croatian nation building was in the creation of civil society and social capital. As public relations' nation building practices have moved from functional (the media relations and information dissemination that we saw in Bosnia) to co-creational roles (organizations cooperating, increased trust in government and NGOs), the idea of public relations creating social capital and civil society has emerged.

As suggested above, social capital is a sociological concept that describes the social relationships that form the foundation for each society (Bourdieu, 1984; Coleman, 1988). Social capital is the invisible wealth of a community. While it can help to create tangible outcomes associated with economic wealth, in the civil society sector social capital is best understood as an intangible asset. We treat social capital as a community benefit that is created by a system of trusting and supportive interconnected organizations (Burt, 1997; Putnam, 2000; Doerfel and Taylor, 2005; Taylor and Doerfel, 2005; Toth, 2006) rather than as a negative force that reproduces inequity, because the 'wealth' of a community is in its relationships that provide new opportunities, information, and access to a variety of resources to people across the community.

Social capital and civil society are created by a system of trusting and supportive, interconnected organizations. These interconnected networks provide opportunities to study how communicatively constructed relationships shape the development of civil society. Taylor and Doerfel (2003; 2005; 2011) analyzed how public relations fosters inter-organizational relationships in the Croatian civil society network over three points in time (2000, 2002, 2004), studying more than 50 organizations. Taylor and Doerfel's studies provide a look at the evolving relationships of leading NGOs that were participating in nation building.

Nation states require certainty and predictable relationships. Uncertainty diminishes social capital because individuals, groups and organizations cannot trust others. Yang and Taylor (2015) hypothesized many roles for public relations in building the networks of a civil society. Public relations as an inter-organizational relationship building function can help organizations coordinate action, reduce uncertainty, build trust, and sustain networks of organizations in civil society. Longitudinal data from the stabilization stage of the Croatian nation building case provide evidence for their hypotheses.

In 1999 and 2000, at the time of heightened mobilization of civil society for the elections, Taylor and Doerfel (2003) found that trust was created when organizations communicated with each other through richer communication channels (face-to-face meetings, and telephone). The civil society network that emerged was a moderately well-connected group of NGOs and media organizations. Foundational organizations (those that had been around the longest) were considered most important and central to the inter-organizational network. All organizations depended on the state and independent media for publicizing their issues. International donors played key facilitating roles in building cross-sector civil society relationships.

In 2002, after the peaceful transition to a new government, Doerfel and Taylor (2005) found that the inter-organizational system of NGOs, INGOs, and media evolved into a relatively unconnected, inefficient network of relations. Organizations more central in terms of the communication networks and perceived importance in 2000, were considered more important and influential in the maintenance of Croatian civil society in 2002.

One key finding that helps us to understand stabilization in civil society is the role of media in the system. The media in the Former Yugoslavia, and throughout most of Eastern Europe, are in a fragile stage of transition. Government-run media have a history of a lack of credibility and objectivity (Taylor and Kent, 2000). In Croatia, the formerly government-run media, HRT, was no different. Indeed, HRT was used by the Tudjman government for over a decade to spread nationalist messages.

To date, no other national media outlet has ever been able to compete with HRT in terms of audience size, distribution of programming, and hiring of talented journalists. In 2000, HRT was on the periphery of the civil society network and the nature of its connections revealed that organizations scrutinized it carefully (Taylor and Doerfel, 2003). However, in 2000, shortly after the election of the new Parliament, HRT ended its long affiliation with the HDZ (Croatian National Party) and instituted a non-partisan editorial policy. And by 2002, HRT had become a full-fledged member of the Croatian civil society movement via its documentaries about NGOs, programming about public agenda issues, and non-partisan reporting. HRT's rehabilitation shows that it evolved into a trusted news source, and according to the data in this study, a valuable information resource for civil society organizations that need to publicize their activities and create shared meaning.

In 2004, nearly five years after the heightened mobilization, Doerfel and Taylor (2009) found the civil society network had again changed. By 2004, HRT was barely functioning under its original purpose of mobilization. The NGOs, donors and media no longer needed to lead political transformation – Croatia was well on its way to EU membership. The NGOs were now part of a wider, diverse civil society sector that allowed for new and capable political and social institutions in Croatia. There is more certainty in relationships and new organizations can enter the civil society sector and begin working toward their goals.

The Croatia network research has implications for public relations' role in building social capital and civil society. Network research and nation building research can help communication theorists, international donor organizations, NGOs and media training organizations to enhance their understanding of and participation in civil society. The organizations that were once important to the election campaign now struggle to find financial and social support for their original causes. The Croatia findings also describe the cyclic nature of partnering, reputation building, and subsequent partnering made possible by public relations communication. Stabilization in the network of NGOs, media and international organizations contributed to civil society in Croatia.

Both the Bosnia and Herzegovina, and Croatia case studies illustrate that the process of building civil society and national identity is a lengthy and ongoing process, made even more difficult by the presence of propaganda in some countries, the lack of a free and open press, or the presence of strong national leaders capable of exercising control as Tito and Tudjman did (cf. Taylor and Kent, 2000). In the decade after Tito's death, countries in the region experienced war atrocities as a direct result of nationalist rhetoric and a lack of crosscutting cleavages (Diamond, 1990; 2000; Taylor and Kent, 2000). Trust in the government, the media and in some cases the international community had been lost. Fortunately, using communication to build trust, foster transparency and engender a collective identity are where public relations excels. The final section of this chapter will highlight some of the lessons learned and what the possibilities are for public relations.

Implications for public relations in rebuilding divided societies: the difference between just communicating and using public relations

Democracies are founded on information from the government, civil society organizations, business interests, and trust by citizens and community leaders (Kent, 2013). For communication professionals working in war-torn and developing regions, theory-based knowledge in a number of areas is needed. *The most important knowledge would be broad, well-rounded communication and public relations skills.* Public relations in divided societies involves more than just producing content, writing news releases and posting social media messages as we see so often in stable societies. Because of issues like trust, professionalism and economic imperatives, the media often make tough choices about obtaining advertising revenue and free content, rather than gathering news or reporting on important social issues (Taylor, 2000b). Indeed, former journalists from communist and totalitarian regimes often lack the skills to deliver unbiased media coverage because their whole career has been devoted to serving as governmental propagandists rather than objective journalists. In light of what we have discussed in this chapter, four issues stand out.

The first issue has to do with *having a thorough understanding of the culture and a deep theoretical knowledge base in order to understand research, rhetoric, and persuasion skills.* The creation of effective messages requires the ability to gather and use a variety of types of research (as noted above, interviews, network data, content analyses of news reports, etc.). Building civil society is not a one-theory or one-method approach. And, more importantly, in countries that lack trust in governmental agencies, the media, business and other people, individuals are guarded about providing personal information and are often known to lie. A broad repertoire of research and rhetorical skills is needed as a basis for developing compelling, persuasive messages and convincing citizens to open themselves to new opportunities and the dialogic possibility of being changed (Kent and Taylor, 2002).

Many academics and communication professionals have only one or two methods in their toolboxes – for example, quantitative methods such as social network analysis or content analysis, or qualitative methods such as focus groups and interviews. The most successful communicators are able to engage in research on many levels, using what was learned from books, articles, their own research, community leaders, interviews, citizens in focus groups, and then using those insights to construct training and development materials for journalists or government communicators, or coming up with an original content analysis tool to address a specific need. The required skill set then includes a broad range of activities, and often the most important skill is the ability to use secondary research and information about the media, political structures, culture, or politics, to inform what is done as a professional communicator.

A second issue would involve *understanding the importance and function of social, political and cultural networks, and becoming a network leader.* As members of civil society, NGOs, INGOs and governmental agencies work together, various individuals and groups inevitably emerge as leaders. On the one hand, being able to *control* which groups will be seen as the most central and will emerge as the most trusted is not really possible. However, on the other hand, communication professionals who understand the nature of networks are able to position their organization more centrally, taking steps to connect other unconnected groups (called a '*tertius iungens*, or the third who joins' [Kent et al., 2016: 91–100]) and build a more cohesive community. A knowledgeable professional who understands how networks or social movements function can heighten an individual or organization's network centrality and ability to have network influence. So although no one can control a complex network of individuals and groups, networks are shaped and influenced by skilled leaders and visionaries.

One of the things that we know from decades of research on social networks is that people and organizations that have broader networks have an increased capacity to succeed – a concept called 'the strength of weak ties' (Granovetter, 1973). In essence, people and organizations that do not have a lot of friends/connections have more trouble achieving their goals than people with many friends/connections. Most people and organizations have a group of strong ties that they go to in times of crisis or difficulty, but access to more weak ties allows for access to novel information, a broader range of information, access to perspectives outside of one's comfort zone, and an increased chance of success.

As discussed previously, one of the big issues in divided societies is a lack of trust in institutions and people. Thus, organizations that are able to position themselves as central have to have something that others want, or want to have access to, and have to share their information or resources freely. Research on networks in divided societies suggests that the most central organizations are often those with the most resources, and those that are supported by external donor organizations (cf. Sommerfeldt and Kent, 2015). Ultimately, organizations that are willing to share more with others are able to engender trust and have a transformative effect on others.

A third issue concerning the body of public relations knowledge and theory in divided societies has to do with *the importance of building trust and identification*. As Kent et al. (2006) suggested, 'In transitional economies, there is a greater need for what public relations does best: build relationships' (p. 11). But relationship building is difficult when there is no social capital or trust. In many ways, what public relations does in the early stages of nation building is akin to marketing. Or, to paraphrase Wiebe (1951–1952), 'selling brotherhood like you sell soap'.

As described above, one of the early goals in Bosnia was to foster a national identity. The tools for this activity are rhetoric and persuasion. Rhetorical skills help public relations professionals understand the importance of the inclusive, nonjudgmental language that is required to help people trust others and see their own interests as being tied up with the interests of others (cf. Kent and Taylor, 2011b). When public relations professionals see their role as building relationships rather than product support, their messages have a greater potential to move people.

A fourth issue when building civil society *is to 'build capacity', or to train journalists and communication professionals how to do their job more effectively* (USAID, 2000). Millions of dollars were spent in Bosnia and Croatia training and retraining journalists in how to report news objectively, how to avoid inflaming passions through the use of objective language, etc. Moreover, in many locations, capacity building also involves creating a market for community journalism, funding news programs by local citizens that report on health and cultural issues, teaching how to provide unbiased content, training journalists how to conduct effective interviews, and even training local journalists in how to use modern news gathering equipment (cf. Kent and Taylor, 2011b). To say that broad communication skills are important is an understatement.

Conclusion

As this chapter explained, the conduct of nation building, building trust and creating civil society in divided nations is not simply the application of writing and conceptual skills, but a theory-based activity. There are no strategies guaranteed to work. There are no magic bullets that will make people trust others, their government or their institutions. Skilled communicators evaluate audience and situations, take into account culture and political circumstances, and gradually, often through trial and error, formulate communication strategies and best practices. This chapter has described many of the outcomes of those practices, and what some of the best practices are.

Building community, civil society, and rebuilding lost or nonexistent trust and relationships is a sophisticated communicative process that requires an understanding of communication, rhetoric, the local culture, the nature of the media and political system, and a knowledge of public issues that have relevance in specific communities (Kent and Taylor, 2007). An outsider cannot simply come into another country and fix their problems, as the US and international aid communities have learned (Taylor and Doerfel, 2011). By the same token, divided societies, whether because of war, political oppression, or other issues, usually cannot deal with all of their problems alone. Communication and public relations skills, coupled with the assistance of international donors, local training, and capacity building initiatives, can have an impact.

Public relations has many roles to play in the nation building process. We would be remiss not to mention that public relations can also hinder relationships. Just as campaigns can be used to bring people together, they can also be used to divide. The same tools that help make public relations a force for social justice and social capital are also used as a force for division, and to convince people to commit atrocities. Public relations researchers and educators can take the lessons of the academy and classroom, and help prepare their students for ways to participate in nation building. Whether in North America, Europe, Africa, Asia or Latin America, there will also be a need to ensure that people have reliable information, the opportunity to learn about each other, forums that allow for dialogue and understanding, and safe spaces where differences can be worked out. We believe public relations theory and practice can provide structures and processes for the nation state.

References

Belloni, R. (2001) 'Civil society and peace building in Bosnia and Herzegovina', *Peace Research*, 38: 163–180.

Botan, C. (1992) 'International public relations: Critique and reformulation', *Public Relations Review*, 18: 149–159.

Botan, C. and Taylor, M. (2005) 'The role of trust in channels of strategic communication in building civil society', *Journal of Communication*, 55: 685–702.

Boulding, K. D. (1977) *The image: Knowledge in life and society.* Ann Arbor: University of Michigan Press.

Bourdieu, P. (1984) *Distinction: A social critique of the judgment of taste.* Cambridge, MA: Harvard University Press.

Burt, R. (1997) 'The contingent value of social capital', *Administration Science Quarterly*, 42: 335–365.

Coleman, J. S. (1988) 'Social capital in the creation of human capital', *American Journal of Sociology*, 94(1): 95–120.

Deutsch, K. W. (1963) *Nationalism and social communication.* Cambridge, MA: MIT Press.

Deutsch, K. W. (1966a) *The nerves of government: Models of political communication and control*. New York: The Free Press.

Deutsch, K. W. (1966b) *Nation-building*. New York: Atherton Press.

Diamond, L. (1990) 'Nigeria: Pluralism, statism and the struggle for democracy', in L. Diamond, J. Linz and S. Lipset (eds) *Politics in developing countries: Comparing experiences with democracy*. Boulder, CO: Lynne Rienner, pp. 351–409.

Diamond, L. (2000) 'Developing democracy in Africa: African and international imperative', *Cambridge Review of International Affairs*, 14(1): 191–213.

Doerfel, M. L. and Taylor, M. (2005) 'Network dynamics of interorganizational cooperation: The Croatian civil society movement', *Communication Monographs*, 71 (4): 373–394.

Doerfel, M. and Taylor, M. (2009) 'The Croatian civil society movement: Implications, recommendations, and expectations for donors and NGOs'. Paper presented to the National Communication Association, Chicago, IL.

Fukuyama, F. (2002) 'Social capital and development', *SAIS Review*, 22: 23–37.

Glenny, M. (1996) *The fall of Yugoslavia: The third Balkan war*. New York: Penguin Books.

Granovetter, M. S. (1973) 'The strength of weak ties', *American Journal of Sociology*, 78(6): 1360–1380.

Hobsbawm, E. (1994/1983) 'The nation as invented tradition', in J. Hutchinson and A. D. Smith (eds) *Nationalism*. New York: Oxford University Press, pp. 76–83.

Huntington, S. (1968) *Political order in changing societies*. New Haven, CT: Yale University Press.

Ihlen, O. (2007) 'Building on Bourdieu: A sociological grasp of public relations', *Public Relations Review*, 33: 269–274.

Karim, H. (1989) 'Development of public relations in Asia/Pacific: A Malaysian view', *International Public Relations Review*, 12: 17–24.

Kennan, W. R. and Hazleton, V. (2006) 'Internal Public relations, social capital, and the role of effective organizational communication', in C. H. Botan and V. Hazelton (eds) *Public relations theory II*. Mahwah, NJ: Lawrence Erlbaum Associates, pp. 311–338.

Kent, M. L. (2013) 'Using social media dialogically: public relations role in reviving democracy', *Public Relations Review*, 39: 337–345.

Kent, M. L., Sommerfeldt, E. J. and Saffer, A. J. (2016) 'Social networks, power, and public relations: *Tertius Iungens* as a cocreational approach to studying relationship networks', *Public Relations Review*, 42(1): 91–100.

Kent, M. L. and Taylor, M. (2002) 'Toward a dialogic theory of public relations', *Public Relations Review*, 28: 21–37.

Kent, M. L. and Taylor, M. (2007) 'Beyond "excellence" in international public relations research: An examination of generic theory in Bosnian public relations', *Public Relations Review*, 33: 10–20.

Kent, M. L. and Taylor, M. (2011a) 'How intercultural communication theory informs global public relations practice', in N. Bardhan and K. Weaver (eds) *Public relations in global public relations contexts: Multiparadigmatic perspectives*. New York: Routledge, pp. 50–76.

Kent, M. L. and Taylor, M. (2011b) 'Ethiopian dialogue: Merging theory and praxis in journalism training'. Competitive paper delivered to the Annual Academic Conference of the International Association for Media and Communication Research (IAMCR), Journalism Research and Education Section, Istanbul, Turkey, July.

Kent, M. L., Taylor, M. and Turcilo, L. (2006) 'Public relations by newly privatized businesses in Bosnia-Herzegovina', *Public Relations Review*, 32: 10–17.

Kruckeberg, D. and Stark, K. (1988) *Public relations and community: A reconstructed theory*. New York: Praeger.

Mamuti, A. and Dzenita, O. (2014) 'Nation branding as a means of attracting FDI: The case of Bosnia and Herzegovina', *International Journal of Business and Globalisation*, 13(2): 197–208.

Martinez, B. and Kiousis, S. (2005) 'Empowering citizens in emerging democracies: Developing effective public relations media strategies for political participation', *Studier i Politisk Kommunikation*, 15: 4–20.

Petritsch, W. (2006, 9 May) 'My lessons learnt in Bosnia and Herzegovina', *Bosnia Daily*, pp. 7–8.

Pratt, C. (1985) 'The African context', *Public Relations Journal*, 41: 11–16.

Putnam, R. (2000) *Bowling alone: The collapse and revival of American community*. New York: Simon and Schuster.

Simões, R. P. (1992) 'Public relations as a political function: A Latin American view', *Public Relations Review*, 18: 189–200.

Somerville, I. and Kirby, S. (2012) 'Public relations and the Northern Ireland peace process: Dissemination, reconciliation and the 'Good Friday Agreement' referendum campaign', *Public Relations Inquiry*, 1(3): 231–255.

Sommerfeldt, E. J. and Kent, M. L. (2015) 'Civil society, networks, and relationship management: Beyond the organization–public dyad', *International Journal of Strategic Communication*, 9: 235–252.

Sriramesh, K. (1992) 'Societal culture and public relations: Ethnographic evidence from India', *Public Relations Review*, 18: 201–211.

Taylor, M. (2000a) 'Toward a public relations approach to nation building', *Journal of Public Relations Research*, 12: 179–210.

Taylor, M. (2000b) 'Media relations in Bosnia: A role for public relations in building civil society', *Public Relations Review*, 26: 1–14.

Taylor, M. (2004) 'Media richness theory as a foundation for public relations in Croatia', *Public Relations Review*, 30: 145–160.

Taylor, M. (2009) 'Civil society as a rhetorical public relations process', in R. Heath, E. L. Toth and D. Waymer (eds) *Rhetorical and critical approaches to public relations II*. Hillsdale, NJ: Lawrence Erlbaum Associates, pp. 76–91.

Taylor, M. and Botan, C. H. (1997) 'Strategic communication campaigns for national development in the Pacific Rim: The case of public education in Malaysia', *Australian Journal of Communication*, 24(2): 115–130.

Taylor, M. and Doerfel, M. L. (2003) 'Building inter-organizational relationships that build nations', *Human Communication Research*, 29(2): 153–181.

Taylor, M. and Doerfel, M. L. (2005) 'Another dimension to explicating relationships: Network theory and method to measure inter-organizational linkages', *Public Relations Review*, 31: 121–129.

Taylor, M. and Doerfel, M. L. (2011) 'The Croatian civil society movement: Implications, recommendations, and expectations for donors and NGOs', *Voluntas: the International Journal of Voluntary Associations*, 22: 311–334.

Taylor, M. and Kent, M. L. (2000) 'Media transitions in Bosnia: From propagandistic past to uncertain future', *Gazette*, 62(5): 355–378.

Taylor, M. and Kent, M. L. (2006) 'Nation-building: public relations theory and practice', in V. Hazelton and C. H. Botan (eds) *Public relations theory II*. Hillsdale, NJ: Lawrence Erlbaum Associates, pp. 341–360.

Taylor, M. and Kent, M. L. (2013) 'Building and measuring sustainable networks of organizations and social capital: Postwar public diplomacy in Croatia', in R. S. Zaharna, A. Arsenault and A. Fisher (eds) *Relational, networked, and collaborative approaches to public diplomacy*. New York: Routledge, pp. 103–116.

Taylor, M. and Napoli, P. (2003) 'Media development in Bosnia: A longitudinal analysis of citizen perceptions of media realism, importance and credibility', *Gazette*, 65(6): 473–492.

Taylor, M. and Napoli, P. (2008) 'An analysis of public perceptions of how media and NGOs contribute to civil society in Croatia', *International Journal of Communication*, 2: 1226–1247.

Toth, E. L. (2006) 'Building public affairs theory', in C. H. Botan and V. Hazelton (eds) *Public relations theory II*. Mahwah, NJ: Lawrence Erlbaum Associates, pp. 441–461.

USAID (2000) *An evaluation of USAID/OTI political transition grants in Croatia and Bosnia and Herzegovina*. Research report. US Doc PN ACK-165. Washington, DC: United States Agency for International Development, Office of Transition Initiatives.

Van Leuven, J. K. (1996) 'Public relations in South East Asia: From nation-building campaigns to regional interdependence', in H. Culbertson and N. Chen (eds) *International public relations: A comparative analysis*. Mahwah, NJ: Lawrence Erlbaum Associates, pp. 207–222.

Van Riel, C. B. M. (1992) 'Corporate communication in European financial institutions', *Public Relations Review*, 18: 161–175.

Wiebe, G. D. (1951–1952) 'Merchandising commodities and citizenship on television', *Public Opinion Quarterly*, 15: 679–691.

Yang, A. and Taylor, M. (2015) 'Looking over, looking out, and moving forward: A network ecology framework to position public relations in communication theory', *Communication Theory*, 25: 91–115.

3 Dialogue with the enemy

Lessons for public relations on dialogue facilitation drawn from the Israeli–Palestinian conflict

Margalit Toledano

Introduction

The process of dialogue involves interacting with, listening to, respecting, empowering, understanding and accommodating less powerful or powerless participants. Often, in the case of organisational dialogue with stakeholders, the less powerful participants are perceived as critical or unfriendly, or in the case of a dialogue between political enemies, can be seen as dangerous and potentially violent. The task of convening a dialogue between antagonistic parties and ensuring that, in spite of the power imbalance, all participants have an equal opportunity to be heard and be respected, presents a significant challenge to the facilitator. This is the situation in both the corporate environment and in cross-national dialogues between opposing parties.

This chapter examines one exceptional case of a dialogue between parties with a history of enmity. It uses evidence from interviews with the public relations expert who facilitated the dialogue and an interview with one of the participants who played a major role in the dialogue process, as well as the author's own involvement in convening the dialogue. The chapter seeks to provide insights into the dialogue experience and to suggest practical ideas about the role of the facilitator that might be applicable to the corporate environment.

Although there are parallel issues with regard to dialogues between organisations and opposing stakeholders in other situations, this chapter directs the field's attention away from strategic corporate conversations to explore the practitioner role as facilitator of dialogue during socio-political conflicts, and to consider public relations' potential contribution to grassroots peace building. This is an exciting role that extends the practitioners' role as builders of relationships and trust into impacting on positive social change and peace.

To understand the context of the dialogue case, the chapter begins with an overview of the history and background of the dialogue participants. It goes on to review relevant literature, to analyse selected evidence from the case, and to conclude with a discussion of the case study's lessons.

History and background

Although the political leaders of both sides signed the 13 September 1993 Oslo Peace Agreement between the Israeli government and the Palestinian Liberation Organisation (PLO), public opinion was not prepared for such a shocking shift from war to peace discourse. The agreement emerged from secret negotiations between Israeli and Palestinian politicians and academics conducted in Oslo. Israelis had experienced no previous civil contact with the Arab enemy; in fact, prior to the Oslo agreement Israelis were forbidden from communicating with members of the PLO. Both sides were influenced by political narratives that emphasised negative stereotypes of the 'other'.

In 1995, as part of its contribution to the Oslo Peace Agreement, the Norwegian government initiated a formal People-to-People programme (P2P), which supported many projects, meetings and dialogues between the parties aiming to remove barriers to interaction (Liel, 2005; 2006). Other international organisations, mainly the European Union, joined the programme and provided funds to non-governmental public and private organisations to enable the implementation of grassroots interaction projects. During the 1990s various organisations promoted P2P under the framework of Oslo. Nevertheless, Israelis and Palestinians who opposed the 'Oslo deal' and/or distrusted the 'other' did not take part in the P2P movement. Nor did the P2P movement enjoy support from either the government of Israel or from the official leaders of the Palestinian Authority. A research paper on the P2P movement published by Herzog and Hai (2005) explained that one fault of the Oslo process was the lack of legitimacy and 'top-down' support for efforts to bridge the gap between the two societies: 'In practice, Israeli and Palestinian leaders failed to assume responsibility for transformational elements within the agreements, were neither pro-active nor consistent in supporting far-reaching governmental and institutional cooperation, and did not articulate clear public messages to this end' (p. 24).

Nevertheless the P2P movement has been active and actually grown in spite of the frustrating deterioration in the relationships, the lack of peace negotiations, and the fact that it has been totally dependent on funding and support from civil organisations and passionate volunteers.

Ifat Maoz (2004: 564), studied the post-Oslo P2P activities and described 'transformative dialogues' as a 'common device for grassroots-level peace building'. She presented a transformative dialogue as:

> a process through which both sides deal with disagreement or conflict between them through expressing themselves, listening to the other, and taking in or empathizing with the emotions, experiences, views, and values of the other. Through such dialogues, the sides come to construct themselves and the other differently, extending the boundaries of the self and including parts of the other within the self, and thus including the other within the realm of relational moral responsibility.
>
> (ibid.)

The Israeli–Palestinian Media Forum (IPMF), which was part of the P2P movement, exemplified the process described by Maoz (2004). It was initiated by an Israeli non-governmental organisation called the International Center for Peace in the Middle East (ICPME). ICPME had been working since 1982 to remove barriers to peaceful co-existence via communication, interaction and dialogues between Israelis, Palestinians and Arabs. Following the Oslo Agreement, ICPME activities focused on organising meetings between Israelis and Palestinians who shared professional interests. Teachers, architects and other groupings from both sides were invited for meetings of between one and four days to get to know each other and discuss the conflict from their professional perspectives. The meetings were funded by international organisations and some of them were held in Europe. The trip abroad provided both Israelis and Palestinians a neutral space and a shared positive experience as tourists in a foreign country. The discussions were held in English so that neither Hebrew nor Arabic could dominate.

Four meetings were organised by the ICPME for politicians from both sides, and were held in Greece. The fourth politicians' meeting, called the Athens Dialogue for Peace and Cooperation in the Middle East took place in July 1998 and ran concurrently with the first Israeli–Palestinian Journalists and Influentials Conference. The latter was sponsored by the Greek government, the European Union and the Adenauer Foundation. Both the politicians' and the journalists' meetings were held in the same hotel on the island of Rhodes. During the four days of the conferences the politicians and journalists conducted separate discussions on separate agendas, although social events and dinner parties were shared by participants from both groups.

The journalists' conference produced a final declaration expressing Israelis' and Palestinians' concerns as professional journalists without referring to political arguments. The statement called for the establishment of an Israeli–Palestinian press club in Jerusalem and for the removal of Israeli restrictions on the free movement of Palestinian journalists between the West Bank, Gaza and Jerusalem. It also proclaimed that 'freedom of expression is an essential condition for the practice of journalism and for fostering the culture of peace in the region through a continuous dialogue with and knowledge of each other through the free flow of ideas' (Conference brochure, 1998: 4); and urged other editors and journalists to fight against prejudices and stereotypes in the media in order to foster mutual understanding.

Following this conference a steering committee, composed of a dozen of the conference participants, met with the conference moderator Mr Alain Modoux, who was at that time UNESCO's director of the Unit for Freedom of Expression and Democracy. Four months after the Rhodes conference, UNESCO announced its sponsorship of a new organisation that was named the Israeli–Palestinian Media Forum (IPMF). According to UNESCO's news release of 2 December 1998, the IPMF's purpose was:

> to organize joint activities, encourage professional exchanges, enhance professional standards in reporting on situations, events and issues of

> common concern or interest, and take action whenever and wherever press freedom and the freedom of movement of journalists are in jeopardy, thus spreading a culture of peace and stimulating a spirit of professional solidarity among all members of the IPMF.
>
> (UNESCO, 1998)

While expressing his great satisfaction with the creation of the IPMF, the director-general of UNESCO, Federico Mayor, said that:

> the setting-up in Jerusalem of the Israeli–Palestinian Media Forum is all the more a significant milestone along the way leading to peace in the Middle East since it concerns a key sector of both Israeli and the Palestinian civil societies. It could and should be a decisive mobilising force for promoting better mutual knowledge and understanding among Israeli and Palestinian people and, in so doing, will foster a culture of peace in the region.
>
> (UNESCO, 1998)

This signalled that the IPMF was set to continue the dialogue between Israeli and Palestinian journalists and to use their influence on public opinion to build bridges between the two former enemies entangled in a long and bloody conflict. The dialogue, which was conducted in the context of the long Israeli–Palestinian history of mutual hostility, sought to achieve mutual understanding and generate joint activities based on professional solidarity. This project lasted barely two years and was dissolved in 2000 when violent conflict in the region (the Second Intifada) prevented meetings between Israelis and Palestinians.

This chapter uses evidence from participants in the July 1998 media conference in Rhodes, and draws from the IPMF's activities. It uses these to gain insight into the process of dialogue, the impact of dialogue, and the role of public relations in dialogues between antagonistic groups.

Literature review

Since the turn of the century the public relations literature has featured dialogue as a core concept. According to Coombs and Holladay (2010), dialogue is a process involving listening and authentic engagement, an effort to understand the other, and an open-ended process that does not lead to outcomes. Participants may feel satisfied that their concerns were heard even though decisions might not go their way. Some schools of thought (Heath et al., 2006; Kent and Taylor, 2002) assume that genuine dialogue is not supposed to lead to agreement or consensus and is different in this way from negotiations or debates.

That said, the focus of PR practice as strategic communication in business is centred on outcomes that benefit the employer's interests, and practitioners tend to use dialogues with organisation stakeholders to achieve a specific goal. The journal *Management Communication Quarterly* published a special forum involving nine scholars addressing the expectations from dialogues (Heath et al., 2006). The forum participants expressed critical reservations about the potential of dialogues to disguise covert agendas or power relations and the risk of manipulative uses of dialogues. They raised questions around the use of persuasive communications in dialogue:

> Dialogue seems to be challenging because it asks us to be more human, less partisan … We should be more human to be open to others' ideas and concerns, but we may be less human because it is so easy to be partisan.
>
> (Heath, in Heath et al., 2006: 353)

This forum's 'dialogue on dialogue', along with most public relations literature that examines the concept of dialogue, relates to dialogue in the context of organisational communication with stakeholders. Or, to use Pearson's (1989) earlier formulation: 'dialogue is a precondition for any legitimate corporate conduct that affects a public of that organisation' (p. 128).

The recent growth of interest in dialogue followed an increase in the public relations industry's use of the internet, especially social media, which some scholars considered a dialogical tool of communication (Kelleher, 2007: 49). However, the public relations literature on dialogue rarely relates to the specifics in the context of national conflicts that involve violence (e.g. people-to-people dialogue). Nevertheless, it is reasonable to assume similarities between dialogues conducted by organisational management with activists and dialogues between two peoples in conflict or post-conflict situations.

Indeed, building on Kent and Taylor's (2002) assumptions, we can look at dialogues in both contexts through the same lens. We can also check the extent to which the specific dialogue featured the following tenets:

> *mutuality*, or the recognition of organisation–public relationships; *propinquity*, or the temporality and spontaneity of interactions with publics; *empathy*, or the supportiveness and confirmation of public goals and interests; *risk*, or the willingness to interact with individuals and publics on their own terms; and finally *commitment*, or the extent to which an organisation gives itself over to dialogue, interpretation, and understanding in its interactions with publics.
>
> (Kent and Taylor, 2002: 24–25)

Theunissen and Wan Noordin (2012) state that 'few, if any textbooks offer useful suggestions on how to create conditions for dialogue to thrive other than entering in dialogue and discussion' (p. 6). In fact, over a decade earlier, Kent and Taylor (2002), based on the work of Pearson (1989), provided the following set of pragmatic dimensions for dialogue as a basis for guidelines and assistance for practitioners who engage in facilitating a dialogue:

1 An understanding of and agreement on the rules governing the opportunity for beginning, maintaining and ending interactions.
2 Public understanding of and agreement on the rules governing the length of time separating messages or questions form answers.
3 Public understanding of and agreement on rules governing opportunities to suggest topics and initialize topic changes.
4 Public understanding of and agreement on rules for when a response counts as a response.
5 Public understanding of and agreement on rules for channel selection;
6 Public understanding of and agreement on the rules of talking about and changing the rules.

(p. 32)

However, the need to provide case studies and facilitation training has been widely ignored in the literature and such criteria might become useful for starting it. Without that, Theunissen and Wan Noordin (2012: 6) question 'whether dialogue truly reflects the pragmatics of public relations practice, whether it is realistically possible for an organisation to engage in "dialogue" with its stakeholders where a specific interest is served, and whether it is even desirable to do so'. That rationale arises from the philosophical concept of dialogue as a process rather than an outcome. For them, dialogue is not supposed to bring about agreement and consensus, whereas organisations pursue goals and objectives, and employ public relations to achieve outcomes.

Accordingly, Theunissen and Wan Noordin (2012: 6) express reservations about the high regard for dialogues in public relations scholarship: 'labeling dialogue as *symmetric communication* and persuasion as *asymmetric* places persuasion in an inferior position'. Instead, they claim that both are actually public relations practices with no hierarchical order between them:

> An organisation will move between publicity, persuasion and dialogue at various stages of its relationships with stakeholders, and this will shift throughout any long-term relationships. Regardless, it is important to keep in mind that dialogue is not a more balanced form of communication, nor will it automatically result in balance with the environment or ensure harmony in organisation–stakeholder relationships.
>
> (Theunissen and Wan Noordin, 2012: 7–8)

Martin Buber and the origins of dialogue

Scholars in public relations and other disciplines often identify the roots of the concept of dialogue in the writings of Martin Buber (1878–1965), a German Jewish philosopher whom Kent and Taylor (2002) titled 'the father of modern concept of dialogue' (p. 22). Pieczka (2010) noted that the 'Publication of Buber's (1958) *I and Thou* is often referred to as the starting point in the story of modern dialogue because of the profound influence of the ideas it contained' (p. 112).

Buber's *I and Thou* was published in 1923 (Kaufmann, 1970) and grounded ethics and theology in a dialogical encounter. *I and Thou* refers to the world and human life experience in relation to an Other. The 'I' does not objectify any 'It' but rather acknowledges a living relationship. Buber characterised I–Thou relations as 'dialogical' and I–It relations as 'monological'. To perceive the other as an It is to take them as a classified and hence predictable and manipulatable object that exists only as a part of one's own experiences. In contrast, in an I–Thou relation both participants exist as polarities of relation, whose centre lies in the 'between' (in German, *Zwischen*) (Scott, 2010).

Buber's thinking helps distinguish between what public relations literature identifies as organisational-centred persuasive strategic communication and the dialogue approach. The former tends to use unethical manipulation to achieve organisational objectives and uses one-way communication with its publics (I–It). The latter sees the organisation as an equal partner in a network of relationships (I–Thou). Coombs and Holladay (2010: 7) describe it as the 'interconnectedness of constituents'.

Buber makes a further distinction between two models of dialogue that Kaufmann (1970) describes as:

> the 'genuine' dialogue of the I–Thou relations, which is the deepening of mutual presence, and technical dialogue, which aims at objective understanding only. The latter would be devisable into the logical, which unfolds in itself, and that which – whatever it may be termed – seeks the human Other for confirmation and/or opposition. Opposed to both of these is monological thinking, which is sheer subjectivism and which often disguises itself as dialogue.
>
> (Buber, cited in Kaufman, 1970: 58)

Heath identified Buber's concept of the Between as the key element of dialogue in regards to the practice of public relations: 'I think the essence of his idea boils down to a mutuality of regard and interest' (Heath et al., 2006: 346). The distinction between different levels of dialogue and the notion of the Between are useful for public relations scholars when analysing specific dialogues, and for practitioners who should consider the different options while planning and facilitating a dialogue.

Methodology

To examine the process and facilitation of dialogue between enemies, this research used ICPME Rhodes conference documents and IPMF activities reports, an email interview with the dialogue facilitator Alain Modoux, and a phone interview with an IPMF board member who participated in the Rhodes conference as a journalist. It also uses evidence based on the author's personal experience as one of the organisers of the Rhodes journalists' conference and the IPMF. My experience as an insider involved in planning and organising the dialogues between former enemies provided an opportunity to evaluate the role of public relations in challenging dialogues during and after violent conflicts.

The self-evidence research approach has the advantage of being based on first-hand knowledge of the events as they were unfolding and the ability to provide informed insider understanding of the case components. However, it has to be acknowledged that the author's personal involvement in the dialogue case might limit the perspective to a subjective selection and interpretation of the facts. Those are well-known advantages and disadvantages of any quantitative research method, especially in the presentation of historical case studies. Stacks (2011: 158) said that the goal of most case studies is to describe and provide examples. The case study described in this paper uses in-depth interviews with major players as well as the author's personal knowledge and involvement in the case to identify major issues and suggest further research and relevant theory.

The case

The ICPME hired the services of the public relations firm that was then owned by the author to support the 1998 Rhodes conferences. The public relations service included consultation during the planning process, construction of the list of invited journalists, negotiations with editors about permissions for journalists to participate, shaping the discussion agendas, identifying an appropriate facilitator from UNESCO and inviting him to moderate the dialogue, pre- and post-conference media publicity, production of the conference brochure, and, as part of the organising team, overseeing the flow of the conference itself. The guidelines for the invitation of media representatives emphasised inclusiveness. The list of over a hundred participants included those who were religious and secular, who were left wing and right wing, and featured Jews, Muslims and Christian journalists, with a few activists, academics and an executive from a public opinion research institution. Five journalists came from Egypt and Jordan, and an additional eight were reporters covering the region for international media channels.

There were about forty representatives for each of the Palestinian and Israeli media people. On the Israeli side there was a significant group of journalists who had, for many years, expressed sceptical or critical views about the Oslo deal and were identified with the right wing. The Palestinian journalists were selected by the International Organisation for Peace and Cooperation, the head of the People-to-People Committee in Gaza, and the Palestinian Ministry of Culture and Information. The list included, in addition to journalists, a few public relations practitioners and representatives from the Palestinian Authority.

The moderator for the journalists' conference was a prominent public relations practitioner, Alain Modoux. At that time Modoux was head of the

Unit for Freedom of Expression and Democracy of UNESCO in Paris, although he later became UNESCO's Assistant Director General for Freedom of Expression, Democracy, and Peace and then UNESCO Deputy Director of Communication and Information. Prior to his role in UNESCO, Modoux served as president of the International Public Relations Association, IPRA, and worked as director of the Communication Department of the International Committee of the Red Cross in Geneva. The author knew Modoux from her participation in IPRA's activities and invited him to moderate the conference, and afterwards concluded that his contribution enabled the conference to become a dialogue rather than a negotiation or a confrontational debate.

Indeed, this chapter further contends that Modoux's work in the process of facilitating dialogue and his skills are worth studying as a model for public relations practitioners aspiring to conduct dialogues. Watching him in action was to observe how his highly developed communication skills and the respect participants had for his fair, professional and impartial moderation helped to calm a very tense meeting. He followed clear guidelines that insisted on silence and listening to each voice. When one side expressed views that upset the other he allowed speakers to proceed and asked the participants to respect their commitment to the dialogue. He smoothly shifted the discussion from its starting focus on political narratives into shared professional experiences as journalists. Deploying a mastery of discourse and diplomacy, he summed up participants' evidence and narratives into statements that were accepted by the speakers. He then helped in shaping the Rhodes Statement and negotiated between the two sides about its wording, finding accurate expressions to satisfy each side's expectations and sensitivities.

The agenda that was distributed to participants in advance included panels titled: 'Culture of peace'; 'National images in the Israeli and Palestinian media before and after the Oslo accords'; 'Peace movement in the Middle East'; 'The involvement of the international media in the Middle East conflict'; 'The role of the media in solving conflicts in times of crisis'; and 'Channels of cooperation – source of information'. Each of these topics had the potential to produce an explosive set of accusations and bitter arguments, especially from those who did not trust the Oslo process and had not previously met the other side for an open discussion. However, following a stormy opening, the tone gradually changed. The political narratives used in the opening session made way for professional exchanges of ideas about journalism. Participants shared experiences and opinions on the role of journalists and the challenges they faced in covering the conflict. A genuine interest in each other's professional work, and personal stories, developed into vivid and increasingly candid conversations.

Media reports about the conference described how the change occurred mainly when both sides decided to use the opportunity to listen and be listened to, while slowly leaving the official narratives and daring to admit responsibility for their side of the violence. Personal testimonials from the others helped the rapprochement, especially in private conversations between sessions and during dinners. Yossi Klein Halevi (1998), a religious Jewish Israeli journalist who at that time reported on religious affairs for the bi-weekly magazine the *Jerusalem Report*, described in a two-page article the process of transformation he himself went through over the four days of the conference. It was especially interesting because Klein Halevi had been a right wing activist in a fundamentalist Jewish group in New York (Klein Halevi, 1995). In a 2015 interview he described his position prior to the conference:

> I was a supporter of the Oslo process in 1993 and gave it a chance but by 1998, following the Jihadist speeches of Yasser Arafat and the horrific terrorist attacks in Israel during the Oslo process years, I became doubtful about the agreement's potential to bring peace.
>
> (Klein Halevi, 2015)

At the start of the conference, he said:

> A complex asymmetry existed between us. On the one hand, they were the occupied and we were the occupiers; yet we represented a free press and they a dictatorship. They mistrusted our insistence on professional interaction, our impatience for what we considered political rhetoric and they considered a simple description of their reality. And we mistrusted their journalistic integrity.
>
> (Klein Halevi, 1998: 3)

However, over the four days of the conference, with many opportunities to socialise as well as talk, the atmosphere changed dramatically:

> On our last night in Rhodes, we danced to Greek music around the swimming pool. All of us – Orthodox Jewish cynics, former administrative detainees [Palestinians held in Israeli prisons] – linked arms, whooping and prancing and swaying our hips. It was wild and moving and a little sad: merely a glimpse into the possible.
>
> (Klein Halevi, 1998: 4)

Back in Israel, in the airport Klein Halevi (1998) described how he found himself pressed in the bus against a Palestinian journalist 'who'd been denied residency in Jerusalem and who'd told me that Haifa and Jaffa were not his to concede. "Welcome home" he said to me, with an exhausted smile. "Welcome home," I replied' (Klein Halevi, 1998: 4).

In retrospect Klein Halevi appreciated the impact of the conference on his life as significant. In a 2015 interview, he explained his continuing interest in dialogue with Muslims (not only Palestinians) as rooted in the 1998 conference and the IPMF experience. In 2015 he was based at the Shalom Hartman Institute, an Israeli think-tank, and headed the Muslim Leadership

Initiative that invited young leaders of Muslim communities in North America (such as Muslim chaplains at US universities, and reporters from Al Jazeera) to explore the Jewish and Zionist story: 'The link between religion, nationality, and state seems to them strange' he explained in the 2015 interview, 'The educational work I do with them actually continues my previous 1998 dialogue':

> Following the Rhodes conference and the IPMF failure I felt that the Oslo agreement had no chance to work because it lacked a religious dimension. It was executed by seculars on both sides. In the Middle East the spiritual component is essential. I started to learn more about Muslims, went to Mosques to pray with them, and then I published a book on this experience: Klein Halevi, 2001. I'm trying to find a religious discourse for peace and see this endeavor as emerging from the 1998 dialogue. I keep trying to communicate with Muslims that wish to speak to me either from the Galilee or Minnesota. Unfortunately there is a metaphoric and physical wall between Israeli and Palestinians right now but I want to stay open and fight despair, though it is so easy and sensible to be in despair these days.
>
> (Klein Halevi, 2015)

All the journalists who participated in the conference later published emotional accounts of an unexpected recognition of the other as human beings. For Moti Zaft, a senior correspondent of *Hatzofe*, the journal of the nationalist-religious party that opposed the Oslo agreement, the conference was his first ever meeting with Palestinians. In spite of the fact that his public oral presentation focused on the reasons he did not like Palestinians, he ended up inviting them to visit him at home:

> When I returned home I told my 10 years old son that five Palestinians will visit us at home two weeks later. His response was: 'I'm going to prepare grenades and stones to protect us in case they would attack us'. At this moment I felt how important it was that I went to meet with Palestinians in Rhodes, and how important it was to continue to try to get closer to each other, if we wish to have normal life here.
>
> (Zaft 1998: 10, author's translation from the Hebrew)

It is hard to conclude from media stories the real impact of dialogues on the individual participant. However, it is possible to deduce more from research that Ifat Maoz (2004) conducted on another dialogue group in 1998. This dialogue was organised by the Israeli–Palestinian Center for Research and Information (IPCRI), a non-governmental organisation involved in peace education. Maoz (2004) evaluated the impact of a workshop IPCRI conducted with 15–16-year-old youths from pairs of Israeli and Palestinian schools, and reported:

> To examine whether participation in the dialogue activities actually transformed mutual attitudes, I compared participants' ratings of their stereotypic perceptions of each other before and after the workshop. Results showed that after participation in the workshops, both Jews and Palestinians viewed each other as more 'considerate of others', 'tolerant', and 'good hearted' than they did before it ... These perceptions are directly relevant to the ability of both sides to trust each other and to build peaceful relations between them.
>
> (Maoz, 2004: 567)

The success of the 1988 journalists' conference in cracking some participants' prejudices was, according to their published reports, remarkable.

However, that would be less significant if it was just a one-off experience. At the last session, following the vote on the Rhodes Statement, a steering committee consisting of journalists from both sides was elected and tasked with the mission of implementation. Modoux, who facilitated the discussion and enabled the change of atmosphere, was again a pivotal player in the wording of the final statement and its emphasis on specific, attainable and long-term professional positive objectives rather than political issues and blame. As a result the steering committee kept in touch with him about the implementation of the statement's ideas once the conference was over.

Modoux used his rich experience in conflict areas around the world, his high position in UNESCO and his excellent skills in public relations and communication to make this come true. Following the conference he travelled twice to Israel in his capacity as head of UNESCO Freedom of Expression and Democracy and met with the steering committee. In December 1998 he was able to announce a UNESCO contribution of $50,000 of seed money to the newly formed IPMF. Two co-directors were selected by the committee – one Israeli and one Palestinian, an office was rented within the complex of the American Colony Hotel in Jerusalem, and an administrative manager from Ramallah, who spoke Arabic, Hebrew and English fluently, was hired. The UNESCO announcement included a commitment by UNESCO to conduct a fundraising campaign for IPMF to secure its long-term operations.

A programme of action to be executed by the co-directors was agreed upon and published in February 1999. It included such activities as: an anti-incitement roundtable with fifty Israeli and Palestinian journalists; a briefing by Miguel Moratinos, the European Union ambassador to the peace process in the Middle East; a campaign by Israeli journalists to put pressure on Israeli security to enable freedom of movement of Palestinian journalists; and setting up a hotline. One of the first activities was a press conference with the American ambassador to Israel, to which Israeli and Palestinian journalists were invited. They were sitting side by side as professional colleagues asking questions and gathering data for their reports. Another one was visits to major Israeli newspapers and TV channel editorial rooms organised by IPMF for both parties, as well as meetings with the

Russian-language Israeli press that promoted a hawkish and anti-Oslo agenda.

The author observed that the Palestinians were more interested in IPMF and used the opportunities it provided to learn about Israel. Only a few Israelis, mainly those on the steering committee, were keen on the joint activities. The Israeli members of the IPMF were the stronger but somewhat cynical partner and were less ready to invest their time in the IPMF's activities. In his interview Klein Halevi commented:

> You could tell that the Palestinian journalists took it more seriously by the way they dressed up and showed up for meetings. I served as co-chair of the 'Committee to Defend Journalists' that was actually trying to defend Palestinian journalists who were harassed by both Israeli and Palestinian authorities. Once my Palestinian co-chair complained about threats from a Palestinian official following a story he had published on corruption of Palestinian leaders. We initiated an extensive IPMF campaign, including a press release and complaint letters to international organisations. The Palestinian Authority did not like the campaign and threatened IPMF members arguing that the organisation actually serves the Zionist cause more than Palestine. This was the last nail in the coffin of IPMF.
>
> (Klein Halevi, 2015)

The reservations from the Palestinian Authority officials grew into what Ron Pundak, one of the initiators of the Oslo Process, described later as the 'anti-normalization movement'. Pundak (2012) explained that 'The notion of anti-normalization, which says that Palestinians should not talk or cooperate with Israelis, until the end of the occupation, has been in existence for years.' The imbalance of power within the IPMF became a significant obstacle for the dialogue. The question 'Who benefits from the dialogue?' would actually be relevant to many other cases of dialogue within the corporate context as well. It offers a major challenge for the dialogue facilitator, who should be prepared for it and ready to consider sensitive responses on both sides.

It is hard to tell how the relationships would have developed if IPMF had a chance to continue to operate over time. The September 2000 Palestinian uprising, the Second Intifada, which continued till 2005, meant the closure of the borders, violent activities, and the freezing of the Oslo process. The IPMF could not continue operating and UNESCO withdrew its support.

Eventually, the IPMF mission was picked up by two other sponsors – the International Peace and Cooperation Center (IPCC) and the Peres Center for Peace. These organisations established a new Israeli–Palestinian Media Forum that continued to organise annual dialogues for about a hundred Israeli and Palestinian journalists, focusing on the same topics – media coverage of the conflict, challenges for journalists in times of conflict, and misrepresentations and stereotypes in the media. This forum held four meetings between 2001 and 2004.

The role of the dialogue facilitator

In an email interview, Alain Modoux (2015) provided retrospective insights into the role of the dialogue facilitator based on his experiences as a public relations expert who facilitated dialogues between antagonistic groups. According to Modoux (2015), the political context is a major precondition to successful dialogues between enemies: 'The global political context at that time was very favorable due to the Oslo Accords that provided Israelis and Palestinians with several windows of opportunity for developing common projects.' Over a decade later Pundak (2012) noticed that the escalation of the conflict hindered the people-to-people activities in the region. The role of the facilitator thus needs to start with 'Sound knowledge of the global political environment (including its historical, cultural and religious dimensions) in which the conflict is taking place' (Modoux, 2015). Identifying the players' interests, allies, opponents, major arguments and narratives of both sides would be relevant to dialogues conducted between organisations with stakeholders as well as between warring enemies. However, the facilitator should not abuse this knowledge for one-sided organisational strategic communication and persuasion, but rather use it for empowering the weaker participants and ensuring their voices are heard, as well as avoiding activities and communications that might be seen as offensive to participants. According to Modoux (2015), the facilitator needs to have a 'capacity to identify, understand and analyze the frustrations and aspirations of the participants and to anticipate their expectations as for the outcomes of the dialogue'.

Another major quality the facilitator should have is trustworthiness. The trust emerges from participants' view of the organisation that the facilitator represents (in this case UNESCO) and the facilitator's experience, reputation and impartiality. Trust matters, since 'only a trusted facilitator is able to build bridges' (Modoux, 2015). He also considers an attractive programme as an asset, and an agenda is needed because it enables participants to prepare for the dialogue and it contributes to overcoming suspicion between the two sides. It is best if participants decide the items to be discussed and are not exposed to undesirable ones. Transparent agendas, according to Modoux, build credibility in the dialogue process. Logistics might have major impact on the success of dialogue, and Modoux emphasised the required facilities – a suitable meeting room where participants feel safe and relaxed, and a secretarial back-up as well as translation services when needed. The facilitator should speak in a common language with the participants. Finally, the facilitator needs to be able 'to conduct a dialogue in a diplomatic, impartial and neutral way and be perceived as such by all participants' (Modoux, 2015).

Discussion

Dialogue during violent conflict is an extreme case and a very challenging emotional process for the participants and the facilitator. This examination of the IPMF case cannot by itself lead to conclusions relating to the diverse functions and responsibilities of public relations within society, but it can suggest some guidelines. Practitioners who communicate on behalf of organisations are expected to conduct dialogues between the organisation and its stakeholders. They could benefit from learning about issues involved in conducting a dialogue during conflict, and use this knowledge to improve communication and understanding between all participants in the process. At this point, the chapter uses Kent and Taylor's (2002) dialogue tenets to analyse the case, consider what can be learned from it, and discuss issues involved in organising and facilitating a dialogue.

Mutuality

Kent and Taylor's first suggested tenet is mutuality. The case does not exemplify mutual relationships – one side, the Israeli, was powerful, confident and less interested, whereas the Palestinians were powerless and restricted. The dialogue's structure allowed equal time for each side to voice thoughts and feelings and to participate in the discussions on an equal basis, but the reality of the relations underpinned the conversation. This chapter argues that this is the case with most dialogues. Balance and mutuality are an aspiration worth keeping; however, the dialogue facilitator should be aware of the imbalance of power and be sensitive in dealing with it. This is true for dialogues during conflict between peoples as well as between organisations and activists.

Propinquity

The case provides evidence of Kent and Taylor's second suggested tenet, propinquity. As seen from the reports on the Rhodes conference, the gap between the two peoples involved in the dialogue narrowed over time and people spontaneously became, for the short period of the dialogue, genuinely interested in each other. The rapprochement was achieved via informal meetings and shared experiences (the space that Buber identified as the Between). To facilitate successful dialogue, opportunities for such informal contact should be included and planned in advance. Shared ground – for example, a prior issue both sides might be concerned about – should be strategically put on the agenda. In the IPMF case an example that worked well was the shift from political debate to shared professional experiences. Also, a strategy of inclusiveness to allow all voices to be heard should be one of the facilitator's responsibilities.

Empathy

The suffering of the Palestinians under the Israeli occupation was a major theme, and many of the Israeli journalists heard about it from first-hand personal experiences during the dialogue. In their reports following the conference it became clear that they were affected and had internalised the stories they heard. On the other hand the fears, anxiety and frustration of the Israelis became clear to the Palestinian participants. Empathy occurred when people spoke about their own private experiences as human beings and as journalists. The dialogue facilitator should consider a strategy that would allow such personal accounts to be spoken and heard in ways that allow the words to enter the hearts of the Other.

Risk

Participants in the dialogue at the Rhodes conference and the IPMF activities took significant risks when they opened themselves to others. Criticism and ridicule might have been the response and the dialogue might have ended in delegitimising the others. Facilitation of dialogue has to be open about it and recognise each voice to ensure respect for anything that is said and done within the dialogue process.

Commitment

The facilitator's major role is to ensure the commitment of all participants in the dialogue to the rules that enable the dialogue to take place. Participants have to listen and stay quiet even when the Other expresses ideas that to them seem upsetting and outrageous. There is a commitment to go on with the process even when it causes pain and anger. The Rhodes conference participants, through a serious commitment to the process, succeeded in agreeing on a joint statement that made the continuation of the dialogue its goal. This would not have been achieved without the involvement of the dialogue facilitator, who navigated between the two groups with excellent public relations skills and sensitivity, as well as calling on participants to adhere to the dialogue procedures.

Additional issues

It is worth noting other issues that a public relations professional facilitating a challenging dialogue should, in addition to the five tenets of dialogue mentioned by Kent and Taylor (2002), consider:

Dialogue outcome

The literature, as mentioned above, emphasises the purpose of dialogues in terms of providing an opportunity to listen, understand and empathise. Dialogue is not a debate, negotiation, or discussion that has to lead to an agreement and consensus. Dialogues are not expected to produce outcomes.

In our case the organisers invested a great deal in sponsoring a challenging dialogue with a goal: to promote a culture of peace. The conference did have an outcome – the Rhodes Statement – that expressed the participants' commitment to the process and their will to continue. The establishment of the IPMF just four months after the conference was a material and significant outcome that enabled the continuation of a dialogue between the two groups. These outcomes have not devalued the dialogue but rather the opposite – they became an asset to the dialogue. Working together on the wording of the Statement and the establishment of the IPMF enabled the aspired rapprochement between participants and made the dialogue a more significant experience for them. The dialogue's facilitator might consider the inclusion of a joint mission in the dialogue process without causing damage if both sides have an equal contribution to this mission and if mutual respectful relationships are maintained by the facilitator.

Dialogue space and resources

A topic often ignored by the literature is the importance of the space in which the dialogue occurs. The Rhodes dialogue and IPMF would not have been successful if it had been held in either Israel or Palestine. The trip abroad and subsequent meetings in the American Colony Hotel in Jerusalem created a neutral space that might be identified as the Between sphere, between I and Thou, that is discussed by Buber (Kaufman, 1970: p. 44). The international organisations that supported the dialogue process were not involved with one side of the conflict. The UNESCO facilitator had a global responsibility for peace and democracy and the representatives of the European Union and the Greek government were interested in promoting and supporting the Oslo peace process for the benefit of both sides.

In drawing lessons for organisational communication, the nature of the space for conducting a dialogue should be seen as essential. When an organisation wishes to conduct a genuine, not a technical dialogue (Buber, 1929, cited in Kaufman, 1970) with, for example, a critical activist group, it needs to be done in a neutral space, not the organisation's facilities. It needs to appoint an uninvolved, universally respected, and skilful facilitator with a public relations rather than, say, a legal background. Allowing space and time for shared personal and group experiences is another aspect contributing to a genuine dialogue. The facilitator has to be aware of communication barriers that might be interpreted as an attempt to persuade and manipulate rather than create understanding and empathy, and avoid any attempt by the organisation to use the dialogue as a tool for achieving an organisational objective. From its organisers, a genuine dialogue might require significant financial investment, time and training, in addition to a commitment to stay out and not impose its agenda on the dialogue.

From organisational agenda to shared professional and personal experiences

The principles and rules for conducting dialogues are helpful in their own right; however, it is important for the facilitator to remember to be flexible and to enable personal accounts and experiences to be voiced and to change the rules according to the dialogue flow and participants' wishes. It is also worth noting that organisations entering a process of dialogue need to understand the strong commitment needed in regard to investment of resources and exposure to risk by opening up to candid disclosures.

Conclusion

Dialogue is supposed to be balanced and collaborative. This chapter argues that in reality, in most cases, there is an imbalance of power between the participating parties. The challenging role of any public relations practitioner in charge of organising the dialogue process is to ensure that all voices are heard, respected, and taken into consideration. To be able to conduct a dialogue, public relations practitioners need to be trained in leadership and to develop facilitation skills that include the ability to listen, to open up the organisations they represent, and to help participants get over their fear of the Other. If the public relations practitioner is not able to become a trusted facilitator, another facilitator who is able to understand the environment, acknowledge the participants' needs, and be trusted as impartial, should be hired to moderate the dialogue. Preconditions for a genuine dialogue require a commitment to neutral space, a highly respected external and objective facilitator, and the creation of shared, positive experiences for participants.

Facilitating a dialogue is a very challenging task that requires serious preparation, commitment and a willingness to take risks. By taking responsibility for genuine dialogues, public relations practitioners can take their role in society to a higher level and make significant contributions to positive social change.

References

Buber, M. (1965) *Between man and man* (trans. R. G. Smith). New York: Macmillan.

Conference brochure (1998) Israeli–Palestinian Journalists and Public Opinion Molders. Conference for Peace in the Middle East. International Center for Peace in the Middle East.

Coombes, T. W. and Holladay, S. J. (2010) *PR strategy and application: Managing influence*. Malden, MA: Wiley-Blackwell.

Friedman, M. (1981) *Martin Buber's life and work: The early years 1878–1923*. New York: E. P. Dutton.

Heath, R. L. (2001) 'A rhetorical enactment rationale for public relations: The good organisation communicates well', in Heath, R. L. (ed.) *Handbook of public relations*. Thousand Oaks, CA: Sage, pp. 31–50.

Heath, R. L., Barnett, P., Shotter, J., Taylor, J. R., Kersten, A., Zorn, T., Roper, J., Motion, J. and Deetz, S. (2006) 'Forum: The process of dialogue: Participation and legitimation', *Management Communication Quarterly*, 19(3): 341–375.

Herzog, S. and Hai, A. (2005) *The power of possibility: The role of people-to-people programs in the current Israeli–Palestinians reality*. Herzeliya, Israel: Friedrich-Ebert-Stiftung.

Kaufmann, W. (1970) *I and thou: Martin Buber. A new translation with a prologue 'I and you' and notes.* 3rd edn. Edinburgh: T. and T. Clark.

Kelleher, T. (2007) *Public relations online.* Thousand Oaks, CA: Sage.

Kent, M. L. and Taylor, M. (2002) 'Toward a dialogic theory of public relations', *Public Relations Review*, 28(1): 21–37.

Klein Halevi, Y. (1995) *Memoir of a Jewish extremist: An American story.* New York: Little, Brown.

Klein Halevi, Y. (1998) 'Meeting with the enemy', *The Jerusalem Report*, 3 August.

Klein Halevi, Y. (2001) *At the entrance to the Garden of Eden: A Jew's search for hope with Christians and Muslims in the Middle East.* New York: Morrow.

Klein Halevi, Y. (2015) Personal communication, 17 July.

Liel, A. (2005 and 2006) 'People-to-people: Telling the truth about the Israeli–Palestinian case', *Palestine–Israel Journal of Politics, Economics and Culture*, 12(4) and 13(1). Retrieved from www.pij.org/details.php?id=397 on 5 November 2015.

Maoz, I. (2004) 'Peace building in violent conflict: Israeli–Palestinian post-Oslo people-to-people activities', *International Journals of Politics, Culture, and Society*, 17(3): 563–574.

Modoux, A. (2015) Personal communication, 20 September.

Paquette, M., Sommerfelt, E. J. and Kent, M. L. (2015) 'Do the ends justify the means? Dialogue, development communication, and deontological ethics', *Public Relations Review*, 41(1): 30–39.

Pearson, R. (1989) 'Business ethics and communication ethics: Public relations practice and the idea of dialogue', in Botan, C. L. and Hazeleton, V. (eds) *Public relations theory.* Hillsdale, NJ: Lawrence Erlbaum Associates, pp. 111–131.

Pieczka, M. (2010) 'Public relations as dialogic expertise?' *Journal of Communication Management*, 15(2): 108–124.

Pundak, R. (2012) 'More relevant than ever: People-to-people peacebuilding efforts in Israel and Palestine', *Palestine–Israel Journal of Politics, Economics and Culture*, 18(2 and 3). Retrieved from www.pij.org/details.php?id=1442# on 5 November 2015.

Scott, S. (2010) 'Martin Buber (1878–1965)', *Internet encyclopedia of philosophy: A peer reviewed academic resource.* Last updated 9 July 2010. Retrieved from www.iep.utm.edu/buber/#SH2b on 28 April 2013.

Stacks, D. W. (2011) *Primer of public relations research.* New York: Guilford Press.

Theunissen, P. and Wan Noordin, W. N. (2012) 'Revisiting the concept "dialogue" in public relations', *Public Relations Review*, 38(1): 5–13.

UNESCO (1998) 'Setting-up in Jerusalem of the "Israeli–Palestinian Media Forum"', press release, Paris, 2 December (no. 98–262). Retrieved from www.unesco.org/bpi/eng/unescopress/98–262e.htm on 25 April 2013.

Zaft, M. (1998) 'Looking for understanding, dreaming about peace', *This Week in Petach Tiqva*, 10 July (author's translation from Hebrew).

4 Making sense of communication in societies divided by terrorism

Lessons from Northern Ireland

Owen Hargie and Pauline Irving

Introduction

Terrorism is now a global disease that has grown rapidly to infect almost every country across the world (Sandler, 2015). For example, the year 2014 witnessed an 81 per cent increase in worldwide deaths from terrorism, from 18,000 in 2013 to 33,000 in 2014, while kidnappings by terrorist groups in 2014 increased by three times the 2013 figure (US State Department, 2015). In some senses this is nothing new, since terrorist activity has a long history, dating back many hundreds of years (Lutz and Lutz, 2013). However, modern methods of communication mean that terrorist acts can now instantly secure publicity and readily reach potential recruits and funders worldwide. Indeed, O'Hair and Heath (2005: 4) argued that 'Terrorism is an inherently communicative process', as communication infuses every level of the activity from the intrapersonal processes involved in adopting and internalising radicalised beliefs, to the interpersonal relations that sustain the group, and the mass communication methods used to publicise and promote their activities.

Communication is fundamental to understanding how people frame terrorism and share meanings to create a common sense of the world. It is this 'sense' which drives our behaviour. As Weick et al. (2005: 409) explain: 'Sensemaking involves turning circumstances into a situation that is comprehended explicitly in words and that serves as a springboard into action'. It is the 'process by which meaning is given to everyday experiences … so that the meaning gained can inform subsequent action' (Arnaud et al., 2016: 41). The sense that is made of events does not reflect an independent objective truth, but rather subjective rationalisations based on the way the individual processes information. Events are filtered by one's perceptions, meaning is attributed and 'sense' is determined by what seems most credible and reasonable. In her analysis, Mills (2009) explains how sensemaking is:

> grounded in identity construction, retrospective interpretations of past events, and enactive of sensible environments (i.e., we create what we can then make sense of), social (i.e., involves shared meanings, common language and social interaction), and focused on and by extracted cues (i.e.,

> familiar structures that provide a simple focus around which sense is developed)
>
> (p. 372)

It is about creating meanings that are defensible rather than 'getting it right' (ibid.: 373).

Sensemaking begins with an individual's personal perspective, or 'frame', which shapes events or cues into meaning. Hargie et al. (2009) point out that 'People do not deal with the world event by event, but rather frame events into larger meaning structures which provide them with an interpretive template within which they can make sense of relevant aspects of the events that they experience' (p. 71). In essence, frames relate to past experience and cues are current experience. Meaning is created when connections are made between the two. Weick (1995: 111) delineates the core processes as follows, 'the content of sensemaking is to be found in the frames and categories that summarize past experience, in the cues and labels that snare specifics of present experience, and in the ways these two settings of experience are connected'. The perceptions and hence sensemaking of a complex event like a terrorist attack and terrorism itself are influenced by a number of key factors.

Rothenberger (2015) identified four main agents and targets of communication of relevance to an understanding of terrorism: the terrorists, civilians/public, government and the media. In the model shown in Figure 4.1, we have portrayed these four 'pieces' as parts of a communication jigsaw, to which we have added the important fifth aspect of the background context within which terrorism occurs. By understanding these five elements we can begin to form a picture of communication in a society divided by terrorism and how sensemaking operates therein. As depicted in Figure 4.1, in such societies the four central pieces of the societal jigsaw are some distance apart, and this results in polar opposite sensemaking, with people from each side of the divide making different sense of the same events. In this chapter we argue that concerted efforts have to be made by all of the four key players to come together so that a more shared form of sensemaking, as portrayed in Figure 4.2, can emerge. The situation as represented in Figure 4.2 also recognises that in reality in most societies, apart from totalitarian regimes, some level of difference and division is inevitable and indeed desirable. This model provides a useful template for the analysis of the key elements that must be addressed if change is to occur to transform divided societies. While all of the five elements included in these figures are inter-related, for the purposes of analysis it is useful to study each separately.

The context: Northern Ireland

Context plays a crucial role in communication and sensemaking (Hargie, 2011). Thus, we develop the cultural or sub-cultural mores of our in-group, interpret historical and contemporary actions selectively through this frame,

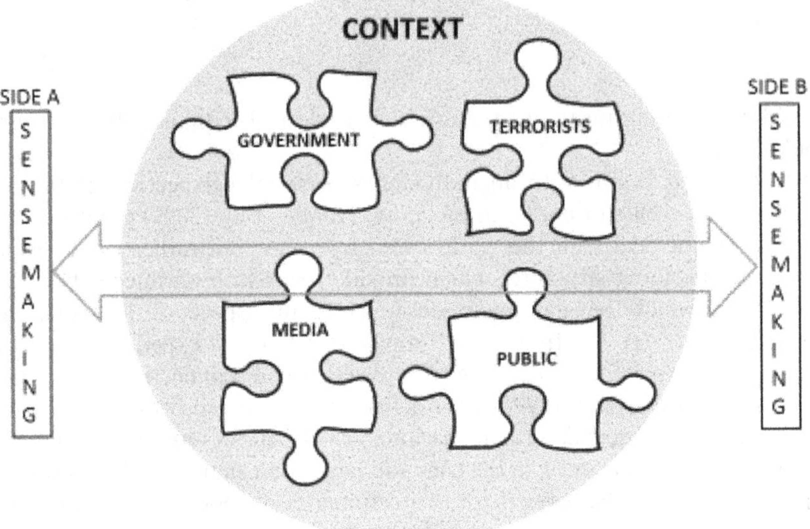

Figure 4.1 The communication sensemaking jigsaw in a society divided by terrorism

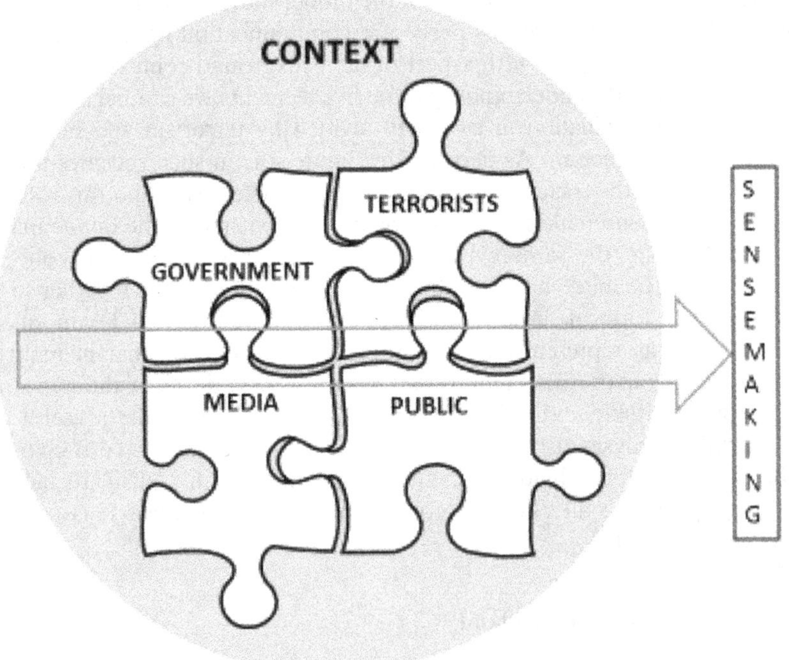

Figure 4.2 The communication sensemaking jigsaw in a unified society

learn the relevant narratives to describe and interpret events, celebrate particular 'heroes', and so on. To understand communication we must therefore be aware of its context and the 'dynamic complexity' of the frames used to shape experience and interpret meaning (Colville et al., 2013: 2010). Within the Northern Ireland (NI) context, the extant societal divisions are driven, shaped and sustained by what has been termed a 'minority-majority conundrum' (Stevenson et al., 2007). The 2012 UK Census revealed that the population of NI is closely divided between Protestants, comprising some 48 per cent of the total population, and Catholics, who make up around 45 per cent. However, in the other part of the island, the Republic of Ireland (RoI), the 2011 Census there showed a tiny Protestant minority, comprising some 5 per cent of the population compared to 84.2 per cent of Catholics. Thus, Protestants constitute a sizable minority of around 20 per cent of the total island population, but are a tiny minority in the RoI. On the other hand, Catholics constitute a significant minority in NI, a very large majority on the island of Ireland, but a small minority of the United Kingdom (UK) as a whole (about 8 per cent). These disparities create a variety of majority and minority perceptions depending upon the territorial perspective within which they are viewed. When taken in conjunction with the historical biases suffered by religious minorities in both parts of Ireland and the role of these in folk memory, together with the toxic effects of the terrorist violence perpetrated by both communities on the other side, this has fostered a culture of mistrust between the two communities in NI and helped to reinforce a dualist division in terms of British or Irish political identities (for a full analysis see Hargie and Dickson, 2003).

While some commentators have attributed the problems in NI solely to the attitudes and behaviour of the Unionist majority and its so-called 'siege mentality' following the partition of the island of Ireland, others have illustrated how the governments in both parts of the island played equal and indeed mirror-image roles in perpetuating division and conflict (Brown, 2010; O'Donnell and Hargie, 2011). Given the way in which Northern Ireland was formed and the operation of a one-party state by unionists with related discrimination and gerrymandering against Catholics, it has been regarded by nationalists as fundamentally sectarian (McVeigh and Rolston, 2007). Equally, the overtly Catholic nature of the Republic of Ireland state from its inception, its territorial claim over NI, and its hostile attitude to Protestants, all played an important role in fostering fear among unionists (Roche and Barton, 2013). This was exacerbated by Protestant flight from the RoI, where their numbers in the early years of the twentieth century dropped by 33 per cent, from 327,179 to 220,723, with up to 60,000 of these as a result of 'forced' departures (Bielenberg, 2013). Suffice it to say that minorities in both parts of the island were not well treated. The result of this is that there have been deep levels of suspicion and indeed animosity between the two communities within NI, and for Catholics towards the UK government and Protestants towards the RoI government. This means that any long-term settlement of the NI problem will have to ensure conducive channels of communication and positive relationships across all of these parties.

Although not exclusively so, Catholics in NI are mainly nationalist and wish to separate from the UK and unite in a new political configuration with the RoI, while Protestants are mostly unionist and wish to remain as an integral part of the UK. The deep-rooted divisions stemming from these equally valid but diametrically opposed aspirations led to a long period of violence and terrorism carried out by republican (Catholic) and loyalist (Protestant) paramilitary groups. The resulting terrorist violence, or 'Troubles', affected the lives of everyone in NI, resulting in the deaths of over 3,700 people (Smyth and Hamilton, 2003) – equivalent pro rata to 600,000 people in the USA or 115,000 in the UK. A much higher number of people were seriously injured or bereaved. It also caused the largest population movements in Europe since the Second World War as many within the two communities, particularly in the cities of Belfast and Derry/Londonderry, physically divided and sought the safety and sanctuary of living with members of their in-group.

The Good Friday (Belfast) Agreement in 1998 attempted to address some of these problems. This agreement formally recognised that NI should remain part of the UK until a majority of the people of NI and the RoI wished otherwise, and that the people of NI should have the right to identify themselves and be accepted as Irish or British, or both. In addition, the RoI withdrew its territorial claim over NI. A new power-sharing assembly was set up in NI, while formal governmental bodies were established between NI and the RoI, and between the UK and Ireland. However, despite this Agreement, and the later more inclusive St Andrews Agreement of 2006 when the main unionist party, the Democratic Unionist Party (DUP) became involved, entrenched divisions between the two communities remain. In their research across six areas of NI, McAlister et al. (2014: 308) found very deep extant divisions between the two communities, concluding that, 'While the external perception of Northern Ireland is a society that has emerged successfully from three decades of war, the impact of the Conflict continues'. While NI is now often described as a 'post-conflict society', a number of smaller, but deadly, 'dissident' republican terrorist groups continue to be actively involved in violence carrying out bomb attacks and shootings, some of which have resulted in fatalities (Cochrane, 2013). NI is therefore a society that is neither at war nor at peace.

During the Troubles, it was described as 'one of the most deeply divided countries in the world and one of the most violent' (Greer, 1985: 275). Despite a decline in violence there is still a deep fault line between the two sides. The body responsible for social housing, the Housing Executive (2015), in noting that over 90 per cent of public sector housing is separated along religious lines, cites a main reason for this as being that NI is part of an 'ethnic frontier' comprised of two opposing traditions rooted in political antagonism. In the capital city of Belfast, social housing is almost entirely segregated, with the two communities divided and protected from one another by physical barriers or 'peace walls', which ironically have increased in number since the Good Friday Agreement (Byrne and Gormley-Heenan, 2014). This led McKeown et al. (2012: 86) to conclude that 'it is often difficult for Protestant and Catholic inhabitants of Northern Ireland to come together or even find a shared space where they could interact if they wanted to'. The segregation affects social relationships, with most adult friendships being in-group, as well as 90 per cent of marriages (O'Donnell and Hargie, 2011).

It also impacts severely on education, with over 90 per cent of pupils being educated with co-religionists, and only 6 per cent attending integrated (desegregated) schools (Borooah and Knox, 2013). For most young people the first educational experience of mixing with the out-group is in further or higher education colleges (Somerville et al., 2011). However, their formative experiences shape them, and students at university have been shown to make self-segregating decisions (Orr et al., 2012), and so although nominally integrated operate in what Cairns (1998) referred to as a state of functional desegregation. Within the workplace, legislation mandates that large employers must recruit a representative workforce and ensure that employees are protected from sectarian abuse. However, while Protestant and Catholic employees work side by side, they rarely socialise outside of work (Dickson et al., 2008a). Even sports witness a high degree of segregation. Gaelic sports (hurling, Gaelic football, camogie) are almost exclusively Catholic, others are mainly Protestant (e.g. cricket, rugby), and only a few are cross-community (e.g. tennis, golf, cycling). Although football is widely played by both communities it also reflects the extant divisions in NI, so that Catholics and Protestants often play for and support different teams (Hargie et al., 2015).

All of these experiences have resulted in a very divided society, where many people from both communities live parallel lives and do not mix. Both sides harbour a sense of being wronged by the other, feeling that they are the victim community. Of particular relevance here is past sensemaking, a retrospective process from which people select interpretations to the comprehension of present cues and events, reflecting what they have seen before (Weick, 1979). In this way, 'ongoing streaming of the present is filtered through the past' (Colville et al., 2014: 219). Each side has its own interpretation of what caused the Troubles and behaviour is shaped as a result, so that each votes for its in-group political parties. The sense they make of their reality is heavily influenced by selective memory of perceived past wrongs by the other side and reinforced by the sensegiving that emanates from leaders within their own homogeneous community, where dissent from the prevailing view is often met with hostility.

The terrorists

As noted by O'Hair and Heath (2005: 1) 'Terrorism is a complex, controversial, and contested concept'. Given the disputed nature of the activity, there is no universally accepted definition of terms such as 'terrorism' or 'terrorist' (Krieger and Meierrieks, 2011; Lutz and Lutz, 2013). For example, terrorists and state governments have very different perspectives on the nature and meaning of the activity (Ganor, 2002; Maikovich, 2005; Matusitz, 2013). The language used by terrorists varies dramatically from the terminology employed by governmental agencies, in terms of, inter alia, the group itself (e.g. 'freedom fighters' or 'terrorists'), those they kill (e.g. 'legitimate targets' or 'innocent people'), their motivation (e.g. 'liberation struggle' or 'criminal activity'), specific activity (e.g. 'justifiable action' or 'callous murder'), and state forces (e.g. 'oppressors' or 'forces of law and order'). Indeed the former would reject the nomenclature of 'terrorist'. The language surrounding terrorism is central to the sensemaking process and bringing this sense back into the world to make it seem more stable and thus controllable.

Schmid et al. (2005) reviewed 109 definitions of terrorism and from these identified twenty-two main component definitional terms. The first five of these were: violence/force, political, fear/terror, threat, psychological effects. This is reflected in recent definitions. There is now a growing consensus that terrorism is activity that is carried out by non-state groups, and is designed to threaten, frighten and coerce mostly non-combatant citizens in order to attain political, social or religious goals (Enders and Sandler, 2012). Examining various defining features of the activity, Hargie and Irving (2016: 87) define terrorism as 'behaviour that has political, social or religious motives, and has the goal of influencing and intimidating a widespread, mostly non-combatant, audience'. This is similar to other recent definitions, where terrorism is defined as: 'the unlawful use of force or violence against persons or property to intimidate or coerce a government, the civilian population, or any segment thereof in furtherance of political or social objectives' (FBI, 2015); 'the use or threat of violence by non-state actors for the purpose of inciting fear in a much wider audience, to bring about political change' (Phillips, 2015: 63); and 'violent attack on civilian populations for the purpose of politically motivated intimidation and issue advancement' (Heath and Waymer, 2014: 230).

Somerville et al. (2011) have illustrated how within most societies there are two broad perspectives surrounding terrorism: the 'official' standpoint and an 'alternative' viewpoint. The former is communicated by government ministers and spokespeople, conservative politicians, right-wing commentators, security experts, etc. It focuses upon the criminality and insanity of terrorism and often argues that dealing with the terrorist threat may necessitate the suspension of normal civil or legal rights or the introduction of more stringent legislation. The alternative perspective, while still accepting that violence is not legitimate, criticises what it terms 'state sponsored terror' by governments, who engage in armed activity either within their own country or in a range of countries, while restricting civil liberties in their own country in the name of security. This perspective tends to be communicated by those who dissent from the official view, such as critical academics, left-wing politicians and commentators, and some journalists. It argues, for example, that in the USA following 9/11 a 'discourse of fear', which accentuated dangers and risks for the population from terrorism, was used by the government to expand 'the new US role in leading the world' (Altheide, 2007: 287). However, as Lutz and Lutz (2013) point out, while alternative views can have legitimacy, one problem is that they are often raised to promote or justify the actions of terrorists and equate their actions to those of democratically elected governments. In sensemaking terms both viewpoints constitute alternative frames which in turn selectively shape perceptions. However, as Colville et al. (2013: 1205) contend, they omit 'cues in other frames, as we fail to notice that we have failed to notice as we have become too familiar with what surrounds us'. In this way, positions become entrenched.

In an early categorisation, Hacker (1976) identified three main categories of terrorists: 'crusaders' who are idealistically driven and believe they are fighting for a just and honourable cause, 'crazies' who are mentally unstable and motivated by irrational beliefs and perceptions, and 'criminals' who use terrorism for personal gain. Of course, the same terrorist organisation may contain all three types. In addition, the perceptions and portrayals of terrorist groups by different constituencies emphasise different aspects of these three types. For example, when ten members of the Provisional Irish Republican Army (PIRA) died on hunger strike in prison in 1981, in a protest designed to secure special category political status, they were portrayed by fellow republicans as heroic and principled freedom fighters making the ultimate sacrifice for their cause. But by unionists they were regarded as crazed, psychopathic, terrorist serial killers who were committing suicide, while the then UK prime minister Margaret Thatcher clearly perceived them to be criminals, stating at a press conference: 'We are not prepared to consider special category status for certain groups of people serving sentences for crime. Crime is crime is crime, it is not political.' In this way, the sensegiving messages from different parties reflected their own positions with regard to the PIRA.

Of course, categorisations of terrorists also can change over time. For example, in 1987 the former UK prime minister Margaret Thatcher described Nelson Mandela as the leader of a terrorist organisation, yet in 2013 he was eulogised by numerous world leaders at his funeral, with President Barack Obama saying that he was 'a giant of history who moved a nation toward justice, and in the process moved billions around the world'. In NI the former PIRA leader Martin McGuinness became deputy first minister in 2007, and shared a very friendly relationship with the first minister, the DUP leader and demagogue Ian Paisley, his former arch-enemy. Paisley had previously castigated PIRA members as the 'spawn of Satan', and asserted 'I am not going to sit down with bloodthirsty monsters who have been killing and terrifying my people'.

It is clear that the objectives of a terrorist group are many and varied (Crenshaw, 2011). Pattwell et al. (2015) developed a fivefold typology for the primary objectives of terrorists:

1 The pursuit of strategic or instrumental goals such as carrying out an atrocity to gain maximum publicity.
2 Attempts to impair governability, by disrupting normal activity, damaging the economic infrastructure and destabilising the state. Thus, PIRA placed no-warning bombs in cities in NI and England, and the UVF (Ulster Volunteer Force) in cities in RoI, to attempt to achieve these aims.
3 Carrying out attacks to create a climate of fear among non-combatants and demonstrate that they have the capacity to continue with their campaign.
4 Attacking what they see as the complicity of citizens. In NI, republican terrorists attacked civilian workers at police stations, claiming they were part of the 'British war machine'. Likewise, loyalist terrorists attacked newsagents who sold republican newspapers since they were part of the 'republican war machine'.
5 Seeking revenge for actions carried out by the government or by opposing terrorists. 'Tit-for-tat' killings by rival paramilitary groups were very common in NI. For example, on Saturday 23 October 1993, shortly after 1 p.m., two PIRA bombers were dropped off by the driver of a getaway car and walked into Frizzell's fishmongers shop on the Shankill Road (a Protestant area of Belfast) intending to leave a Semtex bomb, which was on a short fuse, and make their escape. However, the bomb exploded prematurely and the entire building collapsed, leaving a scene of carnage with ten men, women and children dead (including one of the bombers) and some fifty-seven people seriously injured. Loyalist paramilitary groups reacted with fury to the bombing and vowed retaliation (Silke, 2003). One week later the loyalist Ulster Freedom Fighters (UFF) carried out a revenge shooting at the Rising Sun bar in the mainly Catholic/nationalist village of Greysteel, County Londonderry, in which they murdered eight people (including ironically a Protestant man who was a former member of the security forces).

Other objectives include, inter alia, generation of funds to maintain their campaign, maintenance of in-group morale, recruitment of new members, and activities designed to disseminate and publicise their views or justify their actions. In functionalist terms, judgements about the actions of others are based upon their perceived goals and motives. Terrorists engage in a different form of sensemaking with regard to their actions compared to governments and the public. For this reason, Borum (2003: 7) argued that we must attempt to comprehend not only 'the specific ideology of those who commit or advocate acts of terrorism but also gain an understanding of the process of how these ideas or doctrines develop'. The way in which we make sense of a situation is shaped by our cognitive schema or mindset – how we interpret and represent the world. It is therefore important to attempt to understand the world view of terrorists in order to predict and counteract their planned attacks (Borum, 2014). Thus, suicide is often associated with feelings of despair and futility, but among some terrorist groups a suicide bombing is interpreted as a supreme act of sacrifice and martyrdom by the individual. Understanding the motivations of terrorists is also crucial to the development of strategies to counter their communication strategies.

Richards (2004: 171) argued that a terror attack can be seen as 'a disaster created for PR reasons'. However, he makes an important distinction between 'power-based' PR, where terrorists carry out an atrocity to demonstrate their strength, and 'values-based' PR, which is about promoting 'the reputation or practical goodness of clients and their works. It is about demonstrating the client's adherence to or association with certain values or standards' (p. 173). He argues that the power-based PR of terrorists is antithetical to the world of professional PR. In this way, terrorists validate their legitimacy by self-definition rather than through the mandate of society (Sada, 1985). However, terrorist groups also use public relations strategies to communicate their messages and build their social capital (Heath and Waymer, 2014). They are usually well aware of their stakeholders and of the importance of communicating effectively with, and influencing, them (Mozes-Sadeh and Avraham, 2014). These stakeholders include their core and potential future membership, their immediate non-combative support network, the media, local and international politicians, and local and international public opinion. Key supporters of the group may forgive 'mistakes', where innocent civilians are killed, on the basis that the sense they make of the action is that it was carried out to achieve a wider necessary and valid goal.

However, once a terrorist group becomes actively involved in democratic political activity, it makes their continued campaign of violence more difficult to sustain. This is because their support base is more likely to withdraw political backing if the terrorist arm of an organisation is engaged in killing civilians (Heger, 2015). One of the reasons why activists may adopt a terrorist strategy is because of their failure to establish a viable political base or electoral support, and so they pursue their political aspirations through violence. It is therefore in a government's interests to encourage terrorist groups to engage with a political path. Such sensenegotiation can also help to counteract some of the effects of groupthink, and blinkered thinking, which occur when terrorists only talk with their in-group (Tsintsadze-Maass and Maass, 2014). Jonathan Powell (2014), who was a senior adviser to the UK's former prime minister Tony Blair and spent seventeen years negotiating with terrorists, argues that there is no alternative to face-to-face discussions if solutions are to be found. He also illustrates how terrorists are nearly always keen to talk, and how dialogue with active paramilitary groups in NI was central to achieving agreement. Indeed, in NI the UK government often denied that it was talking with terrorists when in fact it was involved in ongoing backchannel contacts (McLaughlin and Miller, 1996).

Research has shown that when a terrorist group faces 'interfield rivalries' through being violently opposed by another terrorist group with conflicting political aspirations, then violence is likely to be perpetuated and peace becomes more difficult to achieve (Phillips, 2015). This is because the two groups become focused upon fighting, and hopefully defeating, one another. For example, in NI, PIRA was opposed by the UVF and other loyalist paramilitaries. The animosities were so venomous that a perceived concession by government to one group was viewed as a loss by the other group, who often as a result stepped up their attacks on their rivals. For PIRA the time, effort and energies expended on attempting to murder loyalist interfield rivals were at the expense of their core political objectives of attacking the government and destabilising society.

The position becomes even more complicated if there are also 'intrafield rivalries' where two terrorist groups are ostensibly trying to achieve the same objectives. This often leads to internecine conflict between the groups apparently fighting on the same side, not least because of 'turf wars' where each group wants to maintain control of and power within its heartland areas. Thus in NI, the PIRA had other republican groups to contend with such as the INLA (Irish National Liberation Army), while the UVF was faced with rival loyalist groups including the UDA (Ulster Defence Association). The existence of intrafield rivalries makes peace negotiations more difficult and prolonged, since if one group begins to negotiate a possible peace deal it is likely to be denigrated by its internecine rival, being accused of 'selling-out' or weakness. These rival groups, or the outworking from them, may then remain involved in terrorism. For example in NI when the PIRA decommissioned its weapons and disbanded, it was replaced by a number of smaller republican terrorist groups (the Continuity IRA, the Real IRA and Óglaighnah Éireann) who continued to engage in killings and bombings. Such rivalries splinter the sensemaking frames used to interpret events and further add to the complexity of the situation.

The public

The SafeComms (2011) research involved analysing data from case studies in six countries that examined terrorist attacks in Northern Ireland, Spain, Greece, Israel, Turkey and the Arab states. It included media analyses of the incidents together with in-depth interviews with a range of those involved, including first responders (health personnel, police, fire service, etc.), second responders (social workers, clergy, etc.), elected representatives and officials in local and national authorities, journalists and victims. It highlighted the key role the public plays in crisis situations. 'New technologies have allowed the public not only to gain access to multiple versions of reports on the same incident via the internet, but also themselves to become a source that is capable of competing with the Government's official version' (p. 11). Heightened emotions can lead to mobilisation, manifested, inter alia, in mass rallies, public mourning rituals and internet discussions, and even mass rage, leading to violence. All of these responses combine to increase the dynamic complexity of the sensemaking process. An increasingly powerful voice in relation to terrorism is that of victims. In his report on NI, Bloomfield (1998: 14) adopted a broad definition of victims as being, 'the surviving injured and those who care for them, together with those close relatives who mourn their dead'. However, Ferguson et al. (2010: 857), in their empirical study of victims in NI, found that there were definitional problems in this area such that, 'establishing who are victims and the very nature of victimhood has been difficult. In part this is due to the highly contested nature of the labels "victim" and "terrorist".' Thus, there is debate about whether those who are injured when committing terrorist acts can be classed as victims, and whether the relatives of terrorists killed in such acts are victims in the same way that innocent civilians killed by terrorists are victims. As a result, a distinction is often made between 'victims' and 'perpetrators' of terrorist attacks, although in internecine conflicts such as in NI the application of these terms is contested by different groups (Brewer and Hayes, 2011).

In his analysis of victimhood, van Dijk (2009) traces the etymology of the word 'victim' to the Latin term for a sacrificial animal, *victima*, and points out that Western, Hebrew and Arab languages all use words indicating sacrifice to refer to the victims of crime. He further illustrates how victims are often stereotypically portrayed as helpless and passive, and that key characteristics of the 'ideal victim' include being innocent, suffering greatly and in silence, and showing readiness to forgive the perpetrator. The wider community is then expected to give respect to and show compassion for those who comply with these role expectations of the ideal victim. In contrast, those victims who contravene these unspoken norms often do not receive respect or compassion and may instead be viewed and responded to negatively. Indeed, as noted by Hackett and Rolston (2009: 362), 'The victim is not guaranteed a sympathetic hearing'.

However, many people recoil from being described as victims, preferring instead to portray themselves as 'survivors' (Dillenburger et al., 2006) which in sensemaking terms is a more positive frame and so likely to lead to more positive long-term personal outcomes. A common research finding is that victims frequently discover unforeseen reservoirs of inner strength while dealing with the traumatic event and its later consequences. This phenomenon has been referred to as 'victim resilience' (Bonnano, 2004) and 'post traumatic growth' (Dekel et al., 2011). They often have a deep desire to have their story heard, for their loved ones not to be forgotten, and for the perpetrators to be brought to justice. Some remain angry about what has happened to them (van Dijk, 2009). One reason for this is that, 'The person who experiences a traumatic re-enactment is still *inside* the event, present at it … The traumatic event that happened in the past does not belong to a distanced past: it is still present in the present' (van Alphen, 2002: 211). Indeed, Dorahy et al. (2009) argue that the legacy of the NI conflict remains a strong influence on the psychological well-being of individuals affected by the conflict, having an ongoing transgenerational effect.

It has been shown that the sense that victims make of traumatic events, and their need for treatment, is complex and multifaceted (Gilligan, 2006). Furthermore, Manktelow (2007: 46) concludes that, 'the needs of victims of the Troubles in Northern Ireland were left largely unmet for many years by the statutory social work services … the chief support people relied on throughout much of the Troubles was families and friends'. For victims and survivors there is often no sense of positive closure for those who had loved ones killed or maimed in such a cruel and sudden way. They have to live with their loss on an ongoing basis, and function in life, day-by-day, as best as they can. As one victim in the NI part of the SafeComms research expressed it:

> I think the enormity of the incident, and the magnitude of the loss that we had, meant that we could never return to normality in the normal sense of the word. But I think, as in all of these things, I think the pressure of life just forces people to do things. You've got to get up out of your bed. You've got to go and get food. You've got certain things that you have to do in life, tasks that you have to do.

As well as getting on with the routine business of living, victims had to learn to expect many twists and turns in their attitudes and feelings as life progressed, and to realise that many of the emotions that they thought had been dealt with would recur. The advice given by one interviewee, who now worked with other victims, was as follows:

> I would always say to them look, be as you are, if you get up in the morning and feel like crying then cry, if you get up in the morning and feel like laughing then laugh because I think it was CS Lewis in his book A Grief Observed, which [the film] Shadowlands came from, he talks about taking a drive through a mountainside and you see this scenery which you think you have left behind miles ago and you turn a corner and all of a sudden, there it is and you hadn't really left it behind. Grief's like that, you're taking a journey and you're twisting and turning and emotions you had initially, come back much later … and just for somebody to tell you that 'you're not going out of your mind, it's OK, this is all normal'.

In a recent analysis of terrorist communications we developed a model of meaning construction (Hargie and Irving, 2016). This proposes that meaning is created by members of the public as a result of messages being processed through a series of filters, which colour and shape the individual's perceptions and interpretations of terrorist incidents. This involves six main sensemaking filters: media portrayals, culture and context, the nature of the incident, the objectives of the terrorist group, personal beliefs, and the perpetrators of the attack. Each of these impinges upon the sense that is made of terrorism in general and of particular terrorist attacks.

The media

The media play a central role in the framing of terrorism and terrorist incidents and perform a core role in the sensegiving process. For this reason, the former UK prime minister Margaret Thatcher famously argued in 1985 that terrorists had to be starved 'of the oxygen of publicity on which they depend'. This led her government to introduce a ban on representatives from loyalist and republican paramilitary groups speaking on TV or radio, in the years between 1988 and 1994. If they were interviewed their voices had to be overdubbed by those of actors. This ban impacted severely on publicity for terrorist-related groups (Taylor, 1998). In the four months preceding the implementation of the ban the main republican party Sinn Féin (SF) received 471 requests for interview whereas in the four months following the ban this dropped to 110 enquiries. In addition TV producers ran briefer terrorist-related stories if they involved using actors' voices. Given the significant drop in terrorism-related stories, Moloney (2005: 72) concluded that 'Margaret Thatcher's ban has to be judged a success for her government'.

In recent years the media landscape has been heavily influenced by new media which are much less easily controlled or even managed. Conventional media are no longer the only forces shaping the public agenda as social media grow in impact and importance in sensemaking terms. SafeComms (2011) concluded that 'The internet and social media in particular, have become an independent public space characterised by complexity, diversity, anonymity, rapidity … Consquently they are predestined to be hotbeds of rumours and platforms which shape public opinion' (p. 14). In contrast to more traditional media, social media can be seen as:

- Mainly amateur in nature and therefore not dependent on journalistic standards of what may or may not be suitable to publish.
- More or less instant sources of amateur videos and other images;
- Rapid methods of exchanging opinions and propagation of rumour.
- Often containing a mingling of facts and opinion in an unmanaged way.
- Containing a willingness to readily generate scandal and attribute blame.

Furthermore, Diakopoulos et al. (2010) note that journalists increasingly turn to social media to support their reporting of news, thereby embedding social media into more mainstream sensemaking.

The main goal of most journalists is primarily to tell and sell a good story, the essence of which has been shown to include innovation, conflict, drama and an element of the unexpected. Media management is now regarded as very important by paramilitary groups. Yarchi et al. (2013: 265) have shown how 'Many terrorist organizations have come to understand the media's crucial role and to take media considerations into account when planning their activities. Some also employ a relatively sophisticated public relations system.' This has been well known for some time so that, for example, Laqueur

(1977: 223) pointed out that: 'Terrorists have learned that the media are of paramount importance in their campaigns, that the terrorist act by itself is next to nothing, whereas publicity is all.'

Terrorists engage in PR, and strategic communications, to achieve a range of sensegiving goals, not just to obtain publicity for their atrocities (see Rothenberger's analysis of terrorists' use of the internet in Chapter 12). Their communications are also aimed, inter alia, at influencing public opinion, attracting recruits, and shaping an image of strength and determination (Rothenberger, 2015). As mentioned earlier, one clear difference between terrorists and other organisations that use strategic communication is that the former are much less concerned about the social responsibility or moral dimensions of what they do (Falkheimer, 2014). Also, as shown by Somerville and Purcell (2011) in their interviews with spokespersons for the PIRA during the Troubles, there is a tendency for terrorist groups to focus exclusively upon their own goals and messages and so they use one-way or 'arrow' communications (Clampitt, 2013), with no cognisance given to a two-way symmetrical approach. In fact, the PIRA representatives perceived PR purely as a vehicle for disseminating advocacy or propaganda for their own group. This approach is mirrored by terrorist groups on the loyalist side.

In NI the media have played an important role in framing the Troubles, and also in accentuating the in-group and out-group perspectives by using different frames to present their news (Bairner, 1996). The two main morning newspapers have served different audiences: the *News Letter* providing a unionist narrative and the *Irish News* a nationalist one. In this way, the readers of these newspapers have their biases confirmed as the sensegiving messages fit readily with their existing cognitive schemata. By comparison, the daily *Belfast Telegraph* and the weekend *Sunday Life* have played a more neutral role, being read by both communities.

Another communication example provided by Somerville and Purcell (2011) pertains to war murals as a form of communication. The PIRA co-ordinator for wall murals in Belfast at the height of the Troubles gave them what he perceived to be an example of a very effective way to get the republican message across. When Lord Mountbatten was murdered by a bomb explosion on his boat at Mullaghmore on 27 August 1979 (together with an 83-year-old woman and two 14-year-old boys), and this was followed later that day by the Warrenpoint massacre when eighteen soldiers were killed in two roadside bombs, the following mural was painted on walls in republican areas of Belfast: '13 gone and not forgotten [a reference to the number of civilians killed by the army on Bloody Sunday], we got 18 and Mountbatten.' This approach was very typical of terrorist groups from both sides, and of the tit-for-tat mentality that existed. However, these forms of tribal, triumphalist and gloating communications, using a power-based PR frame, only served to cement even more deeply the binary in-group–out-group divide in NI. It also typifies the crude communications of many terrorist groups who have long celebrated the 'propaganda of the deed' (Louw, 2003). This approach to PR is the antithesis of the two definitions of the activity provided by the Public Relations Society of America, that 'Public Relations helps an organization and its publics adapt mutually to each other' and is 'an organization's efforts to win cooperation of groups of people' (cited in Snow, 2006).

Pattwell et al. (2015: 1134) pointed out that, 'Governments have a vested interest in reading terrorist acts in ways that privilege their own interests and ideologies over those of the terrorists. The media, in turn, tend to favor the explanations of the home government.' For example, Canel (2012) shows how in the USA following 9/11 there was ongoing synchrony between the government and the media in the way that the act was portrayed and in the appropriateness of the government's response. In particular the two frames of 'war on terror' and the 'importance of patriotism' were accepted by the public. In terms of terror management theory, the importance of symbolism was palpably evident 'through the inundation of patriotic songs, images, and narratives in the media ... [and] ... unprecedented support for the government, demonstrating both more willingness to embrace increased security measures and less demand for many of the privacy rights formerly considered sacrosanct' (Miller and Landau, 2005: 82–83). By contrast, following the Madrid bombings the media did not follow the patriotic and condemnatory frames as set by the Spanish government. Here there was a disconnect between the government and both the media and large swathes of public opinion, based partly on the fact that the bombings had been initially wrongly blamed on ETA rather than on Al-Qaeda, and also that the perpetrators being Muslim terrorists would place pressure on the ruling Spanish Popular Party in forthcoming elections given its involvement in the Iraq war.

Media system dependency theory argues that when individuals have to make sense of uncertain situations, their reliance on the mass media increases (Ball-Rokeach and Jung, 2003). Although there is increasing emphasis on the importance of social media in preparing for and dealing with crises, there is still a dearth of information about how and in what ways this communication channel can best function as an information dissemination conduit (Spence et al., 2015). As summarised by Sutton et al. (2015: 135), 'relatively little data-driven research exists to inform effective message design when using these media'. In pointing out that there is a great deal of misunderstanding in official circumstances about the nature of communication messages in terrorism, Archetti (2015) identifies three key aspects: the *availability* or accessibility of the message (e.g. whether it is on YouTube), its *reach* (how many potential viewers it has), and most importantly its *impact* (how many people actually watch it and are influenced by it). Of course, terrorists as well as governments attempt to manipulate the sensegiving messages carried by social media. Weimann (2015) has analysed how terrorist groups make use of websites, social networking sites, blogs and so on, to secure maximum publicity for their cause (e.g. by showing shocking and sensational images such as beheadings), shape how their actions should be construed, attract new recruits, and encourage supporters to carry out acts of terrorism against 'the enemy'.

Terrorists also make use of 'geoethnic local media' which allows them to target specific groups and particular geographical areas (Kim and Ball-Rokeach, 2006). Communication infrastructure theory purports that meso-level agents, such as geoethnic local media, can play a central role in providing relevant information for the local community (Literat and Chen, 2014). Terrorist campaigns depend upon the support of their local communities and so they often attempt to develop a 'movement', incorporating an 'army', a related political support and advocacy group, and sympathetic media outlets to advocate and support the movement. Geoethnic local media can play a central role through the way in which they frame news events. Archetti (2015) advises that in relation to dealing with terrorist groups it is important to know the identity of the local community, how its members perceive themselves, and to distinguish the 'relevant others' within the community. In this way, important non-radical networks that are close to the terrorist group can be identified.

The government

The devolved government in NI is based upon a consociational framework. This is a form of democracy by an elite cartel established with the purpose of attempting to transform a fractured political society into a functioning democracy (Lijphart, 2008). In an effort to maintain stability within the arrangement, coalitions between the main parties are the norm as is a mutual veto for both main blocs. However, this means that in NI the political arrangement is a potentially unstable form of government, where, as Kennedy (2009) points out, the two largest parties who share power are those with least in common, who oppose one another vehemently on many fundamental issues. The DUP and SF represent the most extreme forms of unionism and republicanism respectively. They therefore have to sell parallel but contradictory stories to their own constituencies about the gains they are making in the new political arrangement. However, there remains no agreement about the territory they both govern or what its future should be. Thus a major problem with a consociational arrangement is 'its tendency to freeze communal division along ethno-national lines' (Hayes and McAllister, 2012: 124). This is the case in NI where, as Rice et al. (2015: 6) note, 'an "uneasy" peace exists in this current post-conflict consociational environment'.

Maitlis (2005) points out that 'Sensemaking activities are particularly critical in dynamic and turbulent contexts, where the need to create and maintain coherent understandings that sustain relationships and enable collective action is especially important' (p. 21). This description certainly fits the consociational arrangement inherent with the NI devolved government. The sensemaking frames of the two main parties could be described as diametrically opposed, with each determining different significance and interpretation of environmental cues. However, out of this challenge there comes an exceptional opportunity to co-create a new sensemaking structure which can point the way forward. For this to succeed there will have to be extensive sensenegotiations between the two sides in an attempt to produce a narrative with which both can agree.

The aforementioned divisions within NI make such sensenegotiation very difficult. Not surprisingly, the conceptual framework which has driven research in this field is social identity theory (Hargie et al., 2008). A core principle of this theory is that one's self-concept is formed and strengthened by membership of social groups. We distinguish between groups of which we feel part (in-group) and those to which we feel no sense of belonging (out-group). Once a social identity is formed it is then maintained through in-group and out-group comparisons, by accentuating the differences between the two and strongly favouring the former. Individuals adopt the behaviour and attitudes of the in-group through a process of self-stereotyping. This then becomes very resistant to change. The history of NI means that unionists/loyalists and nationalists/republicans have a very strong sense of belonging to their in-group, together with a suspicion of and a tendency to avoid and derogate the out-group. Maitlis (2005) points out that relatively little attention has been paid to the 'dynamics of sensemaking when different parties engage simultaneously or reciprocally in such activities or about the ways in which the accounts they generate are reconciled – or not reconciled' (p. 22). She conducted an extensive longitudinal study which identified four forms of sensemaking relating to leader and stakeholder engagements. These four sensemaking approaches are: 'guided', which involves high levels of leader sensemaking and control leading to intense or animated information flow between stakeholders; 'fragmented', where there is animated engagement but poor control of the process; 'restricted', characterised by high levels of control but low involvement; and 'minimal', which lacks both control and animation. These approaches embody different interaction patterns and lead to different types of sensemaking outcomes. This model could be applied to the analysis of sensemaking in the NI government context, and further research of this type could provide enlightenment regarding how positive outcomes can be attained.

If peace is to become woven into the fabric of NI society then substantive efforts will have to be made to bring the two factions together. Given that they live discrete existences this is not an easy task. However, some steps are being taken. A range of contact schemes has enabled people from both sides to come together, to meet and share activities and ideas. The theoretical basis for such schemes is the Contact Hypothesis (Allport, 1954). This purports that a major cause of conflict is the fact that the feuding parties do not know one another and so increased contact between two opposing groups under conditions conducive to relational development can foster enhanced intergroup relationships. Such contact allows group members to present a positive impression to the out-group and reduces uncertainty about how to handle such encounters. At the same time, the jury is still out in relation to the success of these cross-community initiatives. As McKeown et al. (2012: 92), in their review of such schemes, point out, 'contact interventions in NI have been criticized for failing to encourage intergroup dialogue'. Likewise, in their review of research into sports-based cross-community schemes Hargie et al. (2015: 146) concluded that, while useful, 'such initiatives on their own cannot effect large-scale changes in cross-community relationships'.

One problem is that politicians in NI tend to see negotiations as highly competitive events leading to a zero-sum situation, or win–lose outcome. This somehow has to be transformed into a situation where negotiations are perceived as cooperative events with possible variable-sum gains and a win–win outcome. At present the main parties use PR mainly in an asymmetrical fashion, targeting their own voters with one-sided sensegiving messages. This needs to be replaced by the definition of PR mentioned earlier, which in NI will involve efforts to win the cooperation of both groups in the communal divide. For this to happen, there needs to be large steps towards agreement on contested symbols and aspirations. For example, in line with the common in-group identity model, the growth of a 'Northern Irish' identity in recent years offers the potential for a shared perspective, as this identity has been shown to be associated with more prosocial attitudes towards the former out-group (Lowe and Muldoon, 2014). A Northern Irish identity is more inclusive, being not exclusively 'Irish' or 'British' and so could be embraced by both sides. As Lowe and Muldoon point out, 'The value of this new identity may be that as it develops it can become a vehicle for expressing inclusive political ideals that are not yet evident in Northern Ireland' (p. 615). If such an identity is to take legs it will require agreement on a common flag, anthem, and so on, to which both sides can give at least partial allegiance.

In terms of increased contact, there is now considerable evidence that integrated schools have an important role to play in the changing or softening of attitudes, since those who have attended such schools have been shown to have less sectarian outlooks. As Hayes et al. (2007: 454), in their research into this area, conclude, integrated education: 'has positive long-term benefits in promoting a less sectarian stance on national identity and constitutional preferences … as the numbers experiencing integrated schooling grows, these individuals have the potential to create a new common ground in Northern Ireland politics'. However, rather than forge ahead with a determined drive to desegregate education, the NI government has promoted a segregated policy of 'shared education', where schools will be 'co-located' onto 'shared education campuses' but will stay separate, although with the sharing of some facilities. This serves to maintain the extant divisions among schoolchildren who will walk in the same main entry gate but then go to different buildings to be educated separately. This is a somewhat strange concept of 'sharing' and a poor role model to proffer future citizens.

Knox (2011) has shown how government policy documents such as the 'Programme for Cohesion, Sharing and Integration' abound with well-meaning and idealistic sentiments but, in reality, few concrete time-framed and carefully funded objectives; these documents tend to be 'about managing a divided society rather than about tackling the root causes' (p. 563). Similar criticisms have been levelled at the more recent 'Together: Building a Better Community' government document. Furthermore, while the two main parties agree about the publication of such well-intentioned documents, which espouse the need to build a shared and harmonious society, government ministers and representatives from the DUP and SF appear in the media on a daily basis attacking one another vehemently and delivering asymmetrical and partisan messages to their separate constituencies. In terms of sensemaking, the latter communications serve to negate the impact of the former.

Conclusion

Our NI research illustrates the complexities of communication within divided societies. The SafeComms (2011) study emphasised that the role of communication is often underestimated, pointing out that: 'The way in which communication strategies deal with terrorism becomes an integral part of the fight against terrorism' (p. 6). This research was able to identify international best practice in crisis communication following terrorist acts, but the challenges inherent in facilitating ongoing and meaningful communication between opposing groups in divided societies are even greater and more complex. In sensemaking terms, both the interpretations and actions of individual factions can be understood in terms of the past frames that are used to understand current cues and events. Weick et al. (2005) note that all sensemaking begins with confusion, from which particular cues are noticed and selected for consideration. The labelling of cues is dependent on past experience and so sensemaking is therefore of necessity a retrospective process. In divided societies what we notice and how we interpret our experiences is dependent on previous understanding and beliefs. Sensemaking is presumptive in that 'it connects the abstract with the concrete' (Weick et al., 2005: 413) and is influenced by a range of social factors. However, it is very fundamentally about action, and communication is central at all stages and levels. In their case study analysis of the shooting of Jean Charles Menezes on the London Underground in July 2005, Colville et al. (2013) illustrate how sensemaking is tested in counter-terrorism situations where erroneous decisions can easily be made in light of existing frames and routines.

The 'jigsaw' model presented in this chapter is helpful in both understanding the dynamic nature of communication in divided societies and in highlighting the need for future action to bring the differing sides together. The model is illustrated through an analysis of the NI context but it can readily be applied to other situations where the history and cultural frames are different. SafeComms (2011) illustrated how our understanding of terrorism can be extended and deepened by international comparison and broad lessons can be learned regarding good practice. Although the aims and aspirations of terrorists differ from context to context, there are similarities in modi operandi. In particular, the trend towards terrorists' use of PR to establish their legitimacy is almost universal, characterised by their increasing use of social media to showcase their activities. It is important to note that 'The media all over the world deal with terrorist attacks in different ways, depending on the moment they take place and on the experience that a country already has in terms of terrorism' (SafeComms, 2011: 11), and the continued exponential growth of new media serves to further complicate an already complex situation. Government response is vital in terms of information flow and sensemaking. Politicians are societal leaders who have a positive role to play in sensegiving. They also need to engage in sensenegotiation with their opponents in an attempt to reach some form of agreed and shared view of the past and the future, so that the situation as represented in Figure 4.2 might be achieved. The consociational framework in NI can serve to cement divisions in public opinion when two factions are operating from opposing sensemaking frames. The definition of 'victim' discussed earlier is a good example of this. A consociational government has inherent challenges but in terms of sensemaking we would contend that there are opportunities to develop new ways of understanding the past in NI, thereby leading to more positive future outcomes.

References

Allport, G. (1954) *The nature of prejudice.* Reading, MA: Addison-Wesley.

Altheide, D. (2007) 'The mass media and terrorism', *Discourse and Communication*, 1(3): 287–308.

Archetti, C. (2015) 'Terrorism, communication and new media: explaining radicalization in the digital age', *Perspectives on Terrorism*, 9(1): 49–59.

Arnaud, N., Mills, C., Legrand, C. and Maton, E. (2016) 'Materializing strategy in mundane tools: the key to coupling global strategy and local strategy practice?' *British Journal of Management*, 27: 38–57.

Bairner, A. (1996) 'The media', in Aughey, A. and Morrow, D. (eds) *Northern Ireland politics.* Harlow: Longman, pp. 173–180.

Ball-Rokeach, S. and Jung, J. (2003) 'The evolution of media system dependency theory', in Nabi, R. and Oliver, M. (eds) *Sage handbook of media processes and effects.* Thousand Oaks, CA: Sage, pp. 531–544.

Berger, B. and Meng, J. (2014) 'Making sense of leaders and leadership in public relations', in Berger, B. and Meng, J. (eds) *Public relations leaders as sensemakers.* New York: Routledge, pp. 3–15.

Bielenberg, A. (2013) 'Exodus: the emigration of Southern Irish Protestants during the Irish War of Independence and the Civil War', *Past and Present*, 218(1): 199–233.

Bloomfield, K. (1998) *We will remember them: report of the Northern Ireland Victims Commissioner.* Belfast: Stationery Office.

Bonnano, G. (2004) 'Loss, trauma, and human resilience: have we underestimated the human capacity to thrive after extremely adverse events?' *American Psychologist*, 59(1): 20–28.

Borooah, V. and Knox, C. (2013) 'The contribution of "shared education" to Catholic–Protestant reconciliation in Northern Ireland: a third way?' *British Educational Research Journal*, 39(5): 925–946.

Borum, R. (2003) 'Understanding the terrorist mindset', *FBI Law Enforcement Bulletin*, 72(7): 7–10.

Borum, R. (2014) 'Psychological vulnerabilities and propensities for involvement in violent extremism', *Behavioral Sciences and the Law*, 32(3): 286–305.

Brewer, J. and Hayes, B. (2011) 'Victims as moral beacons: victims and perpetrators in Northern Ireland', *Contemporary Social Science: Journal of the Academy of Social Sciences*, 6(1): 73–88.

Brown, G. (2010) 'Opening Pandora's box? Workplace community relations (WCR) strategies in Northern Ireland: an examination of three case study district councils', Unpublished Ph.D. thesis, University of Liverpool.

Byrne, J. and Gormley-Heenan, C. (2014) 'Beyond the walls: dismantling Belfast's conflict architecture', *City: Analysis of Urban Trends, Culture, Theory, Policy, Action*, 18(4–5): 447–454.

Cairns, E. (1998) 'Community relations in universities: child's play?', in *Report of the NUS–USI Northern Ireland Student Centre Conference: managing diversity in third level education. Promoting effective community relations strategies in Northern Ireland's tertiary education sector.* Belfast: NUS–USI Northern Ireland Students Centre, pp. 10–11.

Canel, M. (2012) 'Communicating strategically in the face of terrorism: the Spanish government's response to the 2004 Madrid bombing attacks', *Public Relations Review*, 38(2): 214–222.

Clampitt, P. (2013) *Communicating for managerial effectiveness: problems, strategies, solutions*, 5th edn. Thousand Oaks, CA: Sage.

Cochrane, F. (2013) *Northern Ireland: the reluctant peace.* New Haven, CT: Yale University Press.

Colville, I., Hennestad, B. and Thoner, K. (2014) 'Organizing, changing and learning: a sensemaking perspective on an ongoing "soap story"', *Management Learning*, 45(2): 216–234.

Colville, I., Pye, A. and Carter, M. (2013) 'Organizing to counter terrorism: sensemaking amidst dynamic complexity', *Human Relations*, 66(9): 1201–1223.

Crenshaw, M. (2011) *Explaining terrorism: causes, processes and consequences.* Abingdon: Routledge.

Dekel, S., Mandl, C. and Solomon, Z. (2011) 'Shared and unique predictors of post-traumatic growth and distress', *Journal of Clinical Psychology*, 67(3): 241–252.

Diakopoulos, N., Naaman, M. and Kivran-Swaine, F. (2010) 'Diamonds in the rough: social media visual analytics for journalistic inquiry', Visual Analytics Science and Technology Symposium, Salt Lake City, Utah, 25–26 October, pp. 115–122.

Dickson, D., Hargie, O. and Nelson, S. (2002) *Relational communication between Catholics and Protestants in the workplace: a study of policies, practices and procedures.* Jordanstown: University of Ulster. Available at: www.ofmdfmni.gov.uk/relatational-communication.pdf (accessed: 9 August 2015).

Dickson, D., Hargie, O., O'Donnell, A. and McMullan, C. (2008a) *Learning to deal with difference in the workplace.* Jordanstown: University of Ulster. Available at: www.ulster.ac.uk/comm/files/2014/10/FinalReport30July.pdf (accessed: 29 June 2015).

Dickson, D., Hargie, O. and Wilson, N. (2008b) 'Communication, relationships, and religious difference in the Northern Ireland workplace: a study of private and public sector organizations', *Journal of Applied Communication Research*, 36(2): 128–160.

Dillenburger, K., Fargas, M. and Akhonzada, R. (2006) 'Victims or survivors? Debate about victimhood in Northern Ireland', *International Journal of the Humanities*, 3(5): 1–13.

Dorahy, M. J., Corry, M., Shannon, M., MacSherry, A., Hamilton, G., McRobert, G., Elder, R. and Hanna, D. (2009) 'Complex PTSD, interpersonal trauma and relational consequences: findings from a treatment-receiving Northern Irish sample', *Journal of Affective Disorders*, 112(1): 71–80.

Enders, W. and Sandler, T. (2012) *The political economy of terrorism*, 2nd edn. New York: Cambridge University Press.

Falkheimer, J. (2014) 'Crisis communication and terrorism: the Norway attacks on 22 July 2011', *Corporate Communications: An International Journal*, 19(1): 52–63.

FBI (2015) 'Protect the United States from terrorist attack'. Available at: www.fbi.gov/albuquerque/about-us/what-we-investigate/priorities (accessed: 6 June 2015).

Ferguson, N., Burgess, M. and Hollywood, I. (2010) 'Who are the victims? Victimhood experiences in post-agreement Northern Ireland', *Political Psychology*, 31(6): 857–886.

Ganor, B. (2002) 'Defining terrorism: is one man's terrorist another man's freedom fighter?' *Police Practice and Research: An International Journal*, 3(4): 287–304.

Gilligan, C. (2006) 'Traumatised by peace? A critique of five assumptions in the theory and practice of conflict related trauma policy in Northern Ireland', *Policy and Politics*, 34(2): 325–345.

Greer, J. (1985) 'Viewing "the other side" in Northern Ireland: openness and attitudes to religion among Catholic and Protestant adolescents', *Journal for the Scientific Study of Religion*, 24(3): 275–292.

Hacker, F. (1976) *Crusaders, criminals, crazies: terror and terrorisms in our time.* New York: Norton.

Hackett, C. and Rolston, B. (2009) 'The burden of memory: victims, storytelling and resistance in Northern Ireland', *Memory Studies*, 2(3): 355–376.

Hargie, O. (2011) *Skilled interpersonal communication: research, theory and practice*, 5th edn. London: Routledge.

Hargie, O., Brataas, H. and Thorsnes, S. (2009) 'Cancer patients' sensemaking of conversations with cancer nurses', *Australian Journal of Advanced Nursing*, 26(3): 70–78.

Hargie, O. and Dickson, D. (eds) (2003) *Researching the troubles: social science perspectives on the Northern Ireland conflict.* Edinburgh: Mainstream Publishing.

Hargie, O., Dickson, D., Mallett, J. and Stringer, M. (2008) 'Communicating social identity: a study of Catholics and Protestants in Northern Ireland', *Communication Research*, 35(6): 792–821.

Hargie, O., Dickson, D. and O'Donnell, A. (2006) *Breaking down barriers: sectarianism, unemployment, and the exclusion of young people from Northern Ireland society.* Jordanstown: University of Ulster. Available at: www.ulster.ac.uk/comm/files/2014/10/report1.pdf (accessed: 28 September 2015).

Hargie, O., Dickson, D. and Rainey, S. (1999) *Communication and relational development among young adult Catholics and Protestants.* Jordanstown: University of Ulster. Available at: www.ulster.ac.uk/comm/files/2014/10/Student-Final-Report.pdf (accessed: 28 June 2015).

Hargie, O. and Irving, P. (in press) 'Crisis communication and terrorist attacks', in Schwarz, A., Seeger, M. and Auer, C. (eds) *Handbook of international crisis communication research*, Chichester: Wiley-Blackwell.

Hargie, O., Somerville, I. and Mitchell, D. (2015) *Social exclusion and sport in Northern Ireland.* Jordanstown: University of Ulster. Available at: www.ulster.ac.uk/comm/files/2014/10/Student-Final-Report.pdf (accessed: 19 January 2015).

Hayes, B. and McAllister, I. (2012) 'Gender and consociational power-sharing in Northern Ireland', *International Political Science Review*, 34(2): 123–139.

Hayes, B., McAllister, I. and Dowds, L. (2007) 'Integrated education, intergroup relations, and political identities in Northern Ireland', *Social Problems*, 54(4): 454–482.

Heath, R. and Waymer, D. (2014) 'Terrorism: social capital, social construction, and constructive society', *Public Relations Inquiry*, 3(2): 227–244.

Heger, L. (2015) 'Votes and violence: pursuing terrorism while navigating politics', *Journal of Peace Research*, 52(1): 32–45.

Housing Executive (2015) 'BRIC: building relationships in communities'. Available at: www.nihe.gov.uk/index/community/community_cohesion/bric.htm (accessed: 10 March 2015).

Kennedy, D. (2009) 'The case against the Belfast Agreement', in Barton, B. and Roche, P. (eds) *The Northern Ireland question: the peace process and the Belfast Agreement*. Basingstoke: Palgrave Macmillan, pp. 246–264.

Kim, Y. and Ball-Rokeach, S. (2006) 'Community storytelling network, neighborhood context, and civic engagement: a multilevel approach', *Human Communication Research*, 32(4): 411–439.

Knox, C. (2011) 'Cohesion, sharing, and integration in Northern Ireland', *Environment and Planning: Government and Policy*, 29(3): 548–566.

Krieger, T. and Meierrieks, D. (2011) 'What causes terrorism?' *Public Choice*, 147(1): 3–27.

Laqueur, W. (1977) *Terrorism*. Boston, MA: Little, Brown.

Lijphart, A. (2008) *Thinking about democracy: power sharing and majority rule in theory and practice*. Abingdon: Routledge.

Literat, I. and Chen, N. (2014) 'Communication infrastructure theory and entertainment-education: an integrative model for health communication', *Communication Theory*, 24(1): 83–103.

Louw, P. (2003) 'The "war against terrorism": a public relations challenge for the Pentagon', *International Communication Gazette*, 65(3): 211–230.

Lowe, R. and Muldoon, O. (2014) 'Shared national identification in Northern Ireland: an application of psychological models of group inclusion post conflict', *Group Processes and Intergroup Relations*, 17(5): 602–616.

Lutz, J. and Lutz, B. (2013) *Global terrorism*, 3rd edn. Abingdon: Routledge.

Maikovich, A. (2005) 'A new understanding of terrorism using cognitive dissonance principles', *Journal for the Theory of Social Behaviour*, 35(4): 373–397.

Maitlis, S. (2005) 'The social processes of organizational sensemaking', *Academy of Management Journal*, 48(1): 21–49.

Manktelow, R. (2007) 'The needs of victims of the Troubles in Northern Ireland', *Journal of Social Work*, 7(1): 31–50.

Matusitz, J. (2013) *Terrorism and communication: a critical introduction*. Thousand Oaks, CA: Sage.

McAlister, S., Scraton, P. and Haydon, D. (2014) 'Childhood in transition: growing up in "post-conflict" Northern Ireland', *Children's Geographies*, 12(3): 297–311.

McKeown, S., Cairns, E. and Stringer, M. (2012) 'Is shared space really shared?' *Journal of Shared Space: A Research Journal on Peace, Conflict and Community Relations in Northern Ireland*, 12(February): 83–93.

McLaughlin, G. and Miller, D. (1996) 'The media politics of the Irish peace process', *International Journal of Press/Politics*, 1(4): 116–134.

McVeigh, R. and Rolston, B. (2007) 'From Good Friday to good relations: sectarianism, racism and the Northern Ireland state', *Race and Class*, 48(4): 1–23.

Miller, C. and Landau, M. (2005) 'Communication and terrorism: a terror management theory perspective', *Communication Research Reports*, 22(1): 79–88.

Mills, C. (2009) 'A case of making sense of organisational communication', in Hargie, O. and Tourish, D. (eds) *Auditing organisational communication: a handbook of research, theory and practice.* London: Routledge, pp. 370–390.

Moloney, E. (2005) 'The peace process and journalism', in *Britain and Ireland: lives entwined II. Essays on contemporary British–Irish relations, with views from the USA.* Dublin: British Council Ireland, pp. 64–82. Available at: www.riverpath.com/wp-content/uploads/2009/11/Lives-Entwined-II-Final.pdf#page=34 (accessed: 11 July 2015).

Mozes-Sadeh, T. and Avraham, E. (2014) 'The use of offensive public relations during a conflict: Hamas's efforts to damage Israel's image during the 2010 flotilla', *Conflict and Communication Online*, 13(2). Available at: http://cco.regener-online.de/2014_2/pdf/avraham2014.pdf (accessed: 20 February 2015).

O'Donnell, A. and Hargie, O. (2011) 'Dealing with the dark side of sectarianism in Northern Irish organisations: guiding principles on inter-group workplace communication', *Australian Journal of Communication*, 38(1): 21–43.

Office of the First Minister and Deputy First Minister, Northern Ireland, (2013) *Together: Building a United Community*, Available at: www.ofmdfmni.gov.uk/together-building-a-united-community-strategy.pdf (accessed: 12 November 2015).

O'Hair, H. and Heath, R. (2005) 'Conceptualizing communication and terrorism', in O'Hair, H., Heath, R. and Ledlow, G. (eds) *Community preparedness and response to terrorism: communication and the media.* Westport, CT: Praeger, pp. 1–12.

Orr, R., McKeown, S., Cairns, E. and Stringer, M. (2012) 'Examining non-racial segregation: a micro-ecological approach', *British Journal of Social Psychology*, 51(4): 717–723.

Pattwell, A., Mitman, T. and Porpora, D. (2015) 'Terrorism as failed political communication', *International Journal of Communication*, 9: 1120–1139. Available at: http://ijoc.org/index.php/ijoc/article/view/2247/1359 (accessed: 11 November 2015).

Phillips, B. (2015) 'Enemies with benefits? Violent rivalry and terrorist group longevity', *Journal of Peace Research*, 52(1): 62–75.

Powell, J. (2014) *Talking to terrorists: how to end armed conflicts.* London: Bodley Head.

Rice, C., Somerville, I. and Wilson, J. (2015) 'Democratic communication and the role of special advisers in Northern Ireland's consociational government', *International Journal of Public Administration*, 38(1): 4–14.

Richards, B. (2004) 'Terrorism and public relations', *Public Relations Review*, 30(2): 169–176.

Roche, P. and Barton, B. (eds) (2013) *The Northern Ireland question: myth and reality.* Tonbridge, Kent: Wordzworth Publishing.

Rothenberger, L. (2015) 'Terrorism as strategic communication', in Holtzhausen, D. and Zerfass, A. (eds) *The Routledge handbook of strategic communication.* New York: Routledge, pp. 481–496.

Sada, S. (1985) 'Trans-national terrorism as public relations?' *Public Relations Review*, 11(3): 26–33.

SafeComms (2011) *The terrorism crisis communication manual for public authorities.* Available at: https://faculty.biu.ac.il/~sshpiro/crisis_manual.html (accessed: 13 October 2015).

Sandler, T. (2015) 'Terrorism and counterterrorism: an overview', *Oxford Economic Papers*, 67(1): 1–20.

Schmid, A., Jongman, A. and Stohl, M., (2005) *Political terrorism: a new guide to actors, authors, concepts, data bases, theories, and literature.* New Brunswick, NJ: Transaction Publishers.

Silke, A. (2003) 'Beyond horror: terrorist atrocity and the search for understanding. The case of the Shankill bombing', *Studies in Conflict and Terrorism*, 26(1): 37–60.

Smyth, M. and Hamilton, J. (2003) 'The human costs of the troubles', in Hargie, O. and Dickson, D. (eds) *Researching the troubles: social science perspectives on the Northern Ireland conflict*. Edinburgh: Mainstream Press, pp. 15–36.

Snow, N. (2006) 'Terrorism, public relations and propaganda', in Kavoori, A. and Fraley, T. (eds) *Media, terrorism, and theory: a reader.* Lanham, MD: Rowman and Littlefield, pp. 145–160.

Somerville, I. and Purcell, A. (2011) 'A history of Republican public relations in Northern Ireland from "Bloody Sunday" to the "Good Friday Agreement"', *Journal of Communication Management*, 15(3): 192–209.

Somerville, I., Purcell, A. and Morrison, F. (2011) 'Public relations education in a divided society: PR, terrorism and critical pedagogy in post-conflict Northern Ireland', *Public Relations Review*, 37(5): 548–555.

Spence, P., Lachlan, K., Lin, X. and del Greco, M. (2015) 'Variability in Twitter content across the stages of a natural disaster: implications for crisis communication', *Communication Quarterly*, 63(2): 171–186.

Stevenson, C., Condor, S. and Abell, J. (2007) 'The minority–majority conundrum in Northern Ireland: an Orange Order perspective', *Political Psychology*, 28(1): 105–125.

Sutton, J., League, C., Sellnow, T. and Sellnow, D. (2015) 'Terse messaging and public health in the midst of natural disasters: the case of the Boulder floods', *Health Communication*, 30(2): 135–143.

Taylor, P. (1998) *Provos: the IRA and Sinn Fein*. London: Bloomsbury.

Tsintsadze-Maass, E. and Maass, R. (2014) 'Groupthink and terrorist radicalization', *Terrorism and Political Violence*, 26(5): 735–758.

US State Department (2015) 'Global terrorism deaths nearly doubled in 2014'. Available at: http://rt.com/usa/268399-global-terrorism-attacks-deaths/ (accessed: 15 October 2015).

van Alphen, E. (2002) 'Caught by images: on the role of visual imprints in Holocaust testimonies', *Journal of Visual Culture*, 1(2): 205–221.

van Dijk, J. (2009) 'Free the victim: a critique of the western conception of victimhood', *International Review of Victimology*, 16(1): 1–33.

Weick, K. E. (1979) *The social psychology of organizing*, 2nd edn. New York: Random House.

Weick, K. E. (1995) *Sensemaking in organizations.* London: Sage.

Weick, K. E., Sutcliffe, K. M. and Obstfeld, D. (2005) 'Organizing and the process of sensemaking', *Organization Science*, 16(4): 409–421.

Weimann, G. (2015) *Terrorism in cyberspace: the next generation*. New York: Columbia University Press.

Yarchi, M., Wolfsfeld, G., Sheafer, T. and Shenhav, S. (2013) 'Promoting stories about terrorism to the international news media: a study of public diplomacy', *Media, War and Conflict*, 6(3): 263–278.

5 Deliberative democracy and government public relations in a deeply divided society

Exploring the perspectives of Government Information Officers in Northern Ireland

Ian Somerville and Charis Rice

Deliberative democracy, public relations and the 'public sphere'

Sanders (2009: 268) notes that studies of 'government communication can hardly avoid discussion of normative issues, nor would it be desirable to do so if our research is to engage with issues that matter not only to the wider scientific community but also to policy makers and our fellow citizens'. Habermas' public sphere model (1962 [trans. 1989]), with amendments and modifications (Habermas, 1984), still serves as a normative vision in much political communication (Davis 2009a), media studies (Lunt and Livingstone 2013) and PR literature (Fairbanks et al., 2007). Although enormously influential, Habermas' original concept was critiqued for several significant failings, notably his 'account of history', his 'simplistic political analysis' and 'his apparent blindness to the many varieties of exclusion (based on gender, class, ethnicity, etc.) endemic to the public discussions he so lauded' (Lunt and Livingstone, 2013: 90). Despite revising the notion of the public sphere in important ways to take account of these criticisms, it is clear that Habermas remains committed to producing a normative democratic theory which stresses transparent government communication as a necessary condition to successfully produce rational, informed and deliberative public discussion of government policies and actions. We agree that this is an important endeavour and concur with Garnham (2007: 203) that the notion of the public sphere remains in many ways a useful 'perspective from which to think about the problem of democracy in the modern world'.

However, it is important to point out that we do diverge somewhat from a strict Habermasian approach in relation to democratic theory. Dryzek (2000: 1) notes that Habermas was quick to embrace and identify with the 'deliberative turn' in democratic theory which has resulted in the idea that:

> the essence of democracy itself is now widely taken to be deliberation, as opposed to voting, interest aggregation, constitutional rights, or even self-government. The deliberative turn represents a renewed concern with the

> authenticity of democracy: the degree to which democratic control is substantive rather than symbolic, and engaged by competent citizens.

However, it is also clear that 'deliberation' for Habermas involves imposing narrow limits on democratic discourse which should consist of purely rational exchanges; 'Participants in argumentation have to presuppose in general that the structure of their communication ... excludes all force ... except the force of the better argument' (Habermas, 1984: 25). In contrast, Dryzek (2000: 2) favours a position which would allow 'rhetoric', 'humour', 'emotion', and 'testimony or storytelling' as contributions to authentic deliberation, insisting only on 'the requirement that communication induce reflection upon preferences in a non-coercive fashion'. Which rules out coercion in the form of 'manipulation', 'indoctrination', 'propaganda', 'deception', 'threats', etc.

While we subscribe to the view that the public sphere concept still 'serves theorists well as an ideal type – that is, as a construct against which different real-world approximations can be evaluated' (Bennett and Entman, 2001: 3), we largely share Dryzek's view that the communicative conditions for deliberative democracy articulated by Habermas and his followers are unnecessarily constraining. The public sphere model is a more fruitful paradigm for democracy if it is much more expansive in the kinds of communication it allows, while still adhering to the important criteria that deliberative discourses must demonstrate that they are concerned with the 'public interest' and that they are 'inclusive and reflexive' (Dryzek, 2000). These conditions are clearly of key importance in what Dryzek (2000) refers to as 'empowered' deliberative spaces such as legislatures. This point has been highlighted by Edwards' (2015) recent work on PR and deliberative democracy which notes that PR is an important and legitimate mechanism for the transmission of positions and preferences between 'empowered spaces' and 'public spaces' (including the media). Edwards (2015: 12) argues that 'In the context of deliberative systems, the effect of public relations on the quality of deliberation is most logically framed in terms of its effects on deliberative capacity', that is to say the degree to which PR can adhere to the conditions of 'generalizable interest' and 'genuine engagement'. The growth of public relations in governmental systems is irreversible and it has become a crucial 'part of the infrastructure of modern political communication' (McNair, 2007b: 337). It is therefore increasingly important to assess and interrogate its role in fostering or diminishing deliberative democracy.

Government public relations and the media

Relationships between the media and political actors are of central importance in contemporary democracies. Some scholars note that these relationships are characterised by contest and antagonism (see Lee, 1999; Wolfsfeld, 1997) with the media tending to be controlled or at least subordinate to powerful institutions who act as 'primary definers' of the news (Hall et al.,

1978: 57). Some commentators emphasise reciprocity between government and media (Negrine, 2008) or note a relationship characterised by exchange and negotiation (Ericson et al., 1989). Gans suggests a symbiotic relationship but notes, 'Although it takes two to tango … sources do the leading' (1979: 116). Others have placed the emphasis more on how politics has become 'mediatised' in the sense that such is the influence of the mass media on political actors and political systems that they have adjusted to the demands of the media (Strömbäck, 2008) or indeed that such is the nature of media saturation that political institutions are inseparable from it (Lilleker 2006; Mazzoleni and Schulz, 1999). Gelders et al. (2007: 374) argue that political actors rely on the media because: 'the news media are *the* platform where the government establishes or loses its credibility … the battle for the public's trust increasingly takes place in the media rather than in the parliament' (italics in original).

Much recent media research has typically argued that the government communication process is affected by micro-level interactions between journalists and their government sources (Davis, 2002; Falasca and Nord, 2013). Davis (2009b) argues that how communicative power is exercised in contemporary societies is best understood through the concept of 'elite-elite relationships', where government and media elites effectively control and exchange information in a closed circuit. At the same time, and related to this point, research has also demonstrated a general point about all communications/PR work (Sriramesh and Verčič 2009) that relationships between journalists and government communicators may be strongly influenced by their immediate political, cultural and economic context (Laursen and Valentini, 2013).

In the UK (and Northern Ireland), two distinct groups of communication professionals coexist: Government Information Officers (GIOs) and ministerial Special Advisers (SpAds) who are personally appointed by a departmental minister. The role of the GIO is (at least theoretically) designed to be apolitical, in that they assist the government of whichever political persuasion in the areas of information management and media relations in an impartial civil servant capacity. The SpAd is *de facto* a temporary civil servant who is appointed by a government minister to assist him/her in a political capacity. In recent times UK research on government communication has raised concerns about the 'politicisation' of the civil service and concomitantly that the neutral GIO is being undermined or supplanted by the partisan SpAd (Gaber, 2004; Negrine, 2008). Fawcett and Gay (2010: 49) argue that: 'It's increasingly difficult (if not impossible) to formally divide the "official" work of civil servants from the "political" work of special advisers'.

Some scholars strongly link the rise of public relations work in government to the notion of 'spinning' information for political purposes (Andrews, 2006; McNair 2007). According to this view government communicators frequently produce: 'information which, far from being rational and motivated by what is in the public interest, is partial, ideologically committed, and at times downright dishonest' (McNair, 2007a: 97). Gaber (2000) argues that there are essentially two categories of government PR efforts, 'above the line' communication and 'below the line' tactics or 'spin'. The 'above the line' category includes those activities that would be considered routine, and that 'would have caused an "old fashioned" civil service press officer no great difficulty' (Gaber, 2000: 508). These are: producing press releases; holding press conferences; using ministerial speeches and answers to Parliamentary questions in the House of Commons to communicate information; and, 'reacting to breaking news events' (Gaber, 2000: 509). 'Below the line' or 'spin' includes those activities which can at times be ethically questionable and, Gaber (2000: 508) suggests, are 'usually covert and as much about strategy and tactics as about the imparting of information'. Such tactics include: 'off the record' briefings to handpicked journalists to set and drive the news agenda (ensuring that government receives coverage on its terms); 'leaks' to discredit political rivals inside one's party or opponents outside it; 'kite flying' (to test reactions to a policy before a formal announcement); and 'fire breaking', planting a another story to deflect attention from a negative one about the government (Gaber, 2000; Somerville and Ramsey, 2012). Spin at its worst can involve blatant lies and manipulation; at its best it still involves various shades of political propaganda (Hiebert, 2003).

Investigating what it is that government and media actors really do in their everyday professional roles is important because it can lead 'to a necessary demystification on the one hand, while at the same time this might allow a first step towards reducing the much lamented *democratic deficit*' (Wodak, 2011: 25, italics in original). Davis echoes this noting that 'to move critical debates about politics, communication and citizenship into new territory … means engaging with "actually existing democracies", contemporary media environments, political actors and political processes' (2009a: 294). This research responds to Davis' call by examining the government–media communicative relationships in Northern Ireland's developing post-conflict democracy.

Post-conflict Northern Ireland: devolution and consociational governance

Bloomfield noted that between 1969 and 1997, the conflict known as the 'Troubles' in Northern Ireland claimed 3,585 lives and that over 50,000 people were injured. He pointed out that:

> Some 3,600 deaths may not seem too calamitous when compared with the scale of the Holocaust, with the local fatalities in the First World War, or with the suffering in Bosnia or Rwanda or Cambodia. But all of this has to be considered against the small scale of Northern Ireland. If the UK as a whole with its population of some 58 million people, had experienced death pro rata, as compared with the 1.6 million population of Northern Ireland, there would have been a total of over 130,000 dead.
>
> (Bloomfield, 1998: 3)

We can extend this comparison further by noting that the 50,000 injured in Northern Ireland during the sectarian conflict is equivalent to 2 million if applied to the UK as a whole or just over 10 million if applied to the USA. Making such comparisons is only useful up to a point but they do illustrate the impact of the sectarian conflict on many of the citizens of Northern Ireland and the fact that recovery from thirty years of political violence is for many a slow and painful process (for a detailed account see Hargie and Dickson, 2003). Stringer et al. (2009: 241) note: 'As Northern Ireland has moved slowly since the paramilitary ceasefires in 1994 from a conflict to a post-conflict region, the underlying problems of social segregation and political mistrust have left an uneasy peace.' A key reason for this 'uneasy peace' is the fact that Northern Ireland remains a highly segregated society in which most people live, learn and worship largely within sectarian groupings. In areas like public housing, 90 per cent is segregated along religious lines with the vast majority of Catholics and Protestants living in areas that are dominated by their own identity group (Hargie et al., 2015). Only 6.8 per cent of children attend integrated schools, with the remainder attending Protestant or Catholic schools and therefore having little opportunity to mix outside their ethnic group until they go to university or work (Somerville et al., 2011).

A key outcome of the Good Friday Agreement (10 April 1998), which formally brought to an end the violent conflict known as the Troubles, was the devolution of powers to a consociational (i.e. mandatory power-sharing) government. This constitutional settlement means that Northern Ireland's political institutions operate in significantly different ways from the majoritarian electoral systems which characterise most Western democratic societies. Governance is by a broad-based, devolved and power-sharing administration, with executive power shared via party lists on the basis of a complex proportional representation mechanism based on the de Hondt system.[1] Between 1998 and 2007 Northern Ireland was characterised by breakdowns in relationships between the political parties in power, leading to a lack of political progress (Gormley-Heenan and Devine, 2010) and difficulties in presenting a centralised and unified position on policy (Fawcett, 2002). However, since 2007's St Andrew's Agreement a complex but functioning consociational administration has governed Northern Ireland. The key tenets of consociational governance are: *grand coalitions* between the key groups are the norm; *mutual veto* is also typical so that a simple majority is never enough in decision-making processes; and *proportionality* is usual with representation based on population guaranteed in political office, the civil service, the police, etc., to ensure widespread confidence in emerging civic institutions (Lijphart, 2008).

Consociationalism has been advocated as a democratic arrangement which can help reconcile and rebuild societies fragmented along religious, racial, or linguistic lines, particularly those which have recently experienced violent conflict (Lijphart, 2008). It has emerged as a political system in deeply divided societies such as those in Bosnia, Switzerland, India, Macedonia, Lebanon,

Belgium and Northern Ireland (Lemarchand, 2007; Rice et al., 2015). While studies of government communication in traditional majoritarian political systems expand rapidly there has been limited research into the communicative relationships of government communicators and the groups they interact with in post-conflict, deeply divided and constitutionally complex societies such as Northern Ireland. The present study addresses this research gap.

Method

A combination of purposive and snowball sampling techniques were employed to recruit individuals for semi-structured in-depth interviews who could provide data relevant to our research questions (Bryman, 2012; Tansey, 2007). Our sample consisted of nine senior GIOs (69 per cent of the total), eight SpAds (42 per cent of the total) and sixteen political journalists, thirty-three interviewees in total. All GIOs interviewed held the rank of Principal Information Officer in the civil service and, as with the SpAds who participated, worked across a number of different government departments for all five coalition government partners. The journalists who participated were from the main press and broadcast organisations in Northern Ireland, and all were at section editor or overall editor level. Interview questions focused on probing participants on their daily work routines of producing and disseminating information on government, and their interactions with the other participant groups.

While our research focuses largely on GIO perspectives, our analysis and conclusions benefit from comparison with the thematic findings from all participant groups (Davis, 2009b). GIO responses are denoted by G1, G2 and so on; SpAd responses by S1, S2 and so on; and journalists responses by J1, J2 and so on. In our findings section below, representative quotations are italicised and have been edited to remove repetitions, stutters and non-verbal sounds for ease of understanding.

Interviewing elites in divided societies is a complex endeavour (McEvoy, 2006) and where possible questions were framed in a manner which avoided inciting political sensitivities or identity issues. All interviews lasted around sixty minutes, were conducted in the participants' workplaces, were audio recorded and later transcribed in full. Interviews were transcribed for analysis, which, in line with recommended interpretative phenomenological analysis (IPA) procedures, was inductive in nature with themes emerging from the narratives (Clarke, 2008; Smith et al., 2009). This involved the process of 'close reading' wherein a detailed reading and re-reading of the text is conducted (Alvesson and Skoldberg, 2009). The content was then coded to identify and delineate themes. The final thematic structure was agreed following detailed collaboration with the other author, who checked the transcripts to confirm themes and ensure that the selected quotes were reflective of the themes.

Our analysis of interview transcripts employed IPA, which gives primacy to the perceptions of respondents, since the objective is to generate knowledge in relation to their lived experience of a phenomenon (Langdridge, 2007). It is a framework which has become a widely employed qualitative analysis system (Walker and Burgess, 2011) and is an approach which is especially relevant for research which focuses upon personal meaning and sense-making in relation to a specific context and with respondents who have similar experiences (Smith et al., 2009). IPA involves 'a double hermeneutic because the researcher is trying to make sense of the participant trying to make sense of what is happening to them' (Smith et al., 2009: 3). Through adopting an approach of empathic hermeneutics, the researcher attempts to garner insight into the meanings being communicated by respondents. To move beyond the surface level of respondent accounts, a critical hermeneutic can then be utilised to interpret and make sense of their narratives (Smith et al., 2009). While accepting the individual meanings allocated to events by individuals, IPA enables various perspectives about similar events to be compared. By combining and interpreting narratives, common themes emerge which can inform our overall understanding of the phenomena under investigation. Two broad themes emerged from our interviews with GIOs, SpAds and journalists: *changing communication roles and working relationships* in the new post-conflict political space; and, *the impact of the new devolved, consociational architecture* upon the communication of politics in Northern Ireland. We analyse these key themes in the next two, strongly empirical, sections and then assess their significance in relation to building deliberative democracy in Northern Ireland's developing public sphere.

Government Information Officers: changing roles and relationships

When asked about how they perceive their role most GIOs typically emphasised a public service ideal: *'we're here to ensure that people on the ground understand what government's doing … I enjoy working here because it's serving the public' (G1)*. However, when probed many also characterised the promotional aspect of their role, one noting: *'the role is to promote the department and its minister and the work that they do … to get as much space for the good news and as little space for the bad news … part of our job is to promote, you know, that* [the government] *is working' (G4)*. Another emphasised this second point: *'it's part of our job to let it be seen that devolution's working' (G3)*. This idea that there are two key promotional tasks is interesting and is what separates GIOs from SpAds, who see the promotion of their minister as where their responsibility begins and ends: *'Everything that goes on around here, you know I am looking with one eye to, where does that leave the … minister's profile, where does that fit in with a communication strategy that we will have rolling forward' (S6)*. When questioned about the role of the GIO, many journalists cast doubt on GIOs' claim to act in the 'public interest' and in fact generally characterise GIOs as concentrating instead on ministerial or departmental reputation management; one journalist said: *'their outlook has become more like a corporation than a public service, you know it's like they're PR chiefs for Shell Oil, rather than there to provide for us journalists, as representatives of the public ... a public service' (J15).* Larsson (2002), in a study of local government in Sweden, notes that journalists and political actors generally display a high level of mutual trust. Journalists in our study accepted they depended on each other but usually emphasised that in their relationships with GIOs: *'I don't entirely trust him and he doesn't entirely trust me' (J3).* The views of GIOs in our study tended to mirror the mild antagonism that journalists expressed and indeed they frequently complained about the poor standards of journalists. When invited to comment on any positive features of their dealings with journalists they usually framed the relationship in terms of instrumentality and reciprocity. One GIO noted: *'we need them to get our stories across ... we need them to understand the issues and they need the hotline to us so that if they get a story at five to five, they want to go on the news at five, they can ring me and ask me X, Y, Z and I give them it' (G1).*

Responses from both GIOs and SpAds build a picture of a gradual reduction in the communication activities of GIOs and increasing control and responsibility being taken by the SpAd. For some GIOs this was a rather suffocating experience: *'now I'm speaking to him more than the wife, like you can't breathe without* [the SpAd], *wanting to know what's going on. So not only do you need to convince the minister, you need to convince the adviser' (G5).* In respect to day-to-day media relations the same GIO stated: *'every media enquiry we receive needs to go through the adviser ... Nothing goes out without their approval'.* Another noted: *'Whatever he says goes, simple as that, I can't over-rule him' (G3).* Some SpAds acknowledged that their role often constrained GIOs, one noting in his government department that the GIO: *'may well say that fella tells me what to do, when to do it and how to do it' (S2).* Another SpAd, reflecting on the shift in power, said: *'I think they're* [GIOs] *much more aware of the need to get out good messages than what was the case previously, they're much more accountable obviously now ... in the old system they didn't have to work to advisers. That might be a sore point' (S6).*

Even though the UK's 'Special Adviser Code of Conduct'[2] explicitly prohibits them from 'managing' or 'directing' civil servants (Fawcett and Gay 2010), it seems that many GIOs have come to accept that there is little they can do to challenge the power of SpAds. Indeed, some have attempted to rationalise this new organisational reality, as one GIO explained: *'the Special Adviser will have the mind of the minister better than any other civil servant, right. So, a Special Adviser can give the press officer like me really good advice and say they'll run with that, he'll not go with that' (G8).* It is debatable whether this kind of interaction illustrates 'advice', indeed arguably it fits rather well with Mumby's (1988) analysis of how organisational power works. Mumby notes:

> A particular group's interests will be best served if those interests become part of the taken-for-granted social reality that structures organizational

> life. Once these interests become part of the organizational structure, then that structure simultaneously mediates in and reproduces those interests.
>
> (Mumby, 1988: 67)

Thus despite a strict code of conduct governing these relationships, the all-pervasive influence of SpAds over communicative activities, by virtue of the associative power which they accrue from their minister (Fawcett and Gay, 2010), means GIOs reluctantly acquiesce to the new reality and/or justify it to themselves in the manner illustrated above.

A number of GIO participants complained that SpAds sometimes liaised 'off the record' with journalists, providing exclusive or 'better' information to that of the GIO, for party political gain, even when this clashed with departmental priorities. According to GIOs, this means they appear as a less valuable source to journalists, which undermines their position. This situation often causes GIOs to feel frustrated and powerless in their role. A GIO articulated a common complaint:

> *they would leak an awful lot of stuff that they shouldn't really leak at all. So, it's unhelpful when they do speak to journalists because I'm in one room trying to sell something and he's in a room just over there talking to the same journalist about something else, it makes us look ... moronic ... but they all do it ... it's just something we're faced with.*
>
> *(G5)*

Some commentators suggest that 'leaking' has become a common means of disseminating information in democratic governments (Flynn, 2006). Indeed interviewees from all three participant groups in this study commented that leaking was a frequent way of disseminating information from the government because it avoided the protracted process of the agreed central government communication mechanism, the Executive Information Service (EIS), which requires information to be politically neutral and often to have cross-departmental/party agreement. It is of course a key way of communicating quickly to one's advantage (which frequently involves undermining rival parties' positions) and belongs in the category which Gaber (2000) defines as 'below the line' spin. The GIO perception that SpAds are supplanting them as the primary departmental communicators is recognised by journalists who speak of SpAds as more productive sources than GIOs. Typical comments were: *'when you're speaking to the Special Adviser you know you're speaking to the minister ... they can be more helpful in sort of steering you ... to stories ... they'll talk to you about what's really going on' (J11)*. In this sense these findings diverge somewhat from research elsewhere; for example, Gaber's work on the UK Westminster system finds that: 'Journalists speak with senior press officers on much the same basis as they speak with special advisers' (2004: 368). A journalist commenting on this situation noted that the EIS: *'does the basic press releases and the road safety campaigns ... all that sort of stuff, but, the really big shouts, the really big decisions are invariably taken by the parties* [i.e. the SpAd]' *(J16)*. This results in SpAds and party press officers increasingly emerging as the preferred point of contact for the media. In this sense our results echo Meyer's (1999) findings in his study of the European Union's communication practices, which found that a significant problem for that polity's public communication and media relations was the lack of political cohesion and the inability of communicators to manage competing political agendas.

There seems to be a distinction emerging in government news management in Northern Ireland between important 'political' news and less important 'government' news, and all of the actors in this communication environment recognise who is responsible for disseminating the different types of news. One way of thinking about this is to characterise it as SpAds controlling the 'below the line' (Gaber, 2000) communication and the important 'good news' stories, leaving GIOs to engage in the more mundane 'above the line' government communication. It does run the risk of producing a situation where the 'everyday' functioning of government is not actually 'news', with higher news value attached to controversial issues and political conflict, a situation hardly unique to Northern Ireland, but nevertheless clearly problematic for emerging democratic institutions and for the provision of the transparent policy information required for authentic deliberation (Flinders and Kelso, 2011; Wodak, 2011). It can also perhaps be viewed as an indication of the 'mediatisation' of politics in Northern Ireland at least in the partial sense identified by Mazzoleni and Schulz (1999), who suggest that: 'political institutions increasingly are dependent on and shaped by mass media but nevertheless remain in control of political processes and functions' (Mazzoleni and Schulz, 1999: 247). The concern with media representation by the parties which make up the coalition government is clearly the main reason why SpAds are constantly trying to exert their control over what they, and their ministerial boss, regard as the most important aspects of information and communication management. Several journalists commented on the increasing involvement SpAds have in all aspects of departmental communication and the decline of GIO control in this area. For some journalists this was all part of the deliberate attempts by the new political elites to undermine civil servants, one suggesting that GIOs: *'at the highest level of the government are absolutely undermined ... not empowered to tell us what's going on, because they* [ministers] *use their own press officers to selectively leak to chosen journalists. Very unhealthy situation' (J14)*. While it is clear that organisational cultures 'do not arise spontaneously and consensually, but are often the product of certain power distributions' (Mumby, 1988: 56), and that this is manifestly the case in Northern Ireland's new political institutions, it is also arguable that difficulties in adapting their professional ideology have played a role in the GIOs' decline as key government sources. The fear of being charged with showing any kind of favouritism to one or other side of the political/cultural/religious divide, is in many ways as significant as the power

SpAds hold over GIOs, when it comes to restricting their work as media sources. Many GIOs have interpreted this 'impartial role' to mean that they work within their departmental 'silo' (Wilford 2007) and focus on managing it (and the minister's) reputation the best they can within the scope they are allowed by the SpAd.

All this should, however, not obscure the fact that our research indicates that the first priority of the SpAd and consequently the government department's communication efforts is how the minister will appear to best advantage in the media and just as importantly how to ensure this is to the detriment of rival ministers in the power-sharing government. We will explore this further in the next section.

The consociational political architecture and 'government' communication

When asked about working in a power-sharing government administration made up of political parties who were fundamentally opposed to each other across a number of key issues, a typical GIO response was: *'as a civil servant, I am not political and it doesn't matter who my minister is, I'm impartial' (G1)*. Journalists we interviewed complained that GIOs tended to be 'overly bureaucratic' and were fond of citing the 'strict guidelines' under which they worked. For journalists this meant that GIOs were viewed as: *'barriers to information flows instead of, helping them' (J7)*. GIOs claimed they had to adhere to political neutrality at all times, one noting: *'it's not worth your job to step over it at any point' (G9)*. They also frequently raised the point that their job was especially difficult in a five-party mandatory coalition government and acknowledged that this may make it appear at times that they are a 'closed' civil service which does not interact enough with journalists. GIOs frequently brought up the dramatic changes that had occurred in governance and government communication since the establishment of a devolved legislature in Northern Ireland. One noted:

> *for many years people thought it was the civil service who ran the country and it probably was … because you know, we had direct rule* [British government] *ministers who literally were only here, maybe a couple of half days a week. So they were relying so much on civil servants to keep them right, that they didn't give full scrutiny to things … there was an amazing difference, going from direct rule ministers, to locally elected ministers who were here, seven days a week, twenty four hours a day, reading the local papers, watching the local news.*
>
> *(G3)*

Many journalists also commented on the detrimental impact of Northern Ireland's new institutional structures on the power of GIOs: *'one of the big differences that we've seen with devolution, with local parties taking over and because of the nature of the government that we have, is that … this is a politically driven government, where as previously it was, a kind of administration that was largely driven by the civil service' (J7).* As noted above, a result of this is that SpAds, with more 'inside' knowledge on political issues, are often journalists' preferred sources.

In respect to the peculiarities which emerge in government administration within the consociational architecture bequeathed by the Good Friday Agreement, GIOs raised a number of issues which explicitly or implicitly relate to this structure. For example, many expressed bemusement at the political infighting between ministers who are supposed to be members of the same government: *'Most of the criticism of government policy ... has come from government ministers ... it's very odd ... if you're responding to criticism from a government minister you know you're quite often hamstrung in what you can say' (G1).* G1 further noted: *'there are arguments in every government, but in most governments they go on behind closed doors. In here, quite often, just because of the nature of it, it will happen in public.'* This participant outlined how he coped with this situation:

> *You have to remember that the Government, it may not appear to be a unified body but ... I operate as if it's a unified body, the ministers may not, so it can be difficult in that regard ... it used to be that we knew who the government was here and who the opposition was, the government was Direct Rule* [British Government] *and the opposition was the local parties. Now, the government is the opposition.*
>
> *(G1)*

Thus traditional ideas about collective government responsibility (including in coalition administrations) for policy decisions do not necessarily apply in Northern Ireland's power-sharing structure which includes parties across the political spectrum. Some GIOs pointed to how other devolved UK administrations have resolved the problem of coalition government while at the same time drawing attention to the limitations combining devolution with consociationalism had produced. One noted:

> *the Scottish government, have a central team that look after all the Scottish government. I don't think that would work here ... The politics isn't right for that to work here ... you could argue that you should have one central press office that looks after all government communications but ... it is a cumbersome organisation, but the Assembly is cumbersome, so it's probably a right fit for what it is.*
>
> *(G7)*

SpAds also recognised the difficulties which GIOs encountered in presenting any sort of unified government communication. When questioned about the changes in government communication since the establishment of consociational government, one SpAd stated that the new political institutions discourage collective government responsibility and encourage competition between ministers from rival parties. They also acknowledged that this can impact both on the autonomy of GIOs, and their ability to develop a common government information dissemination strategy. One SpAd observed: *'the will of the ministers will always over-rule this central* [government communication] *mechanism, which means that you could in any one day have a situation where government could be making three or four very important announcements and they all clash … a lot of them* [ministers] *try and get the best piece of PR for themselves … rather than looking at the Executive as a whole' (S6)*. Another SpAd agreed: *'you get this silo mentality where people are doing separate things … it is very difficult because it's almost a replication of the political structure that sits above it …* [GIOs] *don't at this stage have the power to be able to say to one minister or another no you can't do it, simply because we're built around a coalition government' (S4)*.

Interestingly, however, SpAds don't seem to recognise the GIO view that the political opposition is actually inside the government, instead, and despite the fact that they are very concerned to court the media they also complain that the media frequently take on the role of political opposition: *'the press here, because there's no formal opposition at Stormont probably take the view that, they effectively are the opposition … most of them are just generally hostile here' (S4)*. For their part, many journalists regard the current phase in the development of democratic politics in Northern Ireland as at best a necessary stage along the path to a more majoritarian political system. One stated: *'conventional politics is still in a very infant stage here and I would envisage it would change and mature and eventually we will have government and opposition, and that will be the biggest change and the best thing that can happen' (J11)*. GIOs expressed the concern that the negative media coverage in respect to politics and politicians was problematic for Northern Ireland's nascent democracy. A typical view was:

> *the media, don't seem to take their responsibility in a democratic society seriously … in order for a democracy to work people have to vote, and people have to vote for the people they think are going to represent them as best they can, so they might base that one decision every four years on something that they read, and if they read something that is over-sensationalised, unfair or untrue, that could be the difference in that person voting for a different party, not placing their vote at all.*
>
> *(G2)*

Interestingly, in their book on how journalism has developed in Northern Ireland since the peace process, McLaughlin and Baker (2010) argue that journalists, on the whole, are not adhering to their responsibility to be *critical enough* of the political elites.

It could be argued that underpinning the GIO complaint about the media is a restatement of the classic liberal democratic view that devising the right constitutional arrangements will allow open, undistorted communication flows and result in rational deliberative democracy. As Dryzek notes:

> Liberals are keen to devise constitutional and legal arrangements that will counteract distortion: bills of rights, freely-elected legislatures, and so forth … What liberals fail to recognise is that getting constitutions and laws right is only half the battle. They fail to recognise that extra-constitutional agents of distortion can't easily be counteracted through such means.
>
> (Dryzek, 2000: 21)

In Northern Ireland these extra-constitutional agents include dominant discourses and ideologies intertwined with structural socio-cultural and ethnic identity forces. This is an issue which we will discuss in more detail below but it is worth noting that in consociational systems government communication is frequently tied to the balancing act that is a feature of decision making in this arrangement. As one journalist succinctly put it: *'in our system of government, quite often decisions will be made not on the basis of policy but probably on the basis of a trade-off between the different power blocs … The job of the department is to try and justify what's happened on the basis of policy' (J7)*. One other point should be noted in regard to communication management within Northern Ireland's complex coalition government which is made up of political parties which are ideologically and politically (in respect to constitutional aspirations) opposed to each other. It may be that the consociational architecture in Northern Ireland has opened up a space for the Special Adviser role and reach which is more multifaceted than in other, Westminster-style polities. As one SpAd interviewee stated: *'obviously in a five party coalition, when there's cross-departmental issues, where there's areas of controversy, where there's blockages, special advisers are the people that are sent in to try and resolve those issues' (S4)*. It must be noted, however, that despite their eagerness to embrace this role, up to now SpAds have had little success in resolving the major difficulties besetting the governing administration in Northern Ireland. Other studies of coalition government (Connaughton, 2010; Fawcett and Gay, 2010; Paun, 2011) have identified SpAds playing a highly effective communications role across coalition governments. Eichbaum and Shaw note: 'Clearly, in some jurisdictions, the constitutional context, and specifically a transition to multi-party Government, opens up institutional spaces that … political staff in particular, may be required to fill' (2010: 199).

Discussion and conclusion: deliberative democracy in Northern Ireland?

With the establishment of a devolved governing administration in Northern Ireland – and this is true to an extent in the other devolved UK national regions of Scotland and Wales – significant power has moved from civil servants to locally elected ministers and their support network (Knox, 2010).

One important effect of the devolution in Northern Ireland has been that the pre-devolution 'dominant coalition' (Berger, 2009) in respect to government communication, was overturned to the detriment of GIOs. In this respect it is important to recognise that Northern Ireland mirrors other more stable and 'traditional' (i.e. majoritarian) democratic societies where the increased power and influence of SpAds has been noted within political systems (Blick, 2004; King, 2003). Indeed, our results most certainly also reflect broader changes in the UK political system which have resulted in the curtailing of civil servant autonomy and control over government communication shifting to ministerial SpAds (Winstone, 2003). However, it is also the case that the deeply divided post-conflict context and the relatively unique constitutional political architecture of Northern Ireland's democratic institutions produce some significant findings which diverge from the work on government communication in 'traditional' polities. Northern Ireland has a decentralised governance structure which has rendered futile all attempts to impose any notion of collective cabinet responsibility. One result is that there is no recognisable *government* communication strategy. Northern Ireland's governing coalition is currently made up of what have been described as 'ethnic tribune parties' (Mitchell et al., 2009), who prioritise defending group identities, because it is in their electoral self-interest to maintain distinct identity blocs. A key impact of this consociationalism has been to turn government departments into *de facto* party 'fiefdoms' (Wilford, 2007) ruled by the minister and his/her SpAds. Hayward (2013) notes how the peace agreement and consociational political institutions in Northern Ireland actually did lead to new opportunities for democratic political confrontation and dialogue, but at the same time also consolidated identity cleavages and thus incentivised power politics. She argues:

> although benefitting from the devolved, stable and carefully balanced governance made possible by consociationalism, Northern Ireland's peace process is imbued with a sense of underlying lack of resolution. And as a result of this uncertainty, short-term political capital is gained within competing blocs at the expense of long-term social change in the common interest.
>
> (Hayward, 2013: 11)

So while consociationalism does produce real political power-sharing, as Tonge (2014: 194) observes, the system: 'when unaccompanied by a longer-term plan for societal integration, does not offer the promise of movement towards reconciliation, instead leading to the restatement of difference'.

There is increasing evidence that the institutionalised antagonism and confrontational communication culture has reduced public faith in political institutions. A recent Public Engagement Survey found that only 22 per cent were 'satisfied' or 'fairly satisfied' with the Northern Ireland government and 49 per cent felt they had 'no influence' on decision making in Northern Ireland, with 40 per cent saying they had 'very little influence' (Ipsos MORI,

2013)[3]. A Northern Ireland Life and Times (NILT, 2013)[4] survey produced almost identical results, revealing feelings of pessimism and powerlessness amongst many voters in respect to the influence that they have over decisions that affect them, and this sense was particularly acute among young people and among those with no religious denomination. Yet, if measured in terms of voter turnout it would seem that public interest in politics remains relatively high in Northern Ireland compared to elsewhere in the UK and Europe (52 per cent voted in the May 2013 elections, compared to the EU average of 43 per cent – see Hayward, 2013). However, when the reasons for voting are probed more deeply it is clear that many electors cast their vote out of concern that the 'other side' may be elected. Hayward (2013) notes that all recent public surveys reveal Northern Ireland to be a society with generally low levels of perceived influence in decision making at any level and a society in which those who are often identified as holding the key to a more peaceful future – younger people and those who are free from any one religious denomination – are the people who have the strongest feelings of alienation and pessimism. Galtung (1996), the central contemporary scholar of peace studies, makes an important distinction between 'negative peace' and 'positive peace'. Negative peace refers to the absence of violence, for example, when a ceasefire is agreed. It is 'negative' because something undesirable has stopped happening, violence has ceased, but this is not the same as positive peace. Positive peace, Galtung notes, involves the restoration of relationships through forms of reconciliation, the creation of systems that serve the needs of the whole society and the resolution of conflict in a constructive way. Positive peace does not mean the absence of all conflict; rather it means the absence of violence or the threat of violence as a means of engaging in conflict. A truly peaceful society exists where people manage their conflict positively, interact non-violently and respect the legitimate needs and interest of all. The main challenge for Northern Ireland's political, media and civil society actors is how to make progress toward a more peaceful society and a more deliberative democracy where confrontation, debate and dialogue are all welcome in both public and empowered (legislative) communicative spaces, but coercion, deception and threat are absent.

Research on government communication, Sanders argues, should be research: 'that translates into policy recommendations about structures, resources, processes and outcomes, not driven by managerial imperatives but by normative concerns about the quality of civic life' (2011: 268). It is clear that developing the concept of democratic deliberation in contexts where political antagonisms have violently shattered the social fabric is a difficult task, but it is a task which must be embraced if a more authentic, transparent and accountable democracy is to develop in Northern Ireland. Hayward (2013) argues that institutional reform is required that will allow for a truly deliberative overhaul of the country's political life. This, we suggest, is partially true but equally important is reform of the communicative culture, and key to this is a transformation in the nature of the political rhetoric in

Northern Ireland's public sphere and political institutions. Dryzek (2010) distinguishes between *bonding* and *bridging*[5] political rhetoric in societies where deep divisions exist. Bonding rhetoric is often deployed in ethnically divided democracies and has a tendency 'to deepen divisions with out-groups … to move groups to extremes' (Dryzek 2010: 238). In contrast Dryzek suggests: 'bridging rhetoric takes seriously the outlooks of an intended audience that is different from the speaker – and from the kind of people or discourses the speaker represents' (2010: 328). In order to reach across deep societal divisions, Dryzek (2009: 328) recommends: 'interactive forums composed of individuals from different blocks, at a distance from contests about the construction of sovereign authority, concerned more with particular needs and concrete problems'. In Northern Ireland such forums do exist, indeed they were a requirement of the devolving of certain powers from the UK government level. Forums such as the District Policing Partnerships are required to have cross-community representation in order to agree decisions about local policing policy. They have been an important ground level forum for deliberation and participation where local representatives have been engaged in the hard work of developing bridging rhetoric to reach across to audiences whose dispositions are different to their own in order to deliver successful community policing.

Northern Ireland's legislature, wherein much of the sovereign power resides, has a great deal to learn from such forums about the kind of communication required to foster a more deliberative democratic approach. Indeed, it may be that the political elites are slowly learning such lessons. On 17 November 2015 the political parties came together to announce 'A Fresh Start – *The Stormont Agreement and Implementation Plan*: An agreement to consolidate the peace, secure stability, enable progress and offer hope'.[6] A key clause of the agreement noted:

> It is important that civic voices are heard and civic views are considered in relation to key social, cultural and economic issues. A new engagement model could be achieved, by June 2016, through the establishment of a compact civic advisory panel which would meet regularly to consider key social, cultural and economic issues and to advise the NI Executive.

This is an encouraging development and is perhaps the beginning of institutional changes which will broaden the deliberative democracy process in Northern Ireland. However, as our study has demonstrated, in common with all contemporary representative democracies, government communication in Northern Ireland: 'passes through various expert communicators who package exchanges and discussions for audiences who have little opportunity to contribute' (Bohman, 2012: 48). This is inescapable in representative mass democracy, but the question of what the responsibilities of these publicly funded 'expert communicators' are to the public they serve is also inescapable. Government public relations does not necessarily have to foster the 'mutual understanding' and 'two-way communication' beloved of some PR models (see Cutlip et al., 2000 in the introductory Chapter 1 of this book), but it should be committed to the 'public interest', to fostering 'genuine engagement' and to the recognition that it is legitimate to hold partisan positions while at the same time recognising that opposing voices are treated 'as adversaries rather than antagonists' (Edwards, 2015: 13). In our study it is the GIO participants who speak most clearly of a strong sense of responsibility to inform citizens on government matters and even in facilitating a transition to a shared society. At this crucial stage in the development of its democratic institutions, it is imperative that both GIOs and SpAds build productive working relationships with each other (and with the media) in order to facilitate a post-conflict era of transparent, accountable and participative politics in Northern Ireland. In our view this can only begin to be achieved if these relationships are built on strict adherence to the *Civil Service Code* and Northern Ireland's *Code of Conduct for Special Advisers* (2015)[7], which prohibits SpAd interference in the work of GIOs. A commitment to build an authentic, deliberative and inclusive democracy in Northern Ireland, with bridging communication at the core, will enable the society to continue its path away from the violence and division of the Troubles.

Notes

1 See http://archive.niassembly.gov.uk/io/summary/d'hondt.htm (accessed 14 June 2015).
2 Cabinet Office (2015) *Code of Conduct for Special Advisers*. London: Cabinet Office. Available from: www.gov.uk/government/uploads/system/uploads/attachment_data/file/468340/CODE_OF_CONDUCT_FOR_SPECIAL_ADVISERS_-_15_OCTOBER_2015_FINAL.pdf (accessed 25 January 2016).
3 www.niassembly.gov.uk/globalassets/Documents/RaISe/Publications/2010/General/15710.pdf (accessed 13 December 2015).
4 www.ark.ac.uk/nilt/2013/Political_Attitudes/index.html (accessed 13 December 2015).
5 Dryzek adapts Robert Putnam's terminology from his study of social capital.
6 www.northernireland.gov.uk/a-fresh-start-stormont-agreement.pdf (accessed 8 January 2016).
7 https://www.dfpni.gov.uk/articles/special-advisers.

References

Alvesson, M. and Skoldberg, K. (2009) *Reflexive methodology: New vistas for qualitative research*. 2nd edn. London: Sage.

Andrews, L. (2006) 'Spin: From tactic to tabloid', *Journal of Public Affairs*, 6(1): 31–45.

Bennett, W.L. and Entman, R.M. (2001) 'Introduction', in Bennett, W.L. and Entman, R.M. (eds) *Mediated politics: Communication in the future of democracy*. Cambridge: Cambridge University Press, pp. 1–29.

Berger, B.K. (2009) 'Power over, power with, and power to relations: Critical reflections on public relations, the dominant coalition, and activism', *Journal of Public Relations Research*, 17(1): 5–28.

Blick, A. (2004) *People who live in the dark: The history of the special adviser in British politics.* London: Politico's.

Bloomfield, K. (1998) *We will remember them: Report of the Northern Ireland Victims Commissioner.* Belfast: Stationery Office.

Bohman, J. (2012) 'Representation in the deliberative system', in Parkinson, J. and Mansbridge, J. (eds) *Deliberative systems: Deliberative democracy at the large scale.* Cambridge: Cambridge University Press, pp. 72–94.

Bryman, A. (2012) *Social research methods.* Oxford: Oxford University Press.

Clarke, C. (2008) 'An introduction to interpretative phenomenological analysis: A use approach for occupational therapy research', *British Journal of Occupational Therapy*, 72(1): 37–39.

Connaughton, B. (2010) 'Ireland', in Eichbaum, C. and Shaw, R. (eds) *Partisan appointees and public servants: An international analysis of the role of the political adviser.* Cheltenham: Edward Elgar, pp. 151–179.

Davis, A. (2002) *Public relations democracy: Public relations, politics and the mass media in Britain.* Manchester: Manchester University Press.

Davis, A. (2009a) 'Evaluating communication in the British parliamentary public sphere', *British Journal of Politics and International Relations*, 11(2): 280–297.

Davis, A. (2009b) 'Journalist–source relations, mediated reflexivity and the politics of politics', *Journalism Studies*, 10(2): 204–219.

Dryzek, J.S. (2000) *Foundations and frontiers of deliberative governance.* Oxford: Oxford University Press.

Dryzek, J.S. (2009) 'Democratization as deliberative capacity building', *Comparative Political Studies*, 42(11): 1379–1402.

Dryzek, J.S. (2010) 'Rhetoric in democracy: A systemic appreciation', *Political Theory*, 38(3): 319–339.

Edwards, L. (2015) 'The role of public relations in deliberative systems', *Journal of Communication.* First published online 29 December. DOI: 10.1111/jcom.12199.

Eichbaum, C. and Shaw, R. (2010) 'Conclusion', in Eichbaum, C. and Shaw, R. (eds) *Partisan appointees and public servants: An international analysis of the role of the political adviser.* Cheltenham: Edward Elgar, pp. 198–221.

Ericson, R., Baranek, P. and Chan, J. (1989) *Negotiating control: A study of news sources.* Toronto: University of Toronto Press.

Fairbanks, J., Plowman, K.D. and Rawlins, B.L. (2007) 'Transparency in government communication', *Journal of Public Affairs*, 7(1): 23–37.

Falasca, K. and Nord, L. (2013) 'Structures, strategies and spin: Government communication in Sweden', in Sanders, K. and Canel, M.J. (eds) *Government communication: Cases and challenges.* London: Bloomsbury, pp. 27–44.

Fawcett, L. (2002) 'Who's setting the postdevolution agenda in Northern Ireland?' *The Harvard International Journal of Press/Politics*, 7(4): 14–33.

Fawcett, P. and Gay, O. (2010) 'The United Kingdom', in Eichbaum, C. and Shaw, R. (eds) *Partisan appointees and public servants: An international analysis of the role of the political adviser.* Cheltenham: Edward Elgar, pp. 24–63.

Flinders, M. and Kelso, A. (2011) 'Mind the gap: Political analysis, public expectations and the parliamentary decline thesis', *British Journal of Politics and International Relations*, 13(2): 249–268.

Flynn, K. (2006) 'Covert disclosures: Unauthorized leaking, public officials and the public sphere', *Journalism Studies*, 7(2): 256–273.

Gaber, I. (2000) 'Government by spin: An analysis of the process', *Media, Culture and Society*, 22(4): 507–518.

Gaber, I. (2004) 'Alastair Campbell, exit stage left: Do the "Phillis" recommendations represent a new chapter in political communications or is it "business as usual"?' *Journal of Public Affairs*, 4(4): 365–373.

Gans, H.J. (1979) *Deciding what's news: A study of CBS Evening News, NBC Nightly News, Newsweek and Time*. New York: Pantheon Books.

Galtung, J. (1996) *Peace by peaceful means: Peace and conflict, development and civilization*. London: Sage.

Garnham, N. (2007) 'Habermas and the public sphere', *Global Media and Communication*, 3(2): 201–214.

Gelders, D., De Cock, R., Neijens, P. and Roe, K. (2007) 'Government communication about policy intentions: Unwanted propaganda or democratic inevitability? Surveys among government communication professionals and journalists in Belgium and the Netherlands', *Communications*, 32(3): 363–377.

Gormley-Heenan, C. and Devine, P. (2010) 'The "us" in trust: Who trusts Northern Ireland's political institutions and actors?' *Government and Opposition*, 45(2): 143–165.

Habermas, J. (1962) (1989, trans. Burger, T. and Lawrence, F.) *The structural transformation of the public sphere: An inquiry into a category of bourgeois society*. Cambridge: Polity Press.

Habermas, J. (1984) *The theory of communicative action*. Cambridge: Polity Press.

Hall, S., Critcher, C., Jefferson, T., Clarke, J. and Roberts, B. (1978) *Policing the crisis: Mugging, the state, and law and order*. London: Macmillan.

Hargie, O. and Dickson, D. (eds) (2003) *Researching the troubles: Social science perspectives on the Northern Ireland conflict*. Edinburgh: Mainstream Publishing.

Hargie, O.D.W., Somerville, I. and Mitchell, D. (2015) *Social exclusion and sport in Northern Ireland*. Office of First Minister and Deputy First Minister. University of Ulster.

Hayward, K. (2013) 'Deliberative democracy in Northern Ireland: Opportunities and challenges for consensus in a consociational system', in Ugarriza, E. and Caluwaerts, D. (eds) *Democratic deliberation in deeply divided societies: From conflict to common ground*. London: Routledge, pp. 11–34.

Hiebert, R.E. (2003) 'Public relations and propaganda in framing the Iraq war: A preliminary review', *Public Relations Review*, 29(3): 243–255.

Ipsos MORI (2010) *Public attitude survey 2009: Research report prepared for COI/Northern Ireland Assembly*. Available from: www.niassembly.gov.uk/globalassets/Documents/RaISe/Publications/2010/General/15710.pdf (accessed 5 March 2016).

King, S. (2003) *Regulating the behaviour of ministers, special advisers and civil servants*. London: The Constitution Unit (UCL). Available from: www.ucl.ac.uk/spp/publications/unit-publications/102.pdf (accessed 30 January 2012).

Knox, C. (2010) *Devolution and the governance of Northern Ireland*. Manchester: Manchester University Press.

Langdridge, D. (2007) *Phenomenological psychology: Theory, research and method*. Harlow: Pearson Prentice Hall.

Larsson, L.O. (2002) 'Journalists and politicians: A relationship requiring manoeuvring space', *Journalism Studies*, 3(1): 21–33.

Laursen, B. and Valentini, C. (2013) 'Media relations in the Council of the European Union: Insights into the Council press officers' professional practices', *Journal of Public Affairs*, 13(3): 230–238.

Lee, M. (1999) 'Reporters and bureaucrats: Public relations counter-strategies by public administrators in an era of media disinterest in government', *Public Relations Review*, 25(4): 451–463.

Lemarchand, R. (2007) 'Consociationalism and power sharing in Africa: Rwanda, Burundi, and the Democratic Republic of the Congo', *African Affairs*, 106(422), 1–20.

Lijphart, A. (2008) *Thinking about democracy: Power sharing and majority rule in theory and practice.* Abingdon: Routledge.

Lilleker, D.G. (2006) *Key concepts in political communication*. London: Sage.

Lunt, P. and Livingstone, S. (2013) 'Media studies' fascination with the concept of the public sphere: Critical reflections and emerging debates', *Media, Culture and Society*, 35(1): 87–96.

Mazzoleni, G. and Schulz, W. (1999) '"Mediatization" of politics: A challenge for democracy?' *Political Communication*, 16(3): 247–261.

McEvoy, J. (2006) 'Elite interviewing in a divided society: Lessons from Northern Ireland', *Politics*, 26(3): 184–191.

McLaughlin, G. and Baker, S. (2010) *The propaganda of peace: The role of media and culture in the Northern Ireland peace process.* Bristol: Intellect.

McNair, B. (2007a) 'Theories of government communication and trends in the UK', in Young, S. (ed.) *Government communication in Australia*. New York: Cambridge University Press, pp. 93–109.

McNair, B. (2007b) 'PR must die: Spin, anti-spin and political public relations in the UK, 1997–2004', *Journalism Studies*, 5(3): 325–338.

Meyer, C. (1999) 'Political legitimacy and the invisibility of politics: Exploring the European Union's communication deficit', *Journal of Common Market Studies*, 37(4): 617–639.

Mitchell, P., Evans, G. and O'Leary, B. (2009) 'Extremist outbidding in ethnic party systems is not inevitable: Tribune parties in Northern Ireland', *Political Studies*, 57(2): 397–421.

Mumby, D.K. (1988) *Communication and power in organizations: Discourse, ideology and domination*. Norwood, NJ: Ablex.

Negrine, R. (2008) *The transformation of political communication: Continuities and changes in media and politics.* Basingstoke: Palgrave Macmillan.

NILT (2013) *Northern Ireland Life and Times Survey 2013*. Available from: www.ark.ac.uk/nilt/2013/ (accessed 3 March 2016).

Paun, A. (2011) 'Special treatment? Why the coalition is appointing more special advisers', *Institute for Government Blog*, 18 October. Available from: www.instituteforgovernment.org.uk/blog/3692/special-treatment-why-the-coalition-is-appointing-more-special-advisers/ (accessed 20 June 2012).

Phillis Review (2004) Available from: www.publications.parliament.uk/pa/ld200809/ldselect/ldcomuni/7/704.htm (accessed 17 May 2013).

Rice, C., Somerville, I. and Wilson, J. (2015) 'Democratic communication and the role of special advisers in Northern Ireland's consociational government', *International Journal of Public Administration*, 38(1): 4–14.

Sanders, K. (2009) *Communicating politics in the twenty-first century.* Basingstoke: Palgrave Macmillan.

Sanders, K. (2011) 'Political public relations and government communication' in Strömbäck, J. and Kiousis, S. (eds) *Political public relations: Principles and applications.* New York: Routledge, pp. 254–273.

Smith, J., Flowers, P. and Larkin, M. (2009) *Interpretative phenomenological analysis: Theory, method and research*. London: Sage.

Somerville, I., Purcell, A. and Morrison, F. (2011) 'Public relations education in a divided society: PR, terrorism and critical pedagogy in post-conflict Northern Ireland', *Public Relations Review*, 37(5): 548–555.

Somerville, I. and Ramsey, P. (2012) 'Public relations and politics', in Theaker, A. (ed.) *The public relations handbook*. Abingdon: Routledge, pp. 38–59.

Sriramesh, K. and Verčič, D. (eds) (2009) *The global public relations handbook*. Abingdon: Routledge.

Stringer, M., Irwing, P., Giles, M., McClenahan, C., Wilson, R. and Hunter, J.A. (2009) 'Intergroup contact, friendship quality and political attitudes in integrated and segregated schools in Northern Ireland', *British Journal of Educational Psychology*, 79: 239–257.

Strömbäck, J. (2008) 'Four phases of mediatization: An analysis of the mediatization of politics', *International Journal of Press/Politics*, 13: 228–246.

Tansey, O. (2007) 'Process tracing and elite interviewing: A case for non-probability sampling', *PS: Political Science and Politics*, 40(4): 765–772.

Tonge, J. (2014) *Comparative peace processes*. Cambridge: Polity Press.

Walker, B. and Burgess, M. (2011) 'Creating voice, creating being: An interpretative phenomenological analysis of jazz musicians' experiences', *Existential Analysis*, 22: 119–135.

Wilford, R. (2007) 'Inside Stormont: The Assembly and the Executive', in Carmichael, P., Knox, C. and Osborne, R. (eds) *Devolution and constitutional change in Northern Ireland*. Manchester: Manchester University Press, pp. 167–185.

Winstone, R. (2003) 'Whither the civil service?' House of Commons Library research paper 03/49. Available from: www.parliament.uk/documents/ commons/lib/research/rp2003/rp03–049.pdf (accessed 17 May 2013).

Wodak, R. (2011) *The discourse of politics in action: Politics as usual*. Basingstoke: Palgrave Macmillan.

Wolfsfeld, G. (1997) *Media and political conflict: News from the Middle East*. Cambridge: Cambridge University Press.

6 The entity-agent framework as a starting point for international public relations and public diplomacy research

Diana Ingenhoff and Alexander Buhmann

Introduction

Much contemporary public relations research is said to demonstrate a hegemony of functionalist approaches (Porter, 2009). In the fields of international public relations (IPR) and public diplomacy (PD) research, one such functionalist approach with great influence on the discipline is nation branding (Pamment, 2014; Wang, 2008). This approach has already been criticised in that it favours a marketing focus often unsuited to IPR and PD research (Rasmussen and Merkelsen, 2012; Kaneva, 2011). However, it brings with it another, more implicit, consequence for the field that has so far received little attention: much like other interest-based fields, it widely internalises 'the core conceit' (Meyer and Jepperson, 2000) of modern culture that countries are autochthonous and natural entities. This kind of concretism in IPR and PD research, which is strongly propelled by the nation branding tradition, has important epistemological implications for the field because it tends to take the focus off those aspects that relate to the constructedness and variability of the country as a social entity (Meyer, 2010; Meyer and Jepperson, 2000; Anderson, 1983). However, IPR and PD practices (and nation branding in particular) are necessarily involved in the continuous construction of the country as a social object. Through the strategic communication practices of branding and image management, IPR and PD continuously construct countries as particular entities in society. Furthermore, the way in which a country is culturally and cognitively constructed as a social entity varies greatly: not only do different countries relate to dissimilar attributional properties for constructing them as social entities, but people's perceptions of these countries as social objects also vary depending on the focus of the perceiver as well as the contextual factors of specific situations (Lickel et al., 2000). Such variance in constructing countries as social entities can have significant effects on international relations because it affects how people (domestic and abroad) process information about a country. This applies to the degree of organisation in the cognitive formation of impressions about a country, the drawing of inferences regarding assumed core characteristics of a country, the expectation of consistency in its attributed traits and alleged actions, and the need to resolve perceived inconsistencies in information about a country (Hamilton and Sherman, 1996). This raises the question of how we can conceptually address variations and effects in entity-agent constructions of countries in IPR and PD research.

In the following we address nation branding as an influential functionalist framework that tends to promote a concretist understanding of the country as a central unit of analysis in IPR and PD research. In reviewing the literature, we show how critical works instead provide an alternative view of the country as widely pluralistic and variable in a cultural, ethnic, religious and linguistic sense, and as an inherently and deeply divided entity. Extending this view, we propose to see any entity-agent construction of a country as an ascription, and model possible variations in constructing countries as social entities by drawing on concepts from research on the perception of collective entities and a neo-institutional model of agency (cf. also Buhmann and Ingenhoff, 2015a). We apply these concepts in proposing a framework that focuses on *entitativity* and *agency* as the two central dimensions of constructing countries as social entities. The analytical value of this framework is then demonstrated by elaborating the effects and implications of varying constructions of the country as a social entity in the field of international public relations and public diplomacy.

The functionalist perspective in IPR and PD and the reification of the country

The functionalist approach of nation branding has facilitated a popular and influential stream of studies within international public relations and public diplomacy research (Pamment, 2014; Szondi, 2009; Wang, 2008). Practice-oriented works that use this approach (e.g. Anholt, 2007; Olins, 2002) are grounded in general research on the constitution, measurement and management of brands (see Kaneva, 2011; Papadopoulos, 2004 for an overview of the field). In international public relations and public diplomacy research, the influential concept of the country or nation brand – which is commonly defined as 'the unique, multi-dimensional blend of elements that provide the nation with culturally grounded differentiation and relevance for all of its target audiences' (Dinnie, 2008: 15) – is applied both on the level of branding strategy (output level) as well as the respective perceptions of the country or nation brand in the mind of the perceiver (outcome level) (Buhmann and Ingenhoff, 2015b). In this view, countries themselves appear as products, competing with institutions, commercial products and other countries (Dolea, 2015). As Rasmussen and Merkelsen (2012) show in their recent study, the success of nation branding in international public relations and public diplomacy has strong epistemological consequences for the field as a communication domain because it leads both researchers and practitioners to an almost exclusive focus on economic objectives and facilitates a transformation of international public relations and public diplomacy to the mere marketing of states.

But the success of functionalist approaches leads to yet another consequence for the field of international public relations and public diplomacy. As functionalist approaches aim for competitive advantage they commonly presuppose more or less manifest entities that can be subjected to forms of strategic communication. Strategic branding, for instance, fixates on the idea of a particular object – traditionally a product (Aaker, 1991) – which, through branding efforts, can be defined, communicated and managed in its appearance (Keller, 1993). As a consequence and in its application to international public relations and public diplomacy, such approaches cultivate an understanding of 'competitive countries' and 'countries as products' in a global marketplace as, for example, expressed by Ham (2008: 129): 'Although many countries offer the same "product" – territory, infrastructure, educated people, and an almost identical system of governance – they must compete with each other for investment, tourism, and political power on a global scale'. As Hanna and Rowley (2008) show in a terminological meta-analysis of the field, macro categorisations such as 'nation' and 'country' commonly appear as the stable and pre-fixed units of analysis. This common understanding of the country as a manifest social entity and competitive actor in a global society is visible in the widespread concretist rhetoric in the field. Here countries appear to be able to 'desire' things (Anholt, 2006: 274) and have a 'will' (Fan, 2008: 148) whilst huge collective entities such as China 'understand that they need to move beyond a low cost production model' (Loo and Davies, 2006: 201), and the USA 'assume[s] the role of international sheriff' (Ham, 2008: 140). In this entitative and agentic rhetoric, in which countries desire, want, understand and assume roles, researchers continuously reproduce the common reification of countries as uniform social actors (Meyer and Jepperson, 2000). Like individuals or corporations, countries are being constructed as more or less uniform social entities with capacity for agency. Though any country is endowed with an almost infinite number of characteristics and facets, their common functionalist conceptualisation is guided by presuppositions of coherence, stability and responsibility for action.

Beyond country concretism in IPR and PD research

In recent years the emergence of non-functionalist and critical approaches in international public relations and public diplomacy has helped make explicit the dominant tendencies of marketisation in IPR and PD and problematise prevalent concretist views of the country. In these works, countries are seen as highly complex and fluid discursive phenomena (Dolea, 2015) and cultural and cognitive constructions (Wang, 2008). This line of research focuses more strongly on the fact that modern countries are widely pluralistic in a cultural, ethnic, religious and linguistic sense and can be considered as inherently and deeply divided (Hega, 2011) and 'imagined' social entities (Anderson, 1983).

The notion of the country as a constructed and inherently divided entity poses significant challenges for extant international public relations and public diplomacy research dominated by a nation branding paradigm, when it comes to understanding the role of (strategic and non-strategic) communication in the formation and effects of country images and the cultivation of beneficial relations in the international system (Volčič, 2008; Wang, 2006, 2008; Fan, 2006; Kunczik, 1997). Due to this complexity, the way in which a country, together with its associated national corporations, politicians, people, etc., is constructed as one collective 'social object' and more or less 'uniform actor' can vary strongly: not only do different countries relate to dissimilar properties for constructing them as coherent objects, but peoples' perceptions of these social objects also vary depending on the focus of the perceiver as well as the context factors of specific situations (Lickel et al., 2000). The sheer number and variety of associations that a nation may produce poses manifest challenges in applying strategic communication and branding strategies to 'national image management' (Wang, 2006), and leads to complex interrelations and transfer effects between images of countries and images of sub-country entities such as domestic companies, products and brands (White, 2014; 2012; Newburry, 2012; Gotsi et al., 2011; Wang, 2006; Oh and Ramaprasad, 2003).

In international public relations and public diplomacy research, however, this has so far remained a mostly theoretical realisation and has not yet led to the development and specification of an empirically applicable framework that allows researchers in the field to factor in the possible properties and effects of the variations in constructing the country as a social entity. But once we move beyond the presupposition of the country as a natural social entity we can also apply this non-concretist view to focus on the properties and effects of entity construction in light of people's varying perceptions of countries as social entities. Examples of such properties and effects might be people's varying tendencies to draw inferences about the assumed dispositional properties of a country, to develop an impression of the country, or to resolve inconsistencies in the information acquired about the country. Furthermore, once the social entity is no longer presupposed as a 'natural actor' we can focus on the processes and implications of *how* the country is cognitively and culturally constructed as a more or less authorised social agent. This raises the question of how we can conceptually address variations and effects of cultural and cognitive country entity construction in IPR and PD research.

Towards an entity-agent framework for IPR and PD research

The socio-cognitive construction of entities – from individual persons to large human collectives such as countries – has been studied from a variety of theoretical perspectives over the last century (see, e.g., Prinz, 2012; Luhmann, 1982; Foucault, 1979; Goffman, 1959; Mead, 1934; James, 1890). Functionalist theories, however, such as nation branding, which take the social entity of the country at face value, apply what can be labelled an *implicit theory of the social entity* (Morris et al., 2001): they presuppose that countries possess both self-capacity as well as agency. Below, we draw on two recent concepts to deconstruct these two basic dimensions of 'selfhood' and 'actorhood' and show how they serve the common idea of the country as a more or less manifest social unit (see also Buhmann and Ingenhoff, 2015a). First, we draw on the concept of *entitativity* as developed in research on the perception of collective entities (Yzerbyt et al., 2004; Lickel et al., 2001; Campbell, 1958). Second, we draw on the concept of *agency* as applied in research on the cultivation of micro, meso and macro entities as actors in modern societies (Meyer, 2010; Meyer and Jepperson, 2000).

Constructing the 'selfhood' of countries: the entitativity dimension

Works on the psychology of group perception focus on how 'selfhood' is constructed as a variable property of collective social entities such as families, movements, organisations, or countries (Lickel et al., 2000; Campbell, 1958). The degree to which a country is perceived as a meaningful 'self' can be referred to as the respective country's *entitativity*. Researchers in the psychology of group perception often conceptualise the construct of entitativity to be based on two interrelated components: the ascription of common surface-level attributes (called phenotypic entitativity) as well as common inner qualities (called genotypic entitativity) (Yzerbyt et al., 2001).

Phenotypic entitativity: constructing surface-level attributes of a country

A commonly attributed surface-level property that makes a country appear as a meaningful social self is its relative stability, i.e. its inalterability. This property can be thought of as a combination of continuity on the one hand and permeability on the other (Haslam et al., 2000). While continuity reflects inalterability in a temporal dimension, e.g. the duration of a country and its protracted embeddedness in history (Smith, 2000), permeability refers to inalterability in a spatial dimension, e.g. the discreteness or territoriality of a country as manifested in its physical borders and boundaries of its environment (Benhabib, 2005). As a further property of this phenotypic component, researchers have focused on homogeneity or similarity (Hamilton, 2007), which can be thought of as the construction of uniformity among a country's various sub-units. The degree to which a country is constructed as a more or less homogeneous entity depends, of course, entirely on the relational dimensions or attributes that serve as a point of reference when constructing the relation between the sub-units that come to form the country as an entity. This could be the members of an ethnic group and their assumed physical similarities such as skin colour which serve as a common focus especially in times of conflict (Horowitz, 1985). Or it could be corporate sub-units such as companies and their socially constructed similarities in terms of nationally branded symbols (Feige et al., 2013). In addition to inalterability and homogeneity, Hamilton et al. (1998) suggest internal organisation as an important surface-level determinant of entitativity. The property of internal organisation represents a country's visible coordinative structures, such as the domestic infrastructure, national agencies, and the state as the overarching macro organisation of the country in the sense of a modern nation state (Meyer et al., 1997).

Genotypic entitativity: constructing a country's inner qualities

The component of genotypic entitativity extends beyond the realm of the visible surface of the country, and contributes to its construction on the level of supposed inner qualities. As a common inner quality, social entities are usually endowed with essence (Gelman, 2003), i.e. an ascription of most basic dispositions 'that are regarded as highly enduring and transmitted across time and space' (Rothbart and Park, 2004: 90). Essence can be thought of as a country's constructed 'inherence', i.e. its assumed possession of a distinct and underlying cultural reality. For countries, essence is mainly reproduced within mainstream ideologies of national identity (Hobsbawm and Ranger, 1983; Smith, 1987; Anderson, 1983; Gellner, 1983). Furthermore, on the genotypic level, social objects are also constructed on the basis of common or *shared goals* (Rothbart and Park, 2004). In this sense the social entity of the country is related to particular purposes that entail a common (political, economic, cultural, etc.) agenda and particular 'national interests' (Finnemore, 1996). Last, we can relate to this genotypic component the property of a common fate (Campbell, 1958). Common fate suggests that the sub-units of a country share consequences. In other words: what occurs, happens to the country *as a whole.* Such constructions of common consequences happen commonly within narratives of patriotism and can be seen as the outcomes of shared goal attainment (such as the loss of a war) as well as the result of external events (such as natural disasters) (Li and Brewer, 2004).

Constructing the 'actorhood' of countries: the agency dimension

As with components of entitativity or 'selfhood', any collective social object can vary in the degree to which it is constructed as possessing agency. The neo-institutional approach to social conduct focuses on how 'actorhood' is commonly constructed as a property of micro, meso and macro entities (Meyer, 2010; Meyer and Jepperson, 2000). Following Meyer and Jepperson (2000), modern countries are commonly ascribed with the two basic components of entity-based agency and environment-based agency.

Entity-based agency: constructing agentic capacity for the 'country self'

The first and most basic property of agency construction reflects agency for the self. In this basic form, agency is entirely entity-based, that is, the entity (in this case the country) appears as a sovereign actor in managing goals, which are thought to reside in its 'inner cause' (see the above discussion of genotypic entitativity). This form of self-management is commonly constructed on the macro level of social organisation in which the country or nation state is thought to manage the goals of a sovereign national society. Actions and interactions of the country and its sub-units are thought to be guided by its own underlying principles and serve its own sovereign purposes (Hannum, 1990).

Environment-based agency: constructing a country's agentic capacity for the other

Apart from the basic component of agency for the self we can distinguish more elaborate forms which fall under the category of environment-based agency. First, the modern country is commonly constructed as taking over agency for other internal or external social entities. Meyer and Jepperson argue that this happens based on elaborate structures of *otherhood* and establishment of highly standardised practices, which favour constructions in which countries are thought to apply their agency as a service for others: nation-states can 'collaborate in all sorts of collective activity' and 'serve as agents of their own [...] citizens' (Meyer and Jepperson, 2000: 107). As such, countries may be constructed as collaborators that form alliances to realise collective interests (Wood and Gray, 1991). Second, the country is commonly constructed as possessing the capacity to mobilise actor capacity for entities that do not possess agentic properties themselves. This is evident in how countries are constructed as advocates for unorganised human groups like 'the poor', 'lower classes', or 'cultures'. This constructed capacity of *non-actor advocacy* arises from the country's 'imagined competence in applying natural and moral law' (Meyer and Jepperson, 2000: 108). An example of this is the normatively charged idea of a country's welfare system, which seems to enable a country's agentic capacities in dealing (or not dealing) with unorganised groups such as immigrants (Borjas and Trejo, 1991). Third, modern countries are constructed as taking up agency beyond the self, the other, and the non-actor to reflect their capacity to serve as an agent for general principle. In this form of pure otherhood the country becomes an agent of what is imagined as the status quo of natural and moral law. In highly rationalised models of society this imagined principle is strongly influenced by moral and legal theorists, experts and highly reputed scientists, i.e. social authorities that coin the production of charters, compacts and codes of conduct on the level of transnational organisations such as the UN, which serve as a quasi-global ethic. Country agency is then commonly constructed within discourse on a country's degree of compliance with these principles (Kent, 1999).

Applying the entity-agent framework to IPR and PD research

Just like other social entities, countries differ in the degree to which they are culturally and cognitively constructed as more or less uniform and authorised social agents. On a macro level the importance of such differences in constructing countries may be most obvious when comparing varying cultural contexts. Cultural models of entitativity and agency are emergent concepts that construct the seemingly 'natural states' or 'purposes' of countries. Such models are, as Meyer and Jepperson (2000: 111) put it, 'editing the imagined *true nature* of the nation and its heritages'. In other words, different cultural systems construct countries differently in terms of their entitativity and agency. They argue that in some more corporate or collectivist cultural contexts there tends to be a heightened emphasis on entity attributions and less on agency, Further, in the more liberal systems there is a common understanding of a 'flattened selfhood' and a dominance of exaggerated agency attributions (Meyer and Jepperson, 2000). This assumed systematic difference in entity-agent attributions between cultural contexts is empirically underlined by research on how countries and other human collectives are perceived in different cultures (Kashima et al., 2005; Kashima, 2004; Morris et al., 2001; Menon et al., 1999).

Thus, in the context of IPR and PD, we have to expect that constructions of countries in terms of their entitativity and agency can vary not only in terms of the different properties of different types of countries, but also the same country as it is constructed by different publics in different situational contexts. While the field of IPR and PD research analyses country-level communication between different national agencies and actors and their foreign publics – in order to understand the dynamics of legitimisation, the cultivation of country image and brand, or the development of favourable relations in the international system – the entity-agent framework offers new insights that go beyond the common concretism and allow for the *constructedness* of the 'country entity' to be factored in. In the following we use the conceptual distinctions from the entity-agent framework derived above to elaborate on (a) the role of IPR and PD practice in the construction and deconstruction of countries as social entities, and (b) the effects of varying entity-agent constructions on the country level.

The role of IPR and PD practice in constructing the country as a social entity

The construction of the country as a uniform self

The construction of the 'country entity' in IPR and PD can be observed regarding the attribution of both phenotypic and genotypic properties. As a communicative practice, strategic communication in IPR and PD, and especially in nation branding, is necessarily involved in reproducing surface-level attributes of the country. The property of inalterability is commonly cultivated through the degree of continuity in the categorical use of 'symbolic country identifiers' such as a consistent name, flag, tourism brand and other symbols. Most state and non-state agencies involved in PD and nation branding strongly construct country-level inalterability in this sense when they work with a coherent communication strategy rooted in what is conceived as a particular 'national identity', especially when this strategy – as is often the case – draws heavily on well-established cultural artefacts and even stereotypes associated with a geographic location (Kavaratzis, 2005). Specific challenges arise, of course, when common symbolic identifiers might be altered, as with long-standing national flags being put up for popular vote, as with the Australian (1999) and New Zealand (2015) flag referenda. Homogeneity is communicatively constructed through the representation of the country as a more or less uniform entity. The degree to which entitativity is constructed through similarity on the surface level (i.e. homogeneity) can vary depending on how communicators focus on different units and sub-units of the country. For example, whether a country is framed by repeatedly showing its one presidential political leader or single famous landmark attraction on the one hand, or in terms of its 'eclectic appearance', i.e. its various oppositional parties or diverse cultural regions, on the other hand. This can obviously make a big difference to the resulting sense of homogeneity of the country. Presidential republics, such as the United States, which are headed by one executive leader, and government systems like that of Switzerland, which is headed by a group of parliamentarians in a federal council, tend to produce an entirely different sense of uniformity in this dimension. The construction of internal organisation can also vary from country to country, especially when considering how IPR and PD is organised and practised (centralised vs decentralised) and how the country is portrayed as an institutional structure within strategic communication. Depending on the respective communication strategy the country may be constructed as a highly centralised and manifest body or as a 'loose collective' with decentralised (federal, cultural, etc.) structures. Here the preservation of different language regions as in Belgium, Canada or Switzerland is a good example of the reproduction of decentralised organisation. In Switzerland, for example, these regional structures are supported by a clearly visible state-funded infrastructure (e.g. a separate broadcasting system for each region).

Next to phenotypic properties, the entity-agent framework defines genotypic entitativity properties of essence, shared goals and common fate as forming the second component of country-entity construction. A prominent aspect of constructing essence in IPR and PD is to be seen in practices of engaging and cultivating an inherent culture among internal stakeholders (Haag, 2010). Here, IPR and PD practice continuously contribute to the cultivation of an integral and underlying cultural reality, thereby participating in the overall process of nation building (Toledano and McKie, 2013). Thus, communicative practices of forming national culture become a means for constructing genotypic entitativity. Essence and culture are closely related to the imagined functions of a country or national society, i.e. to the goals it is said to attain as a collective entity. As such, the communication of shared goals in IPR and PD on the macro level of a country reinforces its genotypic entitativity. In the case of Swiss IPR and PD, for instance, we can see how, even in fairly politically and culturally diverse contexts, the communication of national political processes such as referenda necessarily lead to a construction of a common national goal (i.e. a policy choice) (Sciarini and Tresch, 2009). Another example from Switzerland is the persistence of the ideal of neutrality which, inasmuch as it appears as a shared goal, becomes constitutive in ascriptions of country entitativity. The diametric opposite and in this sense deconstructive of Swiss country-level entity ascriptions, are the results of popular referenda which, with very high consistency over time, show results in which particular areas of the country consistently vote differently to others – thus reproducing a sense of a divided country (*Economist*, 2002).

The construction of the country as a social actor

Alongside the construction of entitativity, IPR and PD practice inevitably engages in the construction of countries as social actors; this can be observed on the level of entity-based as well as environment-based agency.

Entity-based agency is constructed, for instance, by 'public pronouncements of plans [for action] and past achievements' (Hamilton, 2007: 1086) that are linked to national (e.g. political or economic) goals. This, of course, is common practice in IPR and PD, most clearly in ex-post communications that justify particular decisions. In Swiss PD we have seen examples of this in the aftermath of national referenda, for instance regarding the ban on minarets (Matyassy and Flury, 2011). As the study by Matyassy and Flury shows, Swiss IPR and PD communication strategies linked reports of national conduct (in this case a plebiscite and its political consequences) with narratives on genotypic properties expressed in testimonies on the underlying national culture (in this case the tradition of participatory democracy in Switzerland). Thus, these communications construct agency as an emergent outcome of what is constructed as the underlying and rationalised interests (essence – see above) of the country as a collective entity.

When looking at the component of environment-based agency we can see that IPR and PD practice engages in the construction of otherhood through the common reification of foreign publics as the 'significant others' of national IPR and PD efforts (Gilboa, 2008). Another example is the distinct communication of country neutrality (as in the case of Switzerland) or even the opposite, distinct country belligerence. Both can be equally constitutive for rather strong country-agency attributions, where the country then appears as an agentic collective actor in a global nation-state system. Furthermore, we can observe the construction of non-actor advocacy when looking at aspects of social responsibility and sustainability communication in value-based IPR and PD. This is specifically visible in the case of 'cultural diplomacy' (L'Etang, 2009). These forms of non-actor advocacy of countries commonly construct the country as an agent for a great variety of social and environmental causes that are often related to unorganised entities or causes such as arts, culture, peace, nature or biodiversity. Last, alongside otherhood and non-actor advocacy, the communication on pure otherhood has clearly become a common part of IPR and PD practice: strategic communicators routinely comment on a country's compliance with social and moral contracts enforced by 'agents of global principle' such as the United Nations, Transparency International or other transnational bodies (Mbaye, 2001).

Effects of varying constructions of the country as an entity and agent in IPR and PD

Based on a non-functionalist perspective, a country is first of all a fluid cultural and cognitive construction. Furthermore, the developed entity-agent framework incorporates the assumption that the way a given country is constructed as an entity and agent varies not only in respect to the different properties of different countries but also in respect to the same country as it is constructed by different publics in different contexts. The arguments above show that the way IPR and PD communicate about a country plays an important role in cultivating more or less concretist ideas about that country. Below, we argue that variances in the construction of entitativity and agency are central for IPR and PD because they affect structures and dynamics of how publics perceive certain countries and, in consequence, influence their expectations and behaviour towards them. This becomes apparent when considering how entity-agent construction relates to specific key concepts in IPR and PD.

First, the properties of entity-agent construction impact upon processes of image and reputation transfer in IPR and PD (Buhmann and Ingenhoff, 2015c; Ingenhoff and Buhmann, 2015; Chen, 2012; Wilson et al., 2008; Oh and Ramaprasad, 2003). Research suggests that the higher the perceived entitativity, the more readily and spontaneously people transfer knowledge or inferred traits between sub-entities of large collective entities such as countries and make implicit comparisons between them (Pickett and Perrott, 2004; Crawford et al., 2002; Pickett, 2001). As a consequence, sub-entities of perceptually highly entitative countries may 'become psychologically interchangeable for the perceiver' (Hamilton, 2007: 1088). As such, factors of entity-agent construction can strongly impact dynamics of image and reputation transfer between countries and their political leaders or national brands (Buhmann and Ingenhoff, 2015c; Ingenhoff and Buhmann, 2015).

Second, the entity-agent framework allows for a new analytical perspective on social responsibility communication and crisis communication in the context of IPR and PD, because the properties of constructing the country-entity affect publics' ascriptions of collective responsibility: Lickel et al. (2003), for instance, show that if perceived entitativity is high then sub-entities are held collectively responsible for an act of wrongdoing that may have only been committed by one particular sub-unit. This happens because when entitativity of a social object is high, stakeholders tend to assume that other members of the collective should have had the capacity to prevent the wrongdoing, or they suspect them of being sympathetic to the act. Ingenhoff and Buhmann (2015) and Buhmann and Ingenhoff (2015c) show, for instance, that the perceived entitativity of a country significantly affects the strength of people's associations between a country and a national corporation and, in turn, affects whether people ascribe crisis responsibility to the corporation on the one hand or the country as a whole on the other.

Third, the introduced properties of entity-agent construction are also relevant for issues of credibility and trustworthiness in IPR and PD. This is because the entitativity of collective actors such as countries has been shown to affect people's need to resolve perceived inconsistencies regarding the entity (Hamilton and Sherman, 1996). In fact, studies suggest that we can expect inconsistent information about a country to be processed more extensively by publics if the country is perceived as a strongly uniform and coherent actor (Stern et al., 1984). This provides an interesting angle for understanding the construction of credibility and trustworthiness in IPR and PD. For instance, entity-agent construction can make a critical difference in the formation and effects of credibility and trustworthiness when comparing highly complex and potentially diverse or even 'culturally divided' countries such as Belgium, Switzerland or Canada with potentially more uniformly constructed/perceived countries such as microstates like Singapore or Lichtenstein.

Conclusion

In this chapter we have argued that mainstream functionalist research in international public relations and public diplomacy, as it is commonly found in studies drawing on a nation branding approach, tends to reify countries and treats them as more or less 'natural entities'. To propose an alternative view we drew on the theory of the perception of collective entities as well as a neo-institutional model of agency to delineate the properties that commonly constitute the country as a social entity. Based on the concepts of entitativity and agency, we propose an entity-agent framework that can be applied to IPR and PD and which suggests that a country-entity is commonly constructed as possessing uniform surface-level characteristics (phenotypic entitativity) and unique inner qualities (genotypic entitativity), and that country-entitativity can be seen as the basis on which its country-agency unfolds. Agency, in turn, is conceptualised as the country's constructed agentic capacity for its own interests (self-management), other social agents (otherhood), non-actor entities (non-actor advocacy) and cultural authority (pure otherhood). The framework emphasises that research in IPR and PD needs to be aware of the fact that entity-agent construction of the country varies not only regarding different properties of different types of countries but also regarding the same country as it is constructed by different publics and in different contexts. And it also needs to be aware of the fact that such variances significantly affect key constructs in IPR and PD.

After introducing the basic properties of entity-agent construction, the framework was used to elaborate on how communicative practices in IPR and PD are necessarily involved in the continuous construction of entitativity and agency on the level of countries. Furthermore, we identified important implications of entity-agent construction that go largely unnoticed in functionalist arguments, which favour a concretist concept of the country. With reference to existing empirical research in the field of social psychology, these implications can be related to a very wide variety of topics, such as the constitution of target constructs in IPR and PD (such as country image and country reputation) or specific communicative challenges (such as the social responsibility of countries and responding to national crises). However, it is a limitation of the current literature that these insights are available more for the entitativity dimension than for the agency dimension, which of course constitutes an interesting research gap for IPR and PD.

These considerations demonstrate how drawing on the entity-agent framework characterises IPR and PD as a communicative practice that is necessarily and continuously involved in the construction of the country as a social object with common surface-level characteristics and unique inner qualities and as a social actor with agentic capacity for its own interests, other social agents, non-actor entities, and cultural authority. Thus, entity-agent construction can be characterised as an underlying phenomenon and challenge in IPR and PD; in light of the constructedness of the country and the specific properties of entity-agent construction, IPR and PD practice ultimately can be seen as a communicative management of the 'entity-agent linkage' on the macro level of the country. In other words: IPR and PD construct country entitativity and country agency and continuously aim to improve the links between these two dimensions. As such, IPR and PD practice has to communicatively deal with the structural tension between the country constructed as a 'principle self' and the country constructed as an 'agentic actor'; it has to produce and reproduce the country as a legitimated self (e.g. draw on a supposed country identity and culture) and at the same time coherently communicate its agency in practical short-term goals and actions (e.g. justify national or international policy decisions). In the case of Swiss IPR and PD this is clearly visible when analysing the communication before, during and after the so-called 'minaret initiative' in Switzerland, where IPR and PD efforts concentrated mainly on justifying the outcome of the plebiscite (a ban on minarets in the whole of Switzerland) based on the Swiss culture of neutrality and participative democracy (Matyassy and Flury, 2011). In another prominent case, with the so-called 'mass immigration initiative' – which resulted in a radical reduction of migration to Switzerland in 2014 – the strategy was to explain to rather upset European neighbours, time and again, just how popular votes in plebescites work in Switzerland and what their importance is within Swiss society.

Apart from focusing on entity-agent construction within IPR and PD practice, or on the effects of entity-agent construction on specific target constructs and topics in IPR and PD, the proposed framework can also serve as a valuable starting point to help clarify how mass media contribute to the construction, reconstruction and deconstruction of countries as relevant social entities. Here, the proposed framework raises the question of how countries as collective entities are medially framed in terms of their entitativity and agency. In this regard, research could focus on how certain logics of mediatisation (e.g. personalisation or scandalisation) or different types of media channels, contents or formats contribute to the social construction of the country as a relevant collective entity and social agent. Last, the proposed framework could be combined with existing models for analysing the constitution and effects of country images in IPR and PD research (Buhmann and Ingenhoff, 2015d), to analyse how the perceived entitativity and agency of a country moderates the effects of country images on behavioural variables.

References

Aaker, D. A. (1991) *Managing brand equity: Capitalizing on the value of a brand name.* New York: The Free Press.

Anderson, B. (1983) *Imagined communities: Reflections on the origin and spread of nationalism.* London: Verso.

Anholt, S. (2006) Public diplomacy and place branding: Where's the link? *Place Branding*, 3(2): 271–275.

Anholt, S. (2007) *Competitive identity: The new brand management for nations, cities and regions.* Basingstoke: Palgrave Macmillan.

Benhabib, S. (2005) Borders, l. *Political Science and Politics*, 4(4): 673–677.

Borjas, G. J. and Trejo, S. J. (1991) Immigrant participation in the welfare system. *Industrial and Labor Relations Review*, 44(2): 195–211. http://doi.org/10.1177/001979399104400201.

Buhmann, A. and Ingenhoff, D. (2015a). Grasping the variability of the 'real organization': Towards a framework for analyzing strategic communication in light of highly variable organizational contexts. Paper presented at the EUPRERA Congress, Oslo, Norway, 2 October.

Buhmann, A. and Ingenhoff, D. (2015b). The 4D-model of the country image: An integrative approach from the perspective of communication management. *International Communication Gazette*, 77(1): 102–124.

Buhmann, A. and Ingenhoff, D. (2015c). Understanding 'reputational fallout': How corporate crises influence the perception of a corporation's home country. Paper presented at the EUPRERA Congress, Oslo, Norway, 2 October.

Buhmann, A. and Ingenhoff, D. (2015d). Advancing the country image construct from a public relations perspective: From model to measurement. *Journal of Communication Management*, 19(1): 62–80.

Campbell, D. T. (1958) Common fate, similarity, and other indices of the status of aggregates of persons as social entities. *Behavioral Science*, 3(1): 14–25. http://doi.org/10.1002/bs.3830030103.

Chen, N. (2012) Branding national images: The 2008 Beijing Summer Olympics, 2010 Shanghai World Expo, and 2010 Guangzhou Asian Games. *Public Relations Review*, 38(5): 731–745. http://doi.org/10.1016/j.pubrev.2012.04.003.

Crawford, M. T., Sherman, S. J. and Hamilton, D. L. (2002) Perceived entitativity, stereotype formation, and the interchangeability of group members. *Journal of Personality and Social Psychology*, 83(5): 1076–1094. http://doi.org/10.1037/0022-3514.83.5.1076.

Dinnie, K. (ed.) (2008) *Nation branding: concepts, issues, practice*. London: Butterworth-Heinemann.

Dolea, A. (2015) The need for critical thinking in country promotion: Public diplomacy, nation branding and public relations. In J. L'Etang, D. McKie, N. E. Snow and J. Xifra (eds) *The Routledge handbook of critical public relations*. London: Routledge, pp. 274–288.

Economist (2002) A country divided. Available at www.economist.com/node/1469593 (accessed 25 November 2015).

Fan, Y. (2006) Branding the nation: What is being branded? *Journal of Vacation Marketing*, 12(1): 5–14. http://doi.org/10.1177/1356766706056633.

Fan, Y. (2008) Soft power: Power of attraction or confusion? *Place Branding and Public Diplomacy*, 4(2): 147–158. http://doi.org/10.1057/pb.2008.4.

FDFA (2015) Presence Switzerland, Swiss Federal Department of Foreign Affairs. Available at: www.eda.admin.ch/eda/en/home/dfa/orgcha/gensec/prs.html (accessed 7 October 2015).

Feige, S., Fischer, P. M., Matt, D. van, and Reinecke, S. (2013) *Swissness Worldwide 2013: Image und internationaler Mehrwert der Marke Schweiz*. St Gallen, Switzerland: Thexis.

Finnemore, M. (1996) *National interests in international society*. Ithaca, NY: Cornell University Press.

Foucault, M. (1979) *Discipline and punish: The birth of the prison*. New York: Vintage.

Gellner, E. (1983) *Nations and nationalism*. Oxford: Basil Blackwell.

Gelman, S. A. (2003) *The essential child: Origins of essentialism in everyday thought*. Oxford: Oxford University Press.

Gilboa, E. (2008) Searching for a theory of public diplomacy. *Annals of the American Academy of Political and Social Science*, 616(1): 55–77. http://doi.org/10.1177/0002716207312142.

Goffman, E. (1959) *The presentation of self in everyday life*. Garden City, NY: Doubleday.

Gotsi, M., Lopez, C. and Andriopoulos, C. (2011) Building country image through corporate image: Exploring the factors that influence the image transfer. *Journal of Strategic Marketing*, 19(3): 255–272. http://doi.org/10.1080/0965254X.2011.581387.

Haag, O. (2010) 'You are German' – 'I am Australian': The construction of national unity through diversity in select examples from Australia and Germany. *National Identities*, 12(4): 333–349. http://doi.org/10.1080/14608944.2010.520968.

Ham, P. van (2008) Place branding: The state of the art. *Annals of the American Academy of Political and Social Science*, 616: 126–149.

Hamilton, D. L. (2007) Understanding the complexities of group perception: Broadening the domain. *European Journal of Social Psychology*, 37(6): 1077–1101. http://doi.org/10.1002/ejsp.436.

Hamilton, D. L. and Sherman, S. J. (1996) Perceiving persons and groups. *Psychological Review*, 103(2): 336–355. http://doi.org/10.1037/0033-295X.103.2.336.

Hamilton, D. L., Sherman, S. J. and Lickel, B. (1998) Perceptions of groups: The importance of the entitativity continuum. In C. Sedikides, J. Schopler and C. A. Insko (eds) *Intergroup cognition and intergroup behavior.* Mahwah, NJ: Lawrence Erlbaum Associates, pp. 47–74.

Hanna, S. and Rowley, J. (2008) An analysis of terminology use in place branding. *Place Branding and Public Diplomacy*, 4(1): 61–75. http://doi.org/10.1057/palgrave.pb.6000084.

Hannum, H. (1990) *Autonomy, sovereignty, and self-determination: The accommodation of conflicting rights.* Philadelphia: University of Pennsylvania Press.

Haslam, N., Rothschild, L. and Ernst, D. (2000) Essentialist beliefs about social categories. *British Journal of Social Psychology*, 39(1): 113–127. http://doi.org/10.1348/014466600164363.

Hega, G. M. (2011) The political functions of education in deeply-divided countries. Coming together apart: The case of Switzerland. In T. Hanf (ed.) *The political function of education in deeply divided countries* (pp. 233–256). Baden-Baden, Germany: Nomos.

Hobsbawm, E. J. and Ranger, T. (1983) *The invention of tradition.* Cambridge: Cambridge University Press.

Horowitz, D. L. (1985) *Ethnic groups in conflict.* Berkeley: University of California Press.

Ingenhoff, D. and Buhmann, A. (2015) Image transfer effects of corporate crises on their home country image: The role of constructed entitativity. Paper presented at the 18th Annual IPRR Conference, Miami, USA, March 4–8.

James, W. (1890) *Principles of psychology.* New York: Holt Rinehart and Winston.

Kaneva, N. (2011) Nation branding: Toward an agenda for critical research. *International Journal of Communication*, 5: 117–141.

Kashima, Y. (2004) Culture, communication, and entitativity: A social psychological investigation of social reality. In V. Yzerbyt, C. M. Judd and O. Corneille (eds) *The psychology of group perception: Perceived variability, entitativity, and essentialism.* Philadelphia, PA: Psychology Press, pp. 257–273.

Kashima, Y., Kashima, E., Chiu, C.-Y., Farsides, T., Gelfand, M., Hong, Y.-Y. and Yzerbyt, V. (2005) Culture, essentialism, and agency: Are individuals universally believed to be more real entities than groups? *European Journal of Social Psychology*, 35(2): 147–169. http://doi.org/10.1002/ejsp.237.

Kavaratzis, M. (2005) Place branding: A review of trends and conceptual models. *Marketing Review*, 5(4): 329–342.

Keller, K. L. (1993) Conceptualizing, measuring, and managing customer-based brand equity. *Journal of Marketing*, 57(1): 1–22. http://doi.org/10.2307/1252054.

Kent, A. (1999) *China, the United Nations, and human rights: The limits of compliance.* Philadelphia: University of Pennsylvania Press.

Kunczik, M. (1997) *Images of nations and international public relations.* Mahwah, NJ: Lawrence Erlbaum Associates.

L'Etang, J. (2009) Public relations and diplomacy in a globalized world: An issue of public communication. *American Behavioral Scientist*, 53(4): 607–626. http://doi.org/10.1177/0002764209347633.

Li, Q. and Brewer, M. B. (2004) What does it mean to be an American? Patriotism, nationalism, and American identity after 9/11. *Political Psychology*, 25(5): 727–739. http://doi.org/10.1111/j.1467-9221.2004.00395.x.

Lickel, B., Hamilton, D. L. and Sherman, S. J. (2001) Elements of a lay theory of groups: Types of groups, relational styles, and the perception of group entitativity.

Personality and Social Psychology Review, 5(2): 129–140. http://doi.org/10.1207/S15327957PSPR0502_4.

Lickel, B., Hamilton, D. L., Wieczorkowska, G., Lewis, A., Sherman, S. J. and Uhles, A. N. (2000) Varieties of groups and the perception of group entitativity. *Journal of Personality and Social Psychology*, 78(2): 223–246. http://doi.org/10.1037/0022-3514.78.2.223.

Lickel, B., Schmader, T. and Hamilton, D. L. (2003) A case of collective responsibility: Who else was to blame for the Columbine High School shootings? *Personality and Social Psychology Bulletin*, 29(2): 194–204. http://doi.org/10.1177/0146167202239045.

Loo, T. and Davies, G. (2006) Branding China: The ultimate challenge in reputation management? *Corporate Reputation Review*, 9(3): 198–210. http://doi.org/10.1057/palgrave.crr.1550025.

Luhmann, N. (1982) *The differentiation of society.* New York: Columbia.

Matyassy, J. and Flury, S. (2011) *Challenges for Switzerland's public diplomacy: Referendum on banning minarets.* Los Angeles, CA: Figueroa Press.

Mbaye, H. A. D. (2001) Why national states comply with supranational law: Explaining implementation infringements in the European Union, 1972–1993. *European Union Politics*, 2(3): 259–281. http://doi.org/10.1177/1465116501002003001.

Mead, G. H. (1934) *Mind, self, and society.* Chicago, IL: University of Chicago Press.

Menon, T., Morris, M. W., Chiu, C. and Hong, Y. (1999) Culture and the construal of agency: Attribution to individual versus group dispositions. *Journal of Personality and Social Psychology*, 76(5): 701–717. http://doi.org/10.1037/0022-3514.76.5.701.

Meyer, J. W. (2010) World society, institutional theories, and the actor. *Annual Review of Sociology*, 36(1): 1–20. http://doi.org/10.1146/annurev.soc.012809.102506.

Meyer, J. W. and Jepperson, R. L. (2000) The 'actors' of modern society: The cultural construction of social agency. *Sociological Theory*, 18(1): 100–120. http://doi.org/10.2307/223284.

Meyer, J. W., Boli, J., Thomas, G. M. and Ramirez, F. O. (1997) World society and the nation-state. *American Journal of Sociology*, 103(1): 144–181. http://doi.org/10.1086/231174.

Morris, M. W., Menon, T. and Ames, D. R. (2001) Culturally conferred conceptions of agency: A key to social perception of persons, groups, and other actors. *Personality and Social Psychology Review*, 5(2): 169–182. http://doi.org/10.1207/S15327957PSPR0502_7.

Newburry, W. (2012) Waving the flag: The influence of country of origin on corporate reputation. In M. L. Barnett and T. G. Pollock (eds) *The Oxford handbook of corporate reputation*. Oxford: Oxford University Press, pp. 240–259.

Oh, M.-Y. and Ramaprasad, J. (2003) Halo effect: Conceptual definition and empirical exploration with regard to South Korean subsidiaries of US and Japanese multinational corporations. *Journal of Communication Management*, 7(4): 317–332. http://doi.org/10.1108/13632540310807458.

Olins, W. (2002) Branding the nation: The historical context. *Journal of Brand Management*, 9(4/5): 241.

Pamment, J. (2014) Articulating influence: Toward a research agenda for interpreting the evaluation of soft power, public diplomacy and nation brands. *Public Relations Review*, 40(1): 50–59. http://doi.org/10.1016/j.pubrev.2013.11.019.

Papadopoulos, N. (2004) Place branding: Evolution, meaning and implications. *Place Branding*, 1(1): 36–49.

Pickett, C. L. (2001) The effects of entitativity beliefs on implicit comparisons between group members. *Personality and Social Psychology Bulletin*, 27(5): 515–525. http://doi.org/10.1177/0146167201275001.

Pickett, C. L. and Perrott, D. A. (2004) Shall I compare thee? Perceived entitativity and ease of comparison. *Journal of Experimental Social Psychology*, 40(3): 283–289. http://doi.org/10.1016/S0022-1031(03)121–125

Porter, L. (2009) Communicating for the good of the state: A post-symmetrical polemic on persuasion in ethical public relations. *Public Relations Review*, 26(2): 127–133.

Prinz, W. (2012) *Open minds: The social making of agency and intentionality*. Cambridge, MA: MIT Press.

Rasmussen, R. K. and Merkelsen, H. (2012) The new PR of states: How nation branding practices affect the security function of public diplomacy. *Public Relations Review*, 38(5): 810–818. http://doi.org/10.1016/j.pubrev.2012.06.007.

Rothbart, M. and Park, B. (2004) The mental representation of social categories: Category boundaries, entitativity, and stereotype change. In *The psychology of group perception: Perceived variability, entitativity, and essentialism*. Philadelphia, PA: Psychology Press, pp. 79–100.

Sciarini, P. and Tresch, A. (2009) A two-level analysis of the determinants of direct democratic choices in European, immigration and foreign policy in Switzerland. *European Union Politics*, 10(4): 456–481. http://doi.org/10.1177/1465116509346388.

Smith, A. D. (1987) *The ethnic origins of nations*. Oxford: Blackwell.

Smith, A. D. (2000) *The nation in history: Historiographical debates about ethnicity and nationalism*. Hanover, NH: University Press of New England.

Stern, L. D., Marrs, S., Millar, M. G. and Cole, E. (1984) Processing time and the recall of inconsistent and consistent behaviors of individuals and groups. *Journal of Personality and Social Psychology*, 47(2): 253–262. http://doi.org/10.1037/0022-3514.47.2.253.

Szondi, G. (2009) International context of public relations. In R. Tench and L. Yeomans (eds) *Exploring public relations*, 2nd edn. New York: Prentice Hall, pp. 117–146.

Toledano, M. and McKie, D. (2013) *Public relations and nation building: Influencing Israel*. London: Routledge.

Volčič, Z. (2008) Former Yugoslavia on the World Wide Web: Commercialization and branding of nation-states. *International Communication Gazette*, 70(5): 395–413. http://doi.org/10.1177/1748048508094292.

Wang, J. (2006) Localising public diplomacy: The role of sub-national actors in nation branding. *Place Branding*, 2(1): 32–42.

Wang, J. (2008) The power and limits of branding in national image communication in global society. *Journal of International Communication*, 14(2): 9–24.

White, C. (2012) Brands and national image: An exploration of inverse country-of-origin effect. *Place Branding and Public Diplomacy*, 8(2): 110–118. http://doi.org/10.1057/pb.2012.6.

White, C. (2014) The building blocks of country reputation: How corporate communication helps brand countries. Paper presented at the 64th Annual Conference of the International Communication Association (ICA).

Wilson, B., Stavros, C. and Westberg, K. (2008) Player transgressions and the management of the sport sponsor relationship. *Public Relations Review*, 34(2): 99–107. http://doi.org/10.1016/j.pubrev.2008.03.012.

Wood, D. J. and Gray, B. (1991) Toward a comprehensive theory of collaboration. *Journal of Applied Behavioral Science*, 27(2): 139–162. http://doi.org/10.1177/0021886391272001.

Yzerbyt, V., Corneille, O. and Estrada, C. (2001) The interplay of subjective essentialism and entitativity in the formation of stereotypes. *Personality and Social Psychology Review*, 5(2): 141–155. http://doi.org/10.1207/S15327957PSPR0502_5.

Yzerbyt, V., Judd, C. M. and Corneille, O. (eds) (2004) *The psychology of group perception: perceived variability, entitativity and essentialism*. New York: Psychology Press.

7 Catalonia's public diplomacy and media relations strategy

A case study of the Eugeni Xammar Programme of International Communication and Public Relations

Jordi de San Eugenio, Xavier Ginesta and Jordi Xifra

Introduction

Catalonia, an autonomous region of Spain, is not the only stateless nation that is currently facing a self-determination process. Several stateless nations have emerged as sovereign states over the past generation – some of these instances have been peaceful constitutional divergences (Czechoslovakia or the Baltic republics), but some have involved conflict (Yugoslavia). Still other territories are in the process of debating their future as sovereign states.

Quebec has held two referendums on its independence from Canada, in 1980 and 1995 (Ridao, 2012). On 18 September 2014, the Scots voted on whether to stay in or leave the United Kingdom. On 1 November 2015, general elections in Turkey allowed the Kurds (HDP party) to keep their representation in the Turkish Parliament with 56 MPs out of 550. Ten years ago in Spain, the Basque Government, led by the Basque nationalist Juan José Ibarretxe, also debated (1 February 2005) a significant reform of its regional Constitution in the Spanish Parliament (Perales, 2014). Social scientists have been active in analysing stateless nations and nationalism from a political point of view (Guibernau, 2014; Ridao, 2012; Gafarot, 2011; Curtice, 2006; Guibernau, 2006; Keating, 1997; Horowitz, 1985). However, this chapter addresses a gap in knowledge because there is little communication or public relations research in this area, despite it being a phenomenon around the world.

A critical moment in recent Catalan history came to pass on 11 September 2012, as 1.5 million people, of a population of 7.5 million, took to the streets to demand that Catalonia be recognised as a sovereign state. Therefore, the elections for the Catalan Parliament on 25 November 2012 were interpreted by some Catalonians as a symbolic plebiscite on independence. The elections resulted in a strong presence in the Parliament of parties that supported independence for Catalonia (74 regional deputies out of 135), both in the present government and in the opposition, and the collective compromise among them to hold a referendum on independence during 2014. Following those elections to the regional Parliament, the Catalan political system has been divided into two main ideological blocks, according to the centre–periphery cleavage: on the one hand parties that want to follow a self-determination process, and on the other parties that prefer to remain a part of Spain (defending also different state models) (Ordeix and Ginesta, 2014).

After three years, in September 2015, independence-oriented parties secured 72 out of 135 seats in regional elections in Catalonia. The MPs now serve in the Catalan Parliament. After the formation of a new government led by nationalist President Artur Mas, the foreign policy strategy adopted in the previous period (2010–2012) was reinvigorated and adapted to the new policy programme of the governing nationalist party, Convergència i Unió (CiU). The CiU had 50 out of 135 deputies in the regional Parliament in 2012 (*Government Plan 2011–2014* [Generalitat de Catalunya, 2011]). Hence, the nationalist government developed a public diplomacy strategy using two main programmes, both depending on the Presidency Department of the regional Catalan Government (Generalitat de Catalunya): On the one hand, the Catalan Public Diplomacy Council (DIPLOCAT), and on the other hand, the Eugeni Xammar Programme of International Communication and Public Relations.

Strategic communication and, more specifically, political public relations play a major role in these new programmes. Catalonia is faced with the challenge of persuading international public opinion that it should become a state in its own right. Spain, however, using arguments based on the Spanish Constitution, is resolutely opposed to Catalonia's right to decide its future and ignores the desire for independence expressed by its people. On 26 March 2014, the Spanish Government thus passed new legislation: the Spanish Law on Foreign Policy Strategy that contravened the actions and aims of Catalonia's foreign policy strategy and opposed some basic principles of the new Catalan Law on External Action and Relations with the EU (CLEARE) that was approved on 26 November 2014.

The aim of this chapter is to analyse the structure and organisation of the Eugeni Xammar Programme of International Communication and Public Relations, as the main project of the Catalan Government, which uses public relations as a basic tool for public diplomacy policies, to gain recognition for its independence on an international scale (Guibernau, 2014; San Eugenio and Xifra, 2015; Xifra and McKie, 2012). In this case study, international public relations emerges as a significant issue in understanding the capacity of stateless nations (such as Catalonia) to favourably influence public opinion. The chapter will also examine which public diplomacy actions different political actors (states, regions) can undertake.

Literature review

The convergence of public diplomacy and public relations

Although the scientific study of public diplomacy emerged in the 1960s, this discipline developed significantly after the fall of the Berlin Wall. According to White and Radic (2014: 460), 'public diplomacy is increasingly multi-directional and has moved from government-to-government propaganda to nation-to-nation communication, dialogue, and relationship building'. However, no single discipline has dominated the study of this phenomenon. As Rasmussen and Merkelsen highlight, 'public diplomacy as a scholarly field is built on the theoretical traditions of international relations and international communication, and for communication scholars the natural host discipline is international public relations' (2012: 810).

Currently, Wang (2006) has organised the existing literature on public diplomacy into four categories. The first group of authors analyse the role of the mass media in public diplomacy (Gilboa, 1998; Kunczik, 1997; Manheim, 1994). Taylor's (2000) research on media relations as a tool for building civil society in Bosnia, and Rice and Somerville's (2013) work on government–press relationships in Northern Ireland's developing democratic institutions inform our study. However, as Wang (2006) states: 'The efficacy of media communication as a primary tool in public diplomacy in certain regions of the world is also called into question' (p. 93).

A second stream of research is an 'exploration of how other disciplines of knowledge may be relevant and useful to public diplomacy' (Wang, 2006: 93). This area explores the convergence of public relations and public diplomacy. Signitzer et al. (1992) argued that, within similar objectives and tactics, 'public relations and public diplomacy are in a natural process of convergence. A process which should be cultivated and not ignored' (p. 146).

L'Etang (2009) also analyses public relations' diplomatic work for states and organisations in a context of globalisation, taking into account its intercultural nature, as well as considering a range of disciplines including public relations, international relations, strategic studies, media studies, peace studies, management studies, cultural studies and anthropology. According to this author 'the integration of public diplomacy concepts with public relations can usefully foreground important issues of power that have been neglected or sidelined in much of the Public Relations literature' (L'Etang, 2009: 609). Moreover, we can consider the relation of this perspective with the 'situational theory' (Grunig, 2011; Grunig et al., 2002), taking into account that:

> the way in which relationships with active publics are framed by both sides [of a conflict] and interpreted in public debates and the media is obviously paramount in the way negotiation (if entered into) proceeds. Merging public relations and public diplomacy perspectives can

> usefully advance our understanding of relational processes in public communication.
>
> (L'Etang, 2009: 611)

Notions of power and globalisation can be considered in the work of Yun and Toth (2009), who conceptualise public diplomacy through sociological globalism, taking into account the role of migrants as public opinion creators. For Yun and Toth, 'a country's soft power resources are nakedly exposed to migrant's living experiences, which make the quality of these resources more substantial in the conduct of public diplomacy. Thus, migration can be either the most conductive or destructive channel of communication' (2009: 500).

The convergence among social disciplines has also been useful for some Catalan scholars in order to develop their research on Spanish and Catalan international communication (San Eugenio and Xifra, 2015; Ordeix and Ginesta, 2014; Xifra and McKie, 2012). In fact, this analysis establishes a new threefold axis when talking about the governance of stateless nations and their international positioning, compared to the Westphalian conception of geopolitics:

> Discourses about public diplomacy, soft power and noopolitik, are discourses about contemporary governance instead of traditional government (diplomacy, hard power and realpolitik). The flows and networks between organisations and their publics provide a more suitable description of a type of governance (as in the Catalan Government's public diplomacy strategy of fostering close relations with its civil society).
>
> (Xifra and McKie, 2012: 823)

A third perspective on public diplomacy research has 'shed light on some of the historical episodes and the inner workings' (Wang, 2006: 93). The analysis of the US public diplomacy institutions and their practices has been a key research object in this area (Dizard, 2004; Haefele, 2001; Malone, 1988; Vaughn, 1980; Creel, 1920). Currently, other studies have highlighted significant episodes outside the US where public diplomacy has become essential for nation branding campaigns. For example, that of Rasmussen and Merkelsen (2012) 'investigates how the role of public relations practice in public diplomacy is undergoing a transformation as a consequence of the influence from nation branding' (p. 810), using a case study of the Danish government's response to the so-called Cartoon Crisis in the autumn of 2005. Another study by White and Radic (2014) explored the message strategies of foreign ministry websites of eight countries that are recent members or candidates to join the European Union. 'For countries vying to enter the European Union, establishing a favourable reputation as a responsible, cooperative, and economically stable nation-state is paramount' (White and Radic, 2014: 461). Other examples include Zhang (2012), who reports on the Chinese government's news conferences from 2001 to 2009; and finally, Ginesta and San Eugenio (2014), who have defined the country branding strategy using sport as a key factor in international communication campaigns in Qatar.

Finally, 'a group of research projects on public diplomacy have recently been conducted by a number of US and British think tanks' (Wang, 2006: 93), such as the Brookings Institution (2004), the Council on Foreign Relations (2003) or the Foreign Policy Centre (2002).

While Wang's (2006) work allows us to follow different research streams when analysing the public diplomacy literature, other authors consider that 'public diplomacy might therefore be seen to contribute to a nation's soft power by generating credibility, fostering values such as the belief in democracy, changing behaviour, and increasing goodwill through activities like broadcasting, cultural diplomacy and exchanges' (Pamment, 2014: 53).

In fact, Pamment (2014: 53) states that 'a number of categorisations of public diplomacy activities emerged'. For example, Leonard et al. (2002) outlined three dimensions of public diplomacy: 'news management', 'strategic communication' and 'relationship building'. According to Pamment (2014) 'short-, medium- and long-term issues are engaged with by using different styles of communication, depending on the problem' (p. 53). Brown (2012) proposed four normative types of public diplomacy according to historical examples: as an 'extension of diplomacy', as an 'instrument of cultural relations', as an 'instrument of conflict' or as a 'tool of nation image construction'. Evans and Steven (2008) and Zaharna (2009) also created their own categorisation of public diplomacy actions. On the one hand, Evans and Steven (2008) consider 'engagement', 'shaping', 'disruptive' and 'destructive' public diplomacy strategies based on a 'nice–nasty continuum'; on the other hand, Zaharna (2009) suggests a spectrum of approaches, ranging from 'informational' to 'relational' actions.

However, the five dimensions of public diplomacy based on Cull's work have been recognised as most accepted categorisations among public diplomacy and public relations researchers. In order to better understand how public diplomacy strategies are designed, Cull (2008) establishes a taxonomy of public diplomacy, dividing its practices into five elements. First, 'listening is an actor's attempt to manage the international environment by collecting and collating data about publics and their opinions overseas and using that data to redirect its policy or its wider public diplomacy approach accordingly' (Cull, 2008: 32). Second, advocacy: 'An actor's attempt to manage the international environment by undertaking an international communication activity to actively promote a particular policy, idea, or that actor's general interests in the minds of a foreign public' (Cull, 2008: 32). Third, cultural diplomacy: 'The attempt to manage the international environment through making its cultural resources and achievements known overseas and/or facilitating cultural transmission abroad' (Cull, 2008: 33). Fourth, exchange diplomacy or willingness 'to manage the international environment by sending its citizens overseas and reciprocally accepting citizens from overseas for a period of study and/or acculturation' (Cull, 2008: 33); and last but not least, international news broadcasting, or the necessity of using mass media or sources based on Information and Communication Technologies (ICTs) in order to engage foreign spectators/viewers.

Public diplomacy in Catalonia as a research topic

There is already an established body of work on Catalan nationalism and the desire of the Catalan people for independence: Perales (2014), Muñoz and Guinjoan (2013), Serrano (2013), Guibernau (2014; 2006; 1999; 1997), and Requejo (2010). However, there is a limited amount of research on Catalonia's public diplomacy in the context of its self-determination agenda.

Few articles have been published on the international relations policies of the Catalan Government. In 2012, Xifra and McKie explored 'ways to advance public relations approaches to nation building by drawing insights from stateless nations and by deploying two sets of theories uncommon in the field: the information society and noopolitik' (Xifra and McKie, 2012, p. 819). This research used a case study based on Catalan Government foreign projects. Following a more legal point of view, Canals et al. (2014) analysed how the Catalan Parliament defined what public diplomacy is in Catalonia, and which actors would undertake it, based on the draft of the Catalan Law on External Action and Relations with the EU (CLEARE)

The grassroots structure of the nationalist movement have also been analysed. Ordeix and Ginesta (2014) analysed how the organisations that defend the self-determination process – close to one hundred – have created a network of interests to help the regional nationalist government to legitimise the popular 'consultation' held on 9 November 2014 by the Catalan people, in the same year as the Scottish independence referendum. As Ordeix and Ginesta (2014) highlight, 'most of the international media that reports on Catalonia have their newsrooms in Madrid. So, their perception of Catalan complexity is shaped by Madrid's cosmovision' (p. 935). Hence, Cull's (2008) taxonomy of public diplomacy can be clearly applied in this study, because international news broadcasting, or the need to use mass media or sources based on ICTs in order to engage a foreign audience, is essential for the Catalan independence strategy. Therefore, use of government–media relations is a basic tool for encouraging the foreign press to report on a country or a region according to the government's political interests. Government–media relations is fundamental to the nation building process (Taylor and Kent, 2006).

Finally, there is the practice of place branding – a strategy of internationally projecting a territory's image and reputation (San Eugenio, 2012). San Eugenio and Xifra (2015) analysed in depth the Catalonian foreign policy strategy (Miralles and Cotxà, 2010) as a starting point for the international promotion of Catalan culture, as well as the basic political documents to structure the creation of the Catalonia brand. In fact, the process of Catalonia's brand building strengthens the public relations focus of Catalan public diplomacy, especially because of the Regional Government's need to establish bridging relations with foreign publics. In this case, we can identify a relationship between place branding perspectives and the executive public relations (Grunig, 2011) in place brand building processes.

Methodology

This research will follow a case study methodology. We can understand a case study as an 'empirical investigation of a contemporary phenomenon, taking [into account] its context, especially when the boundaries between phenomenon and context are not evident' (Yin, 1994: 13). To develop this case study we use an analysis of relevant documents that are representative of the Catalan foreign public diplomacy projects: the *Foreign Policy Strategy 2010–2015* (Miralles and Cotxà, 2010), the *Government Plan 2011–2014* and, finally, the Catalan Law on External Action and Relations with the EU (CLEARE), which was passed in the Catalan Parliament in November 2014. This document has been taken to the Spanish Constitutional Court by the Spanish Government, as it considers that the Parliament of Catalonia is exceeding its authority. A debate on which institution is responsible for regional international representation (the state or the Regional Government) is the core of this conflict.

In addition we conducted four in-depth interviews with relevant sources. To gather personal evidence from executives who were in charge of the Catalan Government communication project we interviewed the Communication Secretary of the Government, Josep Martí Blanch, as well as the former and the current directors of the Eugeni Xammar Programme, Martí Estruch and Jaume Clotet. To contrast this information with the Spanish Government's point of view, we also interviewed Juan Milián, who was the foreign affairs representative of the conservative Popular Party in the Catalan Parliament at the time when the CLEARE was voted. Although Mr Milián is an MP of the Catalan Parliament, he is a member of the Popular Party, which at the time of writing is the ruling party in Spain with an absolute majority. Inside the organisation, he is responsible for the research and political programmes of the Popular Party in Catalonia and he reports on his work to the headquarters of the party in Madrid.

Finally, we attended the conference given by the Permanent Representative of the Generalitat de Catalunya in Brussels, Amadeu Altafaj, in Barcelona on 29 April 2015. The point of view of Mr Altafaj is very interesting, because he represents the Catalan Government to the EU institutions, as well as being the former spokesperson for Olli Rehn, the European Commissioner of Economic and Monetary Affairs (2009–2014).

Case study: the Eugeni Xammar Programme of International Communication and Public Relations of the Catalan Government

According to Ibáñez (2011) Catalonia can be considered an international actor:

> An individual, group, organisation, political or economic body etc. is an international actor according to the extent to which it is able to deploy its

> power to transcend state boundaries, that is, the extent to which it is able to actively participate in international relations.

In this sense, Catalonia may be considered a sub-state political entity with the capacity to exercise foreign policy actions through a public diplomacy strategy which is essentially cultural in nature.

The foreign action strategy deployed by Catalonia since 2010 is currently represented by sixty-five institutional offices: this includes five representative offices (in Belgium, the USA, Germany, France and the UK), thirty-four ACC10 offices (an agency supporting innovation and internationalisation for Catalan companies), ten branches of the Catalan Tourism Agency (ACT), five Catalan Institute of Cultural Businesses offices (ICEC), four Ramon Llull Institute (IRL) branches and, finally, four branches of the Catalan Agency for Development Cooperation in some thirty-one countries and forty cities around the world. All Catalan foreign activities are channelled via the Ministry of the Presidency of the Generalitat and, at a lower level, via the newly created Department of Foreign Affairs and the European Union.

These foreign action structures form part of a working plan within which strategic communication and, more specifically, political public relations play a fundamental role. In fact, Catalonia is faced with the challenge of convincing the international community of why it should become a state in its own right. Spain, however, using arguments based on the Spanish Constitution, is resolutely opposed to Catalonia's right to decide on its future and the desire for independence expressed by its people. Actually, the Spanish Law on Foreign Policy Strategy passed in March 2014 contravenes some of the actions and aims of Catalonia's foreign policy strategy, that in November 2014 was established with the approval of the CLEARE (Canals et al., 2014). The Popular Party's conservative deputy, Juan Milián, emphasises that 'The CLEARE represents Catalonia as a state in the international landscape. It is a very ambitious law taking into account the independence point of view, but it does not follow the Spanish constitutional doctrine' (J. Milián, 2015, personal communication).

Before the approval of the CLEARE, the *Foreign Policy Strategy 2010–2015* promoted by the government of Catalonia became the first internal strategy specifically designed to develop a public diplomacy strategy in an overt, orderly and systematic manner. But, what is the main objective of this plan? It seeks to make Catalonia a global actor, at once responsible, effective, influential and prestigious, orientate its foreign action along the lines of those values which best defend its interests, and promote progress and welfare in Catalan society within the framework of building a more just and supportive global order. Therefore, since 2010, the Catalan Government has activated an international relations policy with a clearly nationalist profile, with a focus on strategic communication in order to favourably influence public opinion.

On the one hand, the Catalonian Public Diplomacy Council (DIPLOCAT) has six fundamental objectives: to support the public diplomacy strategy of the Catalan Government; to promote international recognition of the Catalonia brand; to foster international understanding of Catalonia and its unique values; to encourage links between Catalonia and international organisations; to stimulate the participation of Catalan civil society in public diplomacy activities; and, finally, to promote training in public diplomacy with the aim of raising awareness and increasing the capacity of Catalan society to articulate its interests internationally.

On the other hand, the Eugeni Xammar Programme of International Communication and Public Relations aims to directly influence international public opinion (not just opinion as it appears in the press) without this undergoing a prior process of information and opinion filtering by the Spanish Government. Actually, even the name of the programme, Eugeni Xammar, is not neutral. Eugeni Xammar Puigventós (1888–1973) was a Catalan international correspondent during the 1920s and 1930s. After the Spanish Civil War (1936–1939) he was the representative of the Catalan Government in exile in Paris.

As the Regional Government defines it, the aim of this programme is to promote the creation of a permanent channel of communication with the international media and journalists worldwide and to strengthen 'bridging relations' (Grunig, 2011; Grunig et al., 2002) between the Regional Government and international opinion leaders. Actually, the Communication Secretary of the Catalan Government, Josep M. Martí, states that if Catalonia wants to follow a self-determination process, 'the Catalan Government has to *fight* in a seduction *battle* in the international media landscape' in order to establish a frame where Catalans' wish for independence can be understood as a 'radical democratic process' (J. M. Martí, 2012, personal communication).

Actually, before the approval of this programme by the Catalan Government (25 July 2012), the Generalitat was facing an international challenge to explain to the world why the region had to be better funded by the Spanish Government. As Josep M. Martí points out, this was the first message that the Generalitat tried to strengthen within the mainstream international media. In fact, this policy complemented the grassroots media spin-doctoring activity conducted by some independence-oriented civil society organisations, above all the Emma Collective (J. M. Martí, 2012, personal communication), which started in 2009 and:

> is a network of Catalans and non-Catalans living in different countries who have made it their job to track and review news reports about Catalonia in the international media. Our goal is to ensure that the world's public opinion gets a fair picture of the country's reality today and in history.
>
> (Emma Collective, 2015)

The results of these actions are commented on by Ordeix and Ginesta (2014) in research that analyses the messages published in the mainstream US media regarding the Catalan self-determination process:

> While *Time Magazine* usually reports from Catalonia using pro-independence opinion leaders (i.e. professor Montserrat Guibernau, University of London; professor Ferran Requejo, Pompeu Fabra University) and the *New York Times* also understands the process of self-determination in Catalonia according to the challenges its society has to face in the future, the *Wall Street Journal* presents Catalan vindication as a regional conflict in a dark Spain.
>
> (p. 935)

Initially the Catalan Government promoted a frame for the media and the world based only on economic arguments – the Catalan economics minister is the Harvard chair Andreu Mas-Colell – the development of Eugeni Xammar programme has established other frames: the scientific competitiveness of the region and the tourist attraction of Catalonia, with the city of Barcelona constituting the main Catalan place brand. This is to say that, currently, the Generalitat wants to avoid associating the Catalan wish for independence with a unique argument based on economic reasons, as was presented by the *Wall Street Journal* (28 October 2012): 'Catalonia, beaten down by years of recession, has become the battleground in what threatens to become an economic civil war' (Ordeix and Ginesta, 2014: 935).

As Josep M. Martí states: 'Our action must focus the attention on London, the economic capital of Europe; Brussels, where the EU institutions are located; Berlin, where the real political power in Europe is, and Washington' (2012, personal communication). For this reason, the Eugeni Xammar programme has designed different actions to position these messages worldwide; on the one hand, to use the Catalan representative offices abroad as information hotspots – above all the office in Brussels which is directed by Amadeu Altafaj, the former spokesman of Economic and Monetary Commissioner Olli Rehn (J. Clotet, 2015, personal communication); on the other hand, to appeal to local journalists abroad or to organise media tours with Catalan journalists in order to celebrate debates in different international capitals.

The success of these actions can be considered when we take into account the significance that the international media give to Catalan arguments for independence. Some official data can enable us to shed light on the political significance of this programme. According to the Generalitat de Catalunya, 240 newspapers, radio stations and television channels reported the symbolic referendum of 9 November, 2014; 50 per cent of those were international outlets. Furthermore, 150 journalists covered the independence demonstration on 11 September 2015, and more than 200 covered the following regional elections on 27 September 2015, when the independence parties won 72 out of 135 seats in the regional parliament (J. Clotet, 2015, personal communication). Furthermore, since 2011 the Catalan president, Artur Mas, has been interviewed on eighty occasions by the international media; the Minister of the Presidency, Francesc Homs, was interviewed eleven times; the Minister of Economics Andreu Mas-Colell, ten times; the Foreign Secretary Roger Albinyana, thirty-six times; and finally, the Director of DIPLOCAT, Albert Royo, on twenty-two occasions (J. Clotet, 2015, personal communication).

Additionally, this media 'spin-doctoring' policy is shared with DIPLOCAT, which organises international media tours in Catalonia for European journalists. These tours visit Catalan institutions and seek to create debate with different grassroots opinion leaders. Thanks to this policy, since 2010 more than fifty journalists from nineteen countries have visited Catalonia and have interviewed political and social actors who take part in the Catalan decision-making process (J. Clotet, 2015, personal communication). Moreover, a significant novelty provided by the programme is the beginning of a regular institutional communication policy based on translating the Government's press releases into English and German. Actually, the production of media content in foreign languages is not new. In late August 2010, an English-language website of the Catalan News Agency (CNA) was launched. The CNA is a public corporation owned by the Catalan public administration. It was one of the first digital news agencies in Europe in 1999 and has correspondents in London, Paris and Brussels.

Analysis and discussion

Strategic communication and political public relations are fundamental to the process of state building in Catalonia. As Ordeix and Ginesta (2014) explain, it is very important that the international community offer its support to Catalonia in order for it to become a new European state. In fact, finding this support is a basic mission of Amadeu Altafaj, as a Permanent Representative of the Generalitat at the EU in Brussels: 'Catalan vindications have to be part of the European agenda, they have to be in the decision makers' minds. Actually, they know that Catalan self-determination process is not a soufflé' (A. Altafaj, 2015, personal communication). Even the person responsible for foreign affairs of the Popular Party in the Catalan Parliament, Juan Milián, considers that finding international support is essential for those who want Catalan independence: 'Developing a foreign [policy] … to engage international actors with the Catalan self-determination process is logical for those who want independence. Catalan independence will not occur only through an institutional statement in the Catalan Parliament' (J. Milián, 2015, personal communication).

Hence, 'advocacy' (Cull, 2008) is a basic mission of Catalan foreign policy, as well as the 'cultural diplomacy' strategy led by the international offices of the Ramon Llull Institute. According to Bargalló (2011), cultural diplomacy may be understood as the joint articulation of educational, economic, commercial, financial, cultural and foreign policy, coupled and projected with clear intentions for commercial expansion and increased political influence. As Bargalló (2011) says:

> Catalan culture has the following aptitudes: a) The quantitative and qualitative excellence and relevance of Catalan creators. Good examples of this are Miró, Sert and Dalí in art; Gaudí, Miralles and Calatrava in architecture; Casals in music; Carreras and Caballé in opera; Llull in medieval literature, Rodoreda and Monzó in modern fiction; Adrià and Roca in gastronomy, and Barcelona Football Club and Gasol in sport; b) The relevance of Barcelona as an international capital of culture; and c) The importance of the culture industry itself, particularly in relation to publishing and audiovisual production, as well as music and contemporary art events.

But, these actors and assets will never have enough value if we do not consider the Eugeni Xammar programme as a basic 'tool of nation image construction' (Brown, 2012). This programme represents a 'mediatic accompaniment for those international media corporations that want to understand the situation in Catalonia' (J. M. Martí, 2012, personal communication).

Taking into account Cull's public diplomacy taxonomy, the Regional Government has developed an active policy in 'international news broadcasting' as a 'necessary complement of the foreign political action' (J. M. Martí, 2012, personal communication). Currently, postmodern diplomacy assumes that 'having no hostility [from international organisations and other states] to our vindication' is the basic outcome of our foreign actions (J. M. Martí, 2012, personal communication). Altafaj highlights that, faced with a political crisis, EU decision makers have taken many 'impossible decisions and unthinkable policies'; hence, the EU is based on 'pragmatism, negotiation and legal adaptability' (2015, personal communication).

However, the conservative Popular Party (PP), the ruling party in Spain since 2011, has another vision of this programme. 'It is not a strategy in order to benefit economically either the region or the whole of Spain; it is a programme to produce media impacts internationally in order to glorify them within Catalonia as a success for the independentists' (J. Milián, 2015, personal communication). For this reason, the PP assumes that Catalan foreign actions are not totally aligned with Spanish foreign policy:

> We allow the regional government to do public diplomacy in order to improve its economy or to promote Catalan culture abroad, such as those activities of the Ramon Llull Institute; but some of their basic *paradiplomatic* structures [DIPLOCAT and Eugeni Xammar programme] have been created to internationalise the self-determination process.
>
> (J. Milián, 2015, personal communication)

All in all, we must consider the role of international public relations to build 'relationships with publics that it affects or is affected by' (Grunig, 2011: 16). The significance of the Eugeni Xammar programme in leading media relations in Catalan foreign policy moves is twofold. On the one hand, it contributes to do an 'environmental scanning' of publics; this is to say, 'that they do research and talk to community leaders, leaders of activist groups, or government officials to find out who the publics are and what problems these publics are experiencing' (Grunig, 2011: 16); on the other hand, this programme is basic to a 'scenario building' context, as Grunig (2011: 16) defines it: 'The public relations executive, therefore, needs tools that can be used to show other managers what publics might emerge, what problems they are concerned about, what issues they might create, and what crisis might develop if different decisions are made.' Although Grunig (2011) analyses public relations in a context of 'strategic management', international public relations principles can also be based on this bridging strategy between the organisation and its publics.

The action of state building in Catalonia needs, at the same time, a strategy of place branding to promote the Catalan image. In this sense, the creation and promotion of Catalonia's nation brand is an unresolved critical aspect. For this reason, this is another objective of the Eugeni Xammar programme, as Josep M. Martí recognises: 'In the following years, the brand creation process will be very significant, next to the political discourse. We must follow transversal campaigns, not only based in destination branding or investment attractions, but also in promoting the Catalan values' (2012, personal communication).

However, there is general agreement among our interviewees that, at present, the Catalonia brand does not exist. Catalonia does not have its own brand linked to attributes of identity that offer uniqueness and differentiation. It has not yet created the opportunity to show the world the particular and unique values it has to offer. This outcome is explained by the historical preponderance accumulated by the Barcelona brand since the Olympic Games in 1992, and the international recognition of the FC Barcelona brand after 2003 and the victory of Joan Laporta in the elections for the club's presidency (Ginesta and San Eugenio, 2014). In fact, the duality of Barcelona versus Catalonia has historically been interpreted as a confrontation. As Castells (2011) states, in the world we live in, brands are more important than countries, due to their extraordinary capacity for representation. In this respect, Catalonia still has far to go.

Place branding affects cultural, economic and social aspects of a territory, but place brand creation is, above all, a political matter. For this reason, public diplomacy and place branding are closely interconnected research fields. Although the Catalan Government has been very active in communicating its case for self-determination, not all Catalan political parties support its international communication policy (Canals et al., 2014). As we explained before, the CLEARE has been taken to the Spanish Constitutional Court because the PP, which rules with absolute majority in Spain, considers that Catalonia as a region has no competences in diplomatic affairs and sees Catalonia as seeking to be 'an independent international actor outside the Spanish State' (*El Punt Avui*, 2015). The PP's deputy leader Juan Milián claims that the Catalan Government legislates in international affairs because 'it wants to keep the network of organisations that promote the internationalisation of this conflict, but we want to establish synergies with the Spanish State and its Ministry of Foreign Affairs' (J. Milián, 2015, personal communication). In other words the PP understands that Catalan civil society should be allowed to undertake economic and cultural diplomatic actions if these are aligned with a general strategy to promote the Spanish brand. 'Spain's brand is very valuable internationally, as well as the Barcelona brand, which is considered a Spanish city worldwide. I don't know if we have to spend resources to promote the Catalonia brand when the Barcelona brand has significant positive values for all the region: a European, Mediterranean and open-minded capital' (J. Milián, 2015, personal communication).

Conclusions

The weakening of the nation states and the growing significance of the role exerted by public opinion, and by extension civil society, in matters of the state has led to an evolution in international relations management. Rather than the traditional state diplomacy, with only government involvement, we are moving towards public diplomacy in the case of stateless nations. The example of Catalonia, presented in this article, can be significant in analysing the basic debates that political organisations are facing in order to promote the international communication of this Spanish region (Autonomous Community).

In the context described in this case study, Catalonia seems especially relevant for public relations scholars interested in nation building and nation branding. In 2010, for the first time in its history, the Catalan Government launched a specific public diplomacy strategy, effectively transformed into a cultural diplomacy proposal, and conveyed through the *Foreign Policy Strategy 2010–2015*. In 2014, the Catalan Parliament passed the Catalan Law on External Action and Relations with the EU, the CLEARE (Canals et al., 2014). Therefore, for the first time in its history, Catalonia has a law to regulate its international communication and its public diplomacy efforts. Catalonia, currently an autonomous region of Spain, has an ancient history, a clear international focus and a self-government tradition that goes back thirty years. Among its assets, it has tourist areas of global importance (above all, the tourist attraction of Barcelona, its capital), a culture that the Catalan Government uses to spearhead its international projection (language, literature, modernism, etc.) and a set of promoters who serve as worldwide ambassadors for Catalonia in various fields, for example gastronomy (Ferran Adrià, Joan Roca and Carme Ruscalleda) or sports (FC Barcelona, Pau Gasol or Marc Márquez).

These examples provide evidence of a new world order and a new administrative division of territory, which does not recognise natural obstacles or classic administrative divisions (borders), but rather is committed to empowering the mental borders of territories with the capacity to establish their own values and/or attributes in the imagination of the international community for the purposes of attracting tourists, business and talent, among other possibilities.

The Eugeni Xammar programme provides a useful case study in public relations in order to understand that, for stateless nations, public diplomacy is fundamental activity to ensure that the region has a role in postmodern geopolitics. According to Cull's (2008) taxonomy of public diplomacy, 'international news broadcasting' is the core of this programme established in 2012 by the nationalist Catalan Government. Media spin-doctoring (Ordeix and Ginesta, 2014) is essential, not only at a grassroots level (e.g. the Emma Collective), but also at a government level as a key strategy to avoid 'hostility' to the self-determination process of Catalonia (J. M. Martí, 2012, personal communication). This is to say, international news broadcasting is important in a bridging strategy (Grunig, 2011) in international public relations, to help foreign publics (in this case, the international media) understand Catalan's wish for independent statehood.

References

Bargalló, J. (2011) 'La diplomàcia cultural: creativitat, indústria i identitat (quatre anys pel món)'. Blog. Available at: https://josepbargallo.wordpress.com/2011/06/10/la-diplomacia-cultural-creativitat-industria-i-identitat/ (accessed: 1 June 2015).

Brookings Institution (2004) *The need to communicate: How to improve US public diplomacy with the Islamic world*. Washington, DC: Saban Center for Middle East Policy at the Brookings Institution.

Brown, R. (2012) *The four paradigms of public diplomacy: Building a framework for comparative government external communication research*. San Diego, CA: International Studies Association Convention.

Canals, M., Ginesta, X. and San Eugenio, J. (2014) 'Organizing public diplomacy in Catalonia: The case of Catalan Foreign Affairs Law', paper presented to IABD 2014 Conference, San Diego, CA: 10–12 April.

Castells, M. (2011) 'A network theory of power', *International Journal of Communication*, 5: 773–787.

Conversi, D. (2000) *The Basques, the Catalans and Spain: Alternative routes to nationalist mobilizations*. Reno: University of Nevada Press.

Council on Foreign Relations (2003) *Finding America's voice: A strategy for reinvigorating US public diplomacy*. New York: Council on Foreign Relations.

Creel, G. (1920) *How we advertised America*. New York: Harper & Brothers.

Cull, N. J. (2008) 'Public diplomacy: taxonomies and histories', *Annals of the American Academy of Political and Social Sciences*, 616: 31–54.

Curtice, J. (2006) 'A stronger or weaker Union? Public reactions to asymmetric devolution in the United Kingdom', *Publius, the Journal of Federalism*, 36: 95–113.

Dizard, W. P. (2004) *Inventing public diplomacy: The story of the US Information Agency*. Boulder, CO: Lynne Rienner.

El Punt Avui (2015) 'El Parlament demana al Constitucional que aixe qui el vet a la lleid' acció exterior'. Available at: www.elpuntavui.cat/ma/article/3-politica/17-politica/

855831-el-parlament-demana-al-constitucional-que-aixequi-el-vet-a-la-llei-daccio-exterior.html?cca=1 (accessed: 29 April 2016).

Emma Collective (2015) 'Who we are'. Available at: www.collectiuemma.cat/who-we-are (accessed: 17 August 2015).

Evans, A. and Steven, D. (2008) 'Towards a theory of influence for twenty-first century foreign policy: Public diplomacy in a globalised world', in Welsh, J. and Fearn, D. (eds) *Engagement: public diplomacy in a globalised world.* London: Foreign and Commonwealth Office, pp. 44–61.

Foreign Policy Centre (2002) *Public diplomacy.* London: The Foreign Policy Centre.

Gafarot, M. (2011) *La mort de Bèlgica: La gradual emancipació de Flandes.* Barcelona: Dèria Editors.

Generalitat de Catalunya. (2011) *Pla de Govern 2011–2014* [Government Plan 2011–2014]. Barcelona: Generalitat de Catalunya.

Gilboa, E. (1998) 'Media diplomacy: Conceptual divergence and applications', *Harvard Journal for Press/Politics*, 3(3): 56–75.

Ginesta, X. and San Eugenio J. (2014) 'The use of football as a country branding strategy. Case study: Qatar and the Catalan sports press', *Communication and Sport*, 2(3): 225–241.

Grunig, J. E. (2011) 'Public relations and strategic management: Institutionalizing organization-public relations in contemporary society', *Central European Journal of Communication*, 1: 11–31.

Grunig, J. E., Grunig, L. and Dozier, D. M. (2002) *Excellent public relations and effective organizations.* Mahwah, NJ: Lawrence Erlbaum Associates.

Guibernau, M. (1997) 'Images of Catalonia', *Nations and Nationalism*, 3(1): 89–111.

Guibernau, M. (1999) *Nations without states.* Cambridge: Polity Press.

Guibernau, M. (2006) 'National identity, devolution and secession in Canada, Britain and Spain', *Nations and Nationalism*, 12(1): 51–76.

Guibernau, M. (2014) 'Prospects for an independent Catalonia', *International Journal of Politics, Culture and Society*, 27(1): 5–23.

Haefele, M. (2001) 'John F. Kennedy, USIA, and world public opinion', *Diplomatic History*, 25(1): 63–84.

Horowitz, D. (1985) *Ethnic groups in conflict.* Berkeley: University of California Press.

Ibáñez, J. (2011) 'Actores, autoridades y sujetos: el pluralismo de la política mundial y su incidencia sobre el ordenamiento jurídico internacional', in Rodrigo, A. J. and Garcia, C. (eds) *Unidad y pluralismo en el derecho internacional público y en la comunidad internacional.* Madrid: Tecnos, pp. 107–128.

Keating, M. (1997) 'Stateless nation-building: Quebec, Catalonia and Scotland in the changing state system', *Nations and Nationalism*, 3(4): 689–717.

Kunczik, M. (1997) *Images of nations and international public relations.* Mahwah, NJ: Lawrence Erlbaum Associates.

Leonard, M., Stead, C. and Smewing, C. (2002) *Public diplomacy.* London: The Foreign Policy Centre.

L'Etang, J. (2009) 'Public relations and diplomacy in a globalized world: Qn issue of public communication', *American Behavioral Scientist*, 53(4): 607–626.

Malone, G. D. (1988) *Political advocacy and cultural communication: Organizing the nation's public diplomacy.* Lanham, MD: University Press of America.

Manheim, J. B. (1994) *Strategic public diplomacy and American foreign policy: The evolution of influence.* New York: Oxford University Press.

Miralles, D. and Cotxà, J. (eds) (2010) *Pla de l'acció exterior del Govern de Catalunya 2010–2015* [*Foreign Policy Strategy 2010–2015*]. Barcelona: Generalitat de Catalunya.

Muñoz, J. and Guinjoan, M. (2013) 'Accounting for internal variation in the nationalist mobilization: Unofficial referendums for independence in Catalonia (2009–2011)', *Nations and Nationalism*, 19(1): 44–67.

Nieto, M. (2013) 'Qué es marca España?' Available at: http://elpais.com/especiales/2013/espana-en-positivo/que-es-marca-espana.html (accessed: 29 May 2015).

Ordeix, E. and Ginesta, X. (2014) 'Political engagement principles as basis for new regional self-determination process in Europe: The case of Catalonia', *American Behavioral Scientist*, 58(7): 928–940.

Pamment, J. (2014) 'Articulating influence: Towards a research agenda for interpreting the evolution of soft power, public diplomacy and nation brands', *Public Relations Review*, 40: 50–59.

Perales, C. (2014) *Premsa i autodeterminació: Catalunya i Euskadi dins l'Espanya de la transició*. Barcelona: Editorial UOC.

Public Diplomacy Council of Catalonia (DIPLOCAT) (2014) 'Mission and objectives'. Available at: www.diplocat.cat/en/about-us/mission-and-objectives (accessed: 11 February 2014).

Rasmussen, R. K. and Merkelsen, H. (2012) 'The new PR of states: How nation branding practices affect the security function of public diplomacy', *Public Relations Review*, 38: 810–818.

Redacció [Editorial] (2015) *La llei d'exteriors i dues delegacions, davant la justícia*. Available at: www.elpuntavui.cat/noticia/article/3-politica/17-politica/829751-la-llei-dexteriors-i-dues-delegacions-davant-la-justicia.html (accessed: 3 May 2015).

Requejo, F. (2010) 'Revealing the dark side of traditional democracies in plurinational societies: The case of Catalonia and the Spanish Estado de las Autonomías', *Nations and Nationalism*, 16(1): 148–168.

Rice, C. and Somerville, I. (2013) 'Power sharing and political public relations: Government–press relationships in Northern Ireland's developing democratic institutions', *Public Relations Review*, 39(4): 293–302.

Ridao, J. (2012) *Podem ser independents? Els nous estats del segle XXI*. Barcelona: RBA.

San Eugenio, J. (2012) *Teoría y métodos para marcas de territorio*. Barcelona: UOC.

San Eugenio, J. and Xifra, J. (2015) 'International representation strategies for stateless nations: The case of Catalonia's cultural diplomacy', *Place Branding and Public Diplomacy*, 11(1): 83–96.

Serrano, I. (2013) 'Just a matter of identity? Support for independence in Catalonia', *Regional and Federal Studies*, 23(5). Available at: http://dx.doi.org/10.1080/13597566.2013.775945 (accessed: 26 April 2013).

Signitzer, Benno H. and Coombs, T. (1992) 'Public relations and public diplomacy: Conceptual convergences', *Public Relations Review*, 18(2): 137–147.

Taylor, M. (2000) 'Media relations in Bosnia: A role for public relations in building civil society', *Public Relations Review*, 26: 1–14.

Taylor, M. and Kent, M. L. (2006) 'Public relations theory and practice in nation building', in Botan, C. H. and Hazleton, V. (eds) *Public relations theory II*. Mahwah, NJ: Lawrence Erlbaum Associates, pp. 341–359.

Vaughn, S. (1980) *Holding fast the inner lines: Democracy, nationalsm and the Committee on Public Information*. Chapel Hill: University of North Carolina Press.

Wang, J. (2006) 'Managing national reputation and international relations in the global era: Public diplomacy revisited', *Public Relations Review*, 32: 91–96.

White, C. and Radic, D. (2014) 'Comparative public diplomacy: Message strategies of countries in transition', *Public Relations Review*, 40: 459–465.

Xifra, J. and McKie, D. (2012) 'From realpolitik to noopolitik: The public relations of (stateless) nations in an information age', *Public Relations Review*, 38(5): 819–824.

Yin, R. K. (1994) *Case study research: design and methods.* London: Sage.

Yun, S.-H. and Toth, E. L. (2009) 'Future sociological public diplomacy and the role of public relations: Evolution of public diplomacy', *American Behavioral Scientist*, 53(4): 493–503.

Zaharna, R. S. (2009) 'Mapping out a spectrum of public diplomacy initiatives: information and relational communication frameworks', in Snow, N. and Taylor, P. M. (eds) *Routledge handbook of public diplomacy.* London and New York: Routledge, pp. 86–100.

Zhang, D. (2012) 'A relational perspective on media relations strategies: The Chinese government's news conferences from 2001 to 2009', *Public Relations Review*, 38: 684–696.

8 Government communication in Mozambique

The open presidencies of Armando Guebuza as a public relations strategy to strengthen national identity

Stélia Neta J. Mboene and Gisela Gonçalves

Introduction

After more than four centuries of Portuguese rule, Mozambique gained independence in 1975. Upon independence, its leaders adopted a single-party socialist system and the country became a very close ally of the Soviet Union. Shortly afterwards, in the early 1980s, a bloody sixteen-year civil war broke out between the Mozambique Liberation Front (FRELIMO) and the Mozambican National Resistance (RENAMO). The conflict resulted in the massive destruction of infrastructure and the deaths of thousands of Mozambicans (Mazula, 2002a; 2002b; Alden, 2001). After the collapse of socialist regimes around the world at the end of the Cold War the Mozambican state adopted a democratic system, with elections in 1994, 1999, 2004, 2009 and 2014.

The Mozambican government was led by Armando Emílio Guebuza (of FRELIMO) from 2005 to 2014.[1] From the very beginning, he began a cycle of closer relationships with the citizens using a strategy which became known as 'Presidências Abertas e Inclusivas' or PAIs (open and inclusive presidencies), whereby the President would temporarily leave the Ponta Vermelha, the official presidential residence in Maputo, to live in simple, humble places throughout the Mozambican territory.

The open presidencies governing style had already been used in Mozambique in previous years. After the 'Lusaka Accord' signed by FRELIMO and Portugal on 7 September 1974, which recognized independence and the FRELIMO guerrilla movement as the sole representative of the Mozambican people, Samora Michel (the socialist-inspired revolutionary leader who led Mozambique's war of independence and became the first president, from 1975 to 1986) set out on a trip that became known as the 'triumphal journey'. He started in the north, in Rovuma (on the border with Tanzania), and ended in Maputo, in the south, with the national independence ceremonies at Machava Stadium on 25 June 1975. On this long journey through the country, filled with considerable patriotic symbolism, President Michel engaged in direct contact with his people. He was therefore able to introduce the figure of the President and also, particularly in the context of the country's recent independence, transmit messages of hope for building a single nation founded on peace. As this chapter will show, Armando Emílio Guebuza used the PAIs in a similar way to introduce the figure of the Head of State but also to unite the people under the same ideals of national identity.

Media played a role in Guebuza's national identity efforts in both the production and dissemination of information (Wolton, 1995). Government news management, as an attempt to control the media agenda and public opinion regarding political issues, is common in democratic states (Pfetsch, 1999). Boorstin's idea (1961) that media presence is fundamentally supported by 'pseudo-events' is particularly true of Armando Guebuza's PAIs strategy of high visibility political communication with national and regional media coverage. Management of this strategy includes producing messages that focus on the government's political objectives, a political emphasis on the figure of the President, a dramatization of events, and control over media coverage, particularly through the group of official journalists who travel within the President's entourage.

The President's public speeches, which form the communication action that has the greatest visibility and media repercussion in the scope of the PAIs, constitute an important element of the President's public relations strategy. In this chapter, we seek to analyse the President's speeches from several perspectives with a common objective: to ascertain to what extent public relations can influence the attribution of meaning to the concepts of national identity and unity (Deutsch, 1966a; Emerson, 1966). This is an added challenge within Mozambique's reality since it is a 'deeply divided society' (Guelke, 2012) at socio-economic, cultural and linguistic levels.

Government communication in Mozambique

Overview of the political and media systems

The fifteen years after national independence (1975–1990) were marked by control of the press by the Mozambique Liberation Front's (FRELIMO) single-party regime. State orchestration of the media and censorship served as the mechanisms for protecting the system itself. Interference with and pressure on the press restricted journalists' freedom of expression. This essentially made the media spokespeople for the government bodies and reproducers of political declarations and positions (Magaia, 1994: 137–138). The media were nationalized and the Ministry of Information had control over the management of all written, radio and television media content.

After independence, and thanks to the broadening political arena in Mozambique, an atmosphere developed that was more favourable to the development of free media. Different information organizations emerged, although they were limited in their actions by the notable inequalities in national coverage and were restricted by high levels of illiteracy and poverty in the country. Most of Mozambique's population lives in rural areas, and has never bought or read newspapers. Radio is the only form of media that reaches a significant proportion of the population. The national radio station, Rádio Moçambique, has services in several national languages. There has also been an increasing number of community radio stations that are entirely directed towards serving the rural population.

The creation of the Press Law in 1991 and the passage of the Freedom of Information Law in 2014 are recent advances that support free media. However, the existence of these laws does not mean that there have not been complaints by journalists about government interference in the media (Chichava and Pohlmann, 2010: 132–133). Libel and defamation cases against media are common and can lead to fines, prison terms of up to two years or suspension of the media outlet in question. This in part explains how Mozambique scored 44 on the Press Freedom rating (0 = best; 100 = worst) according to the 2015 Freedom House index.[2]

There are currently seven free-to-air television stations: two are public and nine are private. In the radio sector, Rádio Moçambique is the only public station with national coverage. There are several private radio stations that are mostly based in Maputo and have rather small coverage areas. As far as the press is concerned, there are three daily national newspapers: *Notícias, O País* and *Diário de Moçambique* (published outside the capital, in the city of Beira). Weekly publications include *Zambeze*; *Magazine Independente*; *Canal de Moçambique*; *Savana*; *Domingo*; *Público*; *Sol do Índico*; and *A Verdade*.

The enthusiastic turnout in the first elections in 1994 (87.87 per cent) has been replaced by indifference and apathy in recent years. Official statistics from the Technical Secretariat for Electoral Administration (STAE – Secretariado Técnico de Administração Eleitoral) show that abstention from voting increased from 12.6 per cent in the first multi-party elections in Mozambique in 1994 to around 52 per cent in the 2014 general elections (Conselho Constitucional, 2014; CNE, 2015). Voter apathy is taking place in a country where the political system involves polarization featuring two main parties, RENAMO and FRELIMO; the latter has determined the country's destiny since independence in 1975. The political scene is marked by the dominance of FRELIMO, the leadership of which was built during the fight for freedom and the civil war (Pereira and Nhanale, 2014: 7). The dominance of FRELIMO is also explained by the use of communication campaigns developed by its government, above all with the election of Guebuza in 2004, using a notably nationalist political discourse (Brito, 2008: 8). Nationalist political discourse sought to strengthen the bonds of unity among Mozambicans and address the political divide between the two main political forces. This divide is felt above all in areas of the country where each party has the most influence: FRELIMO in the south and northern tip of the country and RENAMO in the central area and part of the north).

In fact, as Macuane (2009: 175) points out, the democratic regime that was established in 1994 following the General Peace Agreement transferred the bipolar rationale of the armed conflict between FRELIMO and RENAMO to the political institutions. On one side there is FRELIMO, a social democratic, centre-left party that arose from the union of three Mozambican independence movements and abandoned its Marxist-Leninist ideology at the time of its 5th Congress in 1989. It has a solid organizational structure and a history of state leadership inherited from its history of fighting for liberation from Portuguese colonialism (Nuvunga, 2007: 54). On the other side there is RENAMO, known initially as MNR (Mozambican National Resistance), which emerged in 1975 as a reaction to the one-party rule of FRELIMO. It carried out a sixteen-year armed struggle against FRELIMO, and its political formation has military origins. The MNR is inspired by the right and is heavily focused on its leader, Afonso Dhlakama.

Although political participation has broadened with the arrival of a third political party represented in the national Parliament – MDM, the Democratic Movement of Mozambique – the political chess game of Mozambican politics is still essentially dominated by FRELIMO and RENAMO. Today, they share power in bodies such as the Constitutional Council, the National Elections Committee and the Supreme Judicial Council.

The structure of government communication in Mozambique

Mozambique has a presidential political system where the President of the Republic is both head of state and head of government. The President serves in five-year terms that can be renewed only once. The law states that the President must be elected by a single constituency that covers the entire country and the candidate that obtains more than half of the validly cast votes wins.[3] The President of the Republic is therefore at the epicentre of all of Mozambique's government communication.

In general, government communication is the responsibility of the Government Information Bureau (GABINFO – Gabinete de Informação de Moçambique). GABINFO is tied to the Bureau of the Prime Minister. It supervises all the state communication organizations and public media bodies, advises the executive on specific issues in the media field and encourages the dissemination of and access to information about government actions, among other activities. The body is also responsible for the registration and licensing of the media (Law no. 2/2005). The director of GABINFO is appointed by the Prime Minister. GABINFO replaced the Ministry of Information, which was dissolved because of its history of censorship.

Alongside this body for managing government communication, there is the Press Office of the Presidency of the Republic, which is exclusively supervised by the head of state. The press officer who runs it is responsible for all communications of the Ponta Vermelha and reports on his/her activities directly to the President. As in any Western country, the Mozambican government's communications seem to be directed by a professional and political elite which controls information and its dissemination. In recent democracies, there are also broader democratic concerns about how information emanating from the government is controlled and used strategically to exercise power (Bennett, 2001: 16)

In 2005, when President Guebuza started the PAIs, the work of the Presidency's press officer gained greater visibility. During the PAIs, the press officer and his/her team's mission was to establish the best setting for public meetings between the President and the people. Tasks include setting up the sound system, positioning the podium, placing microphones, organizing the press room and press conference room and organizing the journalists.

Interaction between the President and the citizens has also taken place on social networks. Guebuza writes a blog and uses Facebook and Twitter, through which he keeps an open dialogue with Internet users. In fact, in the final years of his second term, PAIs events were broadcast in real time on those platforms, providing both audiovisual communication and instant interaction between President and citizens.

The massive presence of politics in the media is fundamentally provided, according to Boorstin (1961), by 'pseudo-events': self-promotion events designed to obtain media coverage, which is the measure of their success. Armando Guebuza's PAIs clearly match this aim, creating a communication strategy managed by the Press Office of the Presidency of the Republic that is focused on organizing a 'meeting' between the head of state and his people at a rally. The President interacts with people directly at these gatherings and, at the same time is able to gauge the level of local support for the government's five-year programme (Matola, 2009: 8). Media coverage of these events is both national and regional. Regional media include rural radio stations and the national coverage can be found on TV and in the press.

Armando Guebuza's open presidencies

Nation building in Mozambique

In his inaugural speech on 2 February 2005, Guebuza specified rural development as one of the priorities of his government and placed similar emphasis on the fight against poverty. More than half the Mozambican population today lives below the national poverty line (UNDP, 2014: 180).

In 2006, to boost national development, his government passed the Local Initiative Investment Budget (OIIL – Orçamento de Investimento de Iniciativa Local), popularly known as '7 Million'. It is a funding mechanism for individual or collective projects for food production and job and income creation. In a country of more than 24 million people, most of whom (about 70 per cent) live in rural areas, the main governing principle for President Guebuza was to boost the district (*distrito*)[4] as a locus of development, while not forgetting to pay attention to urban problems of crime and poverty.

Mozambique is a young nation at only forty years old.[5] A brief historical overview of the still incipient phenomenon of national identity can be split into three stages: the first stage took place in the 1950s and 1960s when, as in most African countries, feelings of national identity in Mozambique emerged from the fight for independence from European colonialism (Joseph Ki-Zerbo, 2007). In the second stage, in which the major symbols of national identity (e.g. flag, national anthem, emblem) had already been established, the exercise of national unity was tested by a sixteen-year civil war that exacerbated the political and social divides caused by regionalism and tribalism. According to Ngoenha (1998: 31), the existence of a Mozambican state depended on the ability of the political programme to resolve rivalries and conflicts among social, religious, regional and ethnic groups according to the rules acknowledged as legitimate. In fact, the issue of national identity should rightly be thought of in terms of unity and diversity. There still are ethnic and regional divides in the nation as Mozambicans continue to give themselves the labels of *machangana, manhambana, chicondo, machuabo*,[6] etc.

The third stage of building national identity created the conditions for democracy in Mozambique and continues to the present day. The Joaquim Chissano presidency (1994–2005) implemented a reconstruction of national unity (which had been interrupted by civil war) in the guise of dialogue, encouraging peace and reconciliation among Mozambicans, particularly in the political arena. The devastation of the civil war had triggered a strong desire for peace. The starting point would be promoting an atmosphere of peace and good quality of life for all Mozambicans, giving priority to rural areas and providing access to education, health, employment and public services. In other words, Chissano's objectives were the same as Armando Guebuza's PAIs: a 'pedagogy of democratic governance' (Sitoe, 2014).

Public relations and nation building

The PAIs led to a presidential visit to all 128 districts of the country (a number that rose to 152 in 2013).[7] In his first term (2005–2009), Armando Guebuza went to the district capitals and in his second term (2009–2014) he expanded his government action to other locations spread across a territory measuring almost 800,000 km^2.[8]

Data from the Presidency of the Republic shows that the PAIs tours were prepared a year in advance, in a project coordinated by the Presidency of the Republic, the Ministry of State Administration and provincial governments. As a rule, the PAIs took place in the first six months of each year, when the President would visit an equal number of districts per province over four days, except for Nampula and Zambézia – the largest provinces in the country – where he stayed for longer, visiting five districts in each one.

Research carried out by German researchers (Leininger, 2012) identifies three steps involved in the PAIs: preparation, performance and follow-up. The preparation step includes selecting locations to be visited by the President. At this stage, the team would share its recommendations to identify places with the highest standards of services because during the PAIs the district visited would become the Ponta Vermelha. The recommendations would range from how to build the platform for the public meeting to how to furnish and decorate the bedroom or bathroom.

Regarding the performance step – the PAIs themselves – there were meetings, first with the provincial government, then with directors and businesspeople, with visits to local infrastructural and social projects. This is when the high point of the PAIs would take place: the public meeting at which a number of people (from five to fifteen) would have the chance to speak to the President about different topics. These meetings were not spontaneous, and nothing was left to chance. According to Leininger (2012), the district administrators carefully chose those who would participate in meetings with the President. The chance for citizens to address the President was not open to everyone. To avoid overly forceful criticisms of the administration, particular speakers such as members of the opposition and also certain representatives of civil society organizations were avoided. Another equally important moment was undoubtedly the press conference, which took place at the end of the visit. This was when the dialogue with the people was broadened, via the press, to other Mozambicans at both regional and national level.

According to Leininger (2012), the third stage is follow-up. This means that the issues presented by people were incorporated into evaluation frameworks to subsequently monitor the performance of the local administration over time. This step was an attempt to continue the relationship between President and people. The trips to rural areas, all the actions involved in the PAIs, as well as the media coverage that resulted from public meetings in the different provinces, can be seen as a mechanism for building national identity. In fact, the entire event was drawn up with the aim of transmitting messages and positions that would emphasize a feeling of collective belonging among Mozambicans. This is an enormous challenge for any African government, since the context is characterized by different, notable linguistic and ethnic traits. But the issue of national identity should rightly be thought of in terms of unity and diversity.

Against the backdrop of the PAIs, the government's communication strategy plays an important role in the construction of national identity. This importance arises from the PAIs' contribution to the change in attitude towards the government. In fact, the increasing proximity between the political elite and the people demonstrated a desire to embark on a relationship of trust: a classic goal in the relationship paradigm of public relations. Following Taylor and Kent (2006) and Taylor (2000), we also emphasize the importance of public relations to the successful implementation of nation-building objectives: 'communication as a tool for nation building must be understood as that which creates and maintains relationships' (Taylor, 2000: 180).

Taylor (2000) follows an integrationist approach to understanding the role of communication in nation building (Deutsch, 1966a, 1966b), which sees the nation state as a communicatively constructed entity. Contrary to Van Leuven and Pratt's (1996) studies, which showed that Third World countries tend to adhere to the press agency, publicity and public information models, Taylor advocates the adoption of two-way communication in order to foster the relationship between an organization and its publics based on negotiation, trust and mutual respect. For Taylor (2000), relationships play a pivotal role in the public relations approach to nation building. Taylor thoroughly discusses the significance of relationship-centred public relations in emerging democracies prone to ethnic conflicts and violence, and suggests that nation building will be more effective if it adopts a public relations approach focused on establishing and managing relationships, increasing participation, and encouraging cooperation between a government and its people.

Public relations functions already play important roles in the nation-building process of many developing nations (Chaka, 2014; Taylor, 2000; Taylor and Botan, 1997; Taylor and Kent, 2006). In this paper, we follow this line of thought by stating that the PAIs, as a government public relations strategy, and President Guebuza's speeches in particular, have helped to build national unity. The fact that national identities are negotiated through discourse that use repertoires of symbols, narratives and meanings adapted to new needs or historical experiences seems to be largely accepted (Bruner, 2002; Parekh, 1995). In spite of this, there are not many concrete studies of the process. This chapter discusses the case of strengthening Mozambican national identity in a process led by the political elite through the government's public relations strategy of PAIs.

Research questions

This chapter aims to reflect on the PAIs and specifically focus on President Guebuza's speeches as a form of encouraging a strengthened Mozambican nation based on a two-way communication approach that aims to stimulate debate about current affairs. Based on this, three research questions guided the data collection and research:

RQ1 As a government communication strategy, what was/were the main objective(s) of the PAIs?
RQ2 Did the speeches at PAIs events seek to increase feelings of patriotism and unity among Mozambican people?
RQ3 Did the social, cultural and linguistic mosaic of Mozambique restrict the use of the official language (Portuguese) in speeches?

Method

Critical Discourse Analysis (CDA) was used in the study of presidential speeches. All the transcripts were gathered from an official source, the Bureau of Studies of the Presidency of Mozambique (Gabinete de Estudos da Presidência da República de Moçambique). First, an exploratory comparative discourse analysis was conducted in order to select the corpus of analysis. The focus of the analysis was discourse variation. Public meetings aimed at varied audiences (regarding location in the country and language) were chosen, although they had a common speaker, the President of the Republic.

The corpus of analysis selected was comprised of six speeches given at public meetings by President Guebuza during the PAIs that took place in April and May 2007, the third year of his second term. The speeches occurred in provinces in the northern, central and southern regions of the country. The three provinces in the sample were strategically chosen for the following reasons: (1) Niassa is considered the poorest and most disregarded province; (2) Sofala is the political centre for the opposition parties;[9] and (3) Maputo is the seat of government. The selection of the remaining districts by province – Nampula, Tete and Inhambane – was random.

The political speeches were categorized according to the date on which each event took place, and structured as shown in Table 8.1.

There are many different approaches to critical discourse analysis. In our study, we adopted a CDA inspired by Fairclough (2010; 2001) and Van Dijk (1997). Fairclough (2001: 100) suggests a three-dimensional analysis of the texts, contending that any discourse can be considered at the same time a text (linguistic analysis), an example of discursive practice (analysis of text production and interpretation) and an example of social practice (analysis of the institutional and organizational circumstances surrounding a communicative event). Van Dijk highlights the sociocognitive dimension in discourse studies and links three aspects together: discourse, cognition and society. The author focuses on the direct correlation between discourse and society, from which one of the most significant approaches in CDA emerges. It explores the boundaries of ideology as a complex of social, cognitive and sociocognitive beliefs shared by the members of a group. The beliefs can be identified in social interaction settings that may take the form of conflict and struggles related to class, gender or race (Van Dijk, 1997: 107).

Table 8.1 Guebuza's political speeches listed by date

Name	*Location*	*Date*
Public meeting 1	Catembe district Maputo	10 April 2007
Public meeting 2	Changara district Tete province	18 April 2007
Public meeting 3	Mandimba district Niassa province	22 April 2007
Public meeting 4	Mongicual district Nampula province	4 May 2007
Public meeting 5	Búzi district Sofala province	20 May 2007
Public meeting 6	Morrumbene district Inhambane province	30 May 2007

In general, proponents of the CDA approach argue that each speech/text is designed with the purpose of influencing meaning and, logically, to shape knowledge. They say that if the words used and metaphors chosen in a speech are examined carefully, it is likely that they contain aspects that support and justify interests and positions that are often not acknowledged (Daymon and Holloway, 2011; Wood and Kroeger, 2000). Regarding the method, the analysis table produced for the CDA followed the following stages:

1 Carefully reading large blocks of text (comparing and contrasting).
2 Identifying subjects: people, grammar, lexicon and themes.
3 Exploring interpretive repertoires (metaphors and free association).
4 Relating modes of talking to different audiences.
5 Paying attention to the way in which speeches develop (connections with history).
6 Identifying the institutions supported or attacked in speeches.

Presentation and discussion of the data

In general, the comparative analysis of the PAIs speeches showed that the clear focus is on an appeal for unity among Mozambicans to better face the challenge of fighting poverty. This goal is emphasized in the association of the executive with the church. Mozambique is a secular state but the President often mentioned the importance of prayer to 'light and reveal the true way'.

National unity is the central and underlying element of the President's discourse. With an extensive use of symbolism, Guebuza employs the term 'unity' as the catalyst for his message and does so in a simple, effective way that can be understood by his audiences, who are mostly illiterate, by using prosaic, easily understood examples and simple metaphors:

> I could give you the example of a ball. **A group of 11 players**. One of the players is the goalkeeper. He picks up the ball with his hands. The other players use their left feet to finish. Others use their right feet …
>
> (Public meeting 3)[10]

> we are **all in the same boat** and we all need to be motivated to **get our boat to its destination**.
>
> (Public meeting 5)

Another common trait of Guebuza's speeches is related to the chain of ideas itself. Apart from one example, all the texts have the same sequence of topics: they begin with the topic of national unity, followed by the struggle against poverty and then a moment of interaction with the local population. In other words, the President begins with matters that have a macro interest and reach – national unity, in this case – then discusses the struggle against poverty (based on data for the district in question) and ends with a discussion of micro aspects of strictly local interest. Local affairs are only debated at the end of the speech. Although there are also national themes, Guebuza seeks to highlight, among other things, success stories of social projects that aim to boost employment, above all among young people. He seeks to find supporters for the struggle against poverty through these stories.

References to the FRELIMO party are another constant feature of Guebuza's speeches. They are also connected to the issue of national identity: FRELIMO brought the Mozambican people together to 'expel' colonialism; it led the reconciliation of the Mozambican people during the sixteen-year civil war; FRELIMO is the protagonist in strengthening the unity of Mozambicans with the common aim of fighting poverty:

> **FRELIMO** spoke to the people and said: let's work to get rid of the foreigners ... And we won. Then there was another **common problem**. For **all Mozambicans, from Rovuma to Maputo, from Zumbo to the Indian Ocean** (...) the problem was war (...) We were victorious! (...) Now there is a common problem that persists (...) which is poverty (...) We want to get rid of it.
>
> (Public meeting 2)

According to Brito (2008), even before he was elected Guebuza was already an active promoter of FRELIMO and devoted himself to revitalizing the party's system throughout the country: 'Particular attention was paid to the base-level FRELIMO cells and district administrators, who were historically a fundamental part of controlling the land and population' (Brito, 2008: 8).

The interpretation of the speeches as texts, discursive practice and sociocultural practice was analysed using five aspects: (i) lexicon, including vocabulary and grammar; (ii) themes; (iii) historical context; (iv) relationship with the public; and (v) national identity.

(i) Lexicon

Words like *nós* (we/us), *nosso* (our), *somos* (we are), *juntos* (together), *estamos* (we are), *povo* (people) and *Moçambique* (Mozambique) were frequently found in the speeches. The dominance of the personal pronoun *nós* (we/us) transmits the intention of including/involving all of Mozambican society in the ideal of unity, which is understood to be necessary to the success of the anti-poverty campaign.

The President uses three tenses strategically. The present is used mostly at the beginning of the speech. Some examples: *I want to welcome; I want to thank; I have two messages.* The past tense is generally used to give examples of the country overcoming colonialism and civil war thanks to the unity of Mozambicans. The future tense is used at the end of the speeches to give an idea of continuity to the connection between the President and his people.

The use of the past imperfect tense also gives an idea of continuity to actions that began in the past but have not yet been completed, such as the unity of Mozambicans in the struggle against poverty:

> The colonialism that was present in **Mozambique** for 500 years departed because the Mozambicans were **united** (…) we became independent because of **unity, which is the great force** (…) And it is also because of the **unity** that was found here (…) that the war ended. Because **we are stronger united. United**, there is no enemy that can shake us.
>
> (Public meeting 2)

(ii) Themes

Four main themes were identified: (1) national unity, (2) the struggle against poverty, (3) the district, and (4) local needs. Comparison of the speeches revealed that they all mention the same themes and follow the same order. The only exception was the public meeting in Changara district, in Tete province (public meeting 2) in which, right at the start, the topics of provincial elections and the importance of voting were explored. This difference may be the result of the media agenda at the time, which was discussing the legal framework before the provincial assembly elections.[11] Whether it is coincidence or not, the data from the general, presidential and provincial assembly elections on 28 October 2009 show that the turnout in Tete province was over 95 per cent, while the turnout in other districts averaged 30–40 per cent. Furthermore, the results obtained showed that at many polling stations 100 per cent of votes cast were for FRELIMO (MOE-EU, 2009: 34).

Another aspect that stands out in the study of the themes lies in the variation of matters regarding the local needs of each district. It is in this section of the speech that the most important component of the PAIs is revealed, since this is when the issues that are of most direct interest to the different populations are discussed. In most rural districts, matters regarding health, education and management of the '7 Million' are discussed, while the speech given in Maputo, the seat of government, discussed more 'sophisticated' points, such as pharmacies, insurance, public transport, etc.

(iii) Historical context

The use of history, according to Fairclough (2001), helps broader intertextuality processes to occur, which anticipate and shape following texts. In fact, in the speeches, the idea of unity is invoked through stories of breakthroughs and by valorizing national heroes, with particular emphasis on Eduardo Mondlane. Guebuza uses examples that contrast with unity, such as racial or territorial distinctions, to demonstrate the opposite:

> **our different languages, our different traditions, our different ways of singing, dancing** (...) Eduardo Mondlene said that they wouldn't be a problem. On the contrary: **they enrich our heritage** (...) if the Mozambicans want the same thing, while being different, if they bring their differences together and unite, there is no enemy that can defeat them.
>
> (Public meeting 4)

(iv) Relationship with the public

The public is the most important element of the PAIs as a strategy of government communication. Although he recognizes particular racial and cultural features, Guebuza makes an effort to convince people that he represents the interests of all the 'wonderful Mozambican people' (a recurring statement at all public meetings).

In his speeches, the President emulates face-to-face dialogue in his choice of vocabulary which implies presence and proximity (for example listening, sharing, learning) through rhetorical questions, interjections designed to stimulate the audience, and pauses. These silent intervals are elements that help structure the speech, particularly as regards changing themes. These changes are often made by way of a series of good-natured questions:

> Here, where we are standing, we are different: There are men here. There are women here. Are they the same?
>
> There are children here. There are adults here. Are they the same?
>
> There are people with lighter skin here. There are people with darker skin here. Are they the same?
>
> There are slim people here. There are people who are more ... (Laughs) here. Are they the same?
>
> (Public meeting 2)

Furthermore, by emphasising his concern to ensure that the problems presented to him by the people are recorded, he encourages trust in the relationship between people and government bodies and continuity for the relationships that started with the PAIs:

> Some points that I was told about need to be investigated in greater depth (...) That is why **my advisers were working with people who raised issues**; that will allow us to find out later what we can do. But one thing is certain: they will get an answer
>
> (Public meeting 4)

The very fact that the President is accompanied by a government entourage that includes invited guests (ambassadors and cooperation partners) points to the goal of effectively bringing the political class and the citizens closer together.

(v) National identity

Guebuza includes a feeling of 'collective belonging' in his speeches using different tactics: use of the personal pronoun *nós* (us/we), highlighting particular aspects of national identity, specifically language, land, memory, habits and symbols. The use of the official language, Portuguese, a colonial legacy, forced the PAIs to ensure simultaneous translation of the President's speech into different national languages. There are an estimated forty-three national languages in the country; most are Bantu in origin but some are completely different. However, the President does use expressions from national languages in his speeches on several occasions, particularly in the Maputo speech, where all the welcoming and introductory parts of the speech were given in the local language, XiRonga.

References to local folklore in speeches, particularly dances (e.g. Makwai, Mapiko, Mandoa, Wunanga), songs, and local musical instruments (e.g. the chiquissi), are consistent with building up Mozambican national identity. It is assumed that these demonstrations of national culture appear in the President's speeches precisely in order to, once again, deepen the ties of Mozambique's own, exclusive references.

The legitimization of local power, with a decentralization of central power and the institutionalization of Local Consultative Councils (CCLs – Conselhos Consultivos Locais) promoted by the PAIs can only be understood as a reinforcement of national identity. CCLs are the most basic institutions of state administration to ensure the safeguarding of the above-mentioned elements of national identity.

Conclusion

In a multicultural country with deep ethnic differences, governments face the challenge of adopting communication strategies that strengthen a feeling of common belonging. It is in this context that public relations can be used as a catalyst for encouraging dialogue between government and society. Armando Guebuza's *Presidências Abertas e Inclusivas* are the perfect example of this type of effort, since they open up a space for creating a close relationship between the government elite and the most remote and poorest provinces of Mozambique.

The PAIs seem to have helped bring citizens closer to politics. The President's speeches, in particular, emphasized national unity and identity values and, moreover, enabled the opportunity for a dialogue free from mediation, in which people had the chance to speak face to face with the President. However, the conditions for citizens to enter into a dialogue with the President were pre-defined and took into account how favourable each potential speaker was to the government. With this in mind, we cannot help but reflect on whether the PAIs were, deep down, a powerful mechanism for legitimating the government and FRELIMO's discourse and not a symmetrical communication (Grunig, 2001) or participative public relations strategy (Motion, 2005).

There are certainly many variables that influence votes, but the reality is that in 2004 the abstention recorded was around 63 per cent, while in 2009 this fell to 56 per cent.[12] The positive trend in voting extended to FRELIMO and its president, Armando Guebuza, who was elected by 63.74 per cent of votes cast in 2004 and won his second term with 65 per cent of the valid vote in 2009. In this setting FRELIMO and its candidate received a mass of votes in rural areas in 2009, including regions that were traditionally understood to support the opposition. The Búzi district, one of those included in the study sample, is an example of this (Pereira and Nhanele, 2014: 7). In a sense, these electoral data demonstrate how the PAIs, as a government communication strategy, helped achieve one of the main objectives of political public relations: 'to ensure that a party receives maximum favourable publicity, and the minimum of negative' (McNair, 2000: 7). In fact, we have been able to assert that the national press was highly favourable to Guebuza as the PAIs took place, framing the PAIs initiative in a very positive way, even within media usually more critical of the Guebuza administration (interviews by Stelia Neta in 2015).[13]

The CDA analysis suggests that the speeches were effectively a tool for strengthening national unity. In forty years of existence, the concept of national unity for Mozambicans went through three important phases. The first was when Mozambicans put their racial, tribal and ethnic differences aside to fight colonialism and achieve independence in 1975. The second phase was when differences were felt among the Mozambicans themselves, when national unity was put to the test during a sixteen-year civil war. More recently, under democracy, and despite being haunted by ethnic divisions, Mozambicans found an appeal for unity in Armando Guebuza's PAIs, this time in the struggle against socio-economic differences, most specifically in the struggle against the deeply rooted poverty in rural areas.

The anti-poverty message at district level was linked to the Local Initiative Investment Budget (OIIL) project, known as '7 Million', with the aim of funding local projects, and achieved positive results. Despite some setbacks, specifically complaints about the supposed lack of clarity in the criteria for awarding and applying the budget, and alongside some structural reforms in the macroeconomic field of governance, recent data on the progress of the World Bank and International Monetary Fund's Poverty Reduction Strategy Papers (PARP – Plano de Acção para Redução da Pobreza) indicate that Mozambique has risen in its 'doing business' ranking and that poverty levels have also gone down modestly (IMF, 2014: 16).

The multilingual make-up of the country has led to the use of Portuguese, inherited from colonialism, as the language of official presidential communication. The great advantage of this is that it is more widely spread around the country, unlike native languages which are restricted to certain locations and are very different from one another. By prioritizing Portuguese the government shows no bias towards any particular national language, and this decision contributes to the message of unity.

In short, President Guebuza managed to implement a public relations strategy with the aim of educating Mozambican society to create a feeling of national belonging, with undeniable effects on citizens' growing political participation. The order of the speech, the language used and the interconnection of ideas (as suggested by Fairclough, 2001) and, in fact, the President's entire rhetoric were able to boost awareness of the supposed values of 'Mozambiqueness' and, potentially, could have the desired effect of reducing the feeling of 'otherness' grounded in the population's ethnic differences. The President's speeches were also able to establish closer and more effective bilateral communication with citizens by decentralizing and strengthening the local state administration (the Consultative Councils). This tactic helped build the basis for a relationship of trust between the different parties because rural citizens, who were previously lacking in the most basic social services, now had the state's executive power in their community.

Notes

1 The terms of the Constitution prevented Guebuza from running for a third term in the last elections, which were held on 15 October 2014. They were won by Filipe Nyusi and FRELIMO kept the majority of parliamentary seats.

2 Further information on the Freedom House indices is available here: https://freedomhouse.org/report/freedom-press/2015/mozambique

3 Articles 148 to 159, Constitution of the Republic, 2004.

4 In Mozambique, districts (*distritos*) are the main divisions of the country for the organization and functioning of local state administration and the basis for planning economic, social and cultural development. Districts are subdivided into administrative posts (*postos administrativos*), which are in turn divided into localities (*localidades*). In Guebuza's first term there were 128 districts in the country. Since Law no. 26/2013 of 18 December 2013 was passed, Mozambique has had 151 districts.

5 Ten years after the armed fight for national freedom led by the Mozambique Liberation Front (FRELIMO) against Portuguese colonization (25 September 1964–8 September 1974) the independence of Mozambique was proclaimed by Samora Machel on 25 June 1975 and its name was changed to the People's Republic of Mozambique.

6 Names for people according to their ethnic and regional background.

7 Law no. 26/2013 of 18 December 2013.

8 On 15 January 2015 Guebuza was succeeded by Filipe Nyussi.

9 In general elections, votes in the Sofala constituency tend to go to the opposition (RENAMO). The Beira municipality, the capital of Sofala, is managed by the country's third political force, the Mozambique Democratic Movement (MDM) under the leadership of Daviz Mbepo Simango.

10 Several excerpts are included that are representative and characteristic of the speeches made by President Guebuza. Words or sentences are shown in bold whenever necessary to direct the reader's attention.

11 Enshrined in the 2004 Constitution, the provincial assemblies are bodies that exercise sovereign power in Mozambique. The first elections to these assemblies took place on 28 October 2009, the same date on which Guebuza was re-elected.

There are ten provincial assemblies in Mozambique, one per province, except Maputo. They are responsible for supervising, overseeing and monitoring the provincial government programme. Assemblies have a term of five years and are elected by universal suffrage of electors in the relevant province. Their members are elected using the proportional method based on constituencies that correspond to the districts.

12 According to STAE data, the abstention rate was 12 per cent in 1994, 30 per cent in 1999, 63 per cent in 2004 and 56 per cent in 2009.

13 Exploratory interviews with Mozambican journalists in the course of doctoral research were carried out Stelia Neta in 2015.

References

Alden, C. (2001) *Mozambique and the construction of the new African state: From negotiations to nation building*. New York: Palgrave.

Bennett, W. L. (2001) *News: The politics of illusion*. 4th edn. New York: Addison Wesley Longman.

Boorstin, D. J. (1961) *The image: A guide to pseudo-events in America*. New York: Atheneum.

Brito, L. (2008) 'Uma nota sobre o voto, abstenção e fraude em Moçambique', Colecção discussion paper no. 04. Maputo: Instituto de Estudos Sociais e Económicos (IESE).

Bruner, M. L. (2002) *Strategies of remembrance: The rhetorical dimensions of national identity construction*. Columbia: University of South Carolina Press.

Chaka, M. (2014) 'Public relations (PR) in nation-building: An exploration of the South African presidential discourse', *Public Relations Review*, 40: 351–362.

Chichava, S. and Pohlmann, J. (2010) 'Uma breve análise da imprensa Moçambicana', in *Desafios para Moçambique*, Maputo.

Comissão Nacional de Eleições (CNE) (2015) accessed 23 September 2015. www.stae.org.mz/.

Conselho Constitucional (CC) (2014) *A validação e proclamação dos resultados das eleições presidenciais, legislativas e das assembleias provinciais de 15 de Outubro de 2014. Acórdão no. 21/CC/2014 de 29 de Dezembro*. Available at: www.iese.ac.mz/lib/publication/livros/des2010/IESE_Des2010_5.ImpMoc.pdf (accessed: 2 October 2015).

Constituição da República (2004) *República de Moçambique*, Maputo: Imprensa Nacional de Moçambique.

Daymon, C. and Holloway, I. (2011) *Qualitative research methods in public relations and marketing communications*. 2nd edn. New York: Routledge.

Deutsch, K. W. (1966a) *The nerves of government: Models of political communication and control*. New York: The Free Press.

Deutsch, K. W. (1966b) *Nation-building*. New York: Atherton Press.

Emerson, R. (1966) 'Nation building in Africa', in Deutsch, K. W. and Foltz, W. J. (eds) *Nation-building*. Chicago, IL: Atherton Press, pp. 95–116.

Fairclough, N. (2001) *Discurso e mudança social*. Brasília: Universidade de Brasília.

Fairclough, N. (2010) *Critical discourse analysis: The critical study of language*. 2nd edn. New York: Longman.

Grunig, J. (2001) 'Two-way symmetrical public relations: Past, present and future', in Heath, R. (ed.) *Handbook of public relations*. Thousand Oaks, CA: Sage, pp. 11–30.

Guelke, A. (2012) *Politics in deeply divided societies*. Cambridge: Polity Press.

International Monetary Fund (2014) *Poverty reduction strategy paper: Progress report*. IMF country report no. 14/147. Available at: https://www.imf.org/external/pubs/ft/scr/2014/cr14147.pdf (accessed: 16 October 2015).

Ki-Zerbo, J. (2007) *História da África negra II*. Lisbon: Publicações Europa-América.

Leininger, J. (2012) 'Instituições informais e descentralização em Moçambique: A presidência aberta e inclusiva', in Weimer, B. (ed.) *Moçambique: descentralizar o centralismo*. Maputo: Instituto de Estudos Sociais e Económicos (IESE), pp. 216–237.

Macuane, J. (2009) 'O semipresidencialismo em Moçambique (1986–2008)', in Lobo, M. and Neto, O. (eds) *O semipresidencialismo nos países de língua portuguesa*. Lisbon: Imprensa de Ciências Sociais, pp. 171–199.

Magaia, A. (1994) *Informação em Moçambique: A força da palavra*. Maputo: Socieda de Editora Ndjira, Lda.

Matola, A. (ed.) (2009) *Armando Guebuza em Presidência Aberta*. Maputo: Gabinete de Estudos da Presidência da República.

Mazula, B. (2002a) *Moçambique: 10 anos de paz* (vol. 1). Maputo: Imprensa Universitária.

Mazula, B. (2002b) *Moçambique: Dez anos de paz*. Maputo: Centro de Estudos de Democracia e Desenvolvimento (CEDE).

McNair, B. (2000) *An introduction to political communication*. 3rd edn. London: Routledge.

MOE-EU (União Europeia Missão de Observação Eleitoral da União Europeia) (2009) *Relatório Final Eleições Presidenciais, Legislativas e das Assembleias Provinciais de 28 de Outubro, Moçambique*. Brussels: EU.

Motion, J. (2005) 'Participative public relations: power to the people or legitimacy for government discourse?' *Public Relations Review*, 31: 505–512.

Ngoenha, S. (1998) 'Identida de Moçambicana: Já e aindanão', in Serra, C. (ed.) *Identidade, Moçambicanidade, Moçambicanização*. Maputo: Livraria Universitária UEM, pp. 17–34.

Nuvunga, N. (2007) 'Experiências com partidos políticos em novas democracias: O "deixa andar" no quadro institucional em Moçambique', in Themoteo, R. (ed.) *Partidos políticos: Quatro continentes*. Rio de Janeiro: Konrad Adenauer Foundation.

Parekh, B. (1995) 'The concept of national identity', *New Community*, 21(2): 255–268.

Pereira, J. and Nhanale, E. (2014) *As eleições gerais de 2014 em Moçambique: análise de questões fundamentais*. Maputo: AfriMAP, Fundações da Open Society.

Pfetsch, B. (1999) 'Government news management: Strategic communication in comparative perspective'. Discussion paper, FS III 99–101. Available at: http://bibliothek.wzb.eu/pdf/1999/iii99–101.pdf (accessed: 1 December 2014).

Sitoe, R. (2014) 'Presidência aberta e inclusiva: Uma pedagogia de governação democrática', in Matota, A., Zonjo, J. and Padeiro, S. (eds) *Presidência Aberta e inclusiva: Uma pedagogia de governação democrática em Moçambique 2005–2014*. Maputo: Gabinete de Estudos da Presidência da República, pp. 120–153.

Taylor, M. (2000) 'Toward a public relations approach to nation-building', *Journal of Public Relations*, 12(2): 179–210.

Taylor, M. and Botan, C. H. (1997) 'Public relations campaigns for national development in the Pacific Rim: The case of public education in Malaysia', *Australian Journal of Communication*, 24: 115–130.

Taylor, M. and Kent, M. (2006) 'Public relations theory and practice in nation building', in Botan, C. and Hazleton, V. (eds) *Public relations theory II*. Mahwah, NJ: Lawrence Erlbaum Associates, pp. 299–315.

United Nations Development Programme (UNDP) (2014) *Human development report 2014: Sustaining human progress: Reducing vulnerabilities and building resilience*. Available at: www.undp.org/content/dam/undp/library/corporate/HDR/2014HDR/HDR-2014-English.pdf (accessed: 4 October 2015).

Van Dijk, T. (1997) 'Semântica do discurso', in Pedro, E. (ed.) *Análise crítica do discurso: Uma perspectiva sociopolítica e functional*. Lisbon: Caminho.

Van Leuven, J. K. and Pratt, C. B. (1996) 'Public relations' role: Realities in Asia and in Africa south of the Sahara', in Culbertson, H. M. and Chen, N. (eds) *International public relations: A comparative analysis*. Mahwah, NJ: Lawrence Erlbaum Associates, pp. 93–106.

Wolton, D. (1995) 'As contradições do espaço público mediatizado', *Revista de Comunicações e Linguagens*, Lisboa, pp. 167–188.

Wood, L. and Kroeger, R. (2000) *Doing discourse analysis: Methods for studying action in talk and text*. London: Sage.

9 1Malaysia: 'People first, performance now'

A critical perspective on the nation building approach in Malaysia's government public relations

Zeti Azreen Ahmad and Syed Arabi Idid

Introduction

Since independence in 1957, government public relations in Malaysia has striven to accommodate the needs and expectations of multiple ethnic groups to avoid discontent and prejudices that would put social stability at stake. In Malaysia all ethnic groups have equal rights to practise their cultural values rather than being absorbed into the mainstream (dominant group). Malaysia's framework of a pluralistic society resembles Berry's (2011) multiculturalism view that holds pluralism as a resource rather than a problem. This perspective also emphasises that supportive policies and programmes are crucial to uphold inclusivity. Strategic government public relations has been employed since British colonial rule in Malaysia in 1876 (at that time known as Malaya) to maintain the status quo. Similarly, Malaysian leaders used government public relations extensively during the pre- and post-independence period to unite ethnic groups and to win public support.

According to Bowen (2012) the major function of government public relations is to facilitate communication with constituencies and with governmental publics. Meeting the needs and expectations of its pluralistic society remains a challenge for the Malaysian government. According to Lee (2012) responding to public concerns and expectations is not an option for a government. Vandebosche (2004) asserted that government public relations should prioritise citizens' interests instead of mere political gain. Referring to 'communication efforts in which the government/administration tries to be non-partisan, balanced and concise', she stated that: 'These efforts are not aimed to put political party or politician in the picture, but focus on the interest of the receiving citizen who needs to be informed' (cited in Ihlen and Gelders, 2010: 60).

The two-way symmetrical model has been suggested as the most ethical approach to PR and subsequently considered as an excellent model of PR practice that enhances organisational effectiveness (Cutlip et al., 2006; Grunig, 2001; Grunig and Grunig, 1992). Based on this premise, government public relations is likely to be effective when it builds strategic, symmetrical relationships with key publics (Grunig and Jaatiinen, 1998). On the other hand, Ihlen and Gelders (2010) argue that government public relations tends to be persuasive and always attempts to 'influence the knowledge, attitude and/or behavior of citizens' (p. 60). In this context, government public relations will most likely serve the need of the government more than the interests of the people. Therefore, the assumption that government PR functions to establish and maintain mutual understanding and interests of all important publics appears problematic. A major challenge for government public relations in Malaysia is the need to meet the expectations of multiple constituents that at times compete with one another. This study argues that government public relations in a pluralistic society should focus beyond two-way symmetrical communication between government and *rakyat* (citizen). The readiness to negotiate and compromise among the multiple constituents that make up the social landscape in the country is also imperative for the prevention of racial divides.

Alternatively, the critical work which originates from the Frankfurt School has contested the normative theory held by functionalists. Critical scholars have raised the issue of power imbalances that are inherently present in the two-way symmetrical model (Bardhan and Weaver, 2011; Edwards, 2009; L'Etang, 2008; Berger, 2005). Furthermore, Roper (2005) has explored the concept of hegemony that demonstrates how public acceptance is achieved through manufacturing of consent imposed by powerful actors (e.g. the government) rather than through an open discourse (p. 70). In a similar vein, L'Etang (1996: 34) asserted that a two-way symmetrical theory has been 'intrinsically hegemonic' in PR scholarship, and has restrained the development of an alternative world view.

The critical view alleged that PR practitioners work to privilege particular interests, predominantly those with resources and capital, i.e. organisations, governments, the elite or dominant coalition and capitalism (Bardhan and Weaver, 2011; Edwards, 2009) rather than promoting the mutual interests of diverse publics. In fact, PR works in the interests of those who pay for it, whether that be government, commercial interests, NGOs, or activist groups (Edwards, 2011; Berger, 2005). This has implications for government public relations initiatives that by and large support the agendas of powerful actors, including the country's ruling elites. This study examined with a critical perspective the practice of government public relations in its struggle to balance competing demands that were constantly made by multiple ethnic groups in Malaysia.

Over the years, the Malaysian government had initiated numerous PR campaigns to promote national unity, for example the *Kibar Jalur Gemilang* ('Raise the Malaysian Flag') campaign, the *Kempen Kejiranan* or 'Neighbourliness' campaign, the 'Buy Malaysian Products' campaign, and the 'One Heart One Nation' campaign, just to name a few. Taylor (2000) affirmed that the Neighbourliness campaign was a nation-building effort that had been successful in fostering cooperation between people of different ethnic groups in Malaysia but not without unintended consequences. She concluded that other factors have undermined inter-ethnic relations in Malaysia and that includes the government's existing policies and programmes that favoured one ethnic group and thus were in conflict with the campaign's key messages. The literature has affirmed that national policies that preferred one ethnic group over the other have resulted in increased division between them (Noraini and Chan-Hoong, 2013; Chin, 2009; 2010). In the case of Malaysia, the dominant group, the Malays and Bumiputra have been granted a special position due to their long-term discrimination in the past. Such preferred status ignites dissatisfaction and constant debate among other races and may put national unity at stake.

Preserving national unity has always been the top priority of the Malaysian government. The current prime minister, Dato' Seri Najib Tun Abdul Razak, has introduced the '1Malaysia' concept with the tag line 'People First, Performance Now' as a deliberate attempt to keep people together. Critics on the other hand have labelled 1Malaysia as a political attempt to mobilise support for Barisan Nasional (National Front), the ruling coalition party in Malaysia subsequent to its massive defeat in the 12th general election (Noraini and Chan-Hoong, 2013; Chin, 2010). The 1Malaysia concept was depicted by the current leadership as a more inclusive approach that promoted political equality and wealth. The concept revives government's commitment to prioritise the *rakyat* (Malaysians) regardless of race by easing their burden and improving government's delivery system. However, a recent study revealed that the different ethnic groups view the concept as merely a political agenda rather than a genuine attempt to unite the people. The Malays viewed the concept as undermining Malay rights while non-Malays interpreted it as another ploy to win votes (Noraini and Chan-Hoong, 2013: 719).

The campaign titled 1Malaysia is an example of a strategic government public relations that was initiated in response to demands made by the multiple ethnic groups in the country for a greater equity in social, political and economic dimensions. A longitudinal study has been conducted to critically examine public opinion and reaction to 1Malaysia. This study among others has explored public acceptance of the concept since it was implemented in 2009. The study also looked at the gap between government and public in interpreting the 1Malaysia messages.

This chapter is divided into several parts. The literature review presents background information on Malaysia's multicultural and multi-religious features. It also discusses government PR during the colonial period; and national policies, focusing in particular on the concept of 1Malaysia as a PR tool for achieving social and political stability. Next, the paper describes the methodology and the findings of the study. Finally, the concept of 1Malaysia is critically discussed prior to some concluding remarks.

A pluralistic society

Malaysia consists of thirteen states[1] and three federal territories in an area covering 330,290 square kilometres (Department of Statistics Malaysia, 2015: 1). The Department of Statistics recorded a population of 28.3 million based on the 2010 census. The country consists of three main ethnic groups: Bumiputra is the indigenous group which represents 67.4 per cent of the total population (Department of Statistics Malaysia, 2015: 4). The Malays are considered the predominant ethnic group in Peninsular Malaysia, enjoying the status of Bumiputra: the 'sons' and 'daughters' of the soil (Abdullah and Pedersen, 2003) and constituted 63.1 per cent of the population (Department of Statistics Malaysia, 2015: 4). Beside the Malays, other significant indigenous people inhabiting Sabah and Sarawak are also considered as Bumiputra. They include several major ethnic groups such as the Kadazan, Dusun, Bajau, Murut, Iban, Bidayuh and Melanau (Department of Statistics Malaysia, 2015). At present, the Chinese make up 24.6 per cent of the overall population, and a further 7.3 per cent are Indian (Department of Statistics Malaysia, 2015). The Constitution affirmed Islam as the official religion of the Federation (*Federal Constitution*, 2005: 20) and this is largely practised by the Malays. Nevertheless, freedom to practise other religions also applies. Bahasa Malaysia is the official language of the country while English is regarded as the second language and is widely used in the workplace and a few public universities such as the International Islamic University Malaysia (IIUM) and in most private universities that are largely dominated by non-Malay students.

Scholars identified three factors that have contributed to the multicultural set-up of Malaysia: foreign traders, conquest and industrialisation (Shamsul Amri, 1997 in Abdullah and Pedersen, 2003). The ethnic and religious plurality that characterises Malaysia today can be traced back to the Malay kingdom of Malacca[2] (AD 1400–1500) that was once a great trading port. It served as a meeting point for traders and religious missionaries coming from the East and the West. Efficient administrative and legal systems had lured traders from all over the world to Malacca (Adnan, 2009). The plural polity of Malaysia started to take shape when foreign merchants decided to settle there. These immigrants endowed Malaysia with a rich blend of cultures, including religious beliefs.

Colonisation by the Portuguese, the Dutch, and the British from the sixteenth-century Malacca to independent Malaysia in 1957 also greatly affected the Malaysian social landscape, particularly regarding language, religion, culture, law, education and administration (Ibrahim and Joned, 1987; Abdullah and Pedersen, 2003). A massive influx of Chinese and Indian workers into Malaya was evident during British rule and was a further contribution to Malaysia's distinctive pluralistic society. The British divide-and-rule policy kept the three ethnic groups geographically apart in pursuit of a specific economic goal: the Chinese were placed in the urban sites and involved in commerce; the Indians worked on the rubber estates; while the Malays were predominantly village-based peasant farmers (Abdullah and Pedersen, 2003). Unlike those living in the city, the Malays were largely deprived, neither participating in commercial activities nor in education, and thus remained backward. The former prime minister, Tun Mahathir Mohamad (1998), realised that the separation of the economic functions based on race had resulted in huge economic gaps between the three dominant races. The then government under Prime Minister Abdul Razak bin Hussein introduced the New Economic Policy (NEP) that was known as an affirmative action and was designed to help the Malays to take an active part in the economic development of the country.

Political parties in Malaysia are affiliated with the country's racial groups. For example, UMNO (United Malays National Organisation) and PAS (Pan-Malaysian Islamic Party) are dependent on Malay support. Likewise MCA (Malaysian Chinese Association) and DAP (Democratic Action Party) are dependent on the Chinese, while MIC (Malayan Indian Congress) and PPP (People's Progressive Party) depend mainly on Indian support. At the outset, the aspiration of an independent nation has brought people of different ethnic groups together. Tunku Abdul Rahman Putra Al-Haj, the first prime minister of Malaysia, succeeded in forming a coalition of the three main races known as the Alliance party. The Alliance was made up of UMNO, MCA and MIC, and was formed to negotiate independence from the British (Ahmad, 2014). This coalition was enlarged when Barisan Nasional (the National Front) was formed. Other parties that represent other ethnic groups include the PBB (Parti Pesaka Bumiputera Bersatu) representing the Melanaus and Malays and Dayaks in Sarawak; in Sabah the PBS (United Sabah Party) represents the Kadazans and Dusuns; and USNO (Parti Pertubuhan Kebangsaan Sabah Bersatu) represents the Muslim Bumiputra. Ratnam (1965) described Malaysian parties as communal, and this label lingers on although attempts have been made to eradicate the identification of race with party.

Malaysia's parliamentary democracy started with the first national election in 1959. The federal parliament is bicameral with the lower house called the Dewan Rakyat (Lower House of Elected Representatives) and an upper house called the Dewan Negara (Upper House of Nominated Representatives). Governments have a maximum term of five years but in actual practice national elections are more frequent.

Government PR during the colonial period

The role of public relations in advancing government policy in Malaysia was instrumental long before independence. Adnan (2004: 126) asserted that PR during the colonial period was purely propaganda and designed to fight 'for the cause of the imperial master'. Idid (2004) states that the modern practice of PR began before World War II when the British administration formed the Department of Information (1939) and the Department of Information and

Publicity (1941). These departments primarily functioned as a press bureaux to keep British citizens informed about the war. At the same time, public relations was largely used to mobilise support in the colonies and to ward off the Japanese threat in Malaya. These departments ceased to function when Malaya was occupied by the Japanese Imperial Army in January 1942 (Raj, 2007). The British made a comeback when the Japanese withdrew from Malaya in 1945 (Ahmad, 2014). The Department of Public Relations (1946) was established to restore trust among the people of Malaya after the colonial administration's defeat at the hands of the Japanese. An 'Emergency' was declared in Malaya during the Communist insurgency against the government from 1948 to 1960 (Idid, 2004). Subsequently, the British formed the Department of Information and Services (1952) to counter any form of propaganda that might threaten the colonial status quo (Idid, 2004). The British had thrived against the Communists by winning the hearts and minds of the people. They adopted a psychological warfare strategy that attempted to address the different groups' concerns. This included, for example, relocating the Chinese to a new settlement to protect them from the Communists and granting them citizenship. Such initiatives helped the British to secure the support of the Chinese. In a nutshell, government public relations during the colonial period was largely used to pursue the British colonial agenda and was primarily self-serving (Ahmad, 2014).

National policies to sustain racial harmony

Malaysia learned a hard lesson from the dark incident of a racial clash in 1969. The former prime minister, Tun Mahathir Mohamad (1998), affirmed that the race riot could be partly attributed to economic imbalances between races which were inherited from the British divide-and-rule policy. This policy had placed the Malays in remote villages, thus deprived of education and wealth when compared to the urban Chinese. Resentment among the Malays accumulated when their lives changed little even after independence. Furthermore, Idid (2004) asserts that poor communication regarding government policies served as another reason that contributed to the riot: 'the lack of information bred suspicion among the Chinese and the Malays, leading each to believe that the other was getting a better deal from the government' (Idid, 2004: 215).

The aftermath of civil unrest saw PR given a greater role in governmental institutions. Following the riot, public relations officers were appointed in various government agencies. Part of the major function of these officers was to keep the people informed and make sure they understood national policies introduced by the government (Ibrahim, cited in Idid, 2004: 215). PR's role was also to ensure sensitive issues were handled with extra caution to prevent racial conflict. The Ministry of National Unity was also formed to develop programmes that would enhance national cohesion. It is important to note that economic disparity among races was singled out as a major factor of the racial clash. Thus, the government, then under Prime Minister Tun Abdul Razak bin Hussein, introduced the NEP as a remedial action. The NEP was a twenty-year economic plan (1971–1990) which, among other things, 'aimed to eliminate the identification of race with economic function' (Mahathir, 1998: 9). The policy was viewed as a massive effort to 'correct an injustice resulting from past policies and actions' in Malaysia (Mahathir, 1998: 73). Former prime minister Mahathir Mohamad (1998) equated the NEP with a moderate form of affirmative action which was somewhat similar to the 'positive discrimination' which favoured minority groups in the USA. In this regard, the NEP created an opportunity for Bumiputra to participate in the mainstream economy in order to acquire at least 30 per cent of the nation's economic wealth by the year 1990 ('New Economic Policy', 2015). It has been reported that prior to the introduction of the NEP, the Bumiputra (making up 56 per cent of the population) controlled only 2.4 per cent of the nation's economic wealth, while the non-Bumiputra (43 per cent of the population) owned more than 34 per cent, with the remainder (over 60 per cent) in foreign hands (Chin, 2009). Critics affirmed that NEP was a massive government intervention that gave preferential treatment to the Malays and Bumiputra, and thus had affected ethnic relations adversely (Chin, 2009; Noraini and Chan-Hoong, 2013). The policy, among other things, reserved special privileges for the Malays that gave them great opportunities to take part in the socio-economic sphere (Chin, 2009): the Malays were given more places in public universities, and more employment opportunities in the public sector and in businesses. This special position of the Malays continues to be challenged, particularly by the Chinese.

Subsequently, several other key policies were introduced by the government in the 1980s that were purposely designed to bring Malaysia closer to NEP's target: for example, the 'Privatisation' policy and 'Industrialisation' policy that largely succeeded in attracting foreign direct investment (FDI) and subsequently spurred more business opportunities leading to substantial economic growth. Parallel to NEP these policies opened doors for the Bumiputras' participation in business. The 'social restructuring' targets of NEP continue to be part of the Vision 2020 that was formulated during the tenure of Mahathir Mohamad. Among other goals, Vision 2020 aimed to transform Malaysia into a developed nation with its own style ('Key policies', 2015). Vision 2020 has clearly outlined nine challenges that Malaysians need to overcome prior to achieving a developed Malaysia. These include establishing a united Malaysian nation with a sense of common and shared destiny (Mahathir, 2010).

Malaysia has successfully maintained a peace since the 1969 race riot. The ability of the current ruling party, Barisan Nasional, to manage and to overcome the ethnic conflicts over time has been mentioned by several scholars (Ratnam and Milne, 1967). Barisan Nasional's enduring vision is to create a united Malaysian nation or 'bangsa Malaysia' that ideally represents the ability to share a common national identity while pursuing respective ethnic groups' cultural identity (Abdullah and Pedersen, 2003). Mahathir Mohamad (5 April 2013) claimed that the spirit of *kongsi* or sharing adopted by Barisan Nasional (BN) had brought peace and stability to the country. Drawing from the Malaysian context, he defined the concept of sharing as having to give up some things so that other groups can have their share. He stated:

> sharing means having to give up something so that other parties can also enjoy their portions. Taking everything that each believes is his entitlement would not make sharing meaningful.
>
> (Mahathir, 2013)

However, internal conflict and friction remain as part of the Malaysian experience. The founding director of Universiti Kebangsaan Malaysia's Institute of Ethnic Studies (KITA), Professor Shamsul Amri, dubbed Malaysians as living in a state of a 'stable tension' (Halim, 2010).

The national transformation programme

Following Barisan Nasional's huge loss in the 2008 general election a new prime minister, Najib Tun Abdul Razak, assumed leadership in 2009 and began a national transformation programme to win back the people's trust and support.

His administration's transformation programme is based on eight pillars consisting of four key thrusts and four complementary values. The four key thrusts are the '1Malaysia: People First, Performance Now' concept, the Government Transformation Programme (GTP), a New Economic Model (NEM) and the 10th Malaysia Plan (10MP) (see Figure 9.1).

The first two pillars are to unite and give priority to the people of Malaysia. The third and fourth pillars, namely the NEM and 10MP, are two economic strategies that will provide the road map for the country's direction in the immediate, medium and long term. The four complementary values are: establishing a culture of creativity and innovation; prioritising prompt action-taking and decision-making; striving to provide value for taxpayers' money, and emphasising the virtue of integrity at work. The four key thrusts and four complementary values support one another.

The Government Transformation Programme (GTP) is a new way to solve existing issues such as reducing crime and corruption, creating basic rural infrastructures, public transport, and increasing the living standards of low-income households. The programme aims to change the mindset of government ministries and related agencies by prioritising public service above self service. On the economic matters, Najib announced the New Economic Model (NEM) to help Malaysia become a high-income, advanced nation with comprehensiveness and sustainability corresponding to Vision 2020. The plan emphasises ways to increase the income and productivity of workers by encouraging knowledge industries and increasing investment from overseas.

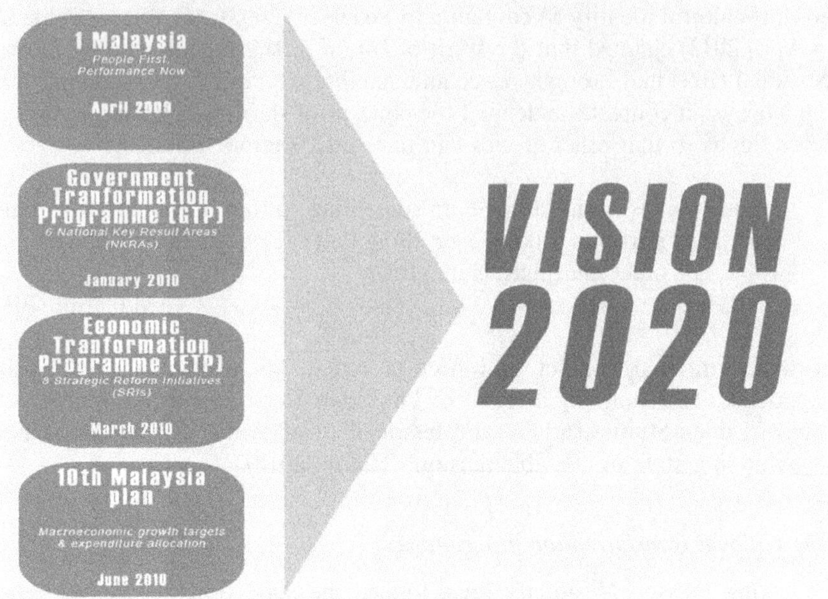

Figure 9.1 The national transformation programme

The changes to the affirmative action policy introduced in the NEM are to reduce poverty and improve the standard of living for all Malaysians. Moreover, Najib gave assurances that the NEM's renewed affirmative action policy would be built on four principles: market-friendly, merit-based, transparent, and needs-driven. It would also promote an inclusive and fair approach for meeting the needs of Malaysia's poorest citizens as a fundamental component of racial harmony.

In the interim, the prime minister also announced the Liberalisation Policy thus cancelling the special quotas that were reserved for the Malays/Bumiputras in dealing with business shares. This policy was not greeted with enthusiasm by the Malays. In addition, the Foreign Investment Committee (FIC) which required the participation of Bumiputra shareholders, was also abolished (Chin, 2010). The Malays realised that they had less than 30 per cent of the business shares but to the non-Malays such promises were not good for business as they indicated a privilege granted on race grounds rather than on merit. The liberalisation was narrowly defined and avoided areas that affected the Malay political base and strategic sectors which are dominated by the government through government linked companies (GLCs). However, the New Economic Model that calls for a greater economic liberalisaton was considered a good start (Kon Yao et al., 2010). This liberalisation idea introduced by Najib marked a reversal of the policy of allocating 30 per cent equity to the Bumiputras in government-related programmes. This policy had been implemented since 1969 when the NEP was introduced as a result of the riot of that year. Perkasa, a right-wing Malay group, was the first to raise objections and asked Najib to withdraw the policy or risk losing Malay support.

1Malaysia concept

1Malaysia did not have a clear definition. Nevertheless, the concept was announced as part of a national agenda that emphasised ethnic harmony, national unity, and efficient administration and governance. 1Malaysia appeared to promote equality for all ethnic groups. Unlike the NEP which was introduced by the second prime minister, Tun Abdul Razak (father of the current prime minister), the concept of 1Malaysia was seen as more inclusive. Chin (2010) affirmed that 1Malaysia appealed to the non-Malays by 'toning down the Malay's supremacy' (p. 166) that was embedded in NEP. Furthermore, 1Malaysia aimed to rally people's support for Najib's wish to change Malaysia into a developed country. Unlike his late father, Najib saw the value of uniting the various races in the country under one mission and vision. Acknowledging the importance for the government to have the trust and confidence of the people, Najib called for a better delivery system in all government departments and agencies.

Along with the spirit of 1Malaysia, Najib also introduced Key Performance Indicators (KPIs) for his ministers to hold them accountable for their work. In the interim, he started using new media such as Twitter, blogs and Facebook to communicate with citizens about the government, opening previously closed government tenders to increase public participation and scrutiny, soliciting public feedback on government spending and also to encourage ministries to make improvements in their services.

The concept of 1Malaysia is renowned for its wide range of products. These include provision of basic goods, services and necessities at lower prices to ease the cost of living. They include schooling aid of RM100 per child and a book voucher scheme for students, in a scheme known as the Back to School Initiative; '1Malaysia People's Aid' (popularly coined as BRIM) for households earning below RM4,000 per month, '1Malaysia Clinic' and and many more (1Malaysia Products, 2015).

1Malaysia is a deliberate initiative to create a new image for Najib's leadership (Chin, 2010). Despite its people-centred approach, 1Malaysia has been criticised by, among others, Malaysia's longest-serving prime minister Tun Mahathir, who lamented that the concept has failed to unite Malaysians (Shazwan Mustafa, 2010a). A public opinion poll by the Merdeka Centre found that the non-Bumiputra perceived 1Malaysia as a mere political gimmick and a tactic to win non-Bumiputra support (Shazwan Mustafa, 2010b). From the start 1Malaysia has been greeted with misgivings by both non-Malays and Malays. Malays feared that their economic position would no longer be given assistance, while non-Malays feared that the slogan was mere rhetoric.

Under the premiership of Najib Tun Razak, the ruling BN party once again failed to garner satisfactory results in the 13th general election. BN experienced a tightly contested general election particularly from the loose coalition of Pakatan Rakyat (PR) (People Alliance) that was comprised of the DAP (Democratic Action party), the PAS (Pan Malaysian Islamic Party) and the PKR (People's Justice Party). The PR had its best result by denying BN a two-thirds majority. But despite its failure to win the popular vote, BN retained a majority of parliamentary seats.

This study argues that 1Malaysia and its tag line 'People First, Performance Now' have been used not only as a strategy to reduce racial disparity but also as a political tactic to win the hearts and minds of the people. This is vital to maintaining the status quo of the current leadership. Building from this premise, the study aims to explore the concept of 1Malaysia and how it was understood and accepted by Malaysians. It questions whether the intended goal of uniting the people as espoused by the slogan '1Malaysia' has been similarly understood by the grass roots. The study also aims to clarify Malaysians' attitude and behaviour towards the current government policy.

Methodology

The study used surveys to measure public perception and understanding of 1Malaysia. The longitudinal study was carried out for five consecutive years with a total of 7,848 respondents nationwide led by the co-author Professor Dr Syed Arabi Idid. The first three surveys (from 2009 to 2011) were funded by a foundation known as Yayasan Sumber Maklumat (YSM). In 2012, the survey was sponsored by National Council of Professors and finally by Yayasan Kepimpinan dan Strategi Malaysia (Foundation of Strategic and Leadership Malaysia). The surveys were administered face to face. The first survey was conducted in August 2009 (1,458 respondents) four months after Najib Tun Razak had become prime minister. The next survey was conducted a year later with 1,367 respondents. The third and the fourth surveys were carried out in July 2011 (1,647 respondents) and 2012 (1,913 respondents) respectively. Finally, in 2013 a nationwide survey was conducted in June with 1,463 respondents. This longitudinal study served to examine Malaysians' acceptance and understanding of 1Malaysia from its inception. The study identified a link between people's perception of and attitudes to 1Malaysia and their attitude and behaviour regarding the government's policy.

Samples were selected using random stratified quota sampling according to racial composition, gender and age. The survey used a closed-ended question to ask whether the respondent agreed with the concept of 1Malaysia, using four item-scales that provide options for respondents to choose from: (1) totally disagree, (2) disagree, (3) agree, and (4) totally agree. In 2013 five item-scales were used to capture a greater variety of responses from respondents by adding 'slightly agree' as part of the scale. The literature had affirmed that 1Malaysia was an ill-defined concept. Therefore, the study decided to ask respondents what they understood by the concept of 1Malaysia using an open-ended question.

Findings

The survey included respondents from the three dominant races in Malaysia. Most respondents were Malays (56 per cent) followed by Chinese (33 per cent) and Indians (11 per cent) (see Table 9.1). In terms of age groups, 39 per cent of respondents were aged between 21 and 35 years old, 38 per cent were aged between 36 and 50 years old, and 24 per cent were above the age of 51 years old (see Table 9.2).

The study found that the1Malaysia concept was well received by Malaysians since it was first announced in 2009. A majority of respondents indicated strong agreement with the idea of 1Malaysia throughout the five-year period (see Figure 9.2). In 2013 the level of acceptance had increased to 86 per cent. However, the intensity of agreement has gradually weakened in comparison to the earlier years. This was evident when the number of respondents who indicated that they totally agreed with the concept fell by 20 per cent in 2013 compared to 2012. Furthermore, the number of respondents who agreed with the concept also fell from 56 per cent in 2012 to 34 per cent in 2013. The Chinese respondents have changed their opinions about the concept in a significant way. For example, the number of Chinese respondents

Table 9.1 Demographic profiles based on ethnicity

Year	*Malay*		*Chinese*		*Indian*		*Total*
2009	811	56%	461	32%	186	13%	1,458
2010	786	57%	426	31%	155	11%	1,367
2011	973	59%	522	32%	152	9%	1,647
2012	1,154	60%	543	28%	216	11%	1,913
2013	723	49%	618	42%	122	8%	1,463
Total	4,447	56%	2,570	33%	831	11%	7,848

Table 9.2 Demographic profiles based on age group

Year	*21–35 y/o*		*36–50 y/o*		*>51 y/o*		*Total*
2009	550	38%	551	38%	357	24%	1,458
2010	543	40%	511	37%	313	23%	1,367
2011	703	43%	654	40%	290	18%	1,647
2012	678	35%	690	36%	545	28%	1,913
2013	559	38%	548	37%	356	24%	1,463
Total	3,033	39%	2,954	38%	1,861	24%	7,848

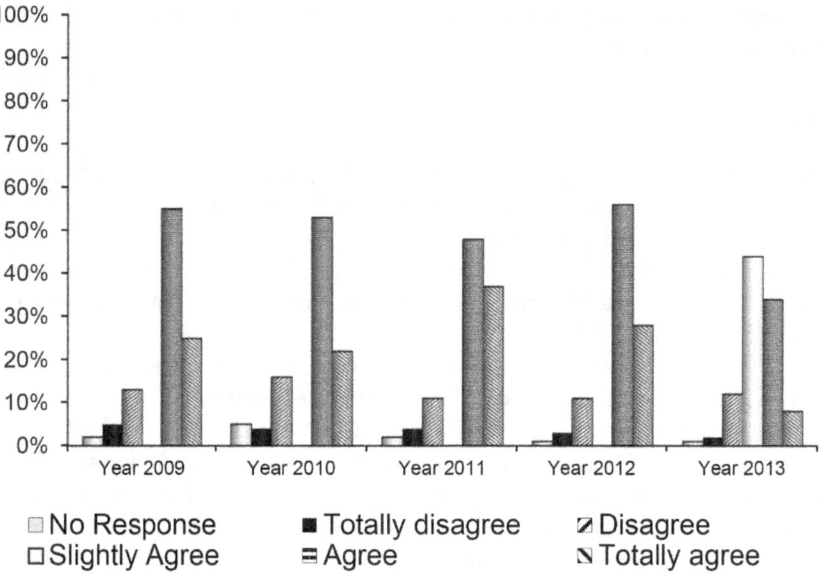

Figure 9.2 Attitudes to the 1Malaysia concept by year

* In the 2013 survey a five-item scale was used. The graph includes those who did not respond to the question.

who indicated that they agreed with 1Malaysia has fallen from 55 per cent in 2012 to 27 per cent in 2013. Furthermore, almost 50 per cent of Chinese respondents indicated that they agreed slightly with 1Malaysia. It is important to note that, as already mentioned, in 2013 the survey adopted five-item scales instead of four-item scales. Thus, despite a high score of agreement (86 per cent) with the idea of 1Malaysia in 2013, more than 40 per cent of respondents indicated only slight agreement with the concept.

In terms of ethnic groups, more than 80 per cent of the Malays and Indians supported the 1Malaysia concept when it was first introduced in 2009 (see Figure 9.3), whereas the level of agreement among Chinese respondents was slightly less (77 per cent). In terms of age group, the survey found that all age groups strongly agreed with the concept of 1Malaysia.

The study demonstrated that the concept of 1Malaysia was not uniformly understood and was subject to many interpretations among Malaysians. Despite being a strategy to promote racial harmony, the survey showed that for the first three years of the study not even half of the respondents interpreted 1Malaysia as representing national unity. However, in 2012 and 2013 the number of respondents who interpreted 1Malaysia as synonymous with national unity has increased from 50 per cent to almost 60 per cent respectively. In the first year of its inception, respondents equated 1Malaysia with 'national unity' (41 per cent) followed by 'living in a multiracial society' (17

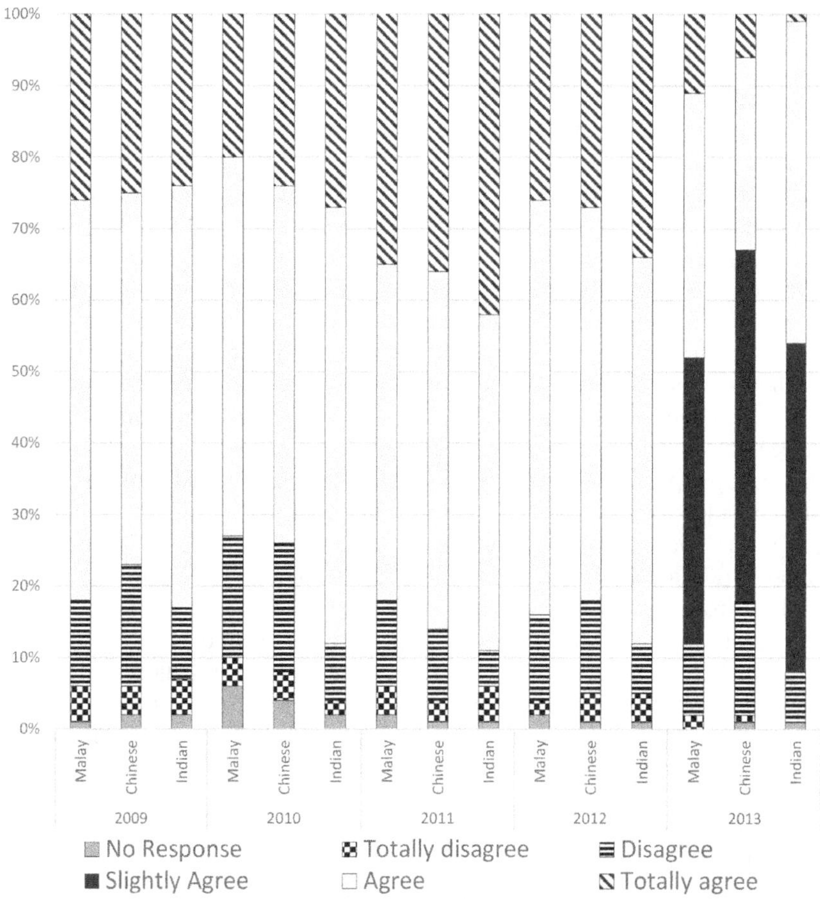

Figure 9.3 Attitudes to the 1Malaysia concept by ethnicity

* In the 2013 survey a five-item scale was used. The graph includes those who did not respond to the question.

per cent) and 'justice and fair treatment' (9 per cent). Beside 'national unity', the respondents frequently defined the meaning of 1Malaysia as giving priority to the people in line with its slogan 'People First …', especially from 2010 to 2012. Respondents also interpreted 1Malaysia as 'helping one another', 'feeling of togetherness' and 'multiracial society' among others. The different levels of understanding of 1Malaysia's meaning may impact the public's different expectations of the current leadership. In other words, 1Malaysia tends to give different hopes to different people. Failure to meet these multiple expectations would lead to frustration among constituents thus affect the *rakyat* (citizen)–government relationship. In such a case, a mutually beneficial relationship between the people and the government will never be achieved.

Discussion

Malaysia: securing a stronger mandate

The Malaysian government has introduced various key policies to address economic and social imbalances that were major obstacles to the national integration of the many ethnic groups in the country. Similarly, numerous programmes have been constantly organised to sustain social cohesion. This is particularly evident when national integration is at stake: for example, the riot in 1969 moved the government to introduce the NEP (1971–1990), a twenty-year plan that aimed to 'lift up the econom[ic] and social status of the Malays' (Torii, 1997: 209). This policy would enable them to catch up with the others, especially the Chinese community that has acquired a dominant share in the economy from an early stage. Over the years, government policies have been designed to accommodate demands and expectations from different ethnic groups, particularly on issues that could spark racial tension. Racial conflict would not only destroy national integration but also have negative implications for socio-economic growth and defeat Malaysia's efforts to become a developed nation by the year 2020. The New Economic Model (NEM) introduced by the current leadership was also responding to the demands of various ethnic groups for equal treatment and fairer distribution of wealth. This accommodative strategy resembles the excellence model of public relations: the two-way symmetrical model of Grunig (2001). In this context, the government remained committed to embark on policies and programmes that would bring mutual benefits to all parties regardless of their differences. These policies were seen as useful for strengthening racial harmony and mitigating conflicts. Alternatively, the policies were considered to be pro-Malay (Torii, 1997; Chin, 2009) as they privileged specific races and were thus portrayed as unjust (Chin, 2009, 2010; Noraini and Chan-Hoong, 2013). However, this study argues that the concept of social justice, including equal distribution of wealth, should be understood within the specific environment of Malaysia, and its historical, socio-cultural, economic and political context.

Likewise, when the ruling Barisan Nasional secured one of its worst results in the 2008 general election, the party searched for a programme to restore public support. It was only in April 2009 when Najib Tun Abdul Razak devised the equitable 1Malaysia programme to draw on the energy and resources of the multi-ethnic society. The programme emphasised a response to the public's needs and improvement of the government's delivery system as reflected in its tag line 'People First, Performance Now'. 1Malaysia was highly recognised by the population. This could be attributed to a strategic and orchestrated effort to promote 1Malaysia and its products through both traditional and new media. Among its popular products that were often highlighted were 1Malaysia People's Aid (BRIM), 1Malaysia Clinic (Klinik 1Malaysia), 1Malaysia Grocery Store (Kedai 1Malaysia), 1Malaysia Voucher

(BRIM), 1Malaysia Housing programme (PRIMA) and many more. At present, there are about twenty-seven 1Malaysia products offered by the current leadership (1Malaysia Products, 2015).

The promotion of 1Malaysia often revolved around Najib's leadership rather than the BN as a party. In many instances, Najib appeared as a single personality rather than accompanied by other BN coalition members to convey the 1Malaysia messages, for example in the television commercial for *Gong Xi Fa Chai* (the Chinese New Year celebration) and during 'meet the people' sessions. The strong association of 1Malaysia with the prime minister could explain the familiarity of Malaysians with the programme and its identification with Najib's premiership. In this case, a high level of public awareness and acceptance of 1Malaysia was not sufficient to secure public support for the current leadership. It could just be an indication of knowledge of the concept and its acceptance as part of government's policy to further develop the nation. However, 1Malaysia's catchphrase and its products were excessively used in the election campaign to secure votes. The current prime minister, who is also the National Front's (BN) chairperson, had included 1Malaysia products as part of the BN's manifesto in the 2013 general election. For example, he pledged to increase BRIM to RM1,200 for those earning below RM3,000 per household ('BN manifesto reflects 1Malaysia spirit', 2013). Other 1Malaysia products served as incentives, for example the 1Malaysia Book Voucher and schooling aid. In other words, 1Malaysia appeared as a strategic tool to win the support of the people. It appeared in the preliminary stages to be a two-way, symmetrical relationship between the government and the people, but evidently there was a mismatch in terms of public acceptance of the 1Malaysia concept in the unfolding years. This could be a reason why the meaning of 1Malaysia was not uniformly understood to be promoting national unity.

On the other hand, the opposition parties viewed 1Malaysia products as a form of enticement to secure votes rather than a genuine tool for social transformation. In this context, 1Malaysia and its products could be seen as a self-serving PR exercise that endows greater benefits to the ruling government without making a real and sustainable impact on the intended recipients. Critical theorists often raised the issue of power imbalances that were inherently present in any relationship. Their critique alleged that the two-way symmetrical approach imparts greater power to organisations, including the government or political actors, thus giving them more control over their environment rather than providing a bridge to the organisation and a voice in management decisions (Grunig, 2009: 10; see also Edwards, 2009). Similarly, Grunig (2001) has reiterated that the symmetrical model actually serves the interests of the organisation better than any asymmetrical model because 'organizations get more of what they want when they give up some of what they want' (p. 13). Based on this argument, the underlying strategy of symmetrical practice is for the government to acquire a better deal from the constituents rather than mutual benefits for all parties.

Despite its popularity, the 1Malaysia concept has yet to win the hearts and minds of the people. The 2013 general election results revealed that 1Malaysia and its products remained ineffective in securing acceptance among Malaysians. The message of 1Malaysia and its benefits were heavily promoted in various forms such as advertisements, billboards, songs, etc. Ashforth and Gibbs (1990), in their discussion of an organisation's legitimacy,[3] argued that corporations that suffered from low legitimacy[4] were more likely to promote their social performance. In the context of government public relations, the quest for legitimacy through symbolic rather than substantive change could easily backfire. In this context, critics lamented that Najib's transformational programme, including 1Malaysia, failed to address real issues such as corruption and national disunity (Chin, 2010; Ramakrishnan, 2015). This study argues that 1Malaysia is a popular slogan but remains in the eyes of the public as political rhetoric. We concur with Ashforth and Gibbs (1990) that publics are not passive constituents in a legitimacy process. Publics are prone to be sceptical of business's explicit attempts to defend legitimacy, particularly when an organisation's reputation is problematic. Therefore, communicating too much about 1Malaysia's achievements and how it has contributed to the people's well-being might have invited greater public scrutiny. More often than not the public would make comparisons between what the government promoted as 'People First, Performance Now' and what really happened on the ground. For example, the Federal Territory Ministry has jumped the gun on banning the soup kitchens in Kuala Lumpur from feeding the poor and homeless, leading to public abhorrence. Referring to this incident in his blog, A. Kadir Jasin (2014), former editor-in-chief of the *New Straits Times*, critically commented that '1Malaysia will be more meaningful if they showed a bit more sincerity and honesty in fulfilling their pledge to prioritize the people as stated in the slogan "People First"'. At the same time, the opposition also could have spun the 1Malaysia concept for their own benefit, thus weakening the government's intended impact of 1Malaysia. This study suggested that the government should walk the talk as it implements the general 1Malaysia concept, as action speaks louder than words. This is imperative in order to instil trust and improve government–*rakyat* (citizen) relationships.

Another major concern is that the implementation of 1Malaysia through its numerous products appears incapable of capturing the essence of national unity and harmony as envisaged by the prime minister. The concept has given much attention to improving government delivery systems or servicing the public. Most initiatives were geared to alleviating the cost of living among the low income group. In other words, these products were merely short-lived support to help the poor rather than a substantive effort to help this sector to improve and pursue a better living in the long term. In this case, economic disparity between the low income group and the high income sector will stay the same. The middle-class urban groups who are largely Chinese resented the wide range of 1Malaysia products that benefited mainly the rural and low income group who were mainly Malays. The recent election results showed that despite 1Malaysia's popularity, Barisan Nasional only won a simple majority of 133 seats out of 222 parliamentary seats. At the outset, the election result showed Chinese voters cast their ballots for the opposition parties instead of BN, and this phenomenon was dubbed the 'Chinese Tsunami' (Anand, 2013) by the premier. This trend appeared worrying as it might shake the social integration that Malaysians have long preserved. Alternatively, local political analysts affirmed that it was due to a major swing among the urban and middle-class electorate rather than a swing based on the race factor (Su-Lyn, 2013). It has been observed that urban middle-class and high income sectors were more likely to commit their votes to the opposition in the last election. Therefore, despite its noble intention to unite a multi-ethnic society, 1Malaysia may have created divisions among social classes and have been perceived as unjust by the deprived groups.

1Malaysia and national integration

In this study we found that people had different interpretations of the concept of 1Malaysia. The country was in need of racial harmony and therefore read 1Malaysia as a rallying point for unity. We argue that understanding the essence of the 1Malaysia concept is fundamental. Sharing a similar interpretation of the concept would help Malaysians to understand the rationale of every policy and programme undertaken by the government without any prejudices. On the contrary, those who failed to grasp the actual meaning of 1Malaysia would continue to be sceptical of the initiative. Furthermore, for those who would be unable to benefit from the government policies such as NEM, 1Malaysia would continue to be perceived as causing discontent, discriminating and threatening. These negative attitudes may lead to constant protest, criticism and racial prejudices among different ethnic groups in Malaysia. Therefore, it becomes imperative for the current leadership to explain the actual meaning of 1Malaysia and illustrate a clear road map for achieving its goal.

1Malaysia has not been used in its totality by the government. The concept has failed to achieve its intended target as it failed to respond to public opinion. The five-year survey presented in this paper provided indicators of people's acceptance of 1Malaysia. Over the years the idea fell out of favour with the public. Government and policy makers ought to have acted on this public reaction by making amendments to the initiative. Drawing from the two-way symmetrical model, there should be negotiation between the government and the public, and any public concern should be addressed properly. In this case, PR needs to play a proactive role in monitoring public attitudes to the concept. The 1Malaysia idea has multiple constituents. A policy announced in favour of one ethnic group may antagonise another ethnic group. The challenge of balancing between different social groups is typical of government PR, and unlike a business's relationship with its stakeholders. The issues are more complex. Government should be sensitive to its multiple constituents, learn and pursue programmes that will work out well for its citizens.

1Malaysia: government–public relationships

1Malaysia has extensively used the Internet and social media, including blogs and video messages, to supply updates on its progress. This is evident from the formation of 1Malaysia.com.my, a personal website of Najib Abdul Razak. The website among other things serves as an interactive platform between the prime minister and other fellow Malaysians. It offers opportunity for the public to engage directly with their leader. In recent years there are more channels of communication available for people to contact government offices and this includes the prime minister, who also has his Facebook and Twitter accounts for interacting with constituents nationwide. Unlike other channels of communication, social media may offer an unprecedented, balanced power relationship between *rakyat* (citizen) and government officials. In this case, the *rakyat* may most likely interact and voice their concerns to leaders. Social media, primarily Twitter and Facebook, were considered vital channels of public communication for Malaysian politicians in the recent general election. However, whether such interaction contributes to more positive and meaningful relationships between *rakyat* and the current leadership is yet to be researched. It is important to note that two-way communication does not necessarily result in mutual understanding. At times, the public feels that its enquiries have not been sufficiently answered by the government, thus opening more space for speculation. Government public relations ought to remain careful to ensure that communications will genuinely contribute to a trusting relationship with a multi-ethnic public.

Conclusion

Preserving national unity in a pluralistic society is indeed an uphill struggle that requires concerted actions not only from the government but also from multiple constituents. Government public relations in Malaysia has adopted an accommodating rather than assimilating approach to sustain social stability in its pluralistic society both before and after independence in 1957. Meeting the competing demands of various ethnic groups remains a challenge. The government must be sensitive to the issues, expectations and needs raised by the *rakyat* (citizen). Furthermore, the multiple ethnic groups' willingness to compromise and negotiate with each other is equally important for avoiding ethnic tension. It is important to note that favouring one ethnic group may create resentment among other groups and be presented and perceived as unjust. Government public relations must play a proactive role in managing public perceptions, being conscious of the inter-group dynamics in its attempts to enhance integration, tolerance and acceptance among the country's many ethnic groups. The two-way symmetrical model that promotes a balanced communication between the organisation and its stakeholders may appear too simplistic for government public relations in a pluralistic society. In other words the two-way symmetrical model needs to be multidirectional instead of just focusing on the government–citizen relationship.

We are postulating that in a pluralistic society, two-way symmetry may be inadequate to explain the necessary relationship between the government and constituents who are basically from different ethnic and religious backgrounds. The socio-economic disparity that underpins these different backgrounds requires an understanding of the dynamics between and among the constituents themselves and their demands on the government. The two-way symmetrical model is limited in seeing a relationship of the government and the public only. There is indeed a tripartite relationship of the government and the multiple constituents. A push by one constituent may affect the other constituents which would inevitably affect government policies and programmes. This had happened to the 1Malaysia plan. A government's programme that appeared favourable to one race was not well received by another race and this brought a negative backlash. The inability of the government to hold multiple dialogues with constituents over its 1Malaysia policy led to its poor acceptance overall, however well-intentioned the original plan might be.

The 1Malaysia concept aims to continue the national agenda set forth by previous and current leaders aiming to unite and develop Malaysia. The concept was well received by all ethnic groups at its inception. However, over the years 1Malaysia has begun to lose steam. The findings presented in this study demonstrate that respondents have started to feel less enthusiastic about the initiative. A lukewarm response was explicit especially among the Chinese and a similar reaction was observed from other groups too. 1Malaysia is an idealistic concept that calls for all ethnic groups to forgo their differences and live together as one nation. Nevertheless, the underlying spirit of 1Malaysia became entangled with politics and thus lost its true meaning of uniting the people. It became a self-serving PR exercise that appeared geared towards meeting a political actor's goal instead of achieving a bigger vision for the people. This study strongly urged that more effort be made to ensure the slogan 'People First, Performance Now' was not mere rhetoric.

This study argues that high public awareness of the concept might have simply implied an effective government PR exercise aiming to reach all segments of society through large-scale and persuasive events and various channels of communication. Nonetheless, the absence of a concrete definition of 1Malaysia invited myriad public interpretations and expectations and thus made the concept problematic. A vague concept has allowed people from different ethnic groups to relate to the concept from their own perspectives, expectations and needs. Subsequently, people may respond differently to 1Malaysia and increase divisions in society.

The 2013 election indicated that the BN government had lost the support of the middle class. It was sustained with the Malay and rural heartland

(Sabah and Sarawak). Politically it will make sense for 1Malaysia to win back the urban middle class with programmes that they will accept. The election result suggested that the middle class were willing to jump the race divide to vote for a party or candidate. In other words, Malaysians were willing to choose a good candidate irrespective of race. The cry for change was loud and clear. This study cautions that 1Malaysia will continue to be another PR effort used by the ruling party to maintain the political status quo rather than make substantive social changes and promote racial integration in Malaysia. Despite being a noble idea in the pursuit of equality within a multi-ethnic setting, 1Malaysia could also be seen as a cynical manipulation of public opinion for short-term political gain. A three-way or tripartite relationship model would have enabled a better appreciation of the issues involved in a pluralist society instead of the two-way symmetry that is the government public relations model today.

Notes

1 Perlis, Kedah, Pulau Pinang, Perak, Selangor, Negri Sembilan, Melaka, Johor, Pahang, Terengganu and Kelantan; whereas Sabah and Sarawak are both located within the island of Borneo.
2 Malacca is one of the states in Peninsular Malaysia.
3 A legitimate organisation is one that is perceived to be pursuing socially acceptable goals in a socially acceptable manner (Ashforth and Gibbs 1990: 177).
4 Low legitimacy organisations include those that are attempting to extend their legitimacy or defend it against a severe challenge (Ashforth and Gibbs 1990: 189).

References

1Malaysia Products (2015) Available at: www.1malaysia.com.my/en/1malaysia-products-1 (accessed 15 April 2015).

Abdullah, A. and Pedersen, P. (2003) *Understanding multicultural Malaysia: delights, puzzles and irritations.* Kuala Lumpur: Prentice Hall.

Adnan, H. (2004) *Government public relations: persuasion, personality and power.* Selangor, Malaysia: Asian Public Relations Academy.

Adnan, H. (2009) *Government and political public relations.* Shah Alam, Malaysia: University Publication Centre.

Ahmad, Z. (2014) 'Malaysia', in Watson, T. (ed.) *Asian perspectives on the development of public relations.* London: Palgrave Macmillan.

A. Kadir Jasin (The scribe A. Kadir Jasin) (2014) 'Soup kitchens vs 1Malaysia', 9 July. Available at: http://kadirjasin.blogspot.com/2014/07/soup-kitchens-vs-1malaysia.html (accessed 12 April 2015).

Anand, R. (2013) 'Najib blames polls results on Chinese tsunami', *Malaysiakini*, 6 May. Available at: www.malaysiakini.com/news/229231 (accessed 10 March 2015).

Ashforth, B. and Gibbs, B. (1990) 'The double edge of organizational legitimation', *Organization Science*, 1(2): 177–194.

Bardhan, N. and Weaver, C. (2011) 'Introduction: public relations in global cultural contexts', in Bardhan, N. and Weaver, C. (eds) *Public relations in global contexts: multi-paradigmatic perspectives.* London: Routledge, pp. 1–28.

Berger, B. (2005) 'Power over, power with, and power to relations: critical reflections on public relations, the dominant coalition and activism', *Journal of Public Relations Research*, 17(1): 5–28.

Berry, J. (2011) 'Integration and multiculturalism: ways towards social solidarity', *Papers on Social Representations*, 20: 1–21.

'BN manifesto reflects 1Malaysia spirit' (2013) *Borneo Post*, 9 April. Available at: www.theborneopost.com/2013/04/09/bn-manifesto-reflects-1Malaysia-spirit/ (accessed 10 August 2015).

Bowen, S. (2012) 'Ethics in government public relations', in Lee, M., Neeley, G. and Stewart, K. (eds) *The practice of government public relations*. London: Taylor & Francis, pp. 157–178.

Chin, J. (2009) 'The Malaysian Chinese dilemma: the Never Ending Policy (NEP)', *Chinese Southern Diaspora Studies*, 3: 167–182.

Chin, J. (2010) 'Malaysia: the rise of Najib and 1Malaysia', *Southeast Asian Affairs*, 1 (January): 165–179.

Cutlip, S., Center, A. and Broom, G. (2006) *Effective public relations*. 9th edn. Englewood Cliffs, NJ: Prentice Hall.

Department of Statistics Malaysia (2015) 'Population update'. Available at: www.statistics.gov.my/ (accessed 10 February 2015).

Edwards, L. (2009) 'Symbolic power and public relations practice: locating individual practitioners in their social context', *Journal of Public Relations Research*, 21(3): 251–272.

Edwards, L. (2011) 'Critical perspectives in global public relations: theorizing power', in Bardhan, N. and Weaver, C. (eds) *Public relations in global contexts: multiparadigmatic perspectives*. London: Routledge, pp. 29–49.

Federal Constitution (2005) Selangor, Malaysia: International Law Book Services.

Grunig, J. (2001) 'Two-way symmetrical public relations: past, present, and future', in Heath, R. (ed.) *Handbook of public relations*. Thousand Oaks, CA: Sage, pp. 11–62.

Grunig, J. (2009) 'Paradigm of global public relations in an age of digitalization', *Prism*, 6(2). Available at: http://praxis.massey.ac.nz/prismon-line journ.html (accessed 15 March 2015).

Grunig, J. and Grunig, L. (1992) 'Models of public relations and communication', in Grunig, J. (ed.) *Excellence in public relations and communication management*. New Jersey: Lawrence Erlbaum Associates, pp. 285–321.

Grunig, J., and Jaatinen, M. (1998) 'Strategic, symmetrical public relations in government: from pluralism to societal corporatism', *Journal of Communication Management*, 3(3): 218–234.

Halim, N. (2010) 'Racial tension will not lead to violence in Malaysia says a UKM don'. Available at www.ukm.my/news/index.php/component/content/article/554-racial-tensions-will-not-lead-to-violence-in-malaysia-says-a-ukm-don.html (accessed 10 April 2015).

Ibrahim, A. and Joned, A. (1987) *The Malaysian legal system*. Kuala Lumpur: Dewan Bahasa dan Pustaka.

Idid, S. (2004) 'Public relations in Malaysia from its colonial past to current practice', in Sriramesh, K. (ed.) *Public relations in Asia: an anthology*. Singapore: Thompson, pp. 207–235.

Ihlen, O. and Gelders, D. (2010) 'Government communication about potential policies: public relations, propaganda or both?' *Public Relations Review*, 36: 59–62.

'Key policies' (2015) Economic Planning Unit. Available at: www.epu.gov.my/wawasan-2020-1991-2020 (accessed 2 February 2015).

Kon Yao, K., Afif, Abdullah and Wan Saiful, Wan Jan (2010) *Liberalising Malaysian economy? A response to the proposed 'new economic model'*. Kuala Lumpur: Institute for Democracy and Economic Affairs.

Lee, M. (2012) 'Government public relations: what is it good for?' In Lee, M., Neeley, G. and Stewart, K. (eds) *The practice of government public relations.* London: Taylor & Francis, pp. 9–25.

L'Etang, J. (1996) 'Public relations as diplomacy', in Pieczka, M. and L'Etang, J. (eds) *Critical perspectives in public relations.* London: Thompson Business Press, pp. 14–34.

L'Etang, J. (2008) *Public relations concepts, practice and critique.* London: Sage.

Mahathir, M. (1998) *The way forward.* London: Weidenfeld & Nicolson.

Mahathir, M. (2010) 'The way forward (Vision 2020)'. Speech presented at the Malaysian Business Council, 20 March.

Mahathir, M. (2013) 'Only Barisan Nasional makes kongsi idea work', *Malaysian Insider*, 5 April. Available at: www.themalaysiantimes.com.my/only-barisan-nasional-makes-kongsi–idea-work (accessed 25 August 2015).

National Economic Advisory Council (2009) *New economic model for Malaysia.* Putrajaya: Percetakan Nasional Malaysia Berhad.

'New Economic Policy' (2015) Economic Planning Unit. Available at: www.epu.gov.my/en/dasar-ekonomi-baru (accessed 10 January 2015).

Noraini, M. Noor and Chan-Hoong, L. (2013) 'Multiculturalism in Malaysia and Singapore: contesting models', *International Journal of Intercultural Relations*, 37: 714–726.

Raj, J. (2007) *The struggle for Malaysian independence.* Selangor, Malaysia: MPH Publishing.

Ramakrishnan, S. (2015) '1Malaysia initiatives finally drowned in debts', *Malaysian Insider*, 19 March. Available at: www.malaysiakini.com/letters/292512 (accessed 10 April 2015).

Ratnam, J. (1965) *Communalism and the political process.* Kuala Lumpur: University of Malaya Press.

Ratnam, J. and Milne, K. (1967) *The Malaya parliamentary election of 1964*. Singapore: University of Malaya Press.

Roper, J. (2005) 'Symmetrical communication: excellent public relations or a strategy for hegemony?' *Journal of Public Relations Research*, 17(1): 69–89.

Shazwan Mustafa, K. (2010a) 'Dr. M says Najib must explain 1Malaysia', *Malaysian Insider*, 2 August. Available at: www.the malaysianinsider.com/Malaysia/article/dr-m-says-najib-must-explain-1malaysia (accessed 21 June 2015).

Shazwan Mustafa, K. (2010b) 'Critics nod as Dr. M pillories 1Malaysia', *Malaysian Insider*, 4 August. Available at: www.the malaysianinsider.com/Malaysia/article/critics-nod-as-dr-m-pillories-1-malaysia (accessed 3 July 2015).

Su-Lyn, B. (2013) 'GE13 an urban, not Chinese swing, say analysts', *Malaysian Insider*, 7 May. Available at: www.themalaysianinsider.com/malaysia/article/ge13-an-urban-not-chinese-swing-say-analysts (accessed 12 March 2015).

Taylor, M. (2000) 'Toward a public relations approach to nation building', *Journal of Public Relations Research*, 12(2): 179–210.

Torii, T. (1997) 'The new economic policy and the United Malays National Organization', *The Developing Economies*, 35(3): 209–239.

Vandebosche, H. (2004) *A reader in government policy and communication.* Antwerpen: University of Antwerp.

10 Propaganda in Czechoslovakia in the 1980s

Life in a ritualised lie

Denisa Hejlová and David Klimeš

Introduction: hard and soft Communist power from 1948 to 1989 as a tool for unifying Czechs and Slovaks

The idea of a common state of Czechs and Slovaks was promoted heavily by Czech sociologist and later president Tomáš Garrigue Masaryk, who lobbied successfully among international political leaders during World War I for one state. The common state of Czechoslovakia was established in 1918, after the collapse of the Austro-Hungarian monarchy. A large minority of citizens of the Czechoslovakia that existed from 1918 to 1938 were Germans in the Czech part, Hungarians in the Slovak part, and Rusyns in Subcarpathia. Problems among nations and ethnic groups were exploited by nationalists on the eve of World War II. According to the Munich Agreement of 29 September 1938 – signed by Britain, France, Germany and Italy – Czechoslovakia lost much of the borderland that was inhabited mainly by German people. Only a few months later, on 12 March 1939, the Slovaks declared their own independent state under the patronage of Hitler's Germany. Masaryk's vision of one Czechoslovak nation seemed to be dead.

After World War II, the state of Czechoslovakia was established again, but with different borders and a different social structure. Ruthenia was now a part of the USSR and the expulsion of more than 3 million German people dramatically changed the ethnic makeup of Czechoslovakia. The Communist Party of Czechoslovakia (KSČ) seized political power in February 1948 in a coup d'état that was supported heavily by the Soviet Union. The events of 25 February are often marked as the start of the Cold War, and a long four decades of Communist dictatorship in Czechoslovakia. Czechoslovakia became one of the horizontally divided societies (Guelke, 2012: 1), whereby a narrow group of ruling Communist elite (nomenklatura) governed the entire society through a one-party system. In 1960, the name of Czechoslovakia was changed to the Czechoslovak Socialist Republic, in order to express the dominant and central role of political ideology. Nevertheless, in 1969, Czechoslovakia became a federation in order to smooth tensions between the Czech and Slovak nations.

In order to maintain its power, the government used both a repressive system and an ideology to create a narrative for its own legitimacy, arising from the 'working class'. Louis Althusser, a neo-Marxist himself, provides a useful understanding of hegemony: the ruling power (in this case not the capitalists but the Communist Party) uses a repressive state apparatus (or so-called hard power) such as the army, the police, the judiciary or the prison system, in order to intimidate and punish its opponents. But it is not only physical coercion or violence that helps to keep the totalitarian regime in power – it is also accompanied by a massive state ideology, as Althusser puts it, an Ideological State Apparatus (or so-called soft power), which embeds the meta-narrative of political ideology in education, schooling system, lifestyle, media and entertainment (Žižek, 2012: 115). Now, despite the fact that this system of a repressive and ideological state apparatus is widely understood by left-oriented or neo-Marxist thinkers, it actually helps us to understand the basics of the operational system of socialist totalitarian regimes – as described here, with Czechoslovakia as the example.

In the 1950s, the Communists used both hard power and repressive methods. Their political opponents were imprisoned or even executed (Courtois and Kramer, 1999: 405). Trials were prepared and completely staged by Soviet 'advisors' (Kaplan, 1995: 20), and used as instruments of Communist propaganda (Formánková and Koura, 2009). The former political, business and intellectual elites (i.e. the bourgeoisie) were systematically eliminated or persecuted. Hard power went hand in hand with soft power, using the socialist ideology as the main narrative.

In the 1950s, the era of massive pro-Soviet and Communist propaganda started. The Czechoslovak coup d'état was named 'Victorious February', and the date of 25 February became an officially celebrated national holiday. In 1918, under the leadership of President Tomáš Garrigue Masaryk, Czechs and Slovaks had formed a unified democratic state – despite some language, cultural and historical differences. But after 1948 Czechoslovakia was embedded under the umbrella of Soviet influence, which used 'Pan-Slavic rhetoric of the nineteenth century to justify its domination of Eastern Europe' (Cull et al., 2003: 31). The era of great adoration of the Soviet Union began. After the death of Stalin in 1953, the regime in Czechoslovakia remained one of his most devoted admirers, and in 1955 it unveiled the world's largest monument, cut in granite and measuring 15 metres in height and 22 metres in length (in Letná, Prague). The tight Soviet–Czechoslovak relationship was marked by the slogan/aspiration 'With the USSR forever' or 'Friendship with the USSR forever'. This became one of the most-quoted slogans for all state and political celebrations and political speeches. Contrary to Hungary, in Czechoslovakia the media came under state control and strong censorship, affecting newspapers, television and radio news, as well as novels, textbooks, and even poetry and song lyrics. During the 1950s most of the Communist 'newspeak' appeared, as will be described in more detail later.

But during the 1960s, the overall situation began to change. Media were partly liberated from strong censorship, the arts blossomed, and in 1962 Stalin's monument was taken down (using 800 kg of explosives). These cultural and intellectual movements, supported by the dissident historical narrative of Czechoslovakia as a country of democratic traditions (Blaive in Kind-Kovacs and Labov, 2013: 130), were brutally oppressed after the Prague Spring in 1968, when the Soviet tanks forced KSČ to change its Communist elite in response to Moscow's demand. In the 1970s, the era of 'normalisation' started (Eidlin, 1980). The Communist propaganda became a staged theatre, which was externally approved by the vast majority of citizens (Havel, 2012). Opposition material and literature circulated clandestinely, and became known as 'samizdat' (Cull et al., 2003: 31). Havel calls this attitude of the Czechoslovak citizens 'the principle of external adaptation': people raised Soviet flags and participated in Communist propaganda to show their dedication to the state politics, but they cared more about their own comfort and easy life, withdrawing from 'politics' (Havel, 2012: 53). However, the mutual relationship between various societal groups and the state propaganda was more complicated.

In 1978, the average Czechoslovak citizen's situation is reflected in Havel's essay 'The Power of the Powerless', where he gives the example of a greengrocer:

> At the greengrocer's, the head assistant placed the slogan 'Proletarians of all countries, unite' in the shop window, between the carrots and the onions. Why did he do so? And doing so, what did he hereby want to impart to the world? As a person, does he really so fervidly support the idea of the world proletarians being united? Does his fervour go so far that he feels a compulsion for presenting his ideal to the public?
>
> (Havel, 2012: 104)

Based upon his observation of Czechoslovak society, Havel's immediate answer was:

> The slogan functions as a sign, and as such, it contains an entirely definite – although hidden – announcement. Its verbal expression could be interpreted as saying: I – a greengrocer named X or Y – am here, well aware of what I am supposed to do; I behave in an expected way; I am reliable and cannot be reproached for anything; I am obedient, and therefore entitled to living in peace and quiet. Of course there is an addressee of this announcement. The slogan is aimed 'upwards', at the greengrocer's superiors; at the same time, it is a shield by which the greengrocer is defended from potential denouncers.
>
> (Havel, 2012: 105)

For the whole communicational dimension of the outward adaptation to the political system, Havel uses the term 'ritual intrapower communication'. Without it, the whole power structure would be unable to exist any longer. According to Havel, for this reason the Czechs and Slovaks during the normalisation epoch knowingly 'live in a lie' (Havel, 2012: 110). To research the practical manifestation of the Communist propaganda of 1980s Czechoslovakia, there is very little specialised literature available – primarily essays written on the topic (Fidelius, 1983; Havel, 2012; Šimečka, 1990). Recent literature connects the examination of propaganda with research of a specific issue (for example, the process of rebuilding, Pullmann, 2011). Further literature maps out the specific development of Communist propaganda (Hejlová, 2014).

The first person to focus on the criticism of the language as an ideological apparatus of approval-making was Petr Fidelius (which was the assumed name of Karel Palek). In the early 1980s he deduced that:

> as the parole of the Communist power, we perceive the compulsive monologue, which is produced by the political system as a means of self-justification. The Communist parole as a term is therefore wider than the actual propaganda. After all, for a long time the parole of Communist power had not been intended to promote any positive ideas and/or to persuade anybody of the truth. Instead of being a device of persuasion, language becomes a device of power. It is not concerned with spreading any ideas; on the contrary, it is concerned with paralysing the ability to think.
>
> (Fidelius, 1983: 8)

The input of Fidelius' work resides especially in the disclosure of the 'semantic inflation' as a phenomenon occurring in the particular terms of the official propaganda – the ones that are most frequently misused:

> Such terms as *people, society, democracy* or *state* are typical examples of the terms which can be understood (and which also usually are understood) as a large number of various, often contradictory meanings. They can be used by practically anybody in a purposeful way – precisely because nobody exactly knows their real meaning.
>
> (Fidelius, 1983: 24)

In his analysis of the contemporary press he points out that the meaning of the term *people* is sometimes global, sometimes restrictive – i.e. occasionally this term is used to denominate only certain citizens. Fidelius deduces that 'there is no possibility that the term *people* objectively includes somebody who is viewed by the Communist Party as an opponent' (Fidelius, 1983, p. 36). The term *people* can thus be reduced to 'the core of the people' and then further to 'the core', which is the Party. The empty phrase 'to go with the people' then actually means 'to go with the Party', and this real meaning is understood by everybody. One of the crucial characteristics of Communist propaganda is also its distinction from the old (Fidelius, 1983: 89). In the contemporary press, the phrases 'working people' or 'people's democracy' or 'real-life socialism' are regularly used; their difference from the original meanings of such terms as *people* or *democracy* or *socialism* is therefore evident.

Consequently, from these individual phenomena, Fidelius deduces the main device for achieving official consensus in Czechoslovakia during the 1980s – nothing but institutionalised violence:

> Totalism is based upon the awareness of the fact that its superiority can be maintained and the obedience of its 'subjects' can be maintained only if the soul of a human being has been successfully subdued. Totalism strives for this aim by means of the specifically adjusted ideology, which is put forward by the perfectly elaborated technique of monopolized propaganda.
>
> (Fidelius, 1983: 161)

Thus, the Communist regime enforced consent in society and blocked the debate about the nature of the totalitarian regime or the relationship between Czechs and Slovaks.

Propaganda, persuasion or PR? Defining the Communist ideology machine

Defining the role, tools and effects of Communist propaganda is not easy, and there is no unified or clear explanation to which we can refer. Jowett and O'Donnell (2014: 1) define propaganda quite broadly as 'a form of communication that attempts to achieve a response that furthers the desired intent of the propagandist', and describe various forms and examples, which give us a more detailed understanding of what propaganda is in various historical and regional contexts. However, the propaganda that was spread under Soviet directives in countries under Soviet influence has not yet been thoroughly examined. Bentele described propaganda in the German Democratic Republic (GDR), where propaganda (or merely agitation, because the word *propaganda* itself has had negative connotations from World War II) was 'spreading the scientific belief (*Weltanschauung*) of Marxism-Leninism, which existed in many forms', such as International propaganda (spreading propaganda to foreign, namely Western countries) – Production propaganda ('sales'), and journalism as a part of propaganda (journalists were taken to be an integral and cooperating part of socialist society, not as watchdogs) (Bentele, 2013: 279).

The propaganda techniques used by the Communists during the second decade of normalisation in the 1980s became subtler and softer than those used when they came to power in 1948 (Hejlová, 2015: 81). Analysing the methods and tools of Communist propaganda in the 1950s, Vladimir Dubnic de Reisky (1960) described the methods of indoctrination and agitation using scientific explanations to promote Sovietisation or propaganda among intellectuals, academics, artists, etc. (Dubnic, 1960). Although ideological persuasion was still a key aspect of Communist power in the 1980s, the techniques and tools became more sophisticated. We can distinguish between 'agitation' in the 1950s, using propaganda methods very similar to those used during World War II, and 'public relations' (*práce s veřejností*) or 'economic or technological progaganda' used in the 1980s. The concept of *práce s veřejností*, derived from the German word *Öffentlichkeitsarbeit*, was introduced by the GDR, or as 'public relations' by Great Britain (Hejlová, 2014).

Öffentlichkeitsarbeit was introduced in the 1960s in the GDR; Bentele described in detail the differences between the totalitarian notion of propaganda and public relations in the GDR (not only in political, but also in economic and media systems), and those can be applied to most of the former Eastern Bloc countries (Bentele et al., 2008: 413–414). In spite of the fact that the notion of 'socialist PR' (Pavlů, 1977) resembles in some ways the Western approach (Grunig and Hunt, 1984) and some authors discuss the existence of PR within socialist societies (Szyszka, 1998, Kocks and Raupp, 2014), we cannot talk about public relations in the sense of a communication process in order to support the required position in 'competing discourses' (Daymon and Demetrious, 2013: 3) or 'dialogic theory' (Kent and Taylor, 2002). Within the context of the authoritarian regime, propaganda (Jowett and O'Donnell, 2014; Bentele, 1998, 2013; Bentele et al., 2008) was used to unify the official discourse of the Communist Party of Czechoslovakia. Bentele et al. (2008) described the organisation of systematic propaganda as a top-down model: 'power, control and the flow of information went only from the top down' (p. 415).

As Grunig et al. (2004: 137) concluded, 'there were no public relations in Eastern Europe before 1989 because the concept was not acceptable for socialism'. However, some local authors are disputing this opinion. Szondi (in Watson, 2014: 42) argues that this conclusion is based on the Yugoslavian example and is thus unbalanced and 'incorrect'. Szondi puts the beginnings of the professional development of the PR field under the Communist regime already in the 1960s, similar to the development in the Czech Republic (then Czechoslovakia) (see Watson, 2014). Both in Hungary and in Czechoslovakia, PR was used mainly 'by the foreign state propagandist … to advertise Hungarian [or Czechoslovakian, notes author D.H.] companies and their products abroad as well as to place advertisements of foreign products and companies in the media' (Szondi in Watson, 2014: 43). Press departments existed in the former Czechoslovakia in major commercial and political bodies, as well as in other countries of the former Eastern Bloc (see Watson, 2014).

The terminology, however, was different. The word PR was only used in communications directed at the West. As Czech PR pioneer Jindřich Lacko stated, the PR was 'only meant to go abroad. Everything that went inside [i.e. to the Czechoslovak public, D.H.] was propaganda' (see Hejlová, 2014: 33). The neutral word, which was used extensively for all forms of persuasive communication in Czechoslovakia, was *propagace* (propagation) or *práce s veřejností* – which derived from the German *Öffentlichkeitsarbeit*, although it translates simply as 'public relations'. Kachlík offers one of the most neutral definitions of *práce s veřejností*:

> communication but also other practices that help to build and maintain positive relations between the public and the subject and lead to an overall climate of creative cooperation, which is necessary for fulfilment of largely societal aims of a certain organization.
>
> (Kachlík, 1985: 6)

Within this newspeak, it is crucial not what is said, but what is unsaid: the clear reference to Marxism-Leninism or socialist society is absent. We can see it clearly when we compare it with another definition by Communist propagandist Dušan Pavlů, who defines propagation (*propagace*) as one of the 'key aspects of ideological and educational tools of socialist society … and as one of the tools of communist upbringing' (Pavlů, 1984: 7).[1]

The Communist 'PR professionals' realised during the 1960s that, in order to be successful in promoting their countries, culture and products in Western societies, they must play by their rules – and started to learn PR from the West (see Watson, 2014). Yet only a very few of them were able to travel abroad or get in touch with Western professionals – and most likely they were under the close watch of the Secret State Police. Only a very limited circle of top professionals had foreign sources (Hejlová in Watson, 2014: 32). Others were following the local teachers of the new method of persuasive communication, who spread the word through specialised courses at select universities (in Czechoslovakia, namely the Faculty of Journalism at the Charles University in Prague or the Czech Economics University).

From the 1970s, local authors published many books, mainly on 'economic propaganda' or 'socialist propagation' or 'technical-economic propaganda' (Kašík, 1987; Kašík and Klimpl, 1982; Košťálová and Seifer, 1979; Zrostlík, 1979; Kachlík, 1985; Nevolová, 1988; Pavlů, 1977; 1978; 1983; 1984; etc.). For example, Zrostlík (1979) published a book concerning the practical implications of socialist propaganda while using how-to examples. Among the most prominent authors – and more importantly, university professors – in the 1960s were Jaroslav Nykryn and Alfons Kachlík, and in the 1980s Milan Kašík, Václav Svoboda and Dušan Pavlů (Hejlová, 2014, 2015). Jaroslav Nykryn and Alfons Kachlík were trying to keep more 'Western' and less political concepts of public relations, but they were a minority among the vast majority of convinced Communist propagandists, namely Kašík, Pavlů and others. Despite their ideological past, these people of influence, who wrote many publications and actively taught Communist views on propagation – and propaganda – in the 1980s maintained their university positions (although not within the dominant Charles University) and kept on teaching and publishing about public relations or marketing communications after 1989 until recently (Pavlů, 2004; 2006a; 2006b; 2009;

etc.; Svoboda, 2003; 2004; 2009; Černá et al., 2006; Kašík and Havlíček, 2012; etc.).

There are ongoing discussions about whether persuasive communication and its forms under Communist rule can be simply called propaganda, because of the lack of freedom of speech and non-democratic political system in the Eastern Bloc countries, or whether they were the same as PR in the Western terminology, or a special form of persuasive communication (for more on PR history-writing see L'Etang, 2008). Kocks and Raupp (2014), using the example of the GDR, analysed the question of whether socialist public relations can conceptually exist. Kocks and Raupp indicate that public relations were indeed existent within the socialist state, both in the political and cultural sector. They analysed the classical functions of PR, such as distribution of information, creating a dialogue (at least at some point) and media relations:

> What we find in analysing 'Socialist Public Relations' in the GDR is anything but a communications oxymoron … Yet 'Socialist Public Relations' is also decisively to be understood as a particular form of PR, a form that tends to have different priorities and a greater emphasis on educational functions.
>
> (Kocks and Raup, 2014: 77)

Kocks and Raupp argue that PR did exist in the GDR on the professional level and thus cannot be simply perceived as 'propaganda'; they prefer the term 'socialist PR'. However, because of deeper differences in political, economic and media systems, as described by Bentele et al. (2008) and quoted above, we use the word propaganda instead of 'socialist PR'.[2]

Methodology

This chapter explores propaganda as an ideological tool that can establish and maintain dominance relationships and uses Thompson's (1990: 60) classification of how individual ideology methods work and reproduce power relations. Ideology was analysed in detail by Thompson (1984, 1990), who defined it not only in the political sense, but also in terms of 'system of thought', 'system of belief' or 'symbolic systems, which pertain to social action or political practice' (Thompson, 1990: 5). Thompson talks about the *modi operandi* of ideology; among these, he ranks the symbolic construction strategies in a particular historical context:

- **Legitimation**. Here, the relationships of dominance are maintained in three ways. By *rationalisation*, the rational reasoning (such as the explanation of the mutually subsequent elements) is linked up. By *universalisation*, the positive aspects for some citizens (such as identifying the 'working' people with the Party) is interpreted as well-being for society.

By *narrativisation*, undeniable timeless stories (such as 'the government of the people') are invented.

- **Dissimulation**. On the other hand, by the methods of dissimulation, relationships are denied and – in this way – reinforced. By shifting the meaning from one person through *displacement*, it is possible to denigrate someone else (e.g. by naming this latter person as an 'enemy of the people'). Through the use of *euphemisation*, a positive evaluation is evoked (e.g. in the term *perestroika* – 'rebuilding'). Dissimulation is also achieved through the use of *tropes* such as metaphors, metonymies and synecdoches.
- **Unification**. By unification, the relationships of inequality within power are eradicated through techniques such as *standardisation* and *symbolisation of unity*. Collective features are attributed to an individual person, who is utilised as a symbol of unity (e.g. in the phrase 'working people's voice').
- **Fragmentation**. By contrast, in fragmentation, the alternative relationships are broken by putting an emphasis upon *discrepancies* and *excluding the ideological opponent from the majority* (e.g. by such labels as 'a disruptor' or 'a hireling of the West').
- **Reification** means 'materialisation', by presenting the processes as unchangeable, eternal and outside time and context (e.g. the system of people's democracy).

To explore the deeper, embedded – or even unsaid – meanings of the text and its relation to the society, the method of critical discourse analysis is very useful (Blommaert and Bulcaen, 2000). Fairclough has contributed widely to the knowledge of relationships between discourse, ideology and social change (Fairclough, 1980; 1993; 2003; 2007; 2013a; 2013b). Other influential thinkers, namely Foucault (2002) and Teun van Dijk (1997; 1998; 2008) also made significant contributions to critical discourse analysis. Fairclough's notion of critical discourse analysis (CDA) will be employed, although other aspects or interpretations of this method are recognised as important.

Fairclough (2013b) describes in detail the methodology of CDA research and also examines the specifics of political discourse and role of the language in 'transition'. He defines discourse as (a) a meaning-making element of the social process, (b) language associated with particular social field or practice (e.g. political discourse), and (c) a way of construing aspects of the world associated with particular social perspective (in our context, a socialist society) (2013b: 232). Whereas Fairclough uses CDA mainly to examine the relations of power, ideology and society in capitalist societies, it can be employed to study its counterparts, i.e. totalitarian Communist regimes. According to Fairclough, CDA has three basic properties that apply to political discourse (2013b: 4):

1 It is relational, focusing on social relations. This aspect is very important when we analyse information or propaganda texts in Communism: they

were meant to shape or constitute social relations and thus also preserve the relations within the political power network. They were multi-layered and carried within them the possibility of multiple interpretations (not only the ideological, but also oppositional, 'between-the-lines').
2 It is dialectical – 'power is partly discourse and discourse is partly power' (2013b: 6) – and when we analyse the discursive conditions of a totalitarian regime (albeit close to its end), where people were persecuted for their opinions, speeches or texts, we have to take this note literally.
3 It is transdisciplinary and can be applied across different fields.

We based our analysis merely on official texts: propaganda textbooks and news, released by the main official source of information, the Czechoslovak Press Agency (ČTK), press agency of the Czechoslovak government. Some may argue that these texts were published as 'compulsory offering' to the state ideology and that they really did not matter to the public. Yet evidence to the contrary can be read literally in between the lines – since the sources are real textbooks which have been used by students at the Faculty of Journalism at Charles University in Prague. We can still see the worn-out, many times read-through pages and underlined sentences. Because of the limits of this chapter, we focus only on these textual sources; however, we derived much information on how to read and interpret the texts from formal and informal interviews and discussions with our colleagues or with journalists.

To answer the main research question 'How was the dominant ideology reproduced in 1980s Czechoslovakia?' we examined the productions of the ČTK in the year 1988. We also comprehensively explored ideology reproduction in enforced public consent: the educational system and the production of propaganda textbooks. The aim was thus to explore possible relations between what was aimed for and what was executed, what existed in theory and how it then translated to day-to-day journalistic practice. We were also trying to tackle possible notions or remarks on the 'deeply divided society', be it socio-political meaning (nomenklatura v. dissent) or national context (Czechs v. Slovaks).

Analyzing ideology in the news: Czechoslovak Press Agency news analysis

In this part, we analyse the news published by the Czechoslovak Press Agency one year before the system collapsed, using Thompson's classification as stated above. The official ideology was trying to bridge the gap between the ruling elite (nomenklatura) and those who were commanded by them, by creating a concept of 'ruling working class' – this means that the vast majority of the 'proletariat' in fact directs the nomenklatura. Thus, the concept of 'working class' was crucial, despite its inner contradictions in meaning (Fidelius, 1983: 165). In the 1988 productions of the ČTK, the phrase 'working people' was found 209 times. Regarding the rigidity of the used term,

Thompson's categories of the symbolic construction strategy were found by means of the CDA method.

By the legitimation of the symbolic order via rationalisation, the items of rational reasoning are linked up:

> We are Marxists, the followers of historical materialism, aware of the fact that social consciousness is determined by its being, by the real-life conditions. However, what matters is the influence upon the changing conditions via the people's purposeful creative activity, via responsible and well-balanced policy. One of the greatest merits of socialism is the fact that, on a large scale, such an activity is enabled by this social order: Provided that by the social revolutionary avant-garde – the Communist Party – society is unified on the basis of a scientifically substantiated programme, that on all the stages of development it remains loyal to the working people, to the items concerning the working class and socialism.
>
> (ČTK, 'The term "activisation of the human factor" had already become familiar', 6 November 1988)

In the text, the items of rational reasoning for the Communist Party procedure are linked together. Yet, paradoxically, the same text gets into a logical inconsistency, inasmuch as the Communist Party is at the same time supposed to be loyal to the scientifically substantiated programme, as well as to the working people, i.e. to the changeable social factor. The working people thus occur here as the completely static legitimation of the Communist Party's aims.

Legitimation by means of universalisation generalises from the positives for some citizens to the well-being of the whole society. This method was used also by President Gustáv Husák in his speech to the army:

> The declaration of the nationalising decrees (the deed by which the bourgeoisie was deprived of its power over the crucial industry, mines and banks) confirmed that the working class and working people, headed by the Communist Party of Czechoslovakia, remain purposeful in putting the aims of the national and democratic revolution into practice. The Victorious February of 1948 opened the journey to socialism, and it enabled the working people to create a truly people's state, filled with social justice, a state of two nations with equal rights – the Czechs and the Slovaks.
>
> (ČTK, 'The command of the President of the Czechoslovak Socialist Republic', 26 October 1988)

The 'working people' here apparently does not stand for all the people who work, because the text implies that the working people cannot include the bourgeoisie. At the same time, it is self-evident that the real aims of the working people are known only to the Communist Party of Czechoslovakia.

By the strategy of legitimation via narrativisation, undeniable stories out of time are created. This was the way 'working people' were presented when the 1918 initiation of the Czechoslovak Republic was explained:

> However, the hopes connected with the initiation of the republic in the minds of the working people did not entirely come true. Despite the undeniable progress and the character of Czechoslovakia, more democratic in comparison with other, neighbouring countries, the capitalist system was not able to solve the elementary rights of the working people and the just arrangement of the relationships between our nations.
>
> (ČTK, 'It was the working people in the Czech lands and in Slovakia', 26 October 1988)

The initiation of the republic thus must be explained only by means of the working people, whose living conditions had improved, but not in a suitable way, because the country had not been governed by the Communist Party of Czechoslovakia.

On the contrary, dissimulations deny the relationships, and in this way these relationships are reinforced. For example by the meaning proposed:

> It was the working people in the Czech lands and in Slovakia, above all the working class, that – influenced by the ideals of the Great October Socialist Revolution – stood up against the Austro-Hungarian monarchy, for the rights of the national self-determination being exerted, for the Czechoslovak statehood.
>
> (ČTK, 'It was the working people in the Czech lands and in Slovakia', 26 October 1988)

In the text, the initiation of the Czechoslovak working people's protest against the Austro-Hungarian Empire is shifted towards the Great October Revolution in Russia. Although this is historically incorrect, during the 1980s this symbolic construction was largely and frequently repeated.

By dissimulation via euphemisation, positive evaluation is evoked:

> The socialist ownership of the means of production enabled a qualitatively new stage of equality to be achieved in the area of political and personal rights, and to the wide social class of the working people it enabled the access to using these rights.
>
> (ČTK, 'For education, for health protection and medical care, for relaxation', 10 December 1988)

Talking about the working people as the reflection of the Communist Party's will is different from a situation where the working people are really supposed to believe in the continual enlargement of their rights. That is why in such a situation, if the talk was related to the 'working people', the propaganda of the 1980s always mentioned 'the wide social class'.

In dissimulation via tropes, metaphors, metonymies and/or synecdoches are used. One of the metaphors frequently used in connection with the 'working people' was 'struggle':

> Our future, the fulfilment of our aims, the growth of the people's living standard, are all going to be determined by the honestly hard building work of each of us. Let us get going with the same steady resolution, determination and self-denial as that which 40 years ago was shown by our working people in the struggle for the socialist future of Czechoslovakia.
>
> (ČTK, 'I want to assure you that the Communist Party Central Committee and the Government of the Czechoslovak Socialist Republic', 25 February 1988)

But the working people's struggle, depending on the context, could take the form of the 1948 constitutional crisis, of the honest fulfilment of the working duties, or of the Communist Party members' internal work. By being used repeatedly, the metaphor was gradually losing its meaning, and eventually became the mere repetitive verbal connection, adopted for propaganda.

In the process of unification, the power relationships are eradicated because collective features are attributed to an individual person, who is standardised as a symbol of unity. Although in West Slovakia the Communists initially got their way with difficulty, the official propaganda left some space only for the class-conscious working people:

> Today, the West-Slovakian region is characterised by nuclear energy, developed industry, the rich vineyards of the Small Carpathian Mountains, and the fertile expanding fields of Rye Island. The journey which has been taken by the working people in this important part of the Czechoslovak Socialist Republic since 1948, is portrayed in the paintings and sculptures by the West-Slovakian artists, an exhibition that has been opened today in the House of the Political Education, attached to the Prague Municipal Communist Party Committee.
>
> (ČTK, 'The West-Slovakian artists in Prague', 29 February 1988)

By contrast, in fragmentation the alternative relationships are broken by the emphasis upon discrepancies and by eliminating the ideological opponent from the majority. One of the classical distinctions of the propaganda in the 1980s is the working people versus the bourgeoisie:

> In the dramatic moments of that time, the fatal questions of the life and future of our nations, of the Czechoslovak state, were at stake. The major focus was the question who would govern our country: Whether it would

> be the working class and, along with it, the working people of the towns and villages, or whether the power would again be grasped by the bourgeoisie, whether the pre-Munich social conditions with the social and national oppression would be restored.
>
> (ČTK, 'Speech of the general secretary of the Czechoslovak Communist Party Central Committee and the chairman of the Czechoslovak National Front Central Committee', 25 February 1988)

The last strategy of the symbolic construction – reification – then means 'materialisation', i.e. presenting the processes as unchangeable, eternal, out of time and context. As an example, we can use the continually repeated slogan 'Long live our working people, socialism and peace!' (ČTK, 'Women and men comrades', 7 November 1988), without anyone asking in the official propaganda about the changes of each significance – i.e. also the class of 'working people' – during the forty years of the Communist government.

Analysing propaganda: critical discourse analysis of propaganda textbooks

The main focus of this part of the critical discourse analysis was to explore the nature and ideological background of propaganda, as it was taught and executed during the 1980s in the Czechoslovak Socialist Republic (ČSSR), with a special focus on the question of whether its philosophical-ideological background can be compared to the contemporary prevalent understanding of PR (compared with the definition of PR as described in Heath, 2013: 722–728, and CIPR, 2014).

First, let us define several terms used to name various aspects of persuasive communication. We have above described the use of *práce s veřejností* according to an East German concept of *Öffentlichkeitsarbeit*, which was more acceptable for the Communist nomenklatura than 'Western' public relations. In Czechoslovakia, the term *propagation* (*propagace*) was used along with the word *propaganda*, but without the primarily political meaning embedded in the word: *propagace* was used mostly as promotion of goods and services, whereas *propaganda* was used to spread ideas or ideology. The English translation of *propagace* is also promotion, but propagation captures a wider sense of 'the spreading of something, as a belief' (Merriam-Webster Dictionary, 2014). Propagation was widely used by a number of institutions, who had propagation departments (*propagačníoddělení*). For example, the headquarters of the Prior department stores had a propagation department, which was responsible for media monitoring, promotional activities, coordination of visual merchandising and window display, and advertising.

The term *advertising* (*reklama*) was considered to be bourgeois and not compatible with the ideological concept of socialist classless society. Yet in practice, the traditional tools of advertising, such as posters, TV spots or newspaper ads were used for both commercial, political and social advertising.

The term *osvěta* (*public awareness*; in the Czech language the meaning is literally 'enlightenment') was used often in public and media communication with merely positive connotations. *Osvěta* was perceived as a public education towards the more modern, future-oriented and advanced society. The claim 'Towards a brighter tomorrow' was used often in communication, and it epitomised the ideology of creating a better (i.e. socialist) society. The same could not have been said about the term *propaganda*, which was remembered mainly by the older generations as a World War I and especially World War II persuasive tool to manipulate the public. But the term *propaganda* was used among the professionals, especially for political communication (Pavlů, 1984; Kašík, 1987). More detailed differences between propagation and propaganda are analysed further below.

It can be concluded that as a common practice among the socialist countries different terminology was used when talking about persuasive communication for the domestic and foreign (meaning: Western) audience. For the domestic audience, there were more subtle and positive terms in the local language used for persuasive communication with the public, such as *Öffentlichkeitsarbeit* in GDR or *work with the public* (*práce s veřejností*) in Czechoslovakia. But for the Western audience, the term *public relations* was used even by professionals of a socialist persuasion, as they wanted to be accepted by Western society and not perceived as some kind of 'propagandists' infiltrating their people (which was more likely when they in fact were cooperating with the intelligence service) (Hejlová, 2014).

Propagation or propaganda?

One of the most widely used terms is *propagation* (*propagace*), which does not bear the political connotations of propaganda. Propagation was defined as:

> one of the tools of managing several social processes and mediated ideological persuasion of the society. Propagation is used for realisation of many societal goals, it is present in many different spheres within the society and it is used by a variety of social subjects and institutions to enforce the interests of the society.
>
> (Pavlů, 1984: 13)

Propagation was used as a 'tool to influence public opinion and behaviour of target groups in [the] wider, not only economic sense', as described in a study text for Charles University students in the Faculty of Journalism (Pavlů, 1984: 6). The goal was to 'deliver the social information from the subject, which was designated to objectively solve the task [i.e. the Communist Party, D.H.], to the target group of recipients, whose aim is to make sure the task is accomplished' (Pavlů, 1984: 6). Propagation was perceived not only as a form of persuasive communication, but as social information *per se*.

However, the term *propaganda* (also called *propaganda* in Czech language), be it specifically economic, technical or related to some other specialisation, was used widely and often as synonymous with *propagace* (propagation or promotion). For example, Kašík uses the term propaganda (propaganda *přestavby hospodářského mechanismu*, i.e. propaganda of the restructuring of the economic system) to describe the state's aim to communicate the massive social, economic and political changes that derived from Gorbachev's perestroika in 1986. Propaganda was also taught at the Charles University in Prague, in the Faculty of Journalism and other institutions.

Persuasive tools for 're-education of the public'

We can see from the above definitions that the goal, far from creating 'mutual understanding between an organisation and its publics' (see the CIPR definition mentioned above, CIPR, 2014), was to create an ideologically cohesive and integrated society. 'After winning the socialist revolution, the working class aims intensively and self-confidently to re-educate the people in the spirit of communist ideology' (Pavlů, 1984: 3). Thus the emphasis on 'education' emerged because education was perceived as a legitimate tool to raise a new, socialist person. Communist ideology was to penetrate the society through:

1 ideological tools of the Communist Party, such as official state and Party resolutions and policies;
2 all parts of the political system of the society, namely cultural revolution and education.

This education was seen as 'scientific *Weltanschauung*', and it was executed through three categories of socialist propagation: (1) economic, also called economic propaganda, (2) social education (*osvěta*, awareness); and (3) state propagation – which was called propaganda (Pavlů, 1984: 3).

The difference between 'Western' promotion and PR and socialist propagation was also perceived from the Eastern point of view through the ideological lens. Whereas Western PR was believed to be used only as a tool for gaining economic profit for businesses in a market society, socialist propagation had much wider and in-depth goals. Propagation was defined as a

> tool, which is being used by social organizations and institutions, ministries, societal organization of National Front and other subjects of social life to significantly influence the ways of public behaviour, both at their workplace and privately, in their working process and leisure time; as a tool, which helps to govern the public towards the meaningful life, rich in cultural impulses, towards the life, whose aim is not consumerism, but harmonious development of personality as a basic precondition and condition for the further development of socialist society.
>
> (Pavlů, 1984: 7)

From the above extract it is evident that the role and aim of what we could possibly call 'socialist PR' was far beyond influencing partial opinions or behaviour, claimed by numerous institutions and groups. The aim was centralised, was directed by the party and had clear goals. It targeted not only the public behaviour of individuals, but also their private life. We can see that sociotechnics, if not social engineering (see Kojder in Podgórecki et al., 1996: 213) was used as a legitimate tool of education by the authoritarian Czechoslovak government to execute political power and ideological control over the public.

One could argue that it is a natural inclination in human society that a minority of the elite rules the majority, and it is a primary function of PR to seek legitimacy for this power game in favour of the dominant players. This is often discussed in Bernays' view of PR as a way for the elite to manipulate the public for their own good (Bernays, 1923, 1947, 1955 – cited in reprint, Bernays 2013). In the socialist propagation, it was the political nomenklatura that was setting the rules for individual and collective behaviour (Kojder in Podgórecki et al., 1996: 215). Their plans and activities were far from a dialogue with the public. And there were clear goals, benchmarks and methods set in advance of the execution:

> propagation in socialist society can be characterised as goal-directed and conceptual communication activity, which mediates specific impulses between the subject [i.e. the sender, D.H.] and its target groups. The goal of the propagation is to achieve socially desirable forms of conscious behaviour of the target group that are in compliance with the social norms.
>
> (Pavlů, 1984: 16)

Journalists as active PRists for the state ideology

Journalists were seen as prominent opinion-makers and mediators of state ideology, not as independent writers watching the behaviour of the state and the politicians, but as active promoters of the state's policies and resolutions. This of course does not reflect the actual state of the socialist society, where many dissidents and underground publishers were actively disseminating the (illegal) information that undermined the official state ideology (and many of them, including the future Czechoslovak president Vaclav Havel, were imprisoned for doing so), but it reflects the official party politics.

Based on Kašík's anthology on the role of journalists in a socialist society, we can find clear evidence that the journalists were seen basically as propagandists themselves, at least from the viewpoint of official Party ideology. It was one of the main research goals of the then Faculty of Journalism of Charles University to bring together the 'scientists' and 'economics journalists' with a clear aim: 'improving the journalistic creative process in order to form the socialist public opinion' (Kašík, 1987: 6) – translated from the newspeak into today's discourse as: actively shaping public opinion towards the acceptance of the socialist ideology. The main goal of Kašík's internally published volume – just two years before the fall of the Berlin Wall – was to reflect Gorbachev's perestroika (1986) and to 'seek new ways to make economic propaganda more efficient and to improve its quality' (Kašík, 1987: 7).

Even in the socialist society, the influencers were aware that, if the propagation was to work, the target groups must like it. Thus the propagation was to respect the current 'fashions' and cultural patterns of the society. According to Pavlů, the propagation should always:

1 Align with the cultural and fashionable standards of the form – have attractive graphics, visual design or packaging.
2 Have attractive content that is interesting for the target group – e.g. that the target group thinks of such content as much needed, actual and right.
3 Be an important mediator of culture – create what we would today call 'cultural memes' and offer high quality cultural experience for its public.
4 Co-create the increase in the standard of living and form a 'new, socialist way of life'.

(Pavlů, 1984: 8)

Journalists were thus essential for conveying the message in forms and ways that were acceptable to and seen to favour the public. But the ideology was also transmitted through a variety of other cultural products and mass media, such as TV series or children's cartoons. Journalists employed in media during 'normalisation' (1970–1980s) were only those who were complying with the totalitarian regime – 'reliable in their opinions' (Bednařík et al., 2011: 326).

Further analysis of this aspect would be very useful – especially the question of how journalists perceived themselves, either as co-creators and servants or as opponents of the regime. In one interview the former TV reporter Jan Martinek claimed that journalists were fully aware that they were participating in and co-creating propaganda. Especially in the 1980s, television was considered the central medium for mass persuasion and thus it was generously supported and meticulously controlled. The main focus was on news production and high-quality entertainment, namely local TV series. Interestingly, we did not find any ideas or information about Czech–Slovak co-existence in any of the propaganda textbooks. Thus the system had to operate on a different level to create this idea of a unified nation. Jan Martinek explained that there were strict rules in Czechoslovak television, which stated that everything had to be divided according to a 2:1 ratio based on the Czech and Slovak populations (there were about 10 million Czechs and 5 million Slovaks). Not only were Czech-speaking and Slovak-speaking[3] citizens proportionally represented as reporters, anchorpersons or actors, but the editors (who served mostly as censors) were also Czechs and Slovaks. 'For example, there were Czech editors for two weeks and then a Slovakian editor had to come to Prague from Slovakia for one week. This was a strict rule which was not possible to bypass' (Martinek, 2015). The editors were instructed to report their regional news. This 2:1 rule also applied to entertainment, the dubbing of foreign films, and so on.

Centralisation of state ideology as a key concept in socialist propaganda

Even if terms like *propagation, awareness* or *economic propaganda* were used to describe the persuasive processes, the main difference between Western PR and the socialist approach lies in the centralisation and state-direction, which penetrated all forms of persuasive communication. 'If the economic propaganda and campaigning should help to enforce the economic policies of the party and the state, then it must be managed on the state-level, to ensure the effective and integrated execution at all levels' (Kachlík, 1987: 8). Of course, the Czechoslovak state propaganda was closely linked to the Soviet Communist Party (Kašík, 1987: 12), and reflected the system and experiences common to the other socialist states.

The propagation was divided into three main categories (Pavlů, 1984: 20):

1 *Economic propagation* – advertising, promotion of goods and services.
2 *Socio-educational propagation* – leisure-time activities and lifestyle shaping, such as public health communication, sport, environmental education, usage of resources and recycling, road safety, culture and hobbies promotion, etc.
3 *State propagation* – state institutional ideological propaganda directed at citizens and foreign countries.

Even in the twilight of the authoritarian regime, the state's aims of centralising communications and taking strong control of the communicated message were evident. In an internal document describing the communication strategy that was to be used to present Gorbachev's perestroika, Kašík (1987: 14–15) states:

> It is essential primarily to:
>
> a Explain on many levels, that the restructuring of the state's economic mechanism is an inevitable part of the Party's progress …
> b Ensure that all the procedures that come along with the restructuring are based on Lenin's principles … deepening of the socialist democracy and consolidating the social ownership …
> c Don't create an illusion that the upcoming changes will bring an instant solution to all problems.

The motivational approach and the social psychology approach to managing public opinion were used efficiently, even by the socialist propaganda. At this point, it is not much different from any other government campaign to promote and motivate rather unpopular state decisions, such as the campaign to gain approval for the USA's involvement in World War II executed by the Creel Committee, or the PR employed to promote Roosevelt's New Deal. Note that both of these campaigns are associated with the boom of PR in the USA and that they can be described as the 'Bernays approach' to PR.

Conclusions

The aim of this chapter has been to examine the role of the propaganda in Czechoslovakia during the second (and final) decade of normalisation, which ended in 1989. At that time Czechoslovakian society was deeply divided between 'two parallel cultural and social spaces with the official sphere, loyal to the regime on one side and colourful various non-official, private-oriented activities ranging from hand-written literature to fine arts on the other side' (Bednařík et al., 2011: 325). The state comprised two nations, of Czechs and of Slovaks, which is not so often mentioned or analysed. The state ideology was meticulously elaborated with Marxist-Leninist philosophy and presented as the objective outcome of scientific research – similar to the situation in the GDR (Bentele et al., 2008; Bentele et al., 2013) and presumably other countries under the Soviet influence. It was conveyed to the wider public through education, culture and, most importantly, mass media. Socialist journalists were educated in order to mediate the state ideology in a likeable and popular way to the public. For the Western audience, the state's image was portrayed in a much less persuasive 'PR approach', creating a 'socialist, yet progressive country' image with high impact on Czechoslovak arts and culture (Hejlová, 2014).

Our research, based on ideological analyses of official information released by the Czechoslovak Press Agency, and critical discourse analysis of propaganda textbooks, demonstrated that the 'official' process of creating propaganda and spreading Communist ideology was thorough, well managed and sophisticated. It created the idea of 'one nation' by expressing and repeating the 'will of the working class', which was 'executed only' by the ruling propaganda. However, when it comes to Czechs and Slovaks, we did not find any evidence of an ideological strategy that was clearly stated in propaganda materials. Instead, the 'brotherhood' between Czechs and Slovaks was kept proportionally by personal politics, which was present from the media to high politics: when the president was Czech, the prime minister had to be Slovak, and vice-versa. In media, proportional representation of Czechs and Slovaks had to be strictly observed: the journalists, the editors, the dubbers and even actors had to represent the population disparity of 2:1 between Czechs and Slovaks respectively. For example, the national anthem began with a Czech song and was followed by a Slovakian song, but it was considered a 'Czechoslovak' song. Probably because of the lack of any ideological reason for the 'forced marriage' between Czechs and Slovaks, there were no substantial disagreements, but the relationship between the two nations within one country came to an end shortly after the collapse of Communism. The two countries were quite easily decoupled in what proved to be an example of amicable divorce (the two independent republics were established on 1 January 1993) – these days a rare phenomenon in international politics – that has often been contrasted to the tragic disintegration of Yugoslavia which led to several civil wars.

The process of forcing the agreement upon the citizens themselves changed considerably during the forty years of Communist rule. In the 1980s the repressive state apparatus was not used as conspicuously as in the 1950s. Rather than that – and on a much larger scale – the state tried to force the citizens' compliance by other means. Petr Fidelius, the first analyst of the Czechoslovak conditions, showed how the language in the public sphere was manipulated by the state (Fidelius, 1983). Such terms as *people, society* and *democracy* all lost their publicly agreed meaning and fell victim to 'semantic inflation'. Despite this fact, the people in the public arena knew how to use them, because these meanings were determined by the Communist Party, mostly with the help of the media. Havel calls this adjustment 'the external adaptation principle' (Havel, 2012), and in this way obedience is forced by the state upon the citizens, who are made to speak the language of official power in public. However, for the accommodation to the official multi-semantic language, schooling by professionals is also required. In Czechoslovakia the PR strategies – of propagation, of cultural activities, of working with the public, of propaganda – were developed under authoritarian conditions (Hejlová, 2014, 2015).

In particular, the analysis shows this well-constructed concept of the ideological impact within the authoritarian political system; this impact is shown in the examples of ČTK productions from 1998 and the related teaching materials, which were then used for educating journalists and propagandists. The phrase 'working people' – which we have analysed here – was strikingly influenced by 'semantic inflation'. This term could mean practically anything: the government, the party, the party leadership, the citizens, the residents, a part of the residents, a class. The certified journalists and propagandists were trying to maintain this semantic inflation until the time of perestroika (Kašík, 1987). Even the principles of perestroika were meant to be explained as a directive to the citizens through the schooling of selected journalists and close work with the media, especially the Czech Press Agency. But in Czechoslovakia, just one more year was left before the 'outward adaptation principle' broke down once and for all. Our main conclusion confirms the findings of Fidelius (1983) and Havel (2012), both of whom, in literary essays, have shown that despite the fact that the system and structure of socialist propaganda was well managed and seemed to be effective, the citizens learned to read between the lines and lived a more or less ritualised lie, and therefore were able to adapt to the new socio-political situation quite quickly.

The chapter brings key insights about specific procedures and perceptions of Communist propaganda that are not only valid for 1980s Czechoslovakia, but were also a reality for most Communist countries of Central and Eastern Europe at that time. It also brings an interesting insight into the mutual relationship between state power, its ideology and propaganda machine, and the society – a relationship that can seem strong, because it is performed in a ritualised, repetitive and symbolic way, but is empty on the inside, and therefore can then collapse easily. Yet our research has been conducted only on a very small scale, and further analysis is much needed, especially in-depth interviews with former journalists and propaganda or communication specialists. This would help us to better understand how the system worked. A more detailed analysis would also be needed to answer the question of how propaganda was perceived by the citizens and to what level and extent it was successful. Also, a multi-national, comparative approach with other countries, for example the GDR, Poland or Hungary, would definitely yield interesting data, which would aid our understanding of propaganda in totalitarian regimes.

Notes

1 More detailed analysis of key terms used by Communist propaganda follows in the analytical part of this text.

2 Also, we have ceased to use the adjective 'socialist (propaganda)', which is more widely used in the Czechoslovak literature, but we stick to the term 'Communist propaganda', which has been coined in the international academic discourse. Some historians might argue that Czechoslovakia (and other Eastern Bloc countries) were on their way to Communism in the stage of 'real socialism', so the term 'Communist propaganda' is not accurate, but the term 'socialist' or 'socialism' is used in current political debate to describe left-wing politics in democratic countries, which is very different from the subject of this paper.

3 Note: the Czech and Slovak languages differ in some aspects, but they are easily understandable for both nations (especially because Czechs and Slovaks were used to listening to the other language from early childhood).

References

Bednařík, P., Jirák, J. and Köpplová, B. (2011) *Dějinyčeskýchmédií: Odpočátku do současnosti*. Prague: Grada.

Bentele, G. (1998) Verständnisse und Funktionen von Öffentlichkeitsarbeit und Propaganda in der DDR, in Liebert. T. (ed.) *Public Relations in der DDR: Befunde und Positionenzu Öffentlichkeitsarbeit und Propaganda*. Leipzig: Institut für Kommunikations- und Medienwissenschaft, Lehrstuhl für Öffentlichkeitsarbeit, PR, pp. 48–59.

Bentele, G. (2013) Propaganda, in Bentele, G., Brosius, H. B. and Jarren, O. (eds) *Lexikon Kommunikations- und Medienwissenschaft*. Wiesbaden: Springer VS, pp. 279–280.

Bentele, G., Fröhlich, R. and Szyszka, P. (eds) (2008) *Handbuch der Public Relations. Wissenschaftliche Grundlagen und Berufliches Handeln*. Wiesbaden: VS Verlag für Sozialwissenschaften.

Bernays, E. L. (1923) *Crystallizing Public Opinion*. New York: Boni and Liveright.

Bernays, E. L. (1947) *The Engineering of Consent*. Norman: University of Oklahoma Press.

Bernays, E. L. (1955) *The Engineering of Consent*. Norman: University of Oklahoma Press.

Bernays, E. L. (2013) *Public Relations*. Norman: University of Oklahoma Press.

Blommaert, J. and Bulcaen, C. (2000) Critical Discourse Analysis. *Annual Review of Anthropology*, 29: 447–466.

Černá, J., Kašík, M. and Kunz, V. (2006) *Public Relations: Komunikace organizací*. Prague: Vysoká škola finanční a správní-EUPRESS.

CIPR (Chartered Institute of Public Relations) (2014) What Is PR?. www.cipr.co.uk/content/careers-advice/what-pr.

Courtois, S. and Kramer, M. (1999) *The Black Book of Communism: Crimes, Terror, Repression*. Cambridge, MA: Harvard University Press.

Cull, N. J., Culbert, D. and Welch, D. (2003) *Propaganda and Mass Persuasion: A Historical Encyclopedia, 1500 to the Present*. Santa Barbara, CA: ABC-CLIO.

Daymon, C. and Demetrious, K. (eds) (2013) *Gender and Public Relations: Critical Perspectives on Voice, Image, and Identity*. London: Routledge.

Dijk, T. A. (1997) *Discourse as Social Interaction*. London: Sage.

Dijk, T. A. (1998) *Ideology: A Multidisciplinary Approach*. London: Sage.

Dijk, T. A. (2008) *Discourse and Power*. London: Palgrave Macmillan.

Dubnic, V. (1960) *Communist Propaganda Methods: A Case Study on Czechoslovakia*. Ann Arbor, MI: Praeger.

Eidlin, F. H. (1980) *The Logic of 'Normalization': The Soviet Intervention in Czechoslovakia of 21 August 1968 and the Czechoslovak Response*. New York: Columbia University Press.

Fairclough, N. (1980) *Critical Discourse Analysis: The Critical Study of Language*. Harlow: Longman.

Fairclough, N. (1993) *Discourse and Social Change*. Chichester: Wiley.

Fairclough, N. (2003) *Analysing Discourse: Textual Analysis for Social Research*. New York: Psychology Press.

Fairclough, N. (2007) *Language and Globalisation*, London: Taylor and Francis.

Fairclough, N. (2013a) *Language and Power*. London: Routledge.

Fairclough, N. (2013b) *Critical Discourse Analysis: The Critical Study of Language*. London: Routledge.

Fidelius, P. (1983) *Jazyk a moc*. Munich: Karel JadrnyVerlag.

Formánková, P. and Koura, P. (2009) *Žádámetrestsmrti! Propagandistic kákampaň provázející proces s Miladou Horákovou a spol*. Prague: Ústav pro studium totalitních režimů.

Foucault, M. (2002) *The Archaeology of Knowledge*. New York: Routledge.

Grunig, J. E., Grunig, L. A. and Verčič, D. (2004) Public Relations in Slovenia: Transition, Change, and Excellence, in Tilson, D. J. and Alozie, E. C. (eds) *Toward the Common Good: Perspectives in International Public Relations*. Boston, MA: Pearson Education, pp. 133–162.

Grunig, J. E. and Hunt, T. (1984) *Managing Public Relations*. New York: Holt, Rinehart and Winston.

Guelke, A. (2012) *Politics in Deeply Divided Societies*. Cambridge: Polity Press.

Havel, V. (2012) *Mocbezmocných a jinéeseje*. Prague: Knihovna Václava Havla.

Heath, R. L. (2013) *Encyclopedia of Public Relations*. London: Sage.

Hejlová, D. (2014) The Czech Republic, in Watson, T. (ed.) *Eastern European Perspectives on the Development of Public Relations.* New York: Palgrave Macmillan, pp. 25–40.

Hejlová, D. (2015) *Public Relations.* Prague: Grada.

Jowett, G. S. and O'Donnell, V. (2014) *Propaganda and Persuasion.* London: Sage.

Kachlík, A. (1985) *Metodika propagační práce: vnitroponiková propagace, ekonomická propaganda a agitace.* Prague: SPN.

Kaplan, K. (1995) *Největší politický proces: 'M. Horáková a spol'.* Prague: Ústav pro soudobédějiny AV ČR.

Kašík, M. (ed.) (1987) *Požadavky urychlování sociálně ekonomického rozvoje na metody a formy ekonomické propagandy. Zdokonalování žurnalistického tvůrčího procesu jako předpoklad účinnějšího působení PMI při utváření socialistkého společenského vědomí.* Prague: Institute of Journalistic Theory and Practice at the Charles University in Prague, Faculty of Journalism.

Kašík, M. and Havlíček, K. (2012) *Podnikovy marketing. Jas ziskataudrzetzakaznika.* Prague: VSFS.

Kašík, M. and Klimpl, V. (1982) *Ekonomicka propaganda a zurnalistika.* Vyd: Novinar.

Kent, M. L. and Taylor, M. (2002) Toward a Dialogic Theory of Public Relations, *Public Relations Review*, 28(1): 21–37.

Kind-Kovacs, F. and Labov, J. (2013) *Samizdat, Tamizdat, and Beyond: Transnational Media During and After Socialism.* Oxford: Berghahn Books.

Kocks, J. N. and Raupp, J. (2014) Socialist Public Relations: A Contradictio in Adiecto? On Conceptualisations and Practices of Political PR in the German Democratic Republic. Proceedings of the International History of Public Relations Conference 2014, Bournemouth.

Košťálová, T. and Seifer, P. (1979) *Ekonomicka propaganda v rozhlasovezurnalistice v letech 1978-1979: Tematicka a zanrovaanalyza.* Prague: Cs. Rozhlas.

L'Etang, J. (2008) Writing PR History: Issues, Methods and Politics, *Journal of Communication Management*, 12(4): 319–355.

Martinek, J. (2015) Personal interview, 9 November, Prague.

Nevolová, L. (1988) *Ekonomicka propaganda aagitace: R. 1988.* Prague: Okr. kult. stredisko.

Pavlů, D. (1977) *Úvod do teorie socialistické propagace.* Prague: ČVTS – Dûmtechniky.

Pavlů, D. (1978) *Čítanka k teorii socialistické propagace: Hospodářská propagace v socialismu a buržoazní reklama.* Prague: Univerzita Karlova.

Pavlů, D. (1983) *Základní otázky teorie socialistické propagace: skripta pro posl. fak. žurnalistiky Univ. Karlovy.* Prague: Univerzita Karlova.

Pavlů, D. (1984) *Propagace – specifická forma sociálníkomunikace. K některým základním otázkám propagačního působení v socialistické společnosti.* Prague: Novinář.

Pavlů, D. (2004) *Marketingové komunikace a firemnístrategie.* Zlín: Univerzita Tomáše Bati, Fakulta multimediálních komunikací.

Pavlů, D. (2006a) *Marketingové komunikace a výzkum.* Zlín: Univerzita Tomáše Bati, Fakulta multimediálních komunikací.

Pavlů, D. (2006b) *Veletrh: multimediální nástroj firemní komunikace v konkurenčním prostředí.* Zlín: Univerzita Tomáše Bati.

Pavlů, D. (2009) *Marketing communications and their new formats.* Prague: Professional Publishing.

Podgórecki, A., Alexander, J. and Shields, R. (1996) *Social Engineering*. Montreal: McGill-Queen's University Press.

Pullmann, M. (2011) *Konecexperimentu: přestavba a pádkomunismu v Československu*. Prague: Scriptorium.

Svoboda, V. (2003) *Corporate identity: učební text*. Zlín: Univerzita Tomáše Bati, Fakulta multimediálních komunikací.

Svoboda, V. (2004) *Základy public relations: učební text*. Zlín: Univerzita Tomáše Bati, Fakulta multimediálních komunikací.

Svoboda, V. (2009) *Public relations: moderně a účinně*. Prague: Grada.

Šimečka, M. (1990) *Obnovení pořádku*. Brno: Atlantis.

Szyszka, P. (1998) Öffentlichkeitsarbeit: Ein Demokratieprodukt? In Liebert, T. (ed.) *Public Relations in der DDR: Befunde und Positionenzu Öffentlichkeitsarbeit und Propaganda*. Leipzig: Institut für Kommunikations- und Medienwissenschaft, Lehrstuhl für Öffentlichkeitsarbeit, PR, pp. 67–79.

Thompson, J. B. (1984) *Studies in the Theory of Ideology*. Oakland: University of California Press.

Thompson, J. B. (1990) *Ideology and Modern Culture: Critical Social Theory in the Era of Mass Communication*. Stanford, CA: Stanford University Press.

Watson, T. (ed.) (2014) *Eastern European Perspectives on the Development of Public Relations*. London: Palgrave Macmillan.

Žižek, S. (2012) *Mapping Ideology*. New York: Verso.

Zrostlík, V. (1979) *Zkušenosti z rozvíjení ekonomické propagandy*. Prague: Práce.

11 Bipolar attitudes in Turkish political PR

The Kurdish question

İlker Bıçakçı, Pelin Hürmeriç and A. Banu Bıçakçı

Introduction

Turkey's Kurdish conflict is a complex and violent trans-state and transnational phenomenon. The Kurdistan Workers Party (Partiya Karkerên Kurdistan, PKK) continues to launch attacks on Turkish security forces and civilians within Turkey, as well as from neighboring Iraq. The war has caused the deaths of up to 40,000 people since 1984 (Somer and Liaras, 2010: 153). In the past 30 years, the Kurdish issue has not been resolved by these armed actions. During this period there have been various weak attempts to resolve the conflict. The recent and the most significant attempt is known as 'The resolution process' that was initiated in 2005 by the Justice and Development Party (Adalet ve Kalkınma Partisi, AKP) government. Over a decade old, this process was suspended on the eve of the first general elections, held on June 7, 2015, with renewed armed struggles between the government forces and PKK. The purpose of this study is to scrutinize the political public relations and/or propaganda efforts of the AKP government by focusing on their media relations regarding the Kurdish question. It is intended to unveil the bipolar shift in these efforts between the resolution process and the following conflict process.

It is clear that the ruling power possesses the advantage in terms of forging public opinion, due to its power to utilize media. President Recep Tayyip Erdoğan and the AKP government suppress the opposition media. In Turkey, the public is not well informed about the Kurdish problem. The 2015 World Press Freedom Index spotlights the negative impact of the lack of freedom of information and free speech advocates in Turkey. Turkey is ranked 149 out of 180 countries (https://index.rsf.org/#!/index-details). This index, generated by 'Reporters Without Borders', ranks the performance of 180 countries according to a range of criteria that include media pluralism and independence, respect for the safety and freedom of journalists, and the legislative, institutional and infrastructural environment in which the media operate. Turkey's rank near the bottom suggests that the Turkish public lacks objective information upon which to make better decisions. Government-controlled media, often following a propagandist approach, further diminish the available information for citizens. In the last decade, media companies have become split into two camps: 'proponents' and 'opponents' of the AKP government. 'The ownership structure has also been changed numerous times by state tenders and privatization where government influence was maintained over mainstream media' (Tunç, 2015: 208).

The media institutions, which shape public opinion, represent bipolar views. According to November 2015 circulation reports, newspapers in Turkey have a total circulation of 4,223,679. Among these newspapers, 53 percent of the circulation belongs to the partisan media (15 newspapers) that support the government. Reflecting the polarity in the media, nearly half of the public support President Erdoğan and the AKP, while the other half of the country rejects the AKP. The results of the last general elections[1] also reflect this near 50–50 split. When there is limitation of press freedom, it negatively affects democracy (de Smaele, 2006: 37).

Public relations is a practice enacted in democratic systems and in times of peace; with its relationship building objective, it serves the mutual interests of all parties. However, when this practice only serves the interests of power elites who aim to impose their will on publics, then it is called 'propaganda'. Public relations and propaganda are both utilized in the political sphere.

The use of public relations in the area of politics has been a controversial issue. It is argued that the main goal of political public relations is the use of media outlets to communicate specific political views, solutions and interpretations of issues in the hope of garnering public support for political policies and campaigns (Froehlich and Rüdiger, 2006: 18). Public relations professionals play central roles in constructing and using frames in the service of groups and organizations (Reber and Berger, 2005: 187). Thus, framing research is utilized for analyzing how the media reflect the news in order to create a precise public opinion. According to Entman (1993) media provide audiences with schemas for interpreting events. The framing and presentation of events and news in the mass media can thus systematically affect how recipients of the news come to understand these events (Price et al., 1997). In this regard, frame analysis is an appropriate method to evaluate the media reflections of the AKP government during both the Kurdish resolution and conflict processes. Hence, in this study, frame analysis, widely used in public relations research (Austin, 2010; Lim and Jones, 2010; An and Gower, 2009; Froehlich and Rüdiger, 2006; Chapman Perkins, 2005; Hiebert, 2003; Anderson, 2001; Knight, 1999; Duhe and Zoch, 1994) will be conducted.

Considering the power relations inherent in public relations, this study aims to contribute to the literature by discussing the political public relations versus propaganda discrepancy, through concepts of democracy and press freedom. The significance of this study, first and foremost, stems from the lack of any national or international study concerning the use of a public relations–propaganda continuum with regards to the Kurdish issue, an issue that has made Turkey a deeply divided society.

Debates on public relations and propaganda

Public relations provides information to the public as they form opinions. Public opinion is characterized by rationality. Rationality in this context is the conscious acquisition of judgments as evidenced by the use of clear language and clear terms (Noelle-Neumann, 1995: 34). As Habermas (1962) claimed, public opinion, as a rational process, focuses on democratic participation and the exchange of different viewpoints in public matters. The government should heed public opinion. There is always a concern that the opinion formation process may be manipulated by the powers of the state and capital, by the mass media and modern technology (Noelle-Neumann, 1995: 45). When this manipulation occurs, this communication process is really more 'propaganda' than public relations. However, the distinction between public relations and propaganda is not that clear-cut. Critical scholars often place propaganda and public relations on a continuum (Gelders and Ihlen, 2010: 60).

> Most academics writing about public relations, including influential modern public relations academics, and non-academic writers (Bernays, Ellul, Grunig, Habermas, Herman and Chomsky etc.) conclude that public relations has been manipulative communication in the very great majority of its practice, or they have conflated it with propaganda.
>
> (Moloney, 2006: 67–68)

As Senne and Moore assert (2015: 328), the main features of a propaganda monopoly might include the following: centralized control of the message, censorship and suppression of information, bribery and other forms corruption, sanctions against media that step out of line, and close personal involvement by a single powerful person. Along with the sanctions that can accompany censorship, extensive censorship and harsh sanctions signal a tightly controlled public communication environment (Senne and Moore, 2015: 330).

The methods of propaganda differ according to the political regime. Authoritarian and totalitarian systems – oppressive regimes such as Hitler's Germany, Mussolini's Italy, etc. – are distinguished by discriminatory, exclusionary and marginalizing discourses in their propaganda methods. Western-type capitalist democracies, on the other hand, utilize more refined persuasion methods. What embodies the distinction between public relations and propaganda is the relative democratic nature of the political regime. Still, in systems where there is inequality between the strong and the weak, public relations makes it easier for the strong party to accomplish its goals. In this context, public relations that serves the interests of power elites is differentiated from propaganda by the sophisticated methods employed under the banner of political public relations.

Strömback and Kiousis (2011) stress that political public relations' purpose is 'building relationships' with others in order to reach political goals. Long-term, mutually beneficial relationships cannot exist when one political party's intention is to deceive, to subdue or to isolate the other from the truth (Martinelli, 2011). In these cases, communication can only be considered as 'propaganda'.

In Turkey, the AKP government utilized both political public relations and propaganda concerning the Kurdish issue. In order to analyze these systematic communication efforts that have been employed to form public opinion, it is crucial to look at the background and the main actors of the so-called 'Kurdish question' in Turkey.

Background and main actors of the 'Kurdish question' in Turkey

The military coup in Turkey on September 12, 1980 was followed by draconian law-and-order measures that virtually annihilated both the left and Kurdish movements. The coup led to the militarization of the Kurdish question (Van Bruinessen, 1999). Kurds constitute the largest nation in the world without a state, and they struggle for their cultural and political rights in the countries where they reside (Çelik, 2015: 260). The Kurdistan Workers Party (Partiya Karkerên Kurdistan, PKK) was established following the Turkish cultural assimilation policies. The PKK began its armed attacks against the government in 1984 (Arslan and Çapan, 2013; Güneş, 2012; Curtis, 2005). In the first attack, 30 Turkish soldiers and citizens were killed (Nachmani, 2003).

Led by Abdullah Öcalan, the PKK has found numerous followers among the Kurdish people, mainly from the eastern and southeastern cities of Turkey. It gradually became more and more powerful, and the conflict between the PKK and the Turkish government resulted in sizable losses on both sides. Indeed, the conflict almost turned into a war. Additionally, since the 1980s, there has been a steady increase in the number of Kurdish refugee communities in many Western European countries (Güneş, 2012: 1). Kurds who went to these countries have formed their own media and have found support for their cause. Western public opinion, as well as many political leaders, grant the Kurds legitimacy in their cause.

Armistices and negotiation attempts by Kurds and Turks in 1993 and 1998 failed, and the clashes continued. After hiding in various countries abroad, Öcalan was captured in 1999 in Kenya and returned to Turkey. For years, the Turkish government's communication machine had framed Öcalan as the 'terrorist leader' and 'baby murderer'. As a result of international pressure (Shatzmiller, 2005), Öcalan's punishment was commuted to a life sentence, following the abolition of the death penalty. Yet despite the fact that its leader was serving a life sentence, the PKK continued its attacks against Turkey.

In 2002 the Justice and Development Party (AKP) became Turkey's ruling party. The AKP defines its ideology within the framework of 'conservative democracy' (Binark et al., 2015: 222). The AKP obtained power through filling a 'rightist-liberal gap' in Turkish politics (Akdenizli and Çetin, 2015). Its leader, Recep Tayyip Erdoğan, comes from a political Islam tradition, as do most of the party leaders. Erdoğan was prime minister of Turkey, and then became president of the Republic in the 2014 elections (Akdenizli and Çetin, 2015: 295). Binark et al. (2015) noted that the AKP is a 'leader oriented' political organization and there is an 'Erdoğan cult' in the party.

After the 1999 prison sentence of Öcalan and through 2005, the Turkish government had ignored the presence of the 'Kurdish problem'. During 1999–2015, the PKK continued to gather more strength by taking advantage of the political developments in the Middle East. The fact that its leader was serving time did nothing to weaken the organization. It continued its military actions against Turkey and it became clear that the PKK would not be defeated by force of arms. Upon this realization, the Turkish government underwent a radical change in its discourse. Prime Minister Erdoğan's early public statements on the Kurdish issue were mixed and confusing, at times denying the existence of a problem (Somer and Liaras, 2010: 154). However, in August 2005, Erdoğan declared that Turkey had a 'Kurdish problem', had made 'grave mistakes' in the past, and now needed 'more democracy to solve the problem'. Never before had a Turkish leader made such an explicit statement regarding the Kurdish problem (Gunter, 2011: 11). Erdoğan played the role of 'chief PR officer' within the context of government and media relations, in order to reach the audience that voted for the AKP.

In 2009 the government initiated the 'Kurdish opening', which was based on a political understanding of giving 'individual cultural rights to Kurds', including permitting the homecoming of PKK militants, initiating Kurdish language education as elective courses in schools and private institutions, and the establishment of TRT6, a state-run Kurdish language television channel (Ayata, 2012; Yeğen, 2011). In September 2009, the Council of Higher Education (YÖK) permitted graduate study in the Kurdish language at the new Mardin Artuklu State University in the Institute for Living Languages (Aslan, 2015). In September 2011, YÖK began to allow undergraduate study in Kurdish and established a Kurdish language and literature department in the same university. Muş Alparslan State University also created this type of language and literature department. The latest democratization package announced in September 2013 allowed Kurdish education in private schools (Aslan, 2015: 159).

The AKP government treated these cultural improvements as public relations tactics in order to gain the sympathy of the Kurdish public. The PKK, with the desire to expand its gains, has increased its political pressure on the government via the Kurdish political parties. One of these parties was the Peace and Democracy Party (Barış ve Demokrasi Partisi, BDP) which was represented in the Turkish Grand National Assembly via 36 independent MPs[2] in the Turkish Grand National Assembly in the 2011 general election. (http://en.hdpeurope.com/?page_id=537). After the BDP, the Peoples' Democratic Party (Halkların Demokratik Partisi, HDP) was founded as a pro-Kurdish and pro-minority, left-wing political party (Akdenizli and Çetin, 2015). The HDP claims that it represents the whole of Turkey, but critics have accused it of mainly representing the interests of the Kurdish minority in southeastern Turkey where the party polls the highest. Selahattin Demirtaş, its co-chair, received 9.76 percent of the vote as a candidate in the presidential elections of August 10, 2014 (http://secim.haberler.com/cumhurbaskanligi-secimi/). Its success was in putting forward party lists instead of running independent candidates in the subsequent June 2015 general election. Exceeding expectations, it polled at 13.12 percent of the vote, becoming the third largest parliamentary group.

The spokespeople of those political parties, representing the Kurdish movement in the Turkish Grand National Assembly, often underlined that Öcalan was one of the negotiators of the resolution process in the eyes of the public. However, as the general public opinion was not quite ready for this idea, the Turkish government did not explicitly state that Öcalan was the person to be negotiated with as a party to the resolution process. Instead, the government was trying to persuade the public of the resolution process itself, which would bring peace. Still, neither the parties involved nor the content of this process were overtly known.

The publics that comprised the strongest opposition to the resolution process were MHP[3] voters and CHP[4] voters. The MHP rejected the process, claiming that it would disturb the territorial integrity of Turkey. The CHP objected on grounds of lack of transparency in the conduct of the process. Still, there is a commonality between the voter bases of MHP and AKP, for they are both nationalistic and conservative – in this context, there is a permeability of votes. Those who support the resolution process are respectively HDP voters and AKP voters (Yılmaz, 2014). While HDP voters support the process, since HDP is among the natural partners of the process itself, AKP voters support the process merely because they support all political decisions Erdoğan makes.

The AKP supporters have distinct demographic characteristics. According to the demographic survey results of the June 7, 2015 general elections (http://survey.konda.com.tr/rapor/KONDA_7HaziranSand percentC4 percentB1kveSe percentC3 percentA7menAnaliziRaporu.pdf), 68 percent of AKP voters have not finished high school, 23 percent are high school graduates, and only 9 percent have an undergraduate or graduate degree. HDP voters and undecided voters' educational profiles are similar and they are below the national average as well. Nevertheless, CHP and MHP voters' educational level is above the Turkish educational average. Considering the income level of the voters, it transpires that AKP voters' income level is also below the national average. It is a significant finding that, as the household income of voters increases, the AKP's vote rate decreases. Voters who have a low income level generally tend to vote in favor of the status quo (Özkan, 2004).

This polarized election challenged the resolution process. To provide a consensus, the government needed to understand the various viewpoints and expectations regarding the Kurdish issue within the country. The AKP government created an initiative, 'The Wise Men Commission'. The Commission attempted to identify the opinions, suggestions, expectations and concerns regarding the resolution process by communicating face to face with people in the country's seven geographic regions[5], including those who are organized and those who are not. Seven different commissions, consisting of scientists, journalists, artists and civil society leaders, all of whom are especially close to the AKP government and Kurdish political movement, conducted this research between April and June 2013.

The social, political, ideological, ethnic, religious and economic landscape of each city in every region was mapped (Wise Men Commission Southeastern Report, June 2013: 5). The Wise Men Commission's reports were built upon the information collected via face-to-face interviews and e-mail group discussions. When the reports from all regions were assessed, the greatest support naturally came from Eastern Anatolia and Southeastern Anatolia. These regions have the largest Kurdish populations and thus largest majority of people supporting the resolution process. Their biggest concern was that the Turkish government would halt the peace process. On the other hand, Turks living in the remaining five regions wanted the peaceful environment to persist but they were also suspicious as to what would happen at the end of the process. Public opinion was particularly resistant in these five regions to the idea that Öcalan might be freed and PKK members be granted amnesty. Public opinion in Turkey's eastern and southeastern parts and in other regions is deeply divided, in terms of the prevailing view of the resolution process (www.yagmurhaber.com/akil-insanlarin-raporu-hazir-1026.html).

Another topic causing deep division between those on different sides of the resolution process focused on the policies of Recep Tayyip Erdoğan. A significant portion of supporters of the process reported quite positive opinions, since he was the one who initiated the process, while the others reported negative opinions for the very same reason (http://hyetert.blogspot.nl/2013/06/akil-insanlar-marmara-bolgesi-raporu.html).

The effort to understand public opinion in detail is part of the research phase in political public relations. Gathered from the Commission's reports, the results presented the opportunity to develop and execute a tailor-made public relations strategy for each and every region, and for the political party that possessed the initiative to govern the resolution process. These findings were delivered to Erdoğan's government and shared with the other regional commissions. However, this opportunity was not taken and the resolution process was halted, under the initiative of Erdoğan.

The political situation in Turkey is always changing and there has been a drastic shift since the general elections of June 7, 2015. Following the 2015 general elections, the AKP lost power after 13 years of governing, while the HDP entered the Turkish Grand National Assembly with 80 MPs, passing the 10 percent election threshold for the first time. The changing political climate made the formation of a coalition government a necessity. Negotiations have started – yet little action has occurred. Without President Erdoğan, the interim AKP government has not continued with the resolution process.

Unhappy with the election results, Erdoğan has created an initiative to hold another round of elections. In this process, Turkish military actions against the PKK have resumed and the peace process has been suspended. Discourses previously aimed at persuading the public that it is crucial to establish peace between the PKK and the Turkish government have now been turned into new discourses that aim to legitimize the Turkey–PKK War.

Strategic shifting in the Kurdish resolution process

The events that occurred in Turkey between the two election campaigns have changed the course of the resolution process. Clashes re-emerged between government forces and the PKK in the east and southeast of the country where the Kurdish population is especially dense.

In the latest period of conflict and violence, President Erdoğan changed his discourse and made official speeches that contradicted his previous position during the resolution process. When he mentioned the 'Kurdish problem' in 2005, and said 'The Kurdish problem is my problem too', that statement became a milestone in the resolution process. However, in March 2015 he asserted that there was no longer a Kurdish issue. The media have played up this message. Basically, Erdoğan has now said, 'The Kurdish problem no longer exists'. The rest of the resolution process is associated with the preservation of the existing rule. Bülent Arınç, deputy prime minister, made the following remarks on the subject in April 2015:

> Their [Kurds'] existence in Turkey was rejected before our government came to power. Kurdish was not accepted as a language. Speaking Kurdish or writing a book, singing in Kurdish or releasing an album was banned. So much so that mothers were not allowed to speak Kurdish to their children in prisons. [...] Our government recognized the Kurdish people and the language. They are now allowed to speak and write in their own language. We respect the Kurdish language. We have launched TV channels, opened courses and paved the way for Kurdish education. We have ensured the preservation of all the rights provided in the Constitution. We consider all these to be within the scope of human rights.
>
> (*HaberTürk*, April 10, 2015)

In his statement of March 2013, Erdoğan asserted that the government was focused on the 'Kurdish resolution process' in order to terminate the terror and stop the bloodshed. He claimed that 'our genuine intention is not to let mothers cry anymore' (www.akparti.org.tr/site/haberler/analar-aglamasin-istiyoruz/40835). In this statement, he mentioned both Turkish and Kurdish mothers whose children were losing their lives in the armed clashes. These kinds of memorable phrases that summarize the main idea and are able to be broadcast quickly through the media are called 'soundbites', and these soundbites are political public relations tactics (Somerville and Ramsey, 2012). This peaceful discourse has also been used by the AKP as a tool to gather votes, especially fom the Kurdish electorate in the Southeast.

In the time of the conflict process, in August 2015, President Erdoğan attended the funeral of a police commissioner who was killed in the armed struggle with the PKK. During his speech he claimed that 'happy are those families, whose sons are martyrs' (www.cumhuriyet.com.tr/haber/turkiye/346947/Erdogan_Ne_mutlu_sehit_ailesine.html). With this emotional soundbite that has religious connotations, he changed his discourse from the language of peace to the language of war. Rather than wanting to build a relationship, Erdoğan aims to impose the legitimacy of the new conflict process on the public. Hence, his discourse can be considered as a propaganda tactic.

Right before the 'Peace Rally' in Ankara in October 10, 2015, which was supported by both the HDP and CHP, there was a double suicide bombing in Ankara which killed more than 100 people (www.reuters.com/article/us-turkey-explosion-erdogan-idUSKCN0SG13F20151022). This terrorist attack caused the HDP and CHP to cancel their own outdoor rallies during the November 1 election campaign. Right after the bombing, President Erdoğan declared 'This incident shows how terror is implemented collectively. This is a completely collective act of terror and it includes ISIS (Islamic State of Iraq and Syria), PKK, the mukhabarat, and the terrorist group PYD from the north of Syria.' President Erdoğan then repeated his claim in a speech broadcast live on Turkish television at the annual meeting of a labor union in Ankara stating, 'They carried out this act all together' (www.reuters.com/article/us-turkey-explosion-erdogan-idUSKCN0SG13F20151022). With these confusing statements of blame, Erdoğan appears to be propagandizing rather than properly informing the public. President Erdoğan has centralized control of the message and is at the same time suppressing information (Senne and Moore, 2015).

Having strong pro-government media support, President Erdoğan has conducted an effective propaganda campaign to build a spiral of violence and fear. Having chosen violence as its strategy, the AKP weakened the HDP and discredited it in eyes of the public. As a result, the AKP regained power on November 1, just five months after losing it.

Framing and communicating issues in Turkish politics

There was a paradigm shift between the pre-election and post-election issues related to the Kurdish policies of the AKP. Issues are the bases around which publics are organized and public opinion is formed (Grunig and Hunt, 1984). Issues can be framed as significant or insignificant to the public interest; but more importantly, issues can be defined in terms of how people should think about an issue (Hallahan, 1999: 227). *The framing of issues* is an approach that examines alternative interpretations of social reality (Hallahan, 1999: 217). In this study, 'the resolution process' is taken as a major issue that is framed by the media.

Once the major power actors define a problem in a particular way, this definition may take on a life of its own in the media, and become superimposed upon other issues (Olien et al., 1995: 304). Framing, defined by Entman (2004) as 'selecting and highlighting some facets of events or issues, and making connections among them so as to promote a particular interpretation, evaluation, and/or solution' (p. 5) might be convenient in explaining the impact of the PR strategies of the power actors on the media.

As Hallahan (1999) stated, interpretation and explanation are of great importance for issues. The political parties in Turkey struggled to dominate how the public interpreted the Kurdish issue. Public relations serves as a means of perception management to create support for a party. The Turkish government had a bipolar attitude to the Kurdish issue before and after the elections. However, the shift in the government's discourse strategy was not so sharp and the arguments rejecting the Kurdish problem evolved gradually over time. This study will focus on the frame transformation strategy that created public opinion via media relations in Turkey.

Kinder and Sanders (1990) suggested that frames serve in this operational process as 'devices embedded in political discourse, invented and employed by political elites, often with an eye toward advancing their own interests or ideologies and intended to make favorable interpretations' (p. 74). Political elites, journalists and audiences have a role in influencing the schematic portrayals of issues. Framing plays an integral part in the process of agenda-building as advocates attempt to communicate with members of affected or sympathetic groups, either directly or indirectly using the media (Hallahan, 1999: 218).

According to Entman (2004: 5) there are two basic types of frames: substantive and procedural. Regarding political events, issues and actors, *substantive frames* serve to fulfill at least two functions: They may define effects or conditions as problematic, identify cause, convey moral judgments and/or endorse remedies or improvements. *Procedural frames* are observed more in number in the news, but they have a narrower focus and function. They are composed of evaluations of political actors' legitimacy, based on their technique, success and representativeness (p. 6). Within this framework, among Turkish media, the researchers selected a sample of four titles representing both mainstream partisan and non-partisan newspapers (*Sabah* and *Haber-Türk; Hürriyet* and *Sözcü*). The coverage of the newspapers included two periods – the first from February 1, 2015 to June 7, 2015, and the second from June 8, 2015 to November 1, 2015[6] – regarding the recent Kurdish resolution process. The before-and-after sample of media content from the first general election will be compared to the second period in order to answer the following research questions:

RQ1 Is the media coverage of partisan media and AKP discourse compatible during periods 1 and 2?
RQ2 Is the media coverage of non-partisan media and AKP discourse compatible during periods 1 and 2?

Method

This empirical study is based on a content analysis of 3,576 news items from four Turkish daily newspapers. According to recent circulation reports (November 16–22, 2015) *Zaman*, *Hürriyet*, *Posta*, *Sabah*, *Sözcü* and *Haber-Türk* newspapers have the highest circulation in Turkey. Among these, four were selected to represent both mainstream partisan and non-partisan newspapers (*Sabah* and *HaberTürk; Hürriyet* and *Sözcü*) were taken. They were selected on their basis of circulation, political orientation and on-line availability (see Table 11.1).

According to the recent circulation reports (November 16–22, 2015), *Zaman*, *Hürriyet*, *Posta*, *Sabah*, *Sözcü* and *HaberTürk* newspapers have the highest circulation in Turkey. *Sabah* is a daily, founded in 1985 by Dinç Bilgin. In 2007 ownership of the newspaper passed to the Savings Deposit Insurance Fund of Turkey. Some of the newspaper's staffers were fired, and the paper was then sold to the Turkuvaz Media Group belonging to Çalık Holding, whose CEO, Berat Albayrak, is the son-in-law of Erdoğan and whose chairman, Ahmet Çalık, has been described as a 'close associate' of Erdoğan. The newspaper supports the AKP government. It has a circulation of 304,000.

HaberTürk is a national daily owned by Ciner Holding. The holding operates in different areas like mining and thermal power. According to leaked wiretaps, then prime minister Tayyip Erdoğan has called M. Fatih Saraç, then deputy head of the Board of Directors of *HaberTürk* and asked him to remove certain media coverage from the paper.

Sözcü is a Turkish daily first published in 2007. Estetik Publishing owns it, and it has a circulation of 290,000. The newspaper has a nationalist and secular stance and it is opposed to the ruling AKP.

Hürriyet is one of Turkey's major newspapers and was founded in 1948 by Sedat Simavi. It is a mainstream, liberal and secular paper owned by Doğan Media Group, with a high circulation of 356,000.

The unit of analysis was the news article, found in the form of featured stories, articles, interviews, opinion pieces and columns, including one of the two key terms 'Resolution process' and 'Kurdish issue'. The timeline of the study was between February 1, 2015 and November 1, 2015. It was divided into two periods by the date of the first general elections on June 7: the first from February 1 to June 7 and the second from June 8 to November 1. *HaberTürk* and *Hürriyet* had on-line archives, which were scanned by the researchers to obtain the data set. During the research process *Sabah* and *Sözcü* limited access to their archives, so that the data set regarding these two

Table 11.1 Analyzed newspapers

	Hürriyet	*HaberTürk*	*Sabah*	*Sözcü*
History	Establshed 1948 by Sedat Simavi	Established 2009 by Ciner Holding	Established 1985 by Dinç Bilgin	Established 2007
Circulation (daily)	356,000	177,405	304,000	290,000
Political standing	Mainstream, liberal and secular	Mainstream, partisan	Mainstream, partisan	Nationalist, secular; opposed to the ruling AKP
Ownership structure	Owner: Doğan Media Group. No known business relationship with the government.	Owner: Ciner Holding. The holding has an ongoing business relationship with the government regarding its operations such as mining and termic station building; their newspaper has a supportive standing with the government. In leaked wiretaps, then prime minister Erdoğan called M. Fatih Saraç (deputy head of the Board of Directors of *HT*) and asked him to remove controversial media coverage from the newspaper.	Owner: Turkuvaz Media Group belonging to Çalık Holding. In 2007 ownership of the newspaper was given to the Savings Deposit Insurance Fund of Turkey. Afterwards the paper was sold to the Turkuvaz Media Group belonging to Çalık Holding, whose CEO Berat Albayrak is the son-in-law of Erdoğan and whose chairman Ahmet Çalık has been described as a 'close associate' of Erdoğan.	Owner: Estetik Publishing. No known business relationship with the government.

newspapers was acquired via Ajans Press, one of Turkey's major media monitoring agencies. News and columns were collected accordingly and classified by category (news item, column), keywords ('Resolution process', 'Kurdish issue') and period (1st period, 2nd period) as shown in Table 11.2. During this process, about 10 percent of the collected news were discarded since they were irrelevant or duplicates. The final data set is composed of 3,576 news stories.

In order to reveal the frames, each of the three researchers read a random sample of 150 news stories (Total N = 450). After creating a list of relevant frames, the researchers discussed and finalized the list, identifying 18 frames. The frames were classified as critical (C), supportive (S) and neutral (N) (indicated in Table 11.3 as C/S/N) regarding their position in terms of the Kurdish question and resolution process. Out of 3,576 news stories, 400 (11.17 percent) of the randomly selected news items were content analyzed by two researchers. In terms of intercoder reliability, a coding of the sample produced acceptable levels on Scott's pi between 0.81 and 0.92.

The researchers looked for difference in the first and second coding periods. A *t*-test was conducted in order to compare the two periods, in both news and columns of the four newspapers. An SPSS 22.0 program was used for the analysis. Thus, N = 144 (18 × 8) comparisons were made. The news and columns that had the value $p < 0.05$ were taken as significant (see Appendix).

Findings

'Substantive frames' fulfill at least two functions in political discourse: They may define effects or conditions as problematic, identify cause, convey moral judgments and/or endorse remedies or improvements. The frames regarding the Kurdish issue and the resolution process are defined as problematic; their reasons are presented; moral ideas or judgments are conveyed and/or resolution, improvement/development suggestions are put forward. The frames in this study are thus evaluated within the 'substantive frame' category. This finding suggests that the news stories, produced as a result of the media relations efforts of political actors, were used as perception management tools; that the resolution process should, first and foremost, be explained to the public, and the support of public opinion be ensured, and that this support should then be withdrawn. No procedural frames are present.

The AKP favored the resolution process in the first period. By the end of this period, the resolution process was suspended by the AKP as a political strategy. Over time, there was a shift to understanding the Kurdish problem as a conflict process. The *t*-test revealed significant differences between the two periods in all of the four newspapers. Values of $p < 0.05$ are taken as significant and indicated bold in the tables. In the study, having no frames in one of the periods, and having a number of frames in another, means that

Table 11.2 Distribution of the news items

1st period (1 February 2015–7 June 2015)				
Newspaper/keyword	*Resolution process*		*Kurdish issue*	
	News	*Column*	*News*	*Column*
Hürriyet	459	144	118	74
HaberTürk	294	103	64	35
Sabah	193	231	9	42
Sözcü	85	51	11	25
Total	1,031	529	202	176
Overall: 1,938				
2nd period (8 June 2015–1 November 2015)				
Newspaper/keyword	*Resolution process*		*Kurdish issue*	
	News	*Column*	*News*	*Column*
Hürriyet	335	196	92	49
HaberTürk	257	50	54	27
Sabah	128	162	35	32
Sözcü	111	88	15	7
Total	831	496	196	115
Overall: 1,638				
Grand total: 3,576 news items				

Table 11.3 News frames

News frames	*C/S/N*
Support for the process	S
Positive reflections on the economic life	S
Glorifying/adressing Öcalan	S
Associating the future of the process with the presidential system (positive relationship)	S
The claim: 'The Kurdish issue has ended'	S
The claim: 'The Kurdish issue persists'	S
The demand to return to the process for the sake of a democratic resolution	S
Associating the future of the process with the presidential system (negative relationship)	C
The cessation of the dialogue between the HDP İmralı Delegation and Öcalan	C
The Kurdish issue becoming an election issue	C
Contradiction regarding the process	C
The demand for a new process for the sake of a democratic resolution	C
Freezing the resolution process	C
Armed conflict	C
Putting HDP on par with PKK	C
Negative reflections on the economic life	C
Neutral news regarding the process	N
The relationship between the Middle East situation and the Kurdish movement	N

there cannot be a comparison between a valid number and zero data. So as to run the *t*-test, the cells having zero data were changed to 0.01.

Regarding the first research question, asking whether coverage by partisan media and AKP discourse are compatible during periods 1 and 2, the results shown in Table 11.4 indicate that coverage by partisan media (*HaberTürk* and *Sabah*) and the AKP discourse are compatible, since in the first period the percentage of supportive frames is higher than that for critical frames, both in the news and columns. In the second period the reverse is the case. Neutral news and columns appear in very small numbers in both periods (see Appendix).

Concerning the second research question asking whether media coverage of non-partisan media reflected the AKP discourse during periods 1 and 2, depending on the small percentage of the significant differences in a few number of frames, it can be asserted that *Sözcü* does not have compatible media coverage. On the other hand, in *Hürriyet*'s columns, there are significant differences. However, differences between the two periods are not polarized to the same degree as observed in the partisan media.

Table 11.4 and Table 11.5 indicate the significant differences, yet the direction of these differences is not clear in the tables. Direction and differences between the two periods are displayed in Table 11.6. In Table 11.6, supportive frames reflect the AKP's discourse in the first period, whereas critical ones are in line with AKP's discourse in the second period. Neutral frames are covering objective news content. The existence of a positive numerical value in the cell concerning a supportive frame demonstrates that data belonging to the newspaper is in line with the AKP's discourse. Meanwhile, the existence of a negative numerical value in the cell regarding a critical frame indicates that data belonging to the newspaper is in line with the AKP's discourse.

Consider for instance the frames 'The cessation of the dialogue between the HDP İmralı Delegation and Öcalan' and 'Neutral news regarding the process'. There are no significant differences.

According to Table 11.6, in the first period the majority of news and columns of the partisan newspapers (*HaberTürk* and *Sabah*), and also the columns of *Hürriyet*, are framed as supporting the resolution process. There are a significant number of news stories that are framed to glorify and/or address the PKK leader, Öcalan. These reveal that when the AKP was supporting the Kurdish resolution process and treating Öcalan as a legitimate actor in the process by treating him respectfully, the partisan newspapers, and some columnists in *Hürriyet*, were reflecting the government's discourse. In the second period, both partisan newspapers present news coverage that reflects the contradictory attitude to the resolution process. The papers reflect AKP's shift in its discourse regarding the process. There is no significant difference in the news coverage of the other two newspapers.

Both in the news stories and opinion columns there is a significant presence of news items that frame positive reflections of the ongoing resolution process on economic life in Turkey. Those newspapers predominantly addressed the news of the boom in regional tourism, the growth in sales figures, and the clearer path for investments as a result of the stable peace environment that would result from the resolution process.

In the second period a large amount of news concerning the suspension of the resolution process is framed in the partisan newspapers. The news content, replete with similes and metaphorical expressions such as 'the process was put into cold storage'; 'was shelved', 'frozen', 'suspended' and so on, also contains the message that this process will begin anew when the parties deem it appropriate. Although there is a slight increase in *Hürriyet*'s coverage of this topic in the second period, there is a noteworthy increase in such coverage by the partisan newspapers.

The partisan newspapers had at first accepted the imprisoned PKK leader Öcalan as a legitimate actor in the resolution process negotiations, then shifted their views and presented numerous stories such as 'HDP: the political puppet of the sanguinary terrorist organization PKK' (*Sabah*, August 2, 2015) and 'PKK's political representative, the HDP (PKK)' (*Sözcü*, July 30, 2015).

Table 11.4 HaberTürk and *Sabah* newspapers' *t*-test table

Frames/Newspaper	*HT_News*		*HT_Col*		*Sabah_News*		*Sabah_Col*	
	t Test Value	*Sig.*	*t Test Value*	*Sig.*	*t Test Value*	*Sig.*	*t Test Value*	*Sig.*
Support to the process	**9,3672**	**p<0.05**	**3,4195**	**p<0.05**	**7,7635**	**p<0.05**	**0**	**p<0.05**
Positive reflections on the economic life	**5,4391**	**p<0.05**	**0**	**p<0.05**		**p<0.05**	**0**	**p<0.05**
Glorifying/Adressing Öcalan	**7,1043**	**p<0.05**	**5,619**	**p<0.05**	**3,8906**	**p<0.05**	**0**	**p<0.05**
Associating the future of the process with the presidential system (positive relationship)	0,5758	p<0.05	0,7595	p<0.05	1,3839	p<0.05	0,5431	p<0.05
The claim: 'The Kurdish issue has ended"	**4,9755**	**p<0.05**	**0**	**p<0.05**	1,4403	p<0.05	0,51512	p<0.05
The claim: 'The Kurdish issue persists'	**2,9855**	**p<0.05**	**0**	**p<0.05**	1,4337	p<0.05	0,149	p<0.05
The demand to return to the process for the sake of the democratic resolution	**1,9621**	**p<0.05**	**0**	**p<0.05**	1,7882	p<0.05	**0**	**p<0.05**
Associating the future of the process with the presidential system (negative relationship)	1,0497	p<0.05	**0**	**p<0.05**	no data		**0**	**p<0.05**
The ceasing of the dialogue between HDP İmralı Delegation and Öcalan	0,8773	p<0.05	1,7099	p<0.05	1,0555	p<0.05	0,3028	p<0.05
The Kurdish issue, becoming an election material	0,8438	p<0.05	0,3093	p<0.05	0,3035	p<0.05	0,4746	p<0.05
Contradiction toward the process	**5,3321**	**p<0.05**	**3,55047**	**p<0.05**	**2,3306**	**p<0.05**	**5,3912**	**p<0.05**

Frames/Newspaper	*HT_News*		*HT_Col*		*Sabah_News*		*Sabah_Col*	
	t Test Value	*Sig.*	*t Test Value*	*Sig.*	*t Test Value*	*Sig.*	*t Test Value*	*Sig.*
The demand of a new process for the sake of the democratic resolution	**2,3312**	**$p<0.05$**	0,5837	$p<0.05$	1,819		**0**	**$p<0.05$**
Freezing the resolution process	**5,3321**	**$p<0.05$**	**3,55047**	**$p<0.05$**	**2,3306**	**$p<0.05$**	**5,3912**	**$p<0.05$**
Armed conflict	**0**	**$p<0.05$**	**0**	**$p<0.05$**	**0**	**$p<0.05$**	**0**	**$p<0.05$**
Putting HDP on par with PKK	**4,385**	**$p<0.05$**	**2,4774**	**$p<0.05$**	**3,1706**	**$p<0.05$**	**6,0965**	**$p<0.05$**
Negative reflections on the economic life	**0**	**$p<0.05$**	**0**	**$p<0.05$**	**0**	**$p<0.05$**	no data	
Neutral news regarding the process	0,7184	$p<0.05$	no data		1,7725	$p<0.05$	no data	
The relationship between the Middle East conjuncture and Kurdish movement	1,616	$p<0.05$	0,9775	$p<0.05$	**0**	**$p<0.05$**	1,2519	$p<0.05$

Table 11.5 *Hürriyet* and *Sözcü* newspapers' *t*-test table

Frames/Newpapers	*Hürriyet_News*		*Hürriyet_Col*		*Sözcü_News*		*Sözcü_Col*	
	t Test Value	*Sig.*	*t Test Value*	*Sig.*	*t Test Value*	*Sig.*	*t Test Value*	*Sig.*
Support to the process	0,8587	p>0.05	**2,6047**	**p>0.05**	0,7103	p>0.05	0,5832	p>0.05
Positive reflections on the economic life	1,2886	p>0.05	1,1221	p>0.05	**0**	**p>0.05**	no data	
Glorifying/Adressing Öcalan	1,8992	p>0.05	**3,7406**	**p>0.05**	0,6927	p>0.05	0,5832	p>0.05
Associating the future of the process with the presidential system (positive relationship)	0,6127	p>0.05	**0**	**p>0.05**	0,1011	p>0.05	no data	
The claim: 'The Kurdish issue has ended'	**3,9345**	**p>0.05**	**2,3581**	**p>0.05**	1,922	p>0.05	1,9283	p>0.05
The claim: 'The Kurdish issue persists'	**3,3954**	**p>0.05**	0,692	p>0.05	**2,0504**	**p>0.05**	**0**	**p>0.05**
The demand to return to the process for the sake of the democratic resolution	0	p>0.05	0	p>0.05	0,3272	p>0.05	0.8699	p>0.05
Associating the future of the process with the presidential system (negative relationship)	0,2055	p>0.05	1,9219	p>0.05	**3,1843**	**p>0.05**	0,5945	p>0.05
The ceasing of the dialogue between HDP İmralı Delegation and Öcalan	0,3608	p>0.05	0,9335	p>0.05	1,3757	p>0.05	0,8708	p>0.05
The Kurdish issue, becoming an election material	1,7749	p>0.05	0,8892	p>0.05	**2,1922**	**p>0.05**	0,5945	p>0.05
Contradiction toward the process	1,6468	p>0.05	0,9466	p>0.05	0,7689	p>0.05	0,1393	p>0.05

Frames/Newpapers	*Hürriyet_News*		*Hürriyet_Col*		*Sözcü_News*		*Sözcü_Col*	
	t Test Value	*Sig.*	*t Test Value*	*Sig.*	*t Test Value*	*Sig.*	*t Test Value*	*Sig.*
The demand of a new process for the sake of the democratic resolution	1,478	p>0.05	**1,9923**	**p>0.05**	0,2384	p>0.05	0,5832	p>0.05
Freezing the resolution process	**2,0887**	**p>0.05**	1,9317	p>0.05	0,9427	p>0.05	0,6058	p>0.05
Armed conflict	**0**	**p>0.05**	**0**	**p>0.05**	**0**	**p>0.05**	**0**	**p>0.05**
Putting HDP on par with PKK	0,5684	p>0.05	0,3165	p>0.05	0,3026	p>0.05	1,1742	p>0.05
Negative reflections on the economic life	**0**	**p>0.05**	**0**	**p>0.05**	**0**	**p>0.05**	**0**	**p>0.05**
Neutral news regarding the process	0,251	p>0.05	0,8247	p>0.05	0,2241	p>0.05	no data	
The relationship between the Middle East conjuncture and Kurdish movement	**3,2997**	**p>0.05**	**2,133**	**p>0.05**	0,8617	p>0.05	0,9335	p>0.05

Table 11.6 Direction and differences between the two periods by percentage

Frames/newpapers	*C/S/N*	*Hür_News*	*Hür._Col*	*Söz._News*	*Söz._Col*	*HT_News*	*HT_Col.*	*Sab._News*	*Sab._Col*
Support to the process	S		(+)9,54			(+)22,93	(+)13,02	(+)23,27	(+)28,23
Positive reflections on the economic life	S			(+)2,42		(+)8,79	(+)8,86	(+)12,38	(+)17,6
Glorifying/Adressing Öcalan	S		(+)9,11			(+)14,44	(+)21,06	(+)7,84	(+)14,62
Associating the future of the process with the presidential system (positive relationship)	S		(-)2						
The claim: 'The Kurdish issue has ended'	S	(+)5,83	(+)4,33			(+)8,73	(+)13,92		
The claim: 'The Kurdish issue persists'	S	(+)4,53		(+)4,19	(+)1,47	(+)3,37	(+)3,79		
The demand to return to the process for the sake of the democratic resolution	S		(-)8,19			(-)2,58			(+)2,99
Associating the future of the process with the presidential system (negative relationship)	C			(-)0,31			(+)0,63		0
The ceasing of the dialogue between HDP İmralı Delegation and Öcalan	C								

Frames/newpapers	*C/S/N*	*Hür_News*	*Hür._Col*	*Söz._News*	*Söz._Col*	*HT_News*	*HT_Col.*	*Sab._News*	*Sab._Col*
The Kurdish issue, becoming an election material	C			(-)2,52					
Contradiction towards the process	C					(-)8,75	(-)11,68	(-)14,18	(-)20,18
The demand of a new process for the sake of the democratic resolution	C	(-)1,93	(-)3,48			(-)2,84			(-)0,89
Freezing the resolution process		(-)3,07				(-)9,66	(-)11,27	(-)10,43	(-)13,02
Armed conflict	C	(-)10,13	(-)9,42	(-)14,54	(-)15,53	(-)18,96	(-)18,82	(-)16,5	(-)11,61
Putting HDP on par with PKK	C					(-)8,44	8,69	(-)9,2	(-)16,4
Negative reflections on the economic life	C	(-)3,15	(-)2,46	(-)3,63	(-)3,88	(-)2,14	(-)1,17	(-)0,5	
Neutral news regarding the process	N								
The relationship between the Middle East conjuncture and Kurdish movement	N	(+)4,35	(+)4,89					(-)2,5	

There is no news framed as armed conflict in the first period, but armed clashes broke out during the second period of the content analysis. In this second period, news of martyrs, interviews with the Rangers and stories specifically emphasizing 'the fear of a return to the 1990s', were to be found in all of the newspapers, both partisan and non-partisan. Considering the news value of such violence, this finding is predictable.

Conclusion

The purpose of this study was to scrutinize the political public relations and/or propaganda efforts of the AKP government by focusing on its media relations regarding the Kurdish question. It was intended to unveil a bipolar shift in these efforts between the resolution process and the following conflict process.

Beginning with Prime Minister Erdoğan's speech in Diyarbakır in 2005, the resolution process has frequently been on the agenda of public opinion. As official speeches are considered as tactics of political PR, his speech was a milestone for the process. Besides speeches, the AKP government utilized several other public relations tactics in order to persuade the public of the legitimacy of the process. One of these moves was to give individual cultural rights to Kurds living in Turkey. By allowing Kurdish language education and broadcasting, the AKP aimed at gaining the sympathy of the Kurdish voters. The AKP government not only wanted to influence those Kurds living in the eastern and southeastern regions of Turkey, but also the rest of the population elsewhere in the country. To understand the opinions and expectations of these publics, another creative public relations tactic was implemented. The committee known as the 'Wise Men Commission' was comprised of opinion leaders in Turkey. The Commission's reports were prolific and they could have been exploited to execute a tailor-made public relations strategy for the resolution process. However, this opportunity was not taken because of the shift in the AKP government's political and communication strategy.

The peace process began to fail in March 2015, and it failed totally after the first general elections of that year. The increase in the popularity of the HDP, which decided to participate in the general elections despite the 10 percent threshold, had a significant influence on the result. Specifically, for Erdoğan to fulfill his wish to become president, the HDP had to remain under the threshold and the AKP, the party he founded, had to come to power alone. The AKP needed to maintain its absolute majority in order to amend the Constitution. In this context, it was understood by Erdoğan that the resolution process would not serve the AKP as an election-winning instrument. The AKP–HDP contest meant that the communication strategy had to change.

Right before the June 7 elections, a spiral of violence broke out, with attacks on HDP buildings and the Diyarbakır rally. The election results then showed that the HDP had passed the threshold with 13 percent of the vote, which meant that they had won 80 seats in the Parliament. AKP's failure to win enough seats for an absoloute majority meant that they would no longer have sole rule.

Later, massacres by unknown perpetrators, PKK actions, and news of military operations and martyrs became the main topics on Turkey's agenda. While the partisan *Sabah* and *HaberTürk* passionately advocated for the resolution process before March 2015, after this date they started to support the government's conflict strategy with the same passion. Ultimately, the fear and worry that the renewed violence brought upon public opinion increased the AKP's votes and led to its coming to power alone as a result of the fresh elections of November 1, 2015. Following these elections, two enormous groups have emerged in Turkey, of equal size and deeply divided in terms of their position, which either supports or opposes President Erdoğan. Turkey is split and so is its media.

This study has ascertained that as the resolution process evolved into the conflict process under the initiative of the government, the news and columns of the partisan newspapers *Sabah* and *HaberTürk* changed, to a large extent, in the same direction. These newspapers served as controlled media that carry out the propaganda, rather than the public relations, of the current government. The pro-Erdoğan group's attitude, in terms of the Kurdish matter, is being reinforced through partisan media propaganda.

On the other side of the resolution process, the anti-AKP *Sözcü* also maintained a similar attitude to the conflict process and criticized the fickle behavior of the government. *Hürriyet*, on the other hand, presented relatively more objective news and comments that reflected the spirit of both periods – the resolution and the conflict processes. The content analysis shows that the ruling power has abused the media's function in order to mold public opinion to serve its own political goals.

The AKP government has the power to take the initiative to either continue or bring an end to the resolution process: either way, it is up to them. The PKK is in a more passive and reactive position. The fact that the media groups that own partisan newspapers such as *Sabah* and *HaberTürk* are privileged and win government tenders in fields such as energy and construction, is yet another piece of evidence of their actions as tools of propaganda. The activities of partisan journalism have proven to be an effective way of winning contracts for Turkey's media owners. Under the control of Erdoğan, the AKP for its part utilizes the partisan newspapers as efficient propaganda tools to win elections and keep itself in power.

Public relations practices serve as strong persuasive tools in comparatively democratic regimes that are based on the separation of powers. However, in authoritarian regimes that limit the public's freedom to be sufficiently informed via the media, a propagandist approach overshadows public relations. The press has never been considered as one of the main pillars of democracy in Turkey; instead, it has been used as a tool for political manipulation and financial benefit (Akser and Baybars Hawks, 2012). For a public considered to have no right to proper information, any sophisticated public relations tactics offering them a freedom of choice would be redundant. It can be observed that this public, mainly consisting of those with low incomes and low levels of education, are being consolidated via propaganda methods that address the 'senses' and 'images', rather than 'reason' (Domenach, 2003). As a consequence, in deeply divided societies such as Turkey, ethical public relations might help to ease the conflict between the parties, bring peace and provide public support for good causes. We see a hope for public relations if power is not monopolized and political actors use their powers sincerely in order to solve the problems.

Appendix

Total number of frames in four newspapers (period 1/period 2)

Table 11.7 Total number of frames, period 1

1st period

Frames/Newspapers	*C/S/N*	*Hür._news*	*%*	*Hür._col.*	*%*	*Söz._news*	*%*	*Söz._col.*	*%*	*HT_news*	*%*	*HT_col.*	*%*	*Sab._news*	*%*	*Sab.col.*	*%*
Support the process	S	113	18,7	72	27,16	11	7,43	4	5,88	88	25,07	28	17,72	56	24,77	85	28,23
Positive reflections on the economic life	S	25	4,13	3	1,13	3	2,02	0	0	33	9,4	12	8,86	28	12,38	53	17,6
Glorifying/Adressing Öcalan	S	42	6,95	35	13,2	13	8.78	4	5,88	55	15,66	37	23,41	20	8,84	44	14,62
Associating the future process with the presidential system (positive relationship)	S	8	1,32	0	0	2	1,35	0	0	41	11,68	26	16,45	18	7,96	46	15,28
The claim: 'The Kurdish issue has ended'	S	57	9,43	18	6,79	9	6,08	5	7,35	36	10,25	22	13,92	22	9,73	12	3,99
The claim: 'The Kurdish issue persists'	S	45	7,45	8	3,01	8	5,4	1	1,47	14	3,98	6	3,79	10	4,42	4	1,33
The demand to return to the process with the presidential system (negative relationship)	C	23	3,8	7	2,64	13	8,78	9	13,23	8	2,27	1	0,63	0	0	0	0
The ceasing of the dialogue between HDP İmralı Delegation and Öcalan	C	20	3,31	8	3,01	9	6,08	3	4,41	7	1,99	1	0,63	5	2,21	2	0,66
The Kurdish issue, becoming election material	C	59	9,76	35	13,2	16	10,8	9	13,23	23	6,55	13	8,22	14	6,19	5	1,66
Contradictions towards the process	C	43	7,11	17	6,41	15	10,1	5	7,35	9	2,56	2	1,26	3	1,32	0	0
The demand if a new process for the sake of the democratic resolution	C	21	3,47	6	2,26	9	6.08	4	5,88	4	1,13	2	1,26	2	0,88	0	0
Freezing the resolution process	C	25	4,13	10	3,77	10	6,75	6	8,82	7	1,99	2	1,26	11	4,86	4	1,33
Armed conflict	C	0	0	0	0	0	0	0	0	0	0	0	0	0	0	15	4,98
Putting HDP on par with PKK	C	33	5,46	17	6,41	15	10,1	14	20,58	9	2,56	3	1,89	12	5,3	6	1,99
Negative reflections on the economic life	C	0	0	0	0	0	0	0	0	0	0	0	0	0	0	0	0
Neutral news regarding the process	N	46	7,61	3	1,13	8	5,4	0	0	8	2,27	0	0	15	6,63	0	0
The relationship between Middle East conjuncture and Kurdish movement	N	44	7,28	26	9,81	5	3,37	2	2,94	3	0,85	1	0,63	0	0	16	5,31
TOTAL		604	99,9	265	99,9	148	100	68	100	351	99,91	158	99,93	224	99,04	301	100

Table 11.8 Total number of frames, period 2

2nd period

Frames/Newspapers	*C/S/N*	*Hür._news*	*%*	*Hür._col.*	*%*	*Söz._news*	*%*	*Söz._col.*	*%*	*HT_news*	*%*	*HT_col.*	*%*	*Sab._news*	*%*	*Sab.col.*	*%*
Support the process	S	74	16,66	43	17,62	9	5,45	4	3,88	7	2,14	4	4,7	3	1,5	0	0
Positive reflections on the economic life	S	12	2,7	6	2,46	0	0	0	0	2	0,61	0	0	0	0	0	0
Glorifying/Adressing Öcalan	S	19	4,27	10	4,09	11	6,66	4	3,88	4	1,22	2	2,35	2	1	0	0
Associating the future process with the presidential system (positive relationship)	S	8	1,8	2	0,82	2	1,21	0	0	13	13,14	11	12,94	24	12	38	17,04
The claim: 'The Kurdish issue has ended'	S	16	3,6	6	2,46	3	1,81	1	0,97	5	1,52	0	0	12	6	11	4,932
The claim: 'The Kurdish issue persists'	S	13	2,92	5	2,05	2	1,21	0	0	2	0,61	0	0	4	2	3	1,345
The demand to return to the process with the presidential system (negative relationship)	S	32	7,2	20	8,19	3	1,81	1	0,97	14	4,28	2	2,35	2	1	0	0
The ceasing of the dialogue between HDP İmralı Delegation and Öcalan	C	13	2,92	7	2,87	8	4,84	2	1,94	10	3,05	4	4,7	8	4	2	0,896
The Kurdish issue, becoming election material	C	30	6,75	26	10,65	22	13,3	17	16,5	27	8,25	8	9,41	11	5,5	5	2,242
Contradictions towards the process	C	21	4,72	11	4,51	15	9,09	7	6,79	37	11,31	11	12,94	31	15,5	45	20,179
The demand if a new process for the sake of the democratic resolution	C	24	5,4	14	5,74	9	5,45	4	3,88	13	3,97	2	2,35	7	3,5	2	0,896
Freezing the resolution process	C	32	7,2	19	7,78	10	6,06	12	11,65	41	12,53	13	15,29	22	11	32	14,349
Armed conflict	C	45	10,13	23	9,42	24	14,5	46	15,53	62	18,96	16	18,82	33	16,5	34	46,591
Putting HDP on par with PKK	C	28	6,3	14	5,74	15	9,09	14	13,59	36	11	9	10,58	29	14,5	41	18,385
Negative reflections on the economic life	C	14	3,15	6	2,46	6	3,63	4	3,88	7	2,14	1	1,17	1	0,5	0	0
Neutral news regarding the process	N	32	7,2	5	2,05	8	4,84	0	0	5	1,52	0	0	6	3	0	0
The relationship between Middle East conjuncture and Kurdish movement	N	13	2,93	12	4,92	3	1,81	6	5,82	8	2,44	2	2,35	5	2,5	7	3,139
TOTAL		444	99,9	244	100	165	100	103	100	327	99,91	85	99,95	2500	100	223	100

Notes

1 AKP votes are 49.5 percent and the cumulation of the other votes are 50.5 percent on 1 November 2015 general elections.
2 Carried into effect in Turkey after the military coup d'état on September 12, the threshold election system claims that political parties under the 10 percent threshold cannot be represented in the Turkish Grand National Assembly. Until the General Elections in 2015, the political parties, which were founded to resolve the Kurdish issue, were based on ethnic foundations. Also possessing the characteristic of being regional, these political parties were often voted for in Eastern and Southeastern Regions, where Kurdish population is dense. These parties were usually taking part in the elections with independent candidates, rather than institutional candidacies, for they could not risk not passing the 10 percent threshold.
3 Nationalist Movement Party (*Milliyetçi Harket Partisi*, MHP) established in 1969. Right-wing party that advocates Turkish–Islamic ideals and Turkish nationalism. www.mhp.org.tr
4 Republican People's Party (*Cumhuriyet Halk Partisi*, CHP) established in 1923. Main opposition party. Positions itself to the left of center. www.chp.org.tr
5 Marmara Region, Mediterranean Region, Aegean Region, Central Anatolia Region, Eastern Anatolia Region, Southeastern Anatolia Region, Black Sea Region.
6 1 November 2015 is the second general election date in 2015.

References

Books and articles

Akdenizli, B. and Çetin, N. (2015) 'Using social media dialogically? Political parties in Turkey and the 2014 local elections', in Akdenizli, B. (ed.) *Digital transformations in Turkey: Current perspectives in communication studies.* Lexington, MD: Lexington Books, pp. 288–312.

Akser, M. and Baybars Hawks, B. (2012) 'Media and democracy in Turkey: Toward a model of neoliberal media autocracy', *Middle East Journal of Culture and Communication*, 5: 302–321.

An, S. Y. and Gower, K. K. (2009) 'How do the news media frame crises? A content analysis of crisis news coverage', *Public Relations Review*, 35(2): 107–112.

Anderson, W. B. (2001) 'The media battle between Celebrx and Vioxx: Influencing media coverage but not content', *Public Relations Review*, 27(4): 449–460. Austin, L. L. (2010) 'Framing diversity: A qualitative content analysis of public relations industry publications', *Public Relations Review*, 36(3): 298–301.

Arslan, H. K. and Çapan, F. (2013) 'Kürt meselesinde şiddet sarmalını aşmak ve çözüm süreci' [Overcoming the spiral of violence in the Kurdish issue and the resolution process], *bilig*, 67: 25–48.

Aslan, S. (2015) *Nation-building in Turkey and Morocco: Governing Kurdish and Berber dissent.* New York: Cambridge University Press.

Ayata, B. (2012) 'Kurdish translation of politics and Turkey's changing Kurdish policy: The journey of Kurdish broadcasting from Europe to Turkey', *Journal of Contemporary Europe Studies*, 19(4): 523–533.

Binark, M., Çomu, T., Aydemir, A. T., Bayraktutan, Y., Doğu, B. and İslamoğlu, G. (2015) "#WeAreErdoğan': The Justice and Development Party's social media campaign during the 2015 general elections', in Akdenizli, B. (ed.) *Digital transformations in Turkey: Current perspectives in communication studies.* Lexington, MD: Lexington Books, pp. 221–256.

Çelik, B. (2015) 'The politics of the digital technoscape in Turkey: Surveillance and resistance of Kurds', in Akdenizli, B. (ed.) *Digital transformations in Turkey: Current perspectives in communication studies.* Maryland: Lexington Books, pp. 256–274.

Chapman Perkins, S. (2005) 'Un-presidented: A qualitative framing analysis of the NAACP's public relations response to the 2000 presidential election', *Public Relations Review*, 31(1): 63–71.

Curtis, A. (2005) *Nationalism in the diaspora: A study of the Kurdish movement.* Available at: http://tamilnation.co/selfdetermination/nation/kurdish-diaspora.pdf (accessed: 27 November 2014).

de Smaele, H. (2006) 'In the name of democracy: The paradox of democracy and press freedom in post-Communist Russia', in Voltmer, K. (ed.) *Mass media and political communication in new democracies.* London: Routledge, pp. 35–48.

Domenach, J. M. (2003) *Politika ve propaganda.* Trans. Yücel, T. (orginal title *La politique et la propagande*). İstanbul: Varlık.

Duhe, S. F. and Zoch, L. M. (1994) 'Framing the media's agenda during a crisis', *Public Relations Quarterly*, 39(4): 42–45.

Entman, R. M. (1993) 'Framing: Towards clarification of a fractured paradigm', *Journal of Communication*, 43(4): 51–58.

Entman, R. M. (2004) *Projections of power: Framing news, public opinion, and U.S. foreign policy.* Chicago, IL: University of Chicago Press.

Froehlich, R. and Rüdiger, B. (2006) 'Framing political public relations: Measuring success of political communication strategies in Germany', *Public Relations Review*, 32: 18–25.

Gelders, D. and Ihlen, Ø. (2010) 'Government communication about potential policies: Public relations, propaganda, or both?', *Public Relations Review*, 36: 59–62.

Grunig, J. E. and Hunt, T. (1984) *Managing public relations.* New York: Holt, Rinehart and Winston.

Güneş, C. (2012) *The Kurdish national movement in Turkey: From protest to resistance.* Abingdon: Routledge.

Gunter, M. (2011) *Historical dictionary of the Kurds.* 2nd edn. Plymouth: Scarecrow Press.

Habermas, J. (1962) (1989 trans. Burger, T. and Lawrence, F.) *The structural transformation of the public sphere: An inquiry into a category of bourgeois society.* Cambridge: Polity Press.

Hallahan, K. (1999) 'Seven models of framing: Implications for public relations', *Journal of Public Relations Research*, 11(3): 205–242.

Hiebert, R. E. (2003) 'Public relations and propaganda in framing the Iraq war: A preliminary review', *Public Relations Review*, 29(3): 243–255.

Kinder, D. R., and Sanders, L. M. (1990) 'Mimicking political debate with survey questions: The case of White opinion on affirmative action for Blacks', *Social Cognition*, 8(1): 73–103.

Knight, M. G. (1999) 'Getting past the impasse: Framing as a tool for public relations', *Public Relations Review*, 25(3): 381–398.

Lim, J. and Jones, L. (2010) 'A baseline summary of framing research in public relations from 1990–2009', *Public Relations Review*, 36(3): 292–297.

Martinelli, D. K. (2011) 'Political public relations: Remembering its roots and classics', in Strömback, J. and Kiousis, S. (eds) *Political public relations: Principles and applications.* Abingdon: Routledge, pp. 33–54.

Moloney, K. (2006) *Rethinking public relations.* 2nd edn. Abingdon: Routledge.

Nachmani, A. (2003) *Facing a new millennium: Coping with intertwined conflicts.* Manchester: Manchester University Press.

Noelle-Neumann, E. (1995) 'Public opinion and rationality', in Glasser, T. L. and Salmon, C. T. (eds) *Public opinion and the communication of consent.* New York: Guilford Press, pp. 33–54.

Olien, C. N., Donohue, G. A. and Tichenor, P. J. (1995) 'Conflict, consensus, and public opinion', in Glasser, T. L. and Salmon, C. T. (eds) *Public opinion and the communication of consent.* New York: Guilford Press, pp. 301–322.

Özkan, A. (2004) *Siyasal iletişim* [*Political communication*]. İstanbul: Nesil.

Price, V., Tewksbury, D. and Powers, E. (1997) 'Switching trains of thought: The impact of news frames on readers' cognitive responses', *Communication Research*, 24: 481–506.

Reber, B. H. and Berger, B. K. (2005) 'Framing analysis of activist rhetoric: How the Sierra Club succeeds or fails at creating salient messages', *Public Relations Review,* 31: 185–195.

Senne, L. and Moore, S. (2015) 'Bismarck, propaganda and public relations', *Public Relations Review,* 41(3): 326–334.

Shatzmiller, M. (2005) *Nationalism and minority identities in Islamic societies.* Montreal: McGill-Queen's University Press.

Somer, M. and Liaras, E. G. (2010) 'Turkey's new Kurdish opening: Religious versus secular values', *Middle East Policy,* 17(2): 152–165.

Somerville, I. and Ramsey, P. (2012) 'Public relations and politics', in Theaker, A. (ed.) *The public relations handbook.* 4th edn. Abingdon: Routledge, pp. 175–195.

Strömback, J. and Kiousis, S. (eds) (2011) *Political public relations: Principles and applications.* Abingdon: Routledge.

Tedesco, J. C. (2011) 'Political public relations and agenda building', in Strömbäck, J. and Kiousis, S. (eds) *Political public relations: Principles and applications.* Abingdon: Routledge, pp. 75–95.

Tunç, A. (2015) 'In quest for democracy: Internet freedom and politics in contemporary Turkey', in Akdenizli, B. (ed.) *Digital transformations in Turkey: Current perspectives in communication studies.* Maryland: Lexington Books, pp. 207–274.

Van Bruinessen, M. (1999) 'The Kurds in movement: Migrations, mobilisations, communications and the globalisation of the Kurdish question', Working paper no. 14, Tokyo: Islamic Area Studies Project.

Yeğen, M. (2011) *The new Kurdish movie.* Available at: www.jadaliyya.com/pages/index/3242/the-new-kurdish-movie.

Yıldız, K. (2005) *Kurds in Turkey: EU accession and human rights.* London: Pluto Press.

Yılmaz, H. (2014) *Türkiye'de kimlikler, Kürt sorunu ve çözüm süreci: kamuoyundaki algılar ve tutumlar.* Available at: www.hakanyilmaz.info/yahoo_site_admin/assets/docs/OSI_Yurttaslik_2014_Cozum_Sureci_Sunum_Basin_v08.259182726.pdf (accessed: 30 November 2014).

Websites

www.akparti.org.tr.
www.hyetert.blogspot.nl.
www.index.rsf.org.
www.reuters.com.
www.secim.haberler.com.
www.survey.konda.com.tr.
www.yagmurhaber.com.

12 Computer-mediated public relations of ethno-nationalist terrorist groups

Liane Rothenberger

Terrorism and PR activities

Terrorist groups are strategic communicators who understand the importance of public relations very well (Holbrook, 2014; Rothenberger, 2012; Richards, 2004; Rada, 1985). However, especially since '9/11', studies primarily deal with religious terrorist groups (e.g. Klausen, 2014) using Al Qaeda as the most prominent example. This article, instead, focuses on public relations of ethno-nationalist terrorist groups and, consequently, on public relations from fringe groups and minorities in deeply divided societies. For these groups, the internet allows them to circumvent traditional media who, for a long time, acted as gatekeepers to any person or group wanting to address the public. Nowadays, some terrorist groups even have press officers or media strategists (Somerville and Purcell, 2011; Bockstette, 2008; Picard, 1989). Hence, terrorism can be seen as strategic communication and PR activity, due to the fact that it not only attempts to convey a certain message, but more importantly, that it aims to satisfy a long-term strategic goal of the terrorists' organization which is building a specific group identity and mobilizing resources. Seen from that angle, the communication is strategic as it tries to fulfill a certain purpose, since 'Strategic communication focuses on how the organization presents and promotes itself through the intentional activities of its leaders, employees, and communication practitioners' (Hallahan et al., 2007: 7).

Although during the last decades researchers have developed different definitions and typologies to categorize different forms of terrorism, they share common features, which are the pre-eminent role of the terrorist groups' ideological backgrounds or identities and the use of media in the furthering of their objectives. Terrorists seek to have an effect on audiences with their message and, additionally, their actions are meant as an exchange of meaning; eliciting a certain response or understanding from the populace or audiences. As discussed by Hargie and Irving in Chapter 4, killing, hijacking, and other acts of terrorism are not the primary goals of these organizations; their aims are to get public attention and to create awareness of their cause (Hirschmann, 2000). The violent acts serve only as mediators of the terrorists' messages. The acts are symbolic and can be understood as a form of communication between the terrorists and the public. As noted by Picard (1993: 4), 'In the majority of incidents, the most important element in communication about terrorist acts is not the acts themselves, but the meaning assigned to the acts by media, authorities and the populace.'

Here, the 'strategy' element of communication comes into play. Smith (2002) describes strategic communication as campaigns which have the following characteristics: 'they have a purpose and a plan, they operate within a specific environment which involves organizations and groups of people who affect it, and finally the communication is subject to eventual evaluation' (cf. also Picard, 1989). To ensure that their messages reach the public, terrorists do not only rely on the news coverage of their actions, they also actively communicate their motives and goals in self-made brochures, pamphlets and periodicals, or in gatherings (Gerrits, 1992) and more recently on the internet. That is why research on the use of the internet for terrorist groups' strategic communication and public relations activities is paramount – also for expanding and refining counterterrorist activities. The internet has gained significant importance per se for public relations because of its unhindered access and reaching of widespread audiences. As PR is also about identity building, this study aims to add to the sparse existing literature on ethnic terrorist groups and the communication strategies they use in identity building and mobilization via online media. This is important, since terrorist 'organizations try to use their websites to change public opinion in their enemies' state, to weaken public support for the governing regime, to stimulate public debate, and, of course, to demoralize the enemy.' (Weimann, 2008: 77).

In this chapter, I will first briefly examine how traditional concepts of public relations are challenged when turning to the special group of terrorist entities as communicators. I will define the conceptual foundation in regard to divergences from traditional PR concepts with a focus on persuasion and mobilization of social movements. I acknowledge that there is a clear difference between social movements and terrorist groups, especially with regard to the use of violence. Often, however, terrorist groups evolve from social movements and share the moment of 'mobilization'. I will describe the segment of ethno-nationalist terrorism which also lays the foundation for the sample building of the empirical study. I will then discuss research in regard to computer-mediated communication of terrorist groups, before, lastly, presenting the methodological design and results of a content analysis of 70 articles from insurgent groups' websites. The empirical study investigates how ethno-nationalist terrorist groups use the internet for public relations, what tools they apply, and to whom they attribute responsibility for the conflict. The study takes a comparative perspective in that it does not just describe the individual characteristics of one group, but of eight different groups. The study aims to reveal the content and public relations activities on terrorist groups' websites, how these 'real' groups create a virtual room for transmitting their ideas, ideology and perception of the conflict. This analysis not only contributes to the existing literature on terrorists' use of the internet but, furthermore, fills the research gap that can be identified in regard to an enlarged view of the public relations of insurgent movements.

Challenging traditional public relations concepts

Hypothesizing that terrorist groups deploypublic relations presupposes an acknowledgment that terrorists are not lunatics or insane but that they are communication strategists and act under the 'rational choice' principle 'as rational and goal-directed' (Walder, 2009: 397). Attributing 'rational choice' to terrorists does not mean one excuses their deeds. The insurgents' motives can be understandable, their violence is not.

This research contradicts traditional concepts of PR, such as the quest for two-way symmetrical communication as proposed by Grunig and Hunt (1984). Their 'ideal' is challenged by insurgent groups. They do not employ two-way-symmetrical communication, but rather power-challenging strategic communication is used as a tool for building relationships and for negotiation. Taken to the extreme, we can call the terrorists' online activities one-way or manipulative models of PR. However, even though the Grunigian paradigm of PR has been very influential, it has always been challenged and critiqued (e.g. L'Etang and Pieczka, 1996).

L'Etang (1996: 29) criticizes the Grunigian concept of mutuality and reciprocity 'in that it presupposes that you can estimate the interests of other parties'. In the case of the terrorists, the terrorist groups' public relations practice is in no way designed to share mutual understanding as an organizational goal. Mutual benefit is not the goal of their negotiations, but instead they seek a better position for their *ethnos* within the divided society. 'It is an appealing ideal, emphasizing dialogue, truth and "win/win" end-states, but possibly underplays negative outcomes such as lying and manipulation, defence-attack spirals and so on' (L'Etang, 1996: 30). The symmetry approach incorporates the so-called 'peacemaker function in public relations' (L'Etang, 1996: 30); the terrorists certainly do not belong to this group but apply public relations in another way. Various stakeholders try to influence public opinion related to the respective ethnic conflict and terrorist action, and to mobilize resources for either side. 'Public relations is profoundly concerned with the establishment and maintenance of the reputation and credibility of client organizations and this is done explicitly to maintain the client's ability to influence key publics' (L'Etang, 1996: 23). The terrorist groups, too, are concerned about their 'credibility' and about making the public aware how seriously they take the conflict.

Kent and Taylor (1998: 323–324) have argued that public relations can assume the shape and characteristics of dialogue; the attitude of the group to its publics and vice versa are important; 'relationship building is the foundation of public relations' (Kent and Taylor, 1998: 324). But even though dialogue is seen as very closely related to ethical communication (Taylor et al., 2001: 265), a 'dialogic approach cannot force an organization to behave ethically, nor is it even appropriate in some circumstances … dialogue can be put to both *moral* and *immoral* ends' (Kent and Taylor, 2002: 24). Free debate and open discourse are essential elements of a relationship created and shaped by public relations. The interests of minorities cannot prevail if their PR experts act upon the mutual benefit and harmony paradigm. The solution of the conflict will not be 'good' in the eyes of all publics and stakeholders. They have to utter conflicting viewpoints and will certainly encounter disagreement. What is good, excellent and ethical is a very normative perception.

Pieczka (1996) described the evolution of paradigms in public relations research and comes to the conclusion that American scholars and textbooks dominate in the field of public relations (p. 143). U.S.-centered theories often focus on 'ethical' PR. Most PR theories are quite normative in nature as their goal is not only to describe organizational communication, but also to improve it (e.g. Heath, 2001). The question remains whether terrorist groups apply 'unethical PR', e.g. for mobilizing newcomers and discrediting the opponent, and how this can be differentiated from traditional PR concepts. In contrast to a terrorist attack, stating causes and grievances on websites is not an act of civil disobedience. However, neither is manipulative language an ethical means, nor do the terrorists use their instruments purely for ethical ends. Their efforts contradict demands for 'ethical' public relations (e.g. Pearson, 1989) and moral relationship building in the framework of dialogue as 'ethical communication' (Taylor et al., 2001: 265). With regard to social movements, which specifically pertain to terrorist groups, we should differentiate two fields where the aspect of ethics arises: the means and the goals or ends. In other words: an arms manufacturer uses 'ethical' two-way-symmetrical PR for cruel ends (selling weapons used for supporting armed conflict). A social movement uses 'unethical' manipulative one-way PR in order to pursue the goal of, for example, animal rights or – as in the case at hand – an autonomous self-determined state for a certain ethnic community. What does this mean for public relations research? It is important not to, a priori, exclude and judge divergent forms of public relations but instead acknowledge the diversity of the efforts of 'selling a message' and to try to describe their characteristics in as detailed a way as possible.

Public relations of terrorist groups cannot be conceptualized as 'the good organization communicating well' (Heath, 2001; for other voices critical of traditional concepts of PR see e.g. Mickey, 1998). It is more a sometimes subliminal, sometimes aggressive (discursive) battle for normative judgments and moral evaluation. PR by terrorist groups and extremist movements is used not only to arouse positive attention and to attract recruits but is also used to deter and threaten the opponent(s) in order to further divide societies – into supporters and enemies. Thus, PR activities of terrorists aim at hardening positions of different parties and deviate from PR as a 'good' product of a corporation or for the 'good work' of an NGO. While companies usually try to show their social responsibility in regard to societal issues on the Web (cf. Esrock and Leichty, 1998), terrorist groups act to the contrary.

Somerville and Purcell (2011: 207) note that except for the notion of the importance of PR, 'there is little conceptual agreement with other features of the Grunigian paradigm. There is, for example, no articulation of a two-way symmetrical approach to communication except when that communication concerns its internal stakeholders.' Somerville and Purcell (2011) examined the public relations strategies of the IRA and their political wing Sinn Féin using semi-structured elite interviews with activists. They discern three phases: the 'propaganda of the deed' phase, the development of a political public relations phase, and the peace process phase. This shows that terrorists apply sophisticated and differentiated PR tactics designed for different purposes such as entering political negotiations or arousing awareness of an international peace-prone audience. With regard to terrorist groups' public relations, the notions of persuasion and mobilization play a pre-eminent role.

Persuasion and mobilization

It is to be assumed that PR of terrorist groups falls into the overarching category of strategic communication, more precisely it is closely linked to techniques of persuasion. Pfau and Wan (2006: 102) argue that 'public relations is best viewed as a form of strategic communication, in which persuasion plays an integral role'. They define persuasion 'as the use of communication in an attempt to shape, change, and/or reinforce perception, affect (feelings), cognition (thinking), and/or behavior' (p. 102). Also Miller (1989: 45) sees a close link between persuasion and public relations 'because both are primarily concerned with exerting symbolic control over relevant aspects of the environment'. At this point, the debate even seems to go backwards to concepts of persuasion and manipulation as defined by Bernays (cf. Pfau and Wan, 2006: 101–102). Moloney (2006) even considers PR as 'weak propaganda'. PR, in the terrorists' case, can be seen as a question of power (Fawkes and Moloney, 2008), as power relations are negotiated by means of communication. The PR strategies on terrorist websites rely on a very sophisticated use of language, sometimes close to manipulation and propaganda, which is something PR practitioners and scientists always try to distance themselves from.

In all mobilization processes, discourse and rhetoric play a pivotal role. Persuading texts often are full of tropes like metaphors, metonyms, synecdoches and the like (cf. Wodak et al., 2009). Gerhards (1991: 234) points out that it is initially the persuasion that an issue constitutes a (social) problem that makes people join social movements and later on terrorist groups. Thereby, the development of group pride as a form of identity work plays an important role (Polletta and Jasper, 2001: 296). In this regard, the online texts of terrorist groups are expected to aim at mobilization in support of challenging the status quo. As terrorist groups commonly evolve from social movements, a combination of enlarged PR theory with mobilization theory is proposed. Klandermans and Tarrow (1988: 4) point out that:

> Resource mobilization theory departed from the traditional social movement approach, according to which the origins of social movements are explained by the existence of grievances in a society … The availability of resources and opportunities for collective action were considered more important.

Social mobilization will only be successful if (a) the benefits or incentives of collective action outweigh the costs of participation, (b) there is a certain degree of organization, and (c) the members expect some success (cf. Klandermans and Tarrow, 1988: 4–7). It is the task of the organization to persuade their audience – via deeds and texts – of these three points. Not only media coverage but also PR activities of the group increase the public awareness of the problem and enhance mobilization: 'The result is a stronger collective actor capable of reaching higher levels of mobilization in the next confrontation with its opponent' (Klandermans, 1988: 174). With regards to resource mobilization Della Porta (1988: 156) assumes 'that the motivation to join terrorist groups can be understood within the framework of categories used for other types of political organizations, especially those which are less well-equipped with institutional resources'. Usually, only symbolic incentives are offered for people joining the group. It is more or less a persuasive narrative that makes new members 'feel' the conflict and the need for change. The trigger for mobilization then is the 'actor's experience of a category, tie, role, network, group, or organization, coupled with a public representation of that experience; the public representation often takes the form of a shared story, a narrative' (Tilly, 2002: 80).

Mobilization theory differentiates between consensus and action mobilization (cf. Klandermans and Tarrow, 1988: 12–13, 31). PR activities primarily fall into the first category. Consensus mobilization is 'a deliberate attempt by a social actor to create consensus among a subset of the population' (Klandermans, 1988: 175). The intended result is a convergence of meaning by the addressees. Thus, the actor (in this case the terrorist groups) wants to influence public opinion by applying persuasive communication. Consensus mobilization precedes action mobilization. Website texts first aim at consensus mobilization, because they are designed to activate recruitment and arouse ideological support. However, this is just the first step in the direction of action mobilization: if one reads about 'the legitimization of action goals in relation to the problems [on the structural level]' (Klandermans and Tarrow, 1988: 14), the individual motivation to participate in deeds might increase.

If the reader experiences a huge gap between the perceived social reality and the textual construction of a problem (in this case ethnic conflict) and if his or her personal identity is stable and quite different from the propagated collective identity, the gap between consensus and action mobilization will not be so easy to overcome. If, however, status inconsistency and relative deprivation make matters worse, radicalization may occur more easily. In addition, 'Rapidly changing societies are singularly prone to disruption' (Walder,

2009: 395). The propagated unruliness can be seen as a deliberate strategy in order to further the terrorist group's goal (Walder, 2009: 397). Counter-actions from the government then often have a negative effect as they reinforce inner-group cohesion within the challenging group. The group-external stimulus provokes resentments a fortiori and boosts 'political protest as an expression of emotional frustration and violent impulses' (Walder, 2009: 397).

It is through communication that insurgents mobilize support before action takes place. The internet seems to be an ideal medium for that purpose. With their cyber presentations the groups try to persuade people and 'construct a broad network around their core community [...] They form communities of interest with members affected by the conflict to varying degrees, where information is exchanged and emotional support is provided, campaigns are invoked and connections to similar cases and contacts are created' (Bräuchler, 2013: 25).

The diaspora then can act as a multiplier and 'convey the interests of their national or ethnic brothers to a broader public' (Bräuchler, 2013: 20). On the internet, the terrorists can mobilize resources like people and money as well as announce activities. The internet is also a means to express frustrations. Conflict groups present their arguments so that 'the Internet becomes a venue for collective identity projects, through which the respective communities define themselves, retain their members, market themselves to prospective new members and project their image to the outside world' (Bräuchler, 2013: 25). Ethnicity is a strong factor in collective identity building and plays a crucial role in the process of mobilization and even as a motivating force for terrorist deeds.

Ethno-nationalist terrorism

Various typologies of sub-categories of terrorism refer to ethno-nationalist/separatist/secessionist entities as a separate group (e.g. Waldmann, 1989; 2001; Farnen, 1990). This segmentation is necessary because the different underlying motives influence the discourse presented on the websites. Purely religious as well as social-revolutionary groups place their emphasis on other topics and neglect, for instance, language and tradition issues. Ethno-nationalist terrorist groups act in societies that are divided along ethnic lines. Cordell and Wolff (2009, pp. 4–5) define the term 'conflict' as 'a situation in which two or more actors pursue incompatible, yet from their individual perspectives entirely just, goals'. In ethnic conflicts, the line of dispute is primarily characterized by ethnic distinction. In this way, 'ethno-national conflicts are a form of group conflict in which at least one of the parties involved interprets the conflict, its causes, and potential remedies along an actually existing or perceived discriminating ethno-national divide' (Wolff, 2011: 163).

In this context, questions of (ethnic) identity building as well as the need for cultural identification play an important role. The concept of identity has been employed for corporations in PR research (e.g. Meech, 1996), but not yet in regard to ethnic identity and PR activities. It should be acknowledged that there is a debate regarding the legitimacy of the concept of ethnicity. For example, Chandra (2006: 398) defines ethnic identities as 'a subset of identity categories in which eligibility for membership is determined by attributes associated with, or believed to be associated with, descent', whereas other researchers associate ethnic identity with the concepts such as a common culture, language, history. The present study examined the attributes of ethnic identity building of separatist terrorist groups. In order to gain insight into the public relations practice of terrorist groups, it is based upon a nearly homogeneous sample of groups whose members were identified by Rothenberger and Müller (2015) to be motivated primarily by ethno-nationalist factors, even though some groups also demonstrate social revolutionary or religious motives. Rothenberger and Müller (2015) made their decision based on the groups' history, founding documents (where available), target selection and statements. All the groups are mentioned on the terrorist groups list published by the Council of the European Union and were identified as having a website in English. Obviously, the list and the EU's definition of terrorism are not free from critique (e.g. Baker-Beall, 2014; Freedman, 2010).

As Table 12.1 shows, there was considerable disparity between the volumes of articles downloaded across groups. One reason for this was the extent of the website, another reason the length and variety of articles: whereas some articles are only short press releases or statements, others are lengthy treatises on historical documents or peace process procedures. Furthermore, 'official' websites could not be found or accessed in all cases. Instead of excluding these groups and thereby significantly reducing the sample, in these cases it was decided to include sites from related extremist groups or the political arm of the organization. It has to be clearly stated that the sites are not fully comparable. The articles on the sites by extremist groups or political wings could have been written by extremist individuals whose ideologies do not necessarily reflect terrorist thinking. This, however, reflects the imponderabilia of research in such a problematic field as terrorism studies – a difficulty that has been acknowledged by others (e.g. Gerstenfeld et al., 2003). Inclusion criteria for the substitute sites were that extremist thoughts were uttered and aspects of separatism/striving for an autonomous region foregrounded. Language of heroism, supremacy and glorification indicated the extremist attitude. Pointing to unity of culture and *ethnos* demonstrated elements of identity building.

Identity 'provides categories by which individuals divide up and make sense of the social world' (Polletta and Jasper, 2001: 298). Construction of identity is not a static, but an emerging relational process (De Fina, 2011: 267), as 'identity' is a multifaceted phenomenon that is connected with social, cultural and (geo)political background. The specific form of *collective identity* is closely linked with 'resource mobilization and political process accounts of the emergence, trajectories, and impacts of social movements' (Polletta and Jasper, 2001: 283). The concept of 'we' in contrast to 'the other' is at the heart of collective identity building and thus of mobilization efforts. Polletta and Jasper (2001: 285) defined collective identity as:

Table 12.1 Sample of terrorist groups, websites and classification of motivation

Terrorist group and respective websites, n = 70 articles (100%)	*Motivation*
Hamas, n = 10 (14%) www.ikhwanweb.com	Ethno-nationalist and religious
Hizbullah, n = 5 (7%) www.hizbmedia.org	Ethno-nationalist and religious
CIRA (Continuity Irish Republican Army) RSF (Republican Sinn Féin), n = 7 (10%) www.rsfnational.wordpress.com www.rsf-ulster.blogspot.de	Ethno-nationalist
UDA (Ulster Defence Association) UVF (Ulster Volunteer Force), n = 2 (3%) www.uvfclansite.webs.com www.freewebs.com/uvfclansite/alliesandenemies.htm	Ethno-nationalist
PFLP (Popular Front for the Liberation of Palestine), n = 9 (13%) www.pflp.ps	Ethno-nationalist and social revolutionary
PKK (Kurdistan Workers Party), n = 15 (22%) www.pkkonline.com/en	Ethno-nationalist and social revolutionary
International Sikh Youth Federation (ISYF), n = 19 (27%) www.khalistan.net www.neverforget84.com www.sikhyouth.com	Ethno-nationalist and social revolutionary
LTTE (Liberation Tigers of Tamil Eelam), n = 3 (4%) www.einnews.com www.tgte-us.org www.eelaminexile.wordpress.com	Ethno-nationalist

> an individual's cognitive, moral, and emotional connection with a broader community, category, practice, or institution. It is a perception of a shared status or relation, which may be imagined rather than experienced directly, and it is distinct from personal identities, although it may form part of a personal identity.

In this context, shared perceptions of the past (crucial events, history of oppression) as well as the experience of solidarity are essential, as will be shown in the present study.

Computer-mediated communication of terrorist groups

Violence and eventually terrorism can be triggered by events such as discrimination against an ethnic group, being non-respectful of their identity, and an ethnic group's wish to separate from a nation state that is perceived as oppressive and suppressive (Forsberg, 2012). Multi-ethnicity in these cases often goes along with multilingualism and multifaith. A conflict arises that manifests itself in numerous disputes over territorial as well as discursive power. The violent acts are accompanied by online communication, which highlights the political role of public relations in trying to purposively influence the meaning-making process:

> Through their web sites separatist groups can now frame their ideologies and their actions to suit their needs and the political and social environment they function in. The Internet enables such movements to focus their message on their cause rather than the actions reported in the mass media … Most importantly for ethno separatist movements such as the Sri Lankan Tamils, it enables the creation of a virtual homeland [Eelam].
>
> (Tekwani, 2004: 9)

Groups like the LTTE use the internet extensively for public relations purposes. A strong virtual collective identity represents the culmination point of effective public relations practice. This, of course, is countered by the nation state government.

Taylor et al. (2001: 281) show how 'The Web offers something unique in mediated organization-public communication: an unobstructed path between publics and organizations. The Web also allows both small and large organizations access to many of the tools of modern public relations.' By communicating through their own website, and using self-produced videos or audio files, terrorists can inform the public about their motives and goals, as well as tailor each message to different audiences (Seib and Janbek, 2011). This enables the group to present its image in a different manner than would be presented by the media. Hence, while the mainstream media focus on the violent actions, the terrorists can justify or even distance themselves from those acts. In this way, terrorist organizations can 'frame their political discourse in a manner that portrays them as statesmen rather than terrorists' (Tekwani, 2004: 9).

However, it is undeniable that this is not the case with all terrorist groups; some religious terrorist groups, for instance, very explicitly portray themselves as brutal. By varying their rhetoric and addressing their issues differently, terrorist groups try to change the public's opinion of the group or even gain support (Seib and Janbek, 2011). Gerstenfeld et al. (2003: 29), who conducted a content analysis of 157 extremist websites, state that only a small percentage of sites 'specifically urged violence. These and other findings suggest that the Internet may be an especially powerful tool for extremists as a means of reaching an international audience, recruiting members, linking diverse extremist groups, and allowing maximum image control.' Anderson (2003), too, emphasizes the importance of the Web for resource building: 'The Internet provides terrorists with a platform with which to reach a mass audience and an important means of fundraising. Also it provides terrorists with much greater direct control over their message compared to the traditional television and print media' (p. 25).

Weimann (2008: 69) provides insights from his '8-year-long monitoring of terrorist presence on the Internet and the analysis of more than 5,000 Web sites'. One of his findings was that terrorists attempt to approach three audiences through their Web content: potential supporters, the international community, and their enemies. He points out that in order to reach out to supporters 'the sites offer appropriate items for sale, including printed shirts, badges, flags, and video and audio cassettes' (p. 77). Here, even an extension of PR into marketing practices can be seen. According to Bräuchler (2013: 13), the Internet makes it possible 'to relocate deterritorialized and delocalized events and movements, that is, in cyberspace'. Due to the internet, terrorists' opportunities for self-presentation have greatly increased. As the internet is a global medium, terrorists are not only able to reach a larger audience, but are also able to reach people outside their region (Seib and Janbek, 2011).

Diani (2000) analyzed the impact of computer-mediated communication on political activism and social movements. He argues that, 'sustained collective action is unlikely to originate from purely virtual ties if they are not sustained by previous interaction' (p. 184). Computer-mediated communication, however, can be used to 'strengthen identities and solidarities' among group members, notably by 'increasing the rate of exchange between geographically very distant activists and organizations' (Diani, 2000: 395). Furthermore, Bräuchler (2013: 20) points out that:

> Internet communities are also often composed of conglomerates of users spread widely across the globe. As with national consciousness, in these cases a feeling of community and identity is conveyed and imagined in cyberspace via the media. Yet in contrast to print media, the Internet also offers interactive modes of communication that appeal to the individual's power of imagination in a far more direct and memorable manner.

It is a key recurring theme that above all for the diaspora, the internet can have a strong influence on exchange of ideas and identity building, and thus mobilization of human as well as financial resources. However, while there has been a considerable amount of research into identity building, strategic online efforts to create collective identity are still under-researched and have not yet been examined in the light of mobilization theory. The present study examined the ways in which the internet is used for such collective identity building, 'self-marketing', framing the conflict and establishing a certain group image by the use of public relations.

Analyzing terrorist groups' public relations practice: study design

When analyzing different terrorist groups, it is, first, possible to conduct an idiographic approach that examines each group as a 'unique case' (Gibbs,

2008: 5). Second, it is possible to compare the groups and look for common features as is suggested by nomothetic approaches which try 'to show what people, events and settings have in common and to explain them in terms of these common features' (Gibbs, 2008: 5). In the study at hand, the focus is on common features; however, unique cases are highlighted when showing peculiarities. The objective of finding general patterns does not deny that each terrorist group and its context of historical development and recent action is unique but that researchers 'must consider the historical, geographical and cultural contexts. There are great insights that we can learn from comparative case studies of terrorism' (Özdamar, 2008: 100).

The websites of the eight groups selected (see Table 12.1) were accessed between December 1 and 14, 2014, and 70 articles were downloaded, applying a purposive sampling technique to gather the most recent articles as well as articles from various sections (e.g. history, culture), a technique similar to that used in similar studies (e.g. Gerstenfeld et al., 2003; Weimann, 2006). The length of the articles ranged from 102 to 4,633 words with a mean of 946 words and a standard deviation (SD) of 839.

Validity and reliability

The design of the study and coding was carried out as part of a research project at Ilmenau University of Technology. The project leader, as well as a group of trained international post-graduates, searched for appropriate websites in order to obtain as much validity as possible. After coder training, a pretest took place. Two texts from LTTE and PKK were chosen for the pretest that did not form part of the later 70-article sample. After the pretest, the codebook was revised, some variables deleted and some descriptions refined. All articles were coded separately by two researchers and an inter-coder reliability test took place in order to ensure a high degree of consistency among the coders, resulting in an overall Holsti reliability coefficient of .72 for the variables presented in this chapter.

Discussion of results

It was evident that, on an English language website, the groups primarily want to target an international audience. Due to language restrictions it was not possible to analyze websites in other languages, but the research showed that one third of the websites offered more than one language version with the PKK leading the sample, offering versions in six different languages. In that these language versions looked different (PKK and PFLP), one can interpret that their content is tailored to particular target audiences, e.g. their own ethnic (language) community versus the (inter) national audience. In this section, I will present the results for the English language websites and articles.

Visual and audio material

PR professionals often emphasize the usefulness of eye-catching material to attract and mobilize recipients. As visual material often is the first thing to look at when opening a site, it could also be the crucial entry to arousing sentiments of consensus. IRA strategists, for instance, have highlighted the importance of photographs (Somerville and Purcell, 2011). Based on this concept, the use of (multi)media elements on the groups' websites was examined. It was found that 65.7 percent of the articles were accompanied by a photograph. Out of these, 35 showed a portrait of a leading figure of the respective group. Audio files were used in 15.7 percent of cases, caricatures in 5.7 percent, and animations in 4.3 percent of the articles. Only four of the 70 articles (5.7 percent) were accompanied by a video; two on the Sikh group's website and two on the Hamas website. The opportunity to access brochures or magazines was offered in only two articles, whereas a reference to a book cover was available in seven articles (10 percent). Often, the websites referred to supremacist literature. The most widespread and sophisticated use of (multi)media elements and visual material was found in the Hamas articles. Most of the websites provided a separate section for multimedia material.

A logo or emblem is described an important element for a high brand recognition value in traditional corporate PR. Like flags of nation states it is a visual element of self-presentation and part of an identity. The logo often combines the name of the group with some symbolic artwork, as 'More than anything else a chosen name is the key symbolic means of identification' (Meech, 1996: 67). All terrorist groups displayed a logo or emblem on their websites, often in an upper corner. Similarly important for group cohesiveness and identity building is the emphasis of the leader or renowned martyrs. A leading figure (e.g. Öcalan for the PKK, Prabhakaran for the LTTE) was presented in pictures or via statements, thus furthering mobilization through appeals and charisma. Also, martyrs and their sacrifices formed part of the personality cult. The texts emphasized the alleged just cause of aiming to collectively change a certain (oppressive) condition by giving voice to experienced high ranking group members. As noted by Holbrook (2014: 147), 'Notions of just and defensive violence as a response to existing aggression that rest on principles of reciprocity represent the strongest case that terrorist leaderships can develop in favor of sustained campaigns of violence'.

Accessibility, site structure and social media use

Even though terrorist groups often act in secrecy, they all demonstrate their accessibility and provide 'contact us' sections on their websites. These do not always include direct contact information such as email or postal addresses, but instead anonymous contact forms. As shown in previous studies (e.g. Rothenberger, 2012), terrorist groups make use of social media such as Facebook or Twitter. In the present sample, all groups except the UVF and LTTE provided a Facebook as well as a Twitter button on their website. Further buttons linked to social media like YouTube channels, Jappy Ticker and Flickr. This indicates that the groups recognize that many people rely on the internet as a source for information as well as for identity building.

An elaborated site structure often guides visitors through a website and helps them to find the information they need. On the terrorist groups' websites, the research team found the following sections (while the exact wording of the headings may have differed from those mentioned here, the concepts were similar): About us, history, events, poetry and literature, information on legal issues, culture and art, leaders, martyrs, crimes of the enemy, befriended organizations, archive, and press releases. This finding confirms those of Weimann (2006: 52):

> A typical Web site usually includes information about the history of the group or organization; biographies of its leaders, founders, heroes, and commanders; information on the political, religious, or ideological aims of the organization; and news bulletins and updates. Most of the sites present a review of the group's social and political background including its notable activities in the past and its current and future plans. The sites of national organizations generally display maps of the areas in dispute.

In the present study, press releases were available on two-thirds of the websites. This illustrates the fight for (media) framing. Even though the use of websites allows direct communication and circumvention of traditional media, the terrorists' discourse is designed to alter broader public opinion and hence also addresses journalists. The aim remains the same: attempting to create consensus in regard to perceptions of the conflict.

Material and ideological support

The extent to which the groups explicitly seek financial funding from external sources (e.g. the site visitors or crowdfunding platforms) was also investigated. This is important, since only if the reader embraces the framing of the conflict as presented on the website, and attains an inner consensus with this conflict presentation, will he or she be willing to donate money or other capital. However, funding was explicitly mentioned in only six articles (8.6 percent). The websites seem to be created more for ideological purposes (consensus mobilization) than for acquisition of financial or material resources (action mobilization). This is also supported by the finding that almost 40 percent of the articles emphasized the importance of (ideological) public support or public participation. The authors of these website articles, by their discourse, made a clear link from consensus mobilization to action mobilization: this indicated that they wanted to move an achieved consensus on the topic of ethnic conflict into a desire for active participation.

Collective identity is constructed, offered and enforced by an external group. Aronoff (2011) points out that collective identities are not natural but, within certain constraints, socially constructed and politically and culturally negotiated, so that 'activists' efforts to strategically "frame" identities are critical in recruiting participants' (Polletta and Jasper, 2001: 291). Their goal is to strengthen the individual's affective connections with the group and thus create loyalty. Social movements function as carriers and transmitters of mobilizing beliefs and ideas and, as shown by Snow and Benford, 1988: 198), they are at the same time:

> actively engaged in the production of meaning for participants, antagonists, and observers. This productive work may involve the shaping and structuring of existing meanings. Movements can thus be construed as functioning in part as signifying agents ... We use the verb framing to conceptualize this signifying work precisely because that is one of the things social movements do. They frame, or assign meaning to and interpret, relevant events and conditions in ways that are intended to mobilize potential adherents and constituents, to garner bystander support, and to demobilize antagonists.

It is via the website texts that this mobilization and identity building takes place. Participant mobilization through framing is directly linked to power: the groups want to make their ethnicity and political issues or demands politically salient for the larger ethnic community, thereby creating an antagonism between the ethnic group and the national state.

Another crucial aspect in this context is to discover to what extent the insurgent groups accept diverging opinions and points of view. Therefore, any statements or quotes within the text, in which they disparage and criticize other sources of information, promises or actions of adversaries, were coded. The research team coded passages where the web content authors state that their point of view is true and that the opposing point of view is false. This creation of demobilizing antagonists (Snow and Benford, 1988) runs like a golden thread through most website texts. The result shows that in 47.1 percent of the articles (n = 33) the author tries to discredit other sources of information and tries to undermine the credibility of the adversaries. The groups further try to turn the audience against alternative messages or against interpretations of a particular circumstance by dispelling alternative interpretations. This means they discredit interpretations of external actors (e.g. 'This was a massacre, not a routine military operation as the state says'). This includes interpretations of history, causes, responsibilities, etc.

Attribution of causes and responsibility

Social movements originate from grievances within a divided society (Klandermans and Tarrow, 1988). This directly leads to the question of attribution of responsibility, which means the 'process of social cognition by which moral accountability is assigned to a person believed to have produced a socially disapproved behavior or effect' (Shaver, 1995: 61). It is subjectively driven and asks who could be morally accountable for the conflict or crisis, and who or what might be blamed for the conflict situation. Kelley (1967) states that individuals attribute effects either to persons (actors), to entities, or to circumstances, i.e. they attribute the observed behavioral outcome to circumstances of the specific situation. The application of active or passive voice in a sentence can indicate the actor's importance, ability and power of social agency. In this way, 'the presence of a linguistic feature in a text is always the sign of the presence of one term from a discursive and ideological system appearing in the context of the copresence of other terms from that system. A linguistic feature or category therefore never appears simply by itself – it always appears as the representative of a system of linguistic terms, which themselves realize discursive and ideological systems' (Kress, 1985: 30).

Attribution of responsibility is closely linked to the concepts of blame and guilt and again to the creation of antagonism. Weimann (2008: 77) remarked that approaches to the enemy are characterized 'by the efforts to demoralize and scare the enemy or to create feelings of guilt'. Holbrook (2014: 151) calls this the 'justificatory narrative that rationalized, glorified and promoted the terrorist acts'. The brutal violence against the enemy and its depiction in discourse seems to be a violation of the group's own (former) moral codes that are praised in other parts of their websites.

In their interpretation of the conflict in the divided society in which they live, the groups named the respective 'recent government' as the 'main person, entity or circumstance held responsible' (30 percent of the articles). 'Former governments' and 'colonialists' (both 8.6 percent) ranked second in the variable 'attribution of responsibility'. 'Military interventions' and 'historical events' were also mentioned quite often (7.1 percent) whereas other alleged causes such as bad laws, particular leaders, or the media, were mentioned in less than five articles. This shows that, even though each group propagates its own view, responsibility for the conflict is primarily attributed to political structures at the macro-level and also to past enforced systemic conditions (e.g. the impact of colonialism).

Helkama (1981: 12) stresses the 'close connection between causality and responsibility … the attribution of moral responsibility is highly dependent on the attributor's grasp of the causal (physical, psychological and social) network in which the actor and his actions with their consequences are enmeshed'. After identifying the grievances and responsibilities, possible treatment recommendation was evaluated.

Treatment recommendation

In order to persuade website visitors of the righteousness, right to exist and usefulness of the groups' (discursive and violent) activities, I expected the authors of the articles to propose some kind of solution to the conflict. Picking up again the social mobilization theory, Klandermans and Tarrow (1988) remind us that social movements will only be successful if enough benefits or incentives are presented, if the groups show that they master of a certain degree of organization and, finally, if the members expect some success. The group can convince the reader of all the three points by featuring concrete treatment recommendations for the solution of the conflict. 'Treatment recommendation' stems from framing research where it refers to text passages that suggest remedies and 'offer and justify treatments for the problems' (Entman, 1993: 52). Thus, treatment recommendations are statements which aim to help, guide or protect people against the consequences within the problematic situation. Additionally, they refer to minimizing the harm or suggest how to avoid future crises. In the present cases, any treatment recommendation coded was related to the ethnic conflict situation.

Most of the articles (55.7 percent; n = 39) mentioned political treatment recommendations to people or organizations that might be affected by the crisis. Political recommendations are changes in law or political regulations made by the government or changes in the political environment or the administrative system, which will help to avoid future conflict. This could be, for example, stricter laws or changes in ministries or political departments. About one third of the articles (35.7 percent; n = 25) contained social treatment recommendations, namely suggestions for how to reorganize social life and to secure people from the conflict during and after the conflict period. Economics was not seen as the major issue in the conflict (see below) and consequently economic treatment recommendations, i.e. suggestions on how to improve the financial aspects of those affected by the conflict, were given in only 8.6 percent (n = 6) of the articles.

Effects of the conflict

As mentioned previously, the websites are meant to further the groups' point of view and interpretation of the conflict and to promote a certain identity building. Therefore, their goal is to distinguish their identity from an opposing identity, most often the national identity. They use nostalgia (positive home country) in order to construct a collective past for the group as historical narratives stress ethnic uniqueness, since:

> Ethnicity is claimed by groups who consider themselves, and are regarded by others, to be culturally distinctive. They share a collective name, tend to stress common descents, and rely frequently on myths of common origin. They share collective historical memories, elements of common culture, association with a homeland, and a sense of solidarity.
>
> (Aronoff, 2011: 169)

The government was often identified as the main entity perceived as responsible for the conflict. Its actions were deemed to have caused or exacerbated the conflict situation. This conflict, according to the groups' texts, has various effects on aspects of life including, inter alia, the economy, politics, social life, culture and language. The effects can be induced by actions from the adversary as well as by the terrorist group, showing that the clash of both groups leads to a change in economy, politics and so on. The effects can occur at different levels (e.g. development blockade of a local region, decrease in international tourism, or change in the global news agenda). In more than half of the articles (58.6 percent) political effects were mentioned. These included any pressure from (national/international) politicians, governments or transnational federations to change laws and regulations that affect the separatist region and have an impact on political parties and/or institutions and officials. Cases of politicians stepping down from their office were also counted as political effects.

Effects on social life and culture were mentioned in 45.7 percent of the articles. These included effects on interpersonal relations, people's daily life, society, folk, nation, and culture in the sense of a shared historical and cultural background, for example myths destroyed, places of worship attacked. Effects on people's health, their physical (illness or injury, e.g. by attacks) and psychological (emotional and behavioral) condition were mentioned in 28.6 percent of articles. Effects on the nation's and/or region's reputation as a result of the conflict were cited in 24.3 percent of the articles. Examples of reputational effects could be a negative portrayal in the media, or mistrust by the international audience, for example not being allowed to host an international conference or sports event due to security concerns. The least important were effects on language and (consistent with the findings above) economy (mentioned by 10.0 and 11.4 percent respectively). This can be interpreted to mean that effects on employment, wages or investment were not the focus of the authors' intention. In regard to identity-building strategies, they were concerned with the groups' standing within the political system, with reputational issues as well as with the social and cultural life and heritage that is disturbed by the conflict situation.

Group cohesion is often a process connected with conflict development, as emotional involvement reinforces allegiance to one's own ethnic group. In this way, 'Collective identity as a process involves cognitive definitions about ends, means and the field of action; this process is given voice through a common language, and enacted through a set of rituals, practices, and cultural artefacts' (Flesher Fominaya, 2010: 395); by these strategies, the groups' leaders want to 'foster reciprocal ties of solidarity and commitment' (p. 398). The idea that identity building can be seen as a strategy has been acknowledged by Polletta and Jasper (2001), who argue that social protest starts when people do not see their identities 'as sufficiently represented in conventional political or nonpolitical arenas' (p. 292). Frequently, when these ethnic groups do not see themselves as being fairly represented, it is a short step for them to act beyond the bounds of legality.

Region affected by the conflict

Another aspect of (ethnic) identity building was measured by the variable 'region affected by the conflict', which indicated in which areas the consequences of the problem were seen. This variable was measured in terms of: global, international, neighboring countries, national and local level (within the nation state, usually the separatist region) as well as ambiguous level (referring to effects beyond the local level, but not decipherable whether regional, international, global, etc.). The results clearly demonstrate that the conflict is framed as an ethnic/local-nationalist complex of problems. The region affected by the conflict was seen as 'ambiguous' in 8.6 percent of the articles, 'global' in 27.1 percent, 'international' in 37.1 percent, 'neighboring countries' in 44.3 percent, 'national' in 67.1 percent and 'local' in 68.6 percent of the articles. The mobilization focuses on the local level, on local identity, but as the internet as a medium is global, the local discourse automatically becomes globalized (cf. Bräuchler, 2013). The percentages show that the 'divided society' is perceived as a trench between the local ethnic separatist group and the rest of the (national) society, and that the terrorist groups quite consciously use communication and discourse strategies to foster this frame. This is in line with Aronoff's (2011: 170) assertion that:

> The more complex and plural a society is, the easier it becomes for groups to acquire greater consciousness of the differences between their identity and that of others. Transnational migrations, communications, economic and cultural transactions, and social networking tend to blur the boundaries of even national cultures, making collective identities more open to negotiation. This, in turn, generates new processes of ethnic revitalization. Paradoxically, it would appear that in order to save a culture, one must first lose it.

Conclusion

The goal of this article was to investigate the extent to which terrorist groups use websites for persuasion and collective identity building and how the texts on the sites contribute to the forming of a 'mobilization campaign'. The persuasion efforts on the websites (consensus), rather than their violent terrorist deeds (action), were the topic of research, because the analysis of how the inclination towards violence accrues requires greater attention. Only if the first step, the indoctrination and identity building, is successful, are attacks and killings in the name of a certain idea, and not for monetary compensation, made possible. Beforehand, a consensus that violent action is legitimate is necessary. Thus, Melucci (1988: 329) argued that, 'The online presence of terrorist groups is emblematic of the collective action needed to mobilize insurgent social movements. From a sociological perspective on collective behavior, such collective action can be seen as a "reactive response" to social anarchy'.

The media and internet representations play a powerful role in the 'defining, redefining, negotiating, renegotiating, and creating our social [individual and collective] identities' (Sparks, 2005: 14). Terrorist groups use online discourse to strategically communicate, and to build and enhance a specific collective identity. We have seen that, to achieve this goal, they use multimedia tools and visuals such as logos and portraits of martyrs. They employ public relations techniques also for relationship building, for example providing a contact facility and social media links. In line with traditional PR concepts, their goal is to create a certain image, but the terrorist groups have two key additional goals: first, to be held in positive regard by recruits and members (by building a collective identity based on shared ethnicity, history, culture, etc.); and second, to deter and threaten their opponents. The coding of 'attribution of responsibility' revealed explicit concepts of 'the enemy' (i.e. mainly the recent government), an antagonist view not used in traditional PR.

In-group consensus is reached by creating dissent along ethnic lines. Thus, the study gives insight into public relations practices of violent groups in ethnically divided societies from across the world. It questions mainstream PR theories, as terrorist groups act with discourse in a power-challenging environment utilizing asymmetrical communication. It demonstrates that a theoretical concept of the PR of terrorist groups differs from concepts that primarily were developed with regard to corporations. A strict 'with us or with them' motto runs like a golden thread through the articles analyzed. From this, we can conclude that terrorist groups try to establish consensus mobilization through antagonistic instead of symmetrical PR. This might sound paradoxical at first glance, but the goal of the terrorist differs from that of the corporation: They want to pass the buck to the nation state. This creation of an 'enemy-other' (Lefebvre, 2003: 3) stands in contrast to 'ideal harmonious PR', as it furthers ethnic division and at the same time forms in-group identity and consensus. In this way, ethnicity sometimes seems to be wrongly depicted as the sole divider in a heterogeneous society even though there are often other deeper divisions that are based, for example, on class, religion, or gender (Lefebvre, 2003).

Ethnic conflict as a political phenomenon is very complex and has yet to be addressed in detail as 'ethnicity may provide the mobilizational basis for collective action, with violence being used as a tactic' (Cordell and Wolff, 2009: 4). As shown in this chapter, violence is often the culmination point that results from the transfer of consensus mobilization (the aim of the website texts) into action mobilization (the riots, and terrorist attacks). To ignore any demands from ethnic groups is often counterproductive: repression can even exacerbate violent conflicts. Also, the physical elimination of ethnic leaders would be counterproductive (cf. Lefebvre, 2003), because – as the results of this empirical study have shown – his or her influence on the ethnic group's identity should not be underestimated.

McCulloch (2014) states that for 'minority groups with aspirations to independence or union with ethnic kin in other states … the ability to represent themselves is paramount' (p. 145). Hence, as also shown in Chapter 3, politicians have to learn that it is important 'to note that peacemaking is based on working and dialoguing with radicals and militants, a point which many academics, government, and law enforcement agencies so easily forget' (Best et al., 2007: 496). In this study, an analysis of the websites very clearly shows whether a group attributes more importance to treatment recommendation in regard to economics, to language issues or to cultural heritage, and whether they attribute responsibility to former governments or even the colonial past. It is the task of the nation state to create a discourse that responds to these demands. If splinter groups vary in their desired outcomes, the government should respond in different ways to each group. This, of course, means that a state cannot have an overall counterterrorism PR strategy which it imposes regardless of the target group. On the contrary, PR concepts have to be tailored to each terrorist group and its specific strategies of consensus and action mobilization. The goal of not letting ethnic minorities feel outcast but belonging to a greater identity is paramount, because 'abandoning a particular identity is possible for the weakly identified' (Sparks, 2005: 25), but if there is strong group identification it is not so easy. For political actors, calling one's own conception of PR into question means to hear the dissenting voices and to accept different 'answers' to ethnic conflicts in deeply divided societies.

References

Anderson, A. (2003) 'Risk, terrorism, and the internet', *Knowledge, Technology and Policy*, 16(2): 24–33.

Aronoff, M. J. (2011) 'The politics of collective identity: contested Israeli nationalisms', in Rosenfeld, J. E. (ed.) *Terrorism, identity and legitimacy: the four waves theory and political violence*. Abingdon: Routledge, pp. 168–189.

Baker-Beall, C. (2014) 'The evolution of the European Union's "fight against terrorism" discourse: constructing the terrorist "other"', *Cooperation and Conflict*, 49(2): 212–238.

Best, S., McLaren, P. and Nocella, A. J. (2007) 'Revolutionary peacemaking: using a critical pedagogy approach for peacemaking with "terrorists"', *Journal for Critical Education Policy Studies*, 5(2): 494–528.

Bockstette, C. (2008) 'Jihadist terrorist use of strategic communication management techniques'. Garmisch-Partenkirchen, Germany: George C. Marshall Center. (Occasional paper series of the George C. Marshall European Center for Security Studies, no. 20, December).

Bräuchler, B. (2013) *Cyberidentities at war: the Moluccan conflict on the internet*. New York and Oxford: Berghahn Books.

Chandra, K. (2006) 'What is ethnic identity and does it matter?' *Annual Review of Political Science*, 9: 397–424.

Cordell, K. and Wolff, S. (2009) *Ethnic conflict: causes, consequences, responses*. Cambridge/Malden, MA: Polity Press.

Council of the European Union (2001) 'Council common position of 27 December 2001 on the application of specific measures to combat terrorism (2001/931/CFSP)', *Official Journal of the European Communities*, 44 (L 344), 28 December, pp. 93–96.

De Fina, A. (2011) 'Discourse and identity', in Van Dijk, T. A. (ed.) *Discourse studies: a multidisciplinary introduction*. 2nd edn. London: Sage, pp. 263–282.

Della Porta, D. (1988) 'Recruitment processes in clandestine political organizations: Italian left-wing terrorism', in *International Social Movement Research*, vol. 1. Supplement to P. G. Coy (series ed.) Research in Social Movements, Conflicts and Change. Bingley, Yorkshire: Emerald Group Publishing, pp. 155–169.

Diani, M. (2000).'Social movement networks virtual and real', *Information, Communication and Society*, 3(3): 386–401.

Entman, R. M. (1993) 'Framing: toward clarification of a fractured pradigm', *Journal of Communication*, 43(4): 51–58.

Esrock, S. L. and Leichty, G. B. (1998) 'Social responsibility and corporate web pages: self-presentation or agenda-setting?', *Public Relations Review*, 24(3): 305–319.

Farnen, R. F. (1990) 'Terrorism and the mass media: a systemic analysis of a symbiotic process', *Terrorism*, 13(2): 99–143.

Fawkes, J. and Moloney, K. (2008) 'Does the European Union (EU) need a propaganda watchdog like the US Institute of Propaganda Analysis to strengthen its democratic civil society and free markets?', *Public Relations Review*, 34: 207–214.

Flesher Fominaya, C. (2010) 'Collective identity in social movements: central concepts and debates', *Sociology Compass*, 4(6): 393–404. DOI: 10.1111/j.1751–9020.2010.00287.x.

Forsberg, O. J. (2012) *Terrorism and nationalism: theory, causes and causers*. Saarbrücken, Germany: Akademikerverlag.

Freedman, B. (2010) 'Officially blacklisted extremist/terrorist (support) organizations: a comparison of lists from six countries and two international organizations', *Perspectives on Terrorism*, 4(2): 46–52.

Gerhards, J. (1991) 'Die Mobilisierunggegen die IWF- und Weltbanktagung 1988 in Berlin: Gruppen, Veranstaltungen, Diskurse', in Roth, R. and Rucht, D. (eds) *NeuesozialeBewegungen in der Bundesrepublik Deutschland. 2. Überarbeitete und erweiterte Auflage*. Bonn: Bundeszentrale für politische Bildung, pp. 213–234.

Gerrits, R. P. J. M. (1992) 'Terrorists' perspectives: memoirs', in Paletz, D. L. and Schmid, A. P. (eds) *Terrorism and the media*. Newbury Park, CA: Sage, pp. 29–61.

Gerstenfeld, P. B., Grant, D. R. and Chiang, C.-P. (2003) 'Hate online: a content analysis of extremist internet sites', *Analyses of Social Issues and Public Policy*, 3(1): 29–44.

Gibbs, G. R. (2008) *Analysing qualitative data*. Los Angeles, CA: Sage.

Grunig, J. E. and Hunt, T. (1984) *Managing public relations*. New York: Holt, Rinehart and Winston.

Hallahan, K., Holtzhausen, D., van Ruler, B., Verčič, D. and Sriramesh, K. (2007) 'Defining strategic communication', *International Journal of Strategic Communication*, 1(1): 3–35.

Heath, R. L. (2001) 'A rhetorical enactment rationale for public relations: the good organization communicating well', in Heath, R. L. (ed.) *Handbook of public relations*. Thousand Oaks, CA: Sage, pp. 31–50.

Helkama, K. (1981) *Toward a cognitive-developmental theory of attribution of responsibility: a critical review of empirical research and some preliminary data*. Helsinki: Suomalainen Tiedeakatemia.

Hirschmann, K. (2000) 'Today's terrorism: a new challenge?' In Hirschmann, K. and Gerhard, P. (eds) *Terrorismus als weltweites Phänomen. Schriftenreihe zur neuen Sicherheitspolitik*. Berlin: Verlag Arno Spitz, vol. 18: 45–56.

Holbrook, D. (2014) 'Approaching terrorist public relations initiatives', *Public Relations Inquiry*, 3(2): 141–161.

Kelley, H. H. (1967) *Attribution theory in social psychology.* Lincoln: University of Nebraska Press.

Kent, M. L. and Taylor, M. (1998) 'Building dialogic relationships through the World Wide Web', *Public Relations Review*, 24(3): 321–334.

Kent, M. L. and Taylor, M. (2002) 'Toward a dialogic theory of public relations', *Public Relations Review*, 28: 21–37.

Klandermans, B. (1988) 'The formation and mobilization of consensus', *International Social Movement Research*, 1: 173–196.

Klandermans, B. and Tarrow, S. (1988) 'Mobilization into social movements: synthesizing European and American approaches', in *International Social Movement Research*, vol. 1. Supplement to P. G. Coy (series ed.) Research in Social Movements, Conflicts and Change. Bingley, Yorkshire: Emerald Group Publishing, pp. 1–38.

Klausen, J. (2014) 'Tweeting the Jihad: social media networks of Western foreign fighters in Syria and Iraq', *Studies in Conflict and Terrorism.* DOI: 10.1080/1057610X.2014.974948.

Kress, G. (1985) 'Ideological structures in discourse', in van Dijk, T. A. (ed.) *Handbook of discourse analysis: discourse analysis in society.* London: Academic Press, pp. 27–42.

Lefebvre, S. (2003) *Perspectives on ethno-nationalist/separatist terrorism.* Camberley, Surrey: Defence Academy of the United Kingdom, Conflict Studies Research Centre.

L'Etang, J. (1996) 'Public relations as diplomacy', in L'Etang, J. and Pieczka, M. (eds) *Critical perspectives in public relations.* London: International Thomson Business Press, pp. 14–34.

L'Etang, J. and Pieczka, M. (eds) (1996) *Critical perspectives in public relations.* London: International Thomson Business Press.

McCulloch, A. (2014) *Power-sharing and political stability in deeply divided societies.* London and New York: Routledge.

Meech, P. (1996) 'Corporate identity and corporate image', in L'Etang, J. and Pieczka, M. (eds) *Critical perspectives in public relations.* London: International Thomson Business Press, pp. 65–81.

Melucci, A. (1988) 'Getting involved: identity and mobilization in social movements', in *International Social Movement Research*, vol. 1. Supplement to P. G. Coy (series ed.) Research in Social Movements, Conflicts and Change. Bingley, Yorkshire: Emerald Group Publishing, pp. 329–348.

Mickey, T. J. (1998) 'Selling the internet: a cultural studies approach to public relations', *Public Relations Review*, 24(3): 335–349.

Miller, G. R. (1989) 'Persuasion and public relations: two "Ps" in a pod', in Botan, C. and Hazleton, V. (eds) *Public relations theory.* Hillsdale, NJ: Lawrence Erlbaum Associates, pp. 45–66.

Moloney, K. (2006) *Rethinking public relations: PR propaganda and democracy.* 2nd edn. London/New York: Routledge.

Özdamar, Ö. (2008) 'Theorizing terrorist behavior: major approaches and their characteristics', *Defence Against Terrorism Review*, 1(2): 89–101.

Pearson, R. (1989) 'Business ethics as communication ethics: public relations practice and the idea of dialogue', in Botan, C. and Hazleton, V. (eds) *Public relations theory.* Hillsdale, NJ: Lawrence Erlbaum Associates, pp. 111–131.

Pfau, M. and Wan, H.-H. (2006) 'Persuasion: an intrinsic function of public relations', in Botan, C. and Hazleton, V. (eds) *Public relations theory II*. New York and London: Routledge, pp. 101–136.

Picard, R. G. (1989) 'Press relations of terrorist organizations', *Public Relations Review*, 15(4): 12–23.

Picard, R. G. (1993) *Media portrayals of terrorism: functions and meaning of news coverage*. Ames: Iowa State University Press.

Pieczka, M. (1996) 'Paradigms, systems theory and public relations', in L'Etang, J. and Pieczka, M. (eds) *Critical perspectives in public relations*. London: International Thomson Business Press, pp. 124–156.

Polletta, F. and Jasper, J. M. (2001) 'Collective identity and social movements', *Annual Review of Sociology*, 27: 283–305.

Rada, S. E. (1985) 'Trans-national terrorism as public relations?' *Public Relations Review*, 11(3): 26–33.

Richards, B. (2004) 'Terrorism and public relations', *Public Relations Review*, 30(2): 169–176.

Rothenberger, L. (2012) 'Terrorist groups: using internet and social media for disseminating ideas. New tools for promoting political change', *Romanian Journal of Communication and Public Relations*, 14(3): 7–23.

Rothenberger, L. and Müller, K. (2015) 'Categorizing terrorist entities listed by the European Union according to the terrorist groups' underlying motives', *Conflict and Communication Online*, 14(2).

Seib, P. and Janbek, D. M. (2011) *Global terrorism and new media: the post-Al Qaeda generation*. London and New York: Routledge.

Shaver, K. G. (1995) 'Attribution of responsibility', in Manstead, A. S. R. and Hewstone, M. (eds) *The Blackwell encyclopedia of social psychology*. Malden, MA, Oxford, and Carlton, VIC: Blackwell, pp. 61–66.

Smith, R. D. (2002) *Strategic planning for public relations*. Mahwah, NJ: Lawrence Erlbaum Associates.

Snow, D. A. and Benford, R. D. (1988) 'Ideology, frame resonance, and participant mobilization', in *International Social Movement Research*, vol. 1. Supplement to P. G. Coy (series ed.) Research in Social Movements, Conflicts and Change. Bingley, Yorkshire: Emerald Group Publishing, pp. 197–217.

Somerville, I. and Purcell, A. (2011) 'A history of Republican public relations in Northern Ireland from "Bloody Sunday" to the "Good Friday Agreement"', *Journal of Communication Management*, 15(3): 192–210.

Sparks, L. (2005) 'Social identity and perceptions of terrorist groups: how others see them and how they see themselves', in O'Hair, D. H., Heath, R. L. and Ledlow, G. R. (eds) *Community preparedness and response to terrorism. Volume 3: Communication and the media*. Westport, CT: Praeger, pp. 13–28.

Taylor, M., Kent, M. L. and White, W. J. (2001) 'How activist organizations are using the internet to build relationships', *Public Relations Review*, 27: 263–284.

Tekwani, S. R. (2004) 'Constructing a nation online: Tamil nationalism and the internet. Paper presented at the Annual Meeting of the International Communication Association, New Orleans, May 2004.

Tilly, C. (2002) *Stories, identities, and political change*. Lanham, MD: Rowman & Littlefield.

Walder, A. G. (2009) 'Political sociology and social movements', *Annual Review of Sociology*, 35: 393–412. DOI: 10.1146/annurev-soc-070308–120035.

Waldmann, P. (1989) *Ethnischer Radikalismus. Ursachen und Folgengewaltsamer Minderheitenkonflikte am Beispiel des Baskenlandes, Nordirlands und Quebecs.* Opladen, Germany: Westdeutscher Verlag.

Waldmann, P. (2001) *Terrorismus: Provokation der Macht.* Munich: Gerling Akademie Verlag.

Weimann, G. (2006) *Terrorism on the internet: the new arena, the new challenges.* Washington, DC: US Institute of Peace Press.

Weimann, G. (2008) 'The psychology of mass-mediated terrorism', *American Behavioral Scientist*, 52(1): 69–86.

Wodak, R., de Cillia, R., Reisigl, M. and Liebhart, K. (2009) *The discursive construction of national identity.* 2nd edn. Edinburgh: Edinburgh University Press.

Wolff, S. (2011) 'Managing ethno-national conflict: towards an analytical framework', *Commonwealth and Comparative Politics*, 49(2): 162–195.

Index